WHAT WENT WRONG?

WHAT WENT WRONG?

The Creation and Collapse of the Black–Jewish Alliance

MURRAY FRIEDMAN

with the assistance of Peter Binzen

THE FREE PRESS

New York London Toronto Sydney Tokyo Singapore

Page 221: Acknowledgment is made of lines excerpted from *Selected Poems* by Langston Hughes.

The Free Press
A Division of Simon & Schuster Inc.
866 Third Avenue, New York, N.Y. 10022

Printed in the United States of America

printing number

1 2 3 4 5 6 7 8 9 10

Library of Congress Cataloging-in-Publication Data

Friedman, Murray
What went wrong?: the creation and collapse of the Black-Jewish Alliance / Murray Friedman.
p. cm.
ISBN 0-02-910910-8
1. Afro-Americans—Relations with Jews. I. Title
E185.61.F858 1995
305.896'073—dc20 92-226616
CIP

CONTENTS

ACKNOWLEDGMENTS

A book of this kind is the work of many hands. I want to acknowledge the assistance of Peter Binzen, a veteran journalist, Nieman Fellow, and friend of more than thirty years. Early drafts of each chapter were sent to Peter for review, pruning, and rewriting, with a view to giving the book the widest readership possible without changing its structure and flow of ideas. Thereafter, I added material and reworked chapters several more times with the advice and assistance of my editor, Adam Bellow. Although Peter sometimes disagreed with some of my interpretations, it has been a delight to work—and argue—with him, and the book has benefited greatly from his involvement.

Adam Bellow and the late Erwin Glikes, the late president and publisher of The Free Press, encouraged me at every stage of the book. They encouraged me also to use as my organizational framework the effort I perceived early on to be under way—among not only racial extremists but some scholars—to minimize and sometimes deny the existence of a black-Jewish alliance. In addition, Adam continually pointed me in the direction of probing deeply each side in the controversies involving blacks and Jews, and I shall always associate the word "nuance" with him. The death of Erwin, as the project neared completion, was a sad moment for me as well as for the publishing field.

Portions of the manuscript or papers that were based on it and delivered at several historical conferences were read and commented on by Leonard Dinnerstein, David Garrow, Robert Weisbrot, Abraham Peck, Lawrence Glasco, Marshall Stevenson, John Bracey, and Clayborne Carson. I profited greatly from their comments even when they differed—sometimes sharply—with my conclusions or interpretations. I am deeply indebted to Midge Decter, who first brought the manuscript to the attention of The Free Press.

The following took time out of their busy schedules to discuss aspects of the book with me: Arnold Aronson, Morris B. Abram, Robert Austin, Steven Bayme, Roy Bennett, Lenora Berson, Taylor Branch, Charney Bromberg, David Brion Davis, Hasia Diner, Seymour Drescher, Joseph H. Filner, Leon Fink, Moe Foner, David Goldenberg, Norman Hill, Milton Himmelfarb, Elaine Hollander, Rachelle Horowitz, Adele Kanter, Jonathan Kaufman, Janet Kennedy, Arthur Kinoy, Harvey Klehr, Guenter Lewy, Will Maslow, Jerald Podair, Victor Navasky, Gary Rubin, Bayard Rustin, Henry Schwartzchild, David Singer, John Slawson, Don Slayman, Harry Wachtel, Arthur Waskow, and Gary Zagon.

I am grateful to the American Jewish Committee for granting me two brief sabbaticals, and to the Muriel and Philip Berman Foundation for the support for one of these. AJC and the various individuals referred to, of course, bear no responsibility for the contents of the book.

The staff of various libraries and collections of materials were immensely helpful. Among the collections utilized were the Moorland-Spingarn Research Project at Howard University, the Martin Luther King Library in Atlanta, and the F.B.I. Reading Room in Washington, D.C. Cyma Horowitz, librarian at the American Jewish Committee, was invariably helpful with ideas and materials. Barbara Lang of St. Joseph's University arranged inter-library loans and bore my numerous requests with extraordinary patience and efficiency.

Ann Frumkin, Vivian Reiben, and Jill Segal typed the manuscript with loving care, and my computer "maven," Steve Applebaum, rescued me at several critical points.

I also wish to recognize Burt Siegel of the Jewish Community Relations Council of Philadelphia and Seymour Samet, a colleague at the American Jewish Committee, for their research assistance on several chapters.

INTRODUCTION

The Rewriting of Black–Jewish History

In recent years a seemingly endless series of conflicts has arisen between blacks and Jews. These conflicts have received wide attention in the press and aroused real concern among Americans of every race and background. Episodes particularly distressing to Jews include the then presidential candidate Jesse Jackson's reference to New York City as Hymietown and his reluctance until very recently to distance himself from the bitter tirades of black Muslim leader Louis Farrakhan; the charges of a Farrakhan associate (Steven Cokely, a Chicago-based "researcher" for the Nation of Islam and former mayoral aide), that Jewish doctors had infected black babies with AIDS; Spike Lee's portrayal of two Jewish nightclub owners as exploiters of black musical talent in his film *Mo' Better Blues*; and the outspoken assertions of Leonard Jeffries, a black professor at City College of New York, that Jews financed the slave trade and conspired, through their control of the Hollywood film industry, to foster racist images of blacks.[1]

College campuses have witnessed numerous unpleasant confrontations between black and Jewish student groups, most often sparked by racial extremists who sometimes denounce Jews in their lectures. Thus, in early 1994, the congressional Black Caucus, NAACP director Benjamin Chavis, and other black leaders found themselves embroiled in a public dispute with Jewish groups after Farrakhan lieutenant Khalid Abdul Muhammad delivered a speech at Kean College in New Jersey that was filled with racist, sexist, homophobic, anti-Catholic, and anti-Semitic remarks.

The most explosive and damaging incident occurred earlier, in the summer of 1991, when anti-Jewish rioting erupted in the Crown Heights section of Brooklyn in the wake of the accidental death of a seven-year-old black boy, Gavin Cato, who was struck by a car in the entourage of the Lubavitcher Rebbe. Over the course of four days, the rioters injured 150 police officers and 38 civilians. Yankel Rosenbaum, a visiting Australian rabbinical student, was stabbed to death in revenge for Gavin Cato's death. This was quite simply one of the worst episodes of violence directed against Jews in American history.

These and other incidents have taken place against a background of intensifying mutual recrimination, with charges of Jewish racism and paternalism on the one hand and countercharges of black anti-Semitism and ingratitude on the other. Some revisionist historians of the civil rights movement maintain that Jews, wishing to enjoy the benefits of assimilation without assuming responsibility for the injustices perpetrated against blacks by the old system of American race relations, betrayed and misled black people by promoting a vision of assimilation that has turned out to be an impracticable option for many. Jews for their part resent this refusal of the moral credit for being virtually the only white group to have gone to the side of blacks in their long and painful struggle for equality at a time when this had little appeal.

Thus, most observers have proclaimed the end of a black-Jewish alliance that existed since the beginning of this century. And the end of that alliance certainly seems to be a fact, despite occasional efforts of both groups to patch things up. Those who lament its passing usually speak from the perspective of the civil rights revolution, which marked—for many Jews, especially—a kind of golden age in black-Jewish relations, when the natural sympathy between the two groups found its highest and most active expression. However, such memories obscure a more complex reality. Conflicts such as those recently experienced erupted long before the halcyon days of the 1960s. Tensions over landlord-tenant disputes, the business practices of merchants in Harlem and Detroit in the thirties and forties, quarrels over racial preferences, the forced resignation of UN ambassador Andrew Young—these and other fractious but largely forgotten incidents are no less typical of this long-standing but troubled relationship. Those who wax nostalgic lack the historical perspective necessary for a full appreciation of this complex American partnership. In light of these recurring conflicts, the remarkable thing is not that the black-Jewish alliance is now in eclipse but that it held together for so long—or indeed that it ever existed.

To all appearances, the present situation is a stalemate. Like Israelis and Palestinians, each side feels wounded and victimized, and each demands a recognition of its special pain and suffering before agreeing to define a new relationship. Clearly, therefore, those concerned with reconciliation and progress between blacks and Jews must recognize that a measure of historical review is in order. Blacks and Jews cannot achieve agreement about their future until they have achieved a common understanding of their past.

What we have been getting, however, is an irresponsible historical revision that aims at writing Jews out of the record of civil rights activism in this country and questions Jewish motives and methods as they relate to blacks today and in the past. At the academic level this effort is sometimes undertaken by serious historians. But at street level there is a strongly politicized effort to promote a worldview that demonizes Jews as conspiratorial and holds them responsible for racial repression in America and throughout the Third World. This effort has been sponsored by extremist elements that arose when the civil rights movement was transformed into a race revolution in the late 1960s. These elements have actively pursued a strategy of confrontation with Jews, hoping to deepen divisions between the two groups and thereby enhance their own power.

A year after Jeffries's inflammatory 1991 speech, in which he promised a series of forthcoming volumes on the subject of black-Jewish relations, the Nation of Islam's "historical research department" published a rambling and disjointed 334-page book entitled *The Secret Relationship between Blacks and Jews*. Replete with bibliography and footnotes, the book was described as Volume I, though no subsequent volume has yet appeared. Noting that both blacks and Jews have begun to question their relationship, the book sought to put such discussion in "historical perspective," going on to argue that the Jews had been "conclusively linked" to the greatest crime ever perpetrated against an entire race of people—the forcible entrapment and exploitation of millions of black Africans. Jewish wealth had been accumulated through the brutal subjugation of blacks, and Jews, more than any other ethnic group, had helped bring slavery to the New World.

Early in 1993 a sharp controversy was set off at Wellesley by the decision of a black professor to use the book in an introductory course on African-American history. Dr. Tony Martin, a tenured professor in the Wellesley Africana department, declared that he had assigned the book as required reading because it was substantially accurate and "a serious attempt at historical scholarship." Martin was denounced by Jewish students and condemned by the chairman of the Africana department and by the president of Wellesley, among others.[2] Nevertheless, these inflammatory charges have since been repeated by a number of racial extremists, including the Nation of Islam's Khalid Mohammad; and Louis Farrakhan, while subsequently distancing himself from the "tone" of Muhammad's remarks, went even further by declaring it was common knowledge that 75 percent of southern slaves were owned by Jews.*

Revisionist projects have not always been aimed at damaging black-Jewish relations, however. Historical distortions have also been sanctioned for "positive" purposes. Thus, at the close of 1992, black and Jewish leaders gathered at the Apollo Theater in Harlem for a special screening of "The Liberators," a PBS documentary that supposedly told the story of the all-black Army units that had liberated the Buchenwald and Dachau concentration camps during World War II. The film's producers intended it as a

---

*This charge about the Jewish role in slavery has lately taken on a broader life. Students repeat it in classrooms, and it is heard in other settings as well. Thus, in a public contretemps in 1989 over a proposed multicultural curriculum for New York State, Adelaide L. Sanford, a former school principal and a member of the New York State Board of Regents, told educator Diane Ravitch, "Some of your grandparents owned the slaveships that we came on." When Dr. Ravitch explained that her grandparents were impoverished Polish Jews who never owned slaves, Sanford had a ready explanation. She said that she had been speaking "ethnically."

means to effect a reconciliation between the two groups. The problem with this plan was that the battalions featured in the film had *not* liberated the camps, according to subsequent reports in the *Jewish Forward* and *New York Times*. After a five-month investigation PBS was forced to withdraw it.[3]

Such efforts to rewrite the history of blacks and Jews from the standpoint of racial extremists and liberal activists could be dismissed as either bigoted nonsense or moralistic propaganda were it not for the fact that the tension and conflict between the two groups is being deliberately exploited for blatant political ends. Testimony to this effect comes from an authoritative source: In a remarkable opinion piece that occupied a full page in the *New York Times* in 1992, Henry Louis Gates, Jr., professor of English and chairman of the Afro-American studies department at Harvard University, called attention to the troubling rise of anti-Semitism among some blacks. "At a time when black America is beleaguered on all sides," he wrote, "there is a strong temptation simply to ignore the phenomenon or treat it as something strictly marginal." Gates pinned the blame on "pseudo-scholars" and other activists who promote wild misconceptions about the historical relationship between blacks and Jews. Gates accused these self-styled scholars and community activists of deliberately seeking to deepen the cultural and social isolation of blacks from the mainstream of American life for political purposes, and he warned, "We must not allow . . . demagogues to turn the wellspring of memory into a renewable resource of enmity everlasting."[4]

The guardians of memory, of course, are—or ought to be—historians, and some fine work has certainly been done on the history of the American civil rights and related social movements, including the relations between blacks and Jews.* But certain distorted notions about the black-Jewish relationship have lately found their way into serious scholarship. Though a far cry from

---

*Some useful studies of black-Jewish relations include Hasia Diner's *In the Almost Promised Land: American Jews and Blacks, 1915–1935*; B. Joyce Ross's biography of Joel Spingarn; Marshall Stevenson's doctoral dissertation on the interaction of the two groups in Detroit; and Claybourne Carson, Jr.'s analysis of the Jewish role in the civil rights movement.[5]

the egregious and manipulative lies of a Leonard Jeffries or Khalid Muhammad, they sometimes have the same effect.

The transformation of the civil rights movement into a race revolution in the latter 1960s gave rise to a scholarly effort that has come to be known as the new black history. Just as black activism came to focus increasingly on issues of group identity, empowerment, and equality of results in public policy, younger black and some white historians on the Left began to take aim at the liberal integrationist assumptions that had hitherto dominated most scholarship about blacks. Liberal historians (many of them Jewish) had tended to see the path of blacks in American life as not unlike that of earlier white immigrant groups. The newer scholars, operating with what Peter Novick has called "a new, assertive, particularist consciousness," were skeptical of claims that blacks had really gained much as a result of the civil rights legislation of the 1960s, and they accordingly tended to focus less on what white liberals had done for blacks in those years than on what blacks had done for themselves.[6]

Thus, it was hardly surprising that as these scholars looked at the African-American experience, they would raise new questions about the "special relationship" between blacks and Jews. Admittedly, some of them raised valid, albeit difficult and sometimes troubling, questions about the role of Jews in the struggle for black equality and the degree to which Jews themselves had become a part of America's racial caste system. Another body of work, however, goes beyond a serious and useful reexamination of the black-Jewish relationship and attempts to rewrite that history from the ideological perspective of the race revolution. These writers maintain that there never was a real black-Jewish alliance; where cooperation did take place, it was of little real importance and indeed was often dysfunctional for blacks.

Such revisionist ideas have their origin in a seminal work by Harold Cruse, *The Crisis of the Negro Intellectual*. Cruse, then a freelance writer and later a founder of the Afro-American studies program at the University of Michigan, published his book in 1967, at a time when racial unrest was exploding in major American cities and Martin Luther King's dream of the "beloved community" had been rejected by black radicals. In this and in a later book, *Plural but Equal*, Cruse sought to free black intellectuals from the domination of a white power structure, which he believed had diverted blacks from the path of black empowerment. A leading cause of the predicament, he argued, was the subservience of blacks to Jews and the inordinate involvement of Jews in black affairs. Cruse assailed as a myth the idea of Jewish friendship for blacks. "American Negroes," he declared, "in deference to Jewish sensibilities tolerated Jewish ambivalence, Jewish liberalism, Jewish paternalism, Jewish exploitation, Jewish radicalism, Jewish nationalism in the same way in which they have lived with similar attributes in the white Anglo-Saxon."[7]

The Crisis of the Negro Intellectual created a major stir among white and black intellectuals and has continued to be strongly influential. In the foreword to the mid-1980s paperback edition, the editors declared the book "as directly relevant to understanding the black condition today as it was in the late 1960s." Historian Marshall Stevenson has noted of Cruse that he "set the tone and direction for the future scholars of Black-Jewish relations."[8]

Cruse is more a polemicist than a historian, and the harshness of his language and his bitter animosity toward Jews have repelled some who have written on the subject. However, even serious revisionist historians occasionally echo Cruse's themes. One of these is David Levering Lewis, author of the Pulitzer-prize-winning biography of scholar-activist W. E. B. Du Bois.

Lewis explores the early stages of the black-Jewish alliance, when a group of upper-class German Jews joined with WASP reformers and black activists to form the NAACP and other biracial organizations. Hasia Diner has suggested in her history of the period that these Jews, who had attained wealth but remained social outsiders, sought to gain respectability by joining with progressive WASPS in efforts for racial equality. Lewis, basing his view on Diner's *In the Almost Promised Land*, asserts that Jews were motivated by self-interest rather than shared experience and goals. "By establishing a presence at the center of the civil rights movement with intelligence, money and influence," Lewis writes, "elite Jews and their delegates could fight anti-Semitism by remote control." This alliance was the fruit of Jewish "caginess," notes Lewis. Far from being a natural or necessary thing, the black-Jewish alliance was "a misconceived ethnic propinquity" that was "minimally" helpful to blacks.[9]

Lewis downplays Diner's focus on the pioneering role of Jewish labor unions (like the ILGWU) in bringing blacks into the labor movement and on the strong support of the Jewish press—another organ of the Jewish working class—for antilynching legislation and other societal reforms. Nor is Lewis unique in doing so. Recent historical studies by Herbert Hill and Robert Laurenz take aim at the ILGWU, arguing that as its Jewish base gave way to new immigrants (mainly Puerto Ricans) in the 1940s and 1950s, Jewish union leaders sacrificed the interests of these new members in order to maintain their own power and enhance the profits of clothing manufacturers.[10]

Clayborne Carson, a professor of history at Stanford and the director of the Martin Luther King, Jr., Papers Project, has introduced an important discussion of what he calls "the Afro-American Jewish radical community." Carson, unlike David Levering Lewis, sees that Jews were genuinely motivated to support the movement for civil rights from an early stage: "[the] existence of substantial Jewish support for black civil rights efforts cannot be seriously doubted." However, in a speech delivered at a Washington conference in 1985, Carson argued that this support derived almost exclusively from highly assimilated Jews with left-wing or radical backgrounds. Leaning on Lewis, Carson noted that the German Jews and black elites who helped found the NAACP in 1909 were assimilationists uncomfortable with their own underclasses. He therefore concluded that Jewish involvement in the civil rights movement should not be seen as "stemming from values that are typical of the Jewish community," and he further observed that there was little evidence "that Judaism as a set of religious beliefs has been associated with support [for] political reform, liberalism or racial tolerance."[11]

Carson is on solid ground, of course, in stressing the important role of alienated and left-wing Jews in social justice efforts, particularly in the labor movement. But was there really no moral imperative at work in the civil rights movement to which Jews as individuals responded? What of the strong support for racial equality that came from white Christian reformers? Were they, too, motivated solely by self-interest, or at best by radical politics? It would be difficult to make this case persuasively. Even if we accept as fact that most of the Jews who went south in the fifties and sixties knew little about the Jewish prophetic tradition, is there nothing in the Jewish historical experience that would cause them to identify with liberal ideas or racial progress and equality? Again, it would be hard to make this argument.

This is hardly to suggest that the relationship of blacks and Jews was always idyllic or that Jews have been unfailing paragons of tolerance, compassion, and commitment. As Vernon J. Williams has recently shown, even a great liberal reformer like anthropologist Franz Boas shared some of the racist assumptions of his day before going on to lead the intellectual attack on racism.[12] Nor can it be maintained that Jews never discriminated against or exploited blacks as other white Americans did, even as many enlisted in efforts to overcome bigotry. But the recent attacks on Jewish motives and behavior, seemingly intended to show that most Jews had little interest in civil rights and to suggest that those who came to oppose such new racial strategies as racial preferences were little more than hypocrites, are both disturbing and, to say the least, offensive.*

It would, of course, be very helpful at this time if we could turn to the historical record for confirmation or disproof of such assertions. However, historians themselves have lately recognized that while much attention has been paid to black-Jewish relations there exist very few historical studies and only a small number of serious articles and doctoral dissertations on the subject.[14]

---

*Ironically, just as the contributions of blacks to American society were ignored for many years in standard American texts, there is a danger that Jews will now be written out of the struggle for racial justice. Thus, in *Freedom Summer*, the most comprehensive study of the social and religious backgrounds of student activists who went south in the 1964 voting rights drive, Doug McAdam ignores the disproportionate number who came from Jewish backgrounds and fails to assess the reasons why they did so. Further, Aldon D. Morris, in *The Origins of the Civil Rights Movement: Black Communities Organizing for Change*, ignores the black-Jewish-labor partnership that spearheaded litigation and legislation campaigns at the city and state level after World War II, helped to launch the social science attack on racist ideology, and set the stage for the protest movement of the 1960s. While his focus undoubtedly is on how blacks organized their fight, absent, from his discussion are key figures like Jack Greenberg, Stanley David Levison, Allard Lowenstein, Joseph Rauh, and Arnold Aronson.[13]

One can only speculate as to why so little history has been written about a topic that has aroused so much interest. For some historians, perhaps, the fact that both groups have been victims of massive injustice made it seem intuitively obvious that they were brought together on the basis of common experience. But many knew, of course, that there was more to the story than that. For one thing the relationship has always lacked the symmetry that characterizes a genuine partnership. Jews, after all, were white people, and while they faced restrictions and a degree of social prejudice, they never confronted the kinds of obstacles and barriers to progress that blacks did in this society.[15]

It has also been known that the black-Jewish partnership was strained long before the stormy 1960s, when the alliance began to break up. Conflicts emerged between the two groups in urban neighborhoods following the migrations of blacks to northern cities after World War I. Few, it may be surmised, were eager to explore these tensions, especially with Nazism on the rise in Europe.[16] And since there was also much truth in the image of a positive special relationship between blacks and Jews, there the matter rested. The idea of a natural and necessary black-Jewish alliance gained even greater credence in the fifties and early sixties when Jews joined the civil rights movement in large numbers.

A start at remedying this dearth of historical writing was recently made with the publication of a useful essay by historians John Bracey and August Meier, laying out an agenda for future research.[17] They call for more attention to the relations between blacks and Jews before the Civil War: Were Jews active in the abolitionist movement as they would later be in the struggle for civil rights? Which Jews joined in these efforts and which remained aloof? What were the motivations of those who did? Why did the two groups come to have such different political rights and economic circumstances? To what degree were the experiences of both with ghettoization and dispersal similar and different?

The list of questions could easily be extended. Did black-Jewish relations differ in different cities, as black historian Marshall Stevenson has suggested? Why did the experience of Jews with exclusion sometimes contribute to their upward movement by spurring them on to create new economic enterprises, while racial discrimination often deepened the outsider status of many blacks?

And certainly high on the list would be the painful subjects of black anti-Semitism and Jewish racism.

On its face, this call for new historical research seems perfectly plausible. Why would we not want to know everything possible about the subject of black-Jewish relations? If knowledge is good, isn't more knowledge better? The answer is, it depends on the question. There are some lines of inquiry that act less to settle questions than to raise them, to create a thought that wasn't there before. Thus, it is somewhat startling to find that Bracey and Meier have also called for systematic study of the Jewish role in the slave trade in Holland, France, and England and in ownership of slaves in the United States. After all, as chapter 1 will show in more detail, the role of Jews in slavery was minimal at worst. There was a statistically significant proportion neither of Jewish slave traders nor of Jewish slave owners. To put it bluntly, there is not much there to know—unless one thinks that there is more than meets the eye.

Bracey and Meier would doubtless object that they intend no such suggestion. Whatever their intentions may be and while there is certainly a great difference between these respectable historians and the tendentious assertions of Louis Farrakhan and his representatives, it is hard to avoid the conclusion that by raising such questions they are lending a degree of credibility to the irrational assertions of the demagogues. For by taking as their premise that next to nothing is known about the relationship of blacks and Jews, they inadvertently suggest that what is thought to be known about the Jewish role in slavery is based not on fact but on myth. And if there is myth, there must be someone with an interest in promoting it. Like it or not, therefore, Bracey and Meier buttress the position of some revisionist historians who, by seeking to adjust the historical record concerning how many Jews were gassed at Auschwitz, lend credence to those who would deny that the Holocaust occurred.

What is worrisome in the seemingly neutral call for more historical research on Jews and slavery is its implied attack upon the moral dimension of the black-Jewish relationship. It is one thing to point out that not all Jews have always been friendly to blacks; it is another to imply by way of an unstated corollary that Jewish friendship toward blacks has been a myth and an illusion, fostered by Jews for political purposes. Nor should it escape notice that this groundless implication bolsters the worldview of left-wing and black nationalist ideologues, for whom anti-Zionism has become a fundamental organizing principle. The roots of this current can be found, once again, in the late-1960s transformation of the civil rights movement into a race revolution. That shift spurred a movement among some elements of the black intelligentsia to link themselves more closely with the struggle of colored peoples throughout the world against colonial oppression, notably including Palestinian Arabs living under Israeli occupation in the West Bank and Gaza.* Israel can be legitimately criticized, of course, for its treatment of its Arab neighbors and citizens. Many have done so, including many Jews. But much of the writing of left-wing and black intellectuals has carried this Third World perspective well beyond the bounds of reasonable criticism of Israel. Thus, rather than recognize Zionism as the national liberation movement of the Jewish people—a movement not unlike the those that gave rise to many newly created African countries—these writers portray the Jewish state as an outpost of Western imperialism and its actions as a counterpart to "Jewish exploitation" in black ghettos. This perspective is summed up in the infamous catchphrase Zionism equals racism.

Throughout the seventies and eighties Israel was sharply attacked for its trade links and alleged military collaboration with South Africa; the fact that many African, Western, and Arab countries engaged in considerably broader trade relations with South Africa was ignored. Critics also failed to take into account Israel's prolonged economic isolation as a result of the decades-long Arab commercial boycott and its deepened political isolation following the Arab oil embargo of 1973. Nevertheless, Israel and South Africa have been portrayed as wicked collaborators in the exploitation of colored peoples.

Again, Harold Cruse was among the first to develop this line.

---

*Ronald Walters, a Howard University political scientist and foreign policy adviser to Jesse Jackson, expressed this view at a conference on black-Jewish relations. Declaring the demise of the black-Jewish relationship, Walters remarked that the moral posture of the Palestinians was "more akin to the black diaspora than to the Jewish diaspora—the former model."[18]

"Can one fight neo-colonialism in Africa without fighting Israel," he asked in *The Crisis of the Negro Intellectual*, going on to argue that the headquarters of some "big trusts" that extracted millions in profits from African copper, gold, and diamonds had "connections in Israel."[19] John Henrik Clarke, an Afrocentrist writer and professor emeritus of African-American world history at Hunter College in New York, similarly argues, "The Israeli confiscation of Arab land and the destruction of their homes by bulldozers is identical with the same act being perpetrated against Africans in South Africa."[20]

Afrocentrism is a movement that has grown both within the academy and elsewhere. An offspring of the race revolution, it sought to provide blacks with a feeling of pride in their heritage and to correct the unfortunate stereotyping of black images in American culture. But as Arthur Schlesinger, Jr., among others, has pointed out, Afrocentrism can be twisted into racial chauvinism by ultranationalist proponents.[21] Thus, alongside legitimate works of Afrocentric history, there exists an extremist literature that is widely circulated in academic circles and through the many black nationalist bookstores that have sprung up around the country. Through Lushena Press, a wholesale distribution network specializing in African-American, Afro-Caribbean, and African literature, black bookstores obtain copies of the *Protocols of the Elders of Zion* and other explicitly anti-Semitic materials. Among featured authors are Dr. Yosef A. A. Ben-Jochannon, who argues that Africans are the real Jews (he maintains that Jesus was black) and white Jews are imposters, and Dr. John Henrik Clarke, who has defended Leonard Jeffries as saying nothing that cannot be authoritatively documented.[22]*

Black history is a story of dreadful oppression, and the anger of those who study it is not only understandable but almost

---

*Some of these materials have recently expanded beyond the network of small bookstores and can be found in major chains like Borders and Barnes and Noble. Extremist materials are sometimes utilized in classrooms as accurate descriptions of the history of blacks and Jews. The highly regarded journal *Black Issues in Higher Education* carried a lead article entitled "Nile Valley Scholars Bring New Light and Controversy to African Studies," citing Ben-Jochannon and Clarke as being among those who "have set about the arduous task of telling the truth."[23]

inevitable. Some of the current writing about blacks and Jews is fueled by such anger, which strikes out in all directions and, as in a family quarrel, is often directed against those who are closest. Since the crucial question for most black intellectuals today is whether liberalism has served black interests well or badly, it should hardly be surprising that Jews—the group most closely identified with liberalism in American society—have become for some blacks the symbol of that conflict. Thus, to the extent that they held out the hope to blacks that liberal ideals could be applied to changing their material and social condition, Jews (as historians Mary Berry and John W. Blassingame put it, writing about the collision over racial preferences) stood in the way of black progress. For revisionist writers Bracey and Meier, the black Jewish alliance has been "romanticized and considerably exaggerated."[24]

Millions of white and black students attending colleges and universities today know little of the long and painful struggle of blacks and Jews, working together, to achieve racial equality. Black students, buffeted by all the pressures that being black in America entails, are told in frequent campus visits by Louis Farrakhan, Khalid Abdul Muhammad, Kwame Touré, Leonard Jeffries, and other ultranationalists that integration does not work, that the black-Jewish alliance was overblown or never existed, that Jews have always been the enemies of blacks (or are at least no better than false friends) and continue to be so. Some revisionist writers provide a "scholarly" gloss to these charges. Whether consciously or not, they seek to obliterate the past and shape a future of acrimony and conflict. It is hardly surprising that the campus has become an increasing area of black-Jewish tension today.[25]

This book seeks to demonstrate that there *was* a black-Jewish partnership, albeit one sometimes marked by conflict and suspicion, that engaged the emotions and efforts of many blacks and Jews for much of this century. Since racism is still prevalent in many areas of the country and anti-Semitism is resurgent both here and throughout the world and since the only possibility for real change in America is through collective effort by different groups, blacks and Jews must recognize that they still have common areas of concern and common enemies, even though their interests sometimes diverge and they may have to go their separate ways at certain points today.

I do not pretend to be neutral on the subject of the black-Jewish alliance; it has meant so much to me for so long. I grew up poor in Williamsburg, Brooklyn, the child of immigrant parents, and was educated at a free municipal college, Brooklyn College, with students from similar circumstances. My generation was profoundly aware of social injustice, and the plight of blacks was a matter of special concern for many of us. I remember the euphoria I felt when the Supreme Court struck down public school segregation on May 17, 1954. Perhaps now, I recall thinking, America is on its way to wiping out prejudice and discrimination once and for all and making amends for its shameful past in regard to race relations.

Several months later I found myself in Richmond, Virginia, heading the Virginia–North Carolina office of the Anti-Defamation League, a Jewish civil rights organization. Richmond, perhaps the least important of the league's network of offices, was seemingly a good place for a young tyro to start. But I had hardly arrived when massive, organized resistance to the Supreme Court's ruling became apparent. I found myself deeply involved in battles against anti-Semitism with the Ku Klux Klan and the white citizens councils, which spearheaded resistance to the high court's edicts. I was also forced to deal with a nervous Jewish constituency, which, although generally inclined to obey the law of the land, was profoundly concerned about the threat of anti-Semitic violence, a threat that often surfaces in periods of profound social change.

After earning a few scars in battles with the southern white resistance, I came to Philadelphia to my present post with the American Jewish Committee, the nation's oldest civil rights organization. For more than thirty years I have been deeply involved in civil rights activities, working closely with black and Jewish leaders over this entire period. There was never any doubt in my mind that the black-Jewish alliance stood at the center of the great American experiment in democracy.

Given my own record of involvement in the civil rights movement, it should not be surprising that I view the destruction of the alliance with a measure of sorrow and anger. But it is precisely because of these emotions that I have tried to write as balanced and objective an account as I can of this highly charged and controversial subject.

This book had its beginnings in an episode at the University of Pennsylvania in 1984, an episode that demonstrated the growing chasm between black and Jewish students. Jesse Jackson's race for the Democratic presidential nomination that year, his reference to New York as Hymietown, and his evident pro-Arab sympathies had engendered fierce debates on the campus. When Jewish students called for dialogue to clear up the "misunderstandings," black students rejected the overture. Three former presidents of the university's black student union wrote a letter to the student newspaper, the *Daily Pennsylvanian*, which was published beneath the headline "Black-Jewish Coalition Cannot Be." "When two groups of unequal power come together at the bargaining table," the letter declared "the final analysis finds the more powerful group coming [away] with all the benefits."[26]

It was clear to me then and has become even more so over the years that they and others like them had heard only one side of the story. I resolved to attempt to set the record straight by writing the history of the black-Jewish partnership. Despite the paucity of historical resources and validity of calls for additional research, enough materials have accumulated to give a broad outline of that history, one that later historians can fill in and, where necessary, correct.[27]

More than a generation has passed since Martin Luther King was murdered in Memphis. He was seemingly the last leader capable of holding together a partnership that is fast receding in memory. The story is a complicated one. The alliance was frequently riven with personal conflicts and tensions, even during the period of its greatest accomplishments. But only if we start from a common understanding of what that partnership was and was not can we put the present conflicts in perspective and lay a foundation for once again establishing normal relations between the two groups.

1

EARLY BLACK–JEWISH RELATIONS

Although the Jewish interest in promoting black equality goes back a century or more, from the outset there also existed certain tensions between the two groups. Until recently, however, these tensions tended to be submerged in order to overcome shared obstacles and barriers. Only in the past thirty years, with the gradual separation of black and Jewish interests and the loss of shared visions in this country, have these conflicts escalated to a point where they now constitute a major confrontation.

In the present atmosphere of mutual suspicion and resentment, acrimonious charges are leveled by both sides with alarming frequency. Among the most serious charges made against Jews has been the assertion by racial demagogues that, despite protestations of historic solidarity, they in reality played a leading role in foisting slavery on African blacks. This charge has even been seen as worthy of further research by several revisionist writers.

On October 17, 1993, the *Washington Post* published a lengthy article called "Half Truths and History: The Debate over Jews and Slavery." The reporter noted that since this matter was now a subject of public discussion, it was the responsibility of the newspaper to present all sides of the issue. The article was sharply criticized by readers of the *Post* as well as by the paper's ombudsman, who wrote that while there might have been some reason to publish such an article immediately following the wide publicity accorded to Leonard Jeffries's charges two years earlier, he wondered why the paper had chosen to publish it now when it would only cause friction. And indeed, the article was soon cited by a columnist for the *New York Daily News*, who used it to support Jeffries; the contents of the *Post* article gained international attention when an English paper, *The Guardian*, later reprinted it.[1]

At this point it is necessary to ask why this matter has come forward again. The question becomes even more germane when one recalls that the slave trade in Africa and in the Muslim world was as great as or greater than that in the Atlantic world. David Brion Davis, a leading student of the subject of slavery, reports that while the precise figures are impossible to establish, the number of free black planters who owned and worked slaves in the South and Caribbean was many times greater than the number of Jews.[2]

Davis writes, "Responsibility for the African slave trade (and even for creating AIDS) has recently been added to the long list of crimes [of Jews]. Given the long history of conspiratorial fantasy and collective scapegoating, a selective search for Jewish slave traders becomes inherently anti-Semitic unless one keeps in view the larger context and the very marginal place of Jews in the history of the overall system."[3]

It is perfectly acceptable, of course, for serious scholars to call for more study of Jewish participation in the slave trade, as some have done, though it is doubtful whether such study will significantly affect the accepted view that the Jewish role was marginal at best. Meanwhile, any historical study of black-Jewish relations must necessarily begin with a review of current knowledge regarding the role of American and European Jews in black slavery.

For four hundred years the African slave trade was a critical element in European colonial expansion and settlement. It was especially important in the tropical and subtropical regions that created the wealth the European nations sought. West Africa was the primary supplier of slave labor, and Arab merchants were the primary dealers in the trans-Sahara slave trade all over the world, aided by African tribes divided by local disputes and rivalries.

Dominated at first by Portugal, the Atlantic slave trade rapidly attracted the Netherlands, France, and England.

Throughout this period European Jews were heavily persecuted. Intermittent violence decimated their numbers, and professing Jews were expelled from Spain and Portugal and were banned from the Spanish and Portuguese colonies in the New World. Such persecution partly resulted in a desperate search for new commercial opportunities. Many Jews settled in Holland, which was then at the peak of commercial expansion. Throughout the seventeenth century the Dutch were predominant in the slave trade. Jews participated in this trade to some extent, the number of Jewish traders in Holland reaching a high of perhaps six to ten percent at this time. However, by the eighteenth century, when even larger numbers of slaves were being sold, Britain had taken the lead, and the Dutch trade, mainly in the hands of Protestants in any case, declined.[4]

Jews played significant roles neither in the Dutch West India Company nor the British Royal African Company. They were also rare among the dealers of Bristol, London, and Liverpool—who bought and sold some two and a half million Africans in the eighteenth century—although they were important in refining and distributing sugar in the "triangular" transatlantic commerce that involved slaves. Since many Jews were forced to become Christians in Spain and Portugal, these Marranos, or secret Jews, sought to find a place in the New World and played a significant role in making Portugal the predominant supplier of slave-grown sugar. David Brion Davis notes, however, that because of intermarriage and loss of identity, "most Marranos were Jewish only in their vulnerability to suspicion, persecution, and anti-Semitic fantasies of conspiracy."[5]

Some Jews and Jewish converts to Christianity were actively involved in trading slaves in Brazil (briefly until expelled). During their dispersion and as experts in sugar technology, they helped the British learn the practice of sugar refining, even as sugar exportation became critical to the British empire during the 1700s. Jewish traders nevertheless did not enjoy the primary benefits of such expansion; they were primarily shopkeepers in the Barbados and Jamaica in the eighteenth century, while the sugar trade was carried on mainly by a small group of sugar planter agents in London. The place of Jews in the slave economy of French-owned Martinique and Guadeloupe was similarly limited. In any case, the French expelled all Jews from the islands in 1685.

Jewish refugees from Brazil also came to Dutch colonies in Suriname and Curaçao, where they thrived in shipping and trading, including slave trading in Curaçao. Their involvement here, however, was mainly in shipping goods. These colonies did not develop extensive plantation systems because they were unable to compete with colonies like Jamaica, St. Domingue, and Brazil, which went directly to Africa to obtain their slaves. It is true that Sephardi sugar planters in Suriname, where the religiously liberal Dutch permitted Jews to create their own town (Joden Savanne), built their lives around slave labor; nevertheless, Suriname was not a major sugar-growing area, and by the 1670s the Dutch sugar boom ended. The French and especially the English quickly came to hold monopolies of trading companies and ultimately of the movement of Africans to New World colonies, excluding Jews from the business. Indeed, during the eighteenth century, when the slave trade reached its height, British ships carried almost forty-two percent of the slaves from Africa, and the Dutch almost six percent.

Researchers can find Jewish slave-trading families like the Belmontes in Amsterdam and the Gradis in Bordeaux, and later individuals, such as Aaron Lopez and Jacob Rivera, in Newport. The important point, David Brion Davis writes, "is not that a few Jewish slave dealers changed the course of history" but that Jews found the ugly system of slavery in place when they came to the New World and a small number became a part of the system briefly. It is hardly to their credit; but they had considerably less involvement in that system than Protestants, Catholics, or even Muslims. With some ninety percent of the four most significant forced African trades—the British and French trades of the late seventeenth and eighteenth centuries and the Brazilian and Cuban of the eighteen and nineteenth centuries—in the hands of these groups, the Jewish role, according to Seymour Drescher, another student of slavery, "ranged from marginal to nil."[6]

When Jews began arriving in this country in significant numbers, they found slavery built into the economy. The Quakers opposed slavery, as did many Unitarians, but white men of virtually all other religious persuasions participated in the lucrative business. Again the Jewish role was minimal. Jacob R. Marcus, in a two-volume study, The *Colonial Jew*, estimated that American Jewish businessmen accounted for considerably less than two percent of the slave imports into the West Indies and North America. Richmond had three Jewish slave dealers out of seventy; Charleston accounted for four out of forty-four and Memphis only one out of a dozen. Bertram Wallace Korn writes in *Jews and Negro Slavery in the Old South, 1789–1865* that the amount of slave business "done by all the Southern Jews was not as much as the single largest non Jewish firm, Franklin and Armfield."[7] In the period before the Civil War, American Jews were few in number and widely scattered. In 1850 there were only fifty thousand Jews living in the United States. In the next decade another one hundred thousand arrived, but they remained an insignificant minority of ethnic outsiders in a nation of twenty-three million people, most of them Protestant Christians.

In most cases Jews took on the values of the regions in which they settled. Southern Jews generally condoned the long-established system of slavery. In the North many probably opposed slavery privately, but only a few joined the abolitionist cause. Given the passions the issue aroused among their countrymen, they undoubtedly preferred to avoid a strong antislavery position.

Before the Civil War the typical southern Jew was a peddler or petty trader eking out a marginal living. A fortunate few were store owners who lived in a few rooms on the floor above the business. The vast majority were far too poor to afford slaves. Nevertheless, there were a few exceptions. Isaiah Moses kept thirty-five slaves on his farm in Goose Creek, South Carolina. And Judah P. Benjamin, who became a major figure in the Confederacy, kept 140 slaves on his splendid plantation, Bellechasse, near New Orleans. Korn reports that it was rare to find even one Jew who served as a plantation overseer.[8]

A handful of Jews like Benjamin felt themselves very much a part of wealthy Southern society, which rested on slavery, and they were ready during the Civil War to defend it to the death. Even after emancipation some southern Jews saw merit in slavery. Solomon Cohen, the distinguished civic leader and merchant of

Savannah, lost a son fighting for the Confederacy but never yielded on the slavery issue. Shortly after Appomattox, Cohen declared:

> I believe that the institution [slavery] was refining and civilizing to the whites, giving them an elevation of sentiment and ease and dignity of manners only attainable in societies under the restraining influence of a privileged class and, at the same time, the only human institution that could elevate the Negro from barbarism and develop the small amount of intellect with which he is endowed.[9]

Such statements may seem barbarous today, but they were commonplace among educated Southerners in the nineteenth century.

While in the North newly arrived Jews were generally at or near the bottom of the social ladder, circumstances were different in the South, where even the poorest, most abject Jews ranked above slaves. This fact apparently worked to the southern Jews' advantage, for they enjoyed greater success in business and politics than did Jews living in other sections of the country. Korn concluded that the road to acceptance and advancement of Jewish Southerners was aided by the ever present assumption of white superiority. "How ironic," he wrote, "that the distinctions bestowed upon men like Judah P. Benjamin were in some measure dependent upon the suffering of the very Negro slaves they bought and sold with such equanimity."[10]

Just as Jewish slave owners benefited from the notion of white superiority, so did the lowly, itinerant, and often foreign-born Jewish peddlers. Oscar S. Straus, later to become Secretary of Labor and Commerce under Theodore Roosevelt, recalled that his father, when peddling in rural areas of Georgia, was treated by plantation owners with "a spirit of equality that is hard to appreciate today. The existence of slavery drew a distinct line of demarcation between the white and Black races."[11]

In 1861, the historian Frederick Law Olmstead described the developing relationship between southern Jews and blacks betraying his own anti-Semitism: "A swarm of Jews, within the last ten years, has settled in nearly every Southern town, many of them men of no character, opening cheap clothing and trinket shops; ruining, or driving out of business, many of the old retailers, and engaging in unlawful trade with the simple Negroes which is found very profitable." Jews apparently also interacted with free Negroes in the South, unmediated by the slaveholding classes. They were thus brought into contact with blacks in ways that other whites were not—through the medium of exchange.[12]

While the number of southern Jews involved in abolitionist causes remains unknown, there are a number of cases on record of southern Jews acting against slavery. In one case the Friedman brothers of Tuscombia, Georgia, bought a slave named Peter Still, without telling his master that their real purpose was to liberate him. In another the abolitionist orator Ernestine L. Rose made an antislavery speech in Columbia, South Carolina, in 1847.[13] There is some further indication that newly arrived European Jews were dismayed when first witnessing black servitude in the South. Cyrus Adler's autobiography, for example, testifies to his immigrant father's shock at slavery in Arkansas.[14]

In the North, where antislavery activities were widespread, Jews were freer to express abolitionist views. They were among the earliest members of the nation's first antislavery organization, the Pennsylvania Society for Promoting the Abolition of Slavery, founded in Philadelphia in 1774. While some northern Jews, like Moses and Myers, owned slaves, many more opposed slavery, and some spoke out against it. In 1838 Senator (later President) James Buchanan of Pennsylvania presented a memorial from twenty-four Jews of Philadelphia, urging abolition of slavery in the District of Columbia. The signers were members of struggling congregations with fewer than 350 worshipers. Despite their own difficulties in creating communal immigrant-aid societies and warding off proselytizing efforts by Christian missionaries, these Jews took a public stand on the most controversial and explosive issue of the day.[15]

For a long time few Jews in the North followed their example. But the 1840s brought Jews of a different outlook to America, the Ashkenazim from central and eastern Europe. Poor and lacking significant business interests, they sought social and economic opportunities that had been denied them at home. Most had no taste for slavery and no stake in the system.

A smaller group of immigrants were refugees from revolutionary movements in Prussia and Austria-Hungary who had fought for equal rights there and would continue do so in their adopted country. It was they who set the precedent for Jewish civil rights activity that has continued to the present day. From their ranks came August Bondi, Theodore Weiner, and Jacob Benjamin, all three of whom joined the most militant of abolitionists, John Brown. (One contemporary observer even saw in Brown's raids in the border states a Jewish plot masterminded by the French Rothschilds.) Michael Greenbaum aided fugitive slaves in Chicago. Moritz Pinner and Wilhelm Rapp edited abolitionist newspapers in Kansas City and Baltimore. Isador Busch—like Bondi, a Viennese émigré—played an important role in Missouri politics. His oratory and leadership at state conventions in 1861 and 1863 were instrumental in keeping Missouri within the Union. He also helped develop the plan that freed slaves in Missouri without compensating their owners.[16] Many northern Jews, however, agreed with Abraham Lincoln that saving the Union was more important than destroying slavery.

Lewis Tappan, a noted New England abolitionist, wrote in 1853 that Jews as a denomination had not formed any opinion on the subject of slavery in America. Tappan found their silence surprising, given the fact they had been the "objects of so much mean prejudice and unrighteous oppression."[17] But there was a rational explanation for this failure. In the pre–Civil War period there were no central religious bodies or national leaders to mobilize Jewish opinion, as there were in the case of Protestant denominations. The slavery issue was therefore left, for the most part, to the individual conscience of each rabbi and each Jew.

Many of the rabbis who took strong abolitionist stands came from the growing Reform movement within Judaism, which focused on the imperatives of social justice rather than religious ritual. The Reform movement encouraged Jews to employ justice and righteousness in attempting to solve the problems and evils of society. A number of these rabbis were immigrants with links to the Jewish Reform movement in Europe and to revolutionary activities there, and some of them made common cause with the abolitionists.[18]

David Einhorn of Baltimore, for example, was an outspoken critic of slavery. Although he lived in Maryland, a border state, he repeatedly declared his belief "in one humanity, all of whose members, being of the same and early origin, possess a like nobility of birth and a claim to equal rights, equal laws, and an equal share of happiness."[19]

But Einhorn's antislavery views received nowhere near the attention paid to the proslavery oratory of Rabbi Morris J. Raphall of B'nai Jeshurun Synagogue in New York. (Einhorn's initial attack on Raphall appeared in his monthly magazine and probably reached a small audience because it was written in German.) The Swedish-born rabbi was a virulent critic of both abolitionism and Reform Judaism. In one of his strongest attacks on abolitionism on January 4, 1861, Raphall excoriated the abolitionists for claiming that biblical law made slavery immoral and unlawful. Reminding his audience that Abraham, Isaac, and Joshua, all of whom had spoken with the Lord, owned slaves, he characterized abolitionism as implicitly blasphemous.[20]

Raphall's sermon contributed little that was new to the slavery debate, since proslavery advocates had used the Bible to sanction slavery since colonial times. But he was a prominent Orthodox rabbi—the first Jewish clergyman to act as chaplain of the day in Congress—so southern newspapers had a field day, with banner headlines telling of the New York rabbi who supported slavery. Another New York rabbi, Michael Heilprin, countered with a critical attack in the influential *New York Daily Tribune*, where Horace Greeley described him as a "learned Jew" who had few living equals. Heilprin accused Raphall of violating the spirit and practice of Judaism. Einhorn charged that only Jews who "prize the dollar more highly than their God and their religion" could approve Raphall's defense of slavery. In Baltimore the reaction was violent. Arsonists burned Einhorn's printing press, and his life was threatened. He fled the city and took a post in Philadelphia.

The debate between Raphall on the one side and Heilprin and Einhorn on the other went beyond the slavery controversy; it represented in some respects the conflict between Reform and Orthodoxy. The latter defended the traditional literal interpretation of the Bible, while Heilprin wanted biblical slavery passages analyzed historically in a critical liberal spirit, according to historian Jayme A. Sokolow. The Republican party in its 1860 campaign endorsed the latter position when it stated that the Mosaic code tried to soften slavery and was therefore the opposite of the American system.[21]

Neither of the two most important Jewish religious leaders in the United States at that time, Isaac Leeser of Philadelphia and Isaac Mayer Wise of Cincinnati, had much to say about slavery. According to his biographer, Leeser was "discreetly pro-South." Commenting favorably on Raphall's views in his monthly journal, *The Occident*, Leeser pointed out that the ancient Jews were described in the Bible as keeping "perpetual servants." He deduced that these servants were in fact slaves, but the word *slave* did not exist in the Hebrew "by any fair construction." Leeser nevertheless rejected the southern and racist version of slavery. The living conditions of Canaanite servants among the Hebrews, he noted, were far more humane than was the harsh treatment of American slaves.[22]

Wise's situation in Ohio, a border state, was delicate. Most of the subscribers to his weekly publication, *the Israelite* (later *The American Israelite*), were southern Jews. Like so many of his fellow citizens in the border states, Wise was a "peace Democrat," who believed that preserving the Union was more important than abolishing slavery. Therefore while not directly challenging Raphall's stand, Wise did question his biblical arguments. "Among all the nonsense imposed on the Bible," he wrote, "the greatest is to suppose the Negroes are descendants of Ham and the curse of Noah [slavery] is applicable to them." After emancipation, when the debate for and against slavery was largely academic, Wise stepped up his attack, charging Raphall with making a grave error in suggesting that divine sanction existed for the inhuman institution of slavery.[23]

But Wise's overriding interest and lifetime work lay in establishing Reform Judaism as a viable form of religious expression in the United States. In seeking to carry out this mission, he was constantly on guard against Protestant efforts to Christianize Jews. What troubled him about opponents of slavery like Lewis Tappan was their belief that the only good abolitionists were evangelical Protestants. Tappan's 1853 report for the American and Foreign Anti-Slavery Society, for example, was clearly directed at antislavery Christians; Jews were treated as outsiders.

In its earlier days abolitionism had enjoyed a broader constituency. Antislavery Quakers, Unitarians, and deists had worked together without much concern about denominational biases. But with the passage of time, the movement became linked to temperance and other Christian causes, which Jews either had no interest in or—as with Sunday closing laws—opposed. Abolitionism itself thus began to reflect the biases of Protestant leaders. Frequently, Protestant clergymen would see no incongruity in citing biblical condemnations of slavery and in the next breath denouncing Jews as guilty of hypocrisy, deceit, and craftiness.[24]

Wise was thus profoundly suspicious of northern abolitionists. In his view they were instigators of war, ethically inconsistent on human rights. He was not alone in his suspicions. Sabato Morais, the Orthodox rabbi of Congregation Mikveh Israel, founded in colonial times in Philadelphia, never hesitated to speak out against slavery but would not join any of the antislavery societies for precisely these reasons.[25] In short, Wise and Morais and other Jews as well believed the nineteenth-century abolitionists to be highly selective in their sympathies, fighting for freedom for black people while trampling on the civil rights of Jews and other "outsiders." Wise and the rest believed that the progressives of his day were willing to identify with the cause of blacks while excluding or ignoring the interests and values of other disadvantaged groups in the society.

If the Jewish view of slavery was equivocal in the antebellum years, the black image of Jews was equally complicated. Prior to Appomattox many blacks had never seen a Jew. Long before the Jewish migration from eastern Europe began, however, slaves on southern plantations shared the Jewish experience of oppression. They saw their own condition reflected in the story of ancient Israel, and they were especially moved by the Israelites' great exodus from Egypt into the land of freedom. James Baldwin would write that just as God had made a covenant with Abraham extending to his children's children in perpetuity, newly freed slaves later felt that such an agreement had also been made with them and would some day be fulfilled.[26]

The slaves seized upon the sacred imagery of the Bible stories and related it to their own suffering, a response reflected in the many surviving spiritual hymns that draw on Old Testament themes. In addition to the spiritual solace afforded by these analogies, they also had a propaganda value for opponents of slavery. Leaders like Harriet Tubman, organizer of the underground railroad, and the slave known as Gabriel, who headed the Virginia slave revolt of 1800, stirred support among Christians and Jews by comparing blacks to the enslaved children of Israel. This tactic was to be repeated in the civil rights struggles of the 1950s and 1960s, when preachers in the South and elsewhere emerged from black pulpits to exhort their followers in the idiom of the Old Testament. In that context, Birmingham police chief Eugene "Bull" Connor was seen as a modern Pharaoh, Martin Luther King, Jr., as Moses, and the freedom marchers were Israelites heading for the Promised Land. The identification of blacks, in and out of slavery, with Jews, the Holy Land, and the Jewish historical experience would thus prove to be a powerful force throughout the history of the black struggle for equality, though it has since been superseded by identification with the African experience.[27]

Although blacks identified with Jews and based their own hopes on the Jewish example, they were also deeply suspicious of Jews. Like many white Christians, blacks often blamed Jews for the betrayal and crucifixion of their Lord and Savior, Jesus Christ. In his autobiography, Richard Wright wrote of his own youthful indoctrination in Mississippi and Tennessee before the First World War: "All of us Black people hated Jews, not because they exploited us but because we had been taught at home and in Sunday School that Jews were 'Christ killers.'" Wright described this anti-Semitism as not merely a prejudice, but a natural part of his cultural heritage."[28] Black jingles and folk rhymes reinforced the stereotype:

Virgin Mary had one son
The cruel Jews had him hung
Bloody Christ killer
Never trust a Jew
Bloody Christ killer
What won't a Jew do?[29]

Yet despite their ambivalence, blacks recognized that Jews were unlike other whites, since for the most part they had not been large slaveholders or farmers. While other whites spurned slaves and free blacks, Jewish peddlers sought them out, grateful for customers of whatever race or background. In some cases their business dealings fostered lasting friendships. After emancipation, when a second generation of German Jews was becoming less distinguishable from other whites, the Negro would unhesitatingly unlock the door of the shanty to the bent figure of a new peddler, this time from eastern Europe, and "experience the Jew all over again." In other instances the peddlers came to be viewed as exploiters of the "simple Negroes."[30] Nevertheless, the black writer Martin R. Delany, in his classic antebellum exposition of black political nationalism, *The Condition, Elevation, Emigration, and Destiny of the Colored Peoples in the United States*, found a fundamental parallel between black aspirations and the Jewish experience.[31]

From the outset, then, the black-Jewish relationship was a complex combination of affection and distrust. Each started out with different views and expectations of the other, Leonora E. Berson writes. These "contradictory concepts of their relationship [ultimately] bewildered the Jews and infuriated the Negroes."[32]

When the break came between North and South, American Jews (who then numbered 150,000) lined up with the section of the country in which they lived. Some six thousand Jews served with the Union and fifteen hundred with the Confederacy. Joining the military was one way in which Jews, as relative newcomers, could show their loyalty.[33] Some 210,000 black men fought in the Union army and navy, and the way they conducted themselves made emancipation and citizenship more conceivable to all Americans.

While Jews fought and died on both sides, there were widespread allegations throughout the war that Jewish businessmen were engaged in profiteering. In one notorious episode in 1862, Gen. Ulysses S. Grant brought the matter to wide public attention with a military order barring "the Jews as a class" from the shifting battle line in Tennessee and Mississippi. President Lincoln later countermanded Grant's order. As the pressures and strains of the war mounted, a movement developed in the North for a constitutional amendment declaring America to be a Christian nation. Anti-Semitic attacks became more frequent and widespread and were also better organized than ever before.[34]

Anti-Semitism was evident in the South, too. Suspicion of the merchant and storekeeper in a society dominated by the plantation owner and foreman fueled an attack on Jews that alleged corruption and disloyalty. In 1862 these suspicions led to calls at a community meeting for the expulsion of German Jews from Thomasville, Georgia—though the threat was not carried out.[35]

The principal target of these attacks, however, was the Confederacy's highest-ranking Jew, Judah P. Benjamin. Next to President Jefferson Davis, Benjamin was the most important figure in the rebel government. According to one historian he "achieved greater political power than any other Jew in the nineteenth century—perhaps even in all American history."[36] Besides serving as secretary of war and then as secretary of state, he was also Davis's chief aide and amanuensis. He wrote the president's speeches, prepared his papers, and ran the Confederacy during Davis's frequent illnesses.

A staunch defender of slavery, Benjamin was nevertheless an ambiguous figure. In 1842, in one of the most famous insurance cases in American history, he was counsel for a group of insurance companies sued by slaveholders who sought compensation for losses incurred in a slave uprising at sea. Gaining control of the ship, the slaves took it to Nassau, a British territory, where some were set free. Benjamin appeared before the Louisiana supreme court, where he argued that slavery was "a controvention of the law of nature." His eloquent plea in his legal brief that a slave was a human being was recognized by abolitionists, who published the brief as a pamphlet.

Because he held such important offices in the Confederacy, Benjamin drew heavy criticism as the South's failures and frustrations mounted. Henry Foote, a member of the Confederate house of representatives and a bitter foe of Davis's administration, labeled his top adviser Judas Iscariot Benjamin. Foote further declared his intention to amend the Confederate constitution so that no Jew would be allowed within twelve miles of the capital. He thus linked the "treasonous" cabinet member with the alleged extortionist merchants and shopkeepers whom he believed were sabotaging the Confederacy.[37]

In the waning days of the war, Benjamin, though a slaveholder and supporter of the southern way of life, recommended that any slaves who agreed to serve in the Confederate ranks be granted their freedom. His motivation was evidently more tactical than moral, since his goal was to expand the size of the Confederate forces as quickly as possible. However, in substance his proposal differed little from Lincoln's Emancipation Proclamation, which granted freedom to slaves only in states that had rebelled.

Benjamin moved carefully to accomplish his goal. Among those supporting the plan was Davis's wife, Varina. Robert E. Lee, commander in chief of the Confederate forces, also gave his approval. In his annual message to the southern congress in November 1864, Davis urged acceptance of the proposal in words written by Benjamin.

What Benjamin sought was an extraordinary change in the principle that had governed slaveholding since the first blacks were imported nearly two centuries earlier. He recommended that the enslaved blacks be granted "certain rights of property, a certain degree of personal liberty, and legal protection for the marital and parental relations" that up to then had gone unrecognized by slaveholders. Such reforms, said Benjamin, would "relieve our institutions from much that is not only unjust and impolitic in itself, but calculated to draw upon us the odium and reprobation of civilized man."

Benjamin used all the power and influence he could muster to win support for the proposal.[38] On February 9, 1865, more than ten thousand people jammed a black church in Richmond and stood in throngs outside to hear Benjamin deliver a stirring defense of the emancipation plan. Jefferson Davis and his wife were there, as were prominent civilians and Confederate military leaders. "Never was he more eloquent or inspiring," Varina Davis later wrote. "He sent those who had come discouraged and desperate, knowing as they did the overwhelming forces which confronted them, back to camp full of hope and ardor, and I think made the most successful effort of his life."[39]

But Benjamin's hopes were defeated. In the final weeks before surrender, the Confederate congress permitted slave volunteers to fight but made no mention of emancipation. The senate, meanwhile, considered but failed to pass a resolution of no confidence in Benjamin. After the war Benjamin settled in England, where he enjoyed another brilliant career as a lawyer and businessman. A truly remarkable figure, Benjamin left an uncertain legacy to future generations of blacks and Jews.

In the years after the Civil War, Jewish peddlers with packs of tinware, clocks, and clothing on their backs or in their carts became a familiar sight in rural areas of the old Confederacy. Unlike the Yankees whom they replaced, the Jewish peddlers, many of them newly arrived immigrants from eastern Europe, sold their goods to black sharecroppers as well as white farmers.[40]

For most southern blacks, dealing with Jews in the flesh (as distinct from the biblical Jew) was an entirely new experience. Now blacks and Jews encountered each other in a free-market setting.[41] A relationship that would last for a hundred years might be said to have begun in just such encounters. For it was from these Jewish peddlers that newly freed blacks frequently gained their "initial sense of dignity," according to the Jewish folk essayist Harry Golden. Through participating in a system of exchange, newly emancipated blacks came to feel themselves active—though still usually poor—members of a free society.[42]

The phenomenon was relatively short-lived. With the passage of time, such peddlers as Benjamin Altman and Adam Gimbel succeeded in accumulating enough capital to go into business for themselves, and their modest dry-goods operations soon evolved into the first modern department stores.[43] The southern Jewish merchants ran their businesses differently from others. While competition generally limited their trade in the white community, the Jewish store operators actively sought business dealings with blacks and sometimes even opened stores in black neighborhoods. In many towns blacks knew that the "Jew store" would extend credit to them, address them as "Mr." and "Mrs.," and permit them to try on clothes before buying.[44]

As early as 1900, when very few white shopkeepers in the North or South employed blacks, they were hired by Jewish stores.[45] While the Jewish owners were occasionally charged with taking advantage of blacks, their openness to blacks, both as customers and employees, and their willingness to disregard caste principles help explain the success of many Jewish merchants and may perhaps explain why there seem to be fewer angry feelings about Jews among blacks born in the South than in the North.[46]

The white southern establishment occasionally perceived the Jewish merchants as unwanted carpetbaggers, agents of the northern victor lording it over the defeated South. More often, however, the Jews were welcomed by white Protestants as "people of the Book." In addition, the South's devastated postwar economy needed help. The advice of Jewish businessmen was often solicited, and they frequently served on policy-making boards and committees.

Not all Jewish immigrants found riches in the South, of course. Some survived as pawnbrokers, others operated "houses of shame" or sold kimonos, stockings, and cosmetics to the prostitutes who worked in them. Ray Stannard Baker noted that many saloons for blacks in Atlanta were foreign-owned, usually by Jewish businessmen.[47] Traveling through the South in the early years of this century, a Jewish socialist named Baruch Charney Vladeck termed such Jews "the most tragic and broken type[s] which modern Jewish life had created." "[I]n chasing after a livelihood," Vladeck reasoned, "he [the Jew] loses his self-respect and the feeling of sympathy that the Jews have evolved during the last couple thousand years of their history."[48]

Influential blacks were divided on the subject of Jews. Some warned of the dangers of growing Jewish wealth and power. In this reaction lay a streak of black populism. Blacks, after all, were not just victims, they were Americans, too. Coming up north in 1883 from the South, where an alliance of black and white populists had been gaining strength, journalist T. Thomas Fortune charged in the black-owned *New York Globe* that Jews controlled the southern money markets, keeping white planters in thralldom and oppressing poor black laborers. Other black newspapers, like the *New York Freeman* and the *Age* (the *Globe*'s successors) made similar statements in subsequent years. Enshrined in this rhetoric was the popular perception of Jews as "crossroads storekeepers" who charged high interest and exorbitant prices for mortgages and other financial arrangements.[49]

Such expressions, however, were not the norm. Black anger was more often directed toward their direct oppressors and the European immigrants who threatened their jobs.[50] Blacks found much to admire in the Jewish experience, viewing Jews as people who despite humble beginnings and minority status overcame discrimination and achieved economic success. To them it appeared that prejudicial treatment had only made the Jews strive harder, thereby establishing a pattern on which former slaves could model themselves.

In the *Age* and other papers the oft-repeated message was "Let us learn from the Jews." Instead of wallowing in despair and brooding about their unjust treatment, blacks were urged to reclaim self-respect through Jewish-style group cohesion. "Where everything else had been denied him—political rights, social standing, even the privilege of owning real estate—the Jew yet conquered," the A.M.E. Church Review reported in 1892. The secret, it said, lay in acquiring money and education, and it encouraged blacks to do the same.[51] Clearly the image of the Jew held by poor and often uneducated blacks was more benign than their view of the "cracker," and frequently implicit within it was a bond of sympathy. Thus, quite early in their relationship, it would appear, blacks held a view of Jews that mixed admiration and respect with suspicion and hostility.

A central figure in promoting the idea that blacks should emulate Jews was the most prominent black in the America of that time—Booker Taliaferro Washington. Born into slavery in 1856, Washington became a nationally known educator, whose gradualist racial philosophy won wide acceptance at a time when blacks enjoyed few civil rights. He founded a new school for blacks, Tuskegee Institute, at Tuskegee, Alabama, in 1881 and acquiesced publicly in policies of racial separation in schools and some social settings, whatever his private feelings may have been. The ideology he shaped at Tuskegee, one that found favor with some blacks as well as whites, was well stated in a speech at the Atlanta Exposition in 1885: "Cast down your buckets where you are."[52] To this end he encouraged blacks to respect the laws and get along as best they could with southern whites. He favored industrial and agricultural training and self-help strategies for blacks.

After a brief period of freedom during Reconstruction, blacks were once again subjected to harsh repression throughout the

South. Black codes were enacted to deprive them of basic liberties. The Ku Klux Klan was organized as a terrorist group that preyed on blacks. In this grim atmosphere Booker T. Washington became more heavily influenced by the Jewish example. "Ever since I can remember," he wrote, "I have had a special and peculiar interest in the history and progress of the Jewish race. As I learned in slavery to compare the condition of the Negro with that of the Jews in bondage in Egypt, so I have frequently, since freedom, been compelled to compare the prejudice, even persecution, which the Jewish people have to face and overcome in different parts of the world with the disadvantages of the Negro in the United States and elsewhere."*

What particularly impressed Washington was the pride that Jews took in their Jewishness, their faith in themselves, and the way they supported one another. In *The Future of the American Negro*, he wrote: "These people [Jews] have clung together. They have had a certain amount of unity, pride and love of race; and, as the years go on, they will be more influential in this country—a country where they were once despised, and looked upon with scorn and derision. It is largely because the Jewish race has had faith in itself. Unless the Negro learns more and more to imitate the Jew in these matters, to have faith in himself, he cannot expect to have any high degree of success."

Washington was careful to distinguish Jews from other European immigrants, whom he dismissed as beggars, anarchists, or superstitious peasants. He admired Jews, however, not only for withstanding centuries of persecution but for gaining a measure of wealth and position in society. Washington was fond of recounting the story of a Jewish immigrant who happened to be traveling through Alabama with all of his possessions in a single satchel. Passing through a prosperous cotton-growing region sixteen miles from Tuskegee, the immigrant noted the absence of nearby stores. That keen observation changed his life. He halted his travels on

---

*The *New York Times* once asked Washington to name his favorite passage from Shakespeare. He selected Shylock's "Hath not a Jew eyes?" speech in *The Merchant of Venice*. To Washington, Shylock's plea on behalf of Jews and brotherhood had an echo in the appeal of blacks to be treated as men and brothers.[53]

the spot, rented property, and opened a store. Within four years he was a wealthy businessman and the owner of hundreds of acres of rich farmland.

The extraordinary strides Jews made in overcoming disadvantages gave Washington hope for blacks. He believed they could become the architects of their own future in the new South.[54] He ignored, however, the major differences between the black and Jewish experiences, including the long Jewish mercantile tradition, the important fact that Jews were whites, and as a result of this, the freedom of opportunity that Jews generally found here.

Although Washington greatly admired Jews, he is reported by his biographer, Louis Harlan, as being full of misunderstandings about them. Harlan sees Washington as sharing the small-town American anti-Semitism of his day that identified Jews with the image of overpricing storekeepers and the usurious lender. Washington criticized Jews in some of his early speeches, but after affluent German Jews began contributing to Tuskegee and other black causes, he either discarded or concealed his prejudice.[55]

Washington's recommendation that blacks place economics ahead of politics, as Jews did, was not without black critics. William Monroe Trotter, editor of the *Boston Guardian*, rejected the notion that Jews had won acceptance through the accumulation of wealth. In fact, Trotter argued, their business success only intensified hatred against them. By the same token, he believed, the hostility that blacks encountered stemmed from prejudice, not poverty. He was convinced that Jews got attention by using the vote, and blacks, he said, must do the same. Meanwhile, the *St. Paul Appeal*, a black newspaper, dismissed as bunk the view, widely circulated in the black press, that Jews never raised their voices in political protest because of their obsession with moneymaking.

Thus, while there was certainly no formal black-Jewish alliance in the years immediately after the Civil War, there was at least an indirect relationship, as the Jewish example became central to the debate over strategies for the future of blacks.

Southern Jews, meanwhile, found themselves in the middle of a postwar power struggle between opposing white groups. On one side were former plantation owners who, while building a new South, longed for a return to the old feudal order. On the other were upcountry farmers who advocated a populist and racist government with power in the hands of poor whites. Both groups were opposed to black liberation.[56]

Individual Jewish reactions to the South's defeat varied. Still few in number and anxious to get along with their white neighbors, most southern Jews tended to identify with the more moderate forces of Bourbon restoration and the new South. Typical was attorney Edwin Moise of Charleston, a member of the local Jewish aristocracy, who was installed as adjutant and inspector general in South Carolina in 1876 to battle radical reconstruction. Moise opposed the violent methods of the Ku Klux Klan—which would later turn its wrath on Jews—but he maintained a discreet silence out of a combination of opportunism and fear. Most southern Jews tried to distance themselves from the newly liberated black population for much the same reason.[57]

The South had always been culturally and economically separate from other parts of the country, and it had held on to its intrinsic differences even after the war as a way of maintaining its distinctiveness and cohesion. Leaders of the new South recognized that the region's recovery was imperiled by self-imposed historic isolation. Southern bourbons therefore encouraged northern investment, fostered immigration, and promised cheap labor. Over time these initiatives succeeded in strengthening a region that lacked industry and had been prostrated by war. But poor whites, already suffering from ruinous agricultural prices and joblessness, viewed the newly arrived outsiders with undisguised hostility. While blacks were the central focus of their hostility, all "foreigners"—meaning those who differed in any way from the dominant Anglo-Saxon culture—became targets of xenophobia.

Jews presented a special case. They had been in the South since colonial times, and attitudes toward them were decidedly varied, as has already been suggested. During periods of calm, they had suffered no special difficulties. But now a sustained crisis gripped the South, and all the latent fears and jealousies about Jewish success came to the surface. Welcomed earlier, they were now often denounced as economic exploiters, loan sharks, and agents of a conquering northern imperialism. In the Bible Belt, Jews were often labeled Christ killers; white populists considered them eternal aliens, the embodiment of all the evils that white Southerners feared and hated.

The suspicion that Jews were colluding with freed slaves became entwined with the belief that they were exploiting white Southerners. In Franklin, Tennessee, in 1868, Klansmen lynched a young Russian Jew who operated a dry goods store and had a reputation as a radical Republican. He was close to blacks and employed a black clerk, who was also slain. Another Jew who counseled blacks to retaliate against the Klan was murdered.[58] Physical attacks on Jews mounted across the South in the 1880s and 1890s. With the coming to power of "Pitchfork" Ben Tillman in South Carolina, the reign of harassment and terror intensified. Edwin Moise was vilified as "an outsider and a member of a despised and despicable race" by Tillman and defeated in his race for Congress in 1890. The difficulties that Jews now began to face in the South would culminate a generation later in the highly publicized lynching of Leo Frank.[59]

As the wave of anti-Jewish and anti-black feeling increased throughout the South, relations between Jews and blacks became more complex. There was much that still drew them together. Blacks often rallied to the support of Jews, whose sufferings were seen as similar to their own. Thus, when Alfred Dreyfus, a Jewish officer in the French army, was sent to Devil's Island in 1895 on trumped-up charges of treason, black newspapers were harsh in their condemnation of French anti-Semitism. The *Washington Bee* condemned this outrageous persecution of an innocent man and compared the Dreyfus court proceedings with those that American Negroes experienced.[60]

Before long, however, the editorial tone of some black newspapers changed. Jews were often seen as a favored group, even if still outsiders, and some papers accused the U.S. government of employing a double standard in its dealings with Jews abroad and blacks in this country. When Russian and Romanian Jews were hounded by pogroms, black newspapers pointed out, Washington filed formal protests with Moscow and Bucharest. Yet despite a sharp rise in lynchings of blacks in the South, federal officials were silent, ignoring their duty to protect the rights of Negro citizens guaranteed under the Fourteenth and Fifteenth Amendments. As one black newspaper wrote, it was regrettable that "so industrious, sober and intelligent a class as the Jews should have to be discriminated against," while going on to argue that the nation's press was devoting too much space to condemnations of anti-Semitism in Europe and not enough to advancing the cause of underprivileged Negroes at home.[61]

The black press's tiny audience, of course, did not include influential Americans in business or government. Its complaints about government indifference or worse, though certainly valid, were barely noticed at the time because the nation's mainstream newspapers paid them no heed.

Some of this resentment was directed against the Jewish-owned *New York Times*, which blacks found guilty of myopically ignoring the plight of southern blacks while concentrating on Russian pogroms. In 1891 the *Times* underwrote a reporter's trip to czarist Russia to investigate anti-Semitism there; it subsequently published regular reports on the problems encountered by Russian Jews. At first the *Freeman*, a black weekly published in Indianapolis, was sympathetic toward the *Times*'s coverage of Russian atrocities. But before long, the *Freeman* and its successor, *The Age*, began to sound a persistently negative note. "Jews through their instrument, the *New York Times*, influenced foreign policy, but hurt Negroes in America," the *Age* alleged. Additionally, the *Times* was accused of "sowing seeds of race prejudice against Negroes" by publishing letters to the editor that emphasized black crime instead of black accomplishment.[62] Strains with the *Times* would continue well into the twentieth century.

Following the widely publicized 1903 pogrom in Kishinev in which forty-nine Jews were killed, five hundred were injured, and many more were driven from their homes, President Theodore Roosevelt forwarded to the czar a B'nai B'rith petition denouncing the killing and looting. Booker T. Washington was among the Americans who spoke out publicly on behalf of the victims.[63] Many blacks could not help noting, however, that the petition signers included senators from Mississippi who had favored the lynching of Negroes as necessary for the maintenance of law and order. Other signers included the mayor of Evansville, Indiana, and members of the city council. (Evansville had been the scene of a riot earlier in 1903 in which more than a thousand blacks had been driven from their homes into nearby woods.) "Negroes are fleeing from the American Kishineff [sic], Evansville, Indiana," the *Freeman* wrote bitterly on July 25, 1903. "Shall the Negroes look to the czar of Russia for protection, since neither the President of the United States nor the Mayor of Evansville seem interested in protecting them?"[64]

Blacks were also aware that Roosevelt was concerned enough about the Jewish situation abroad to discuss the matter with such prominent leaders as Leo N. Levi, Simon Wolf, and Oscar Straus at the White House. Roosevelt was practicing what Henry Feingold, in a different context, has called the "politics of gesture." But even so, Jewish access to people in high positions contrasted sharply with the impotence of blacks.[65]

Jewish leaders occasionally exacerbated these tensions with their own insensitivities. Thus, when the *Public*, a Chicago liberal weekly, urged Jews in 1903 to recognize the parallel experiences of American blacks and Russian Jews, it provoked an outburst of criticism from Jewish spokesmen. Dr. Solomon Cohen, a leader of B'nai B'rith in Philadelphia, insisted in a letter endorsed by his organization that there were simply no grounds for comparing the two groups, considering the advanced intellectual and moral development of the Jews in comparison with the limited progress made by Negroes in America.[66] Cohen's comments were widely reprinted and sharply criticized by the black press, which waited for Jews to take issue with them. None did, however.

Just when black-Jewish friction over Kishinev was easing, an episode in Maryland stirred further rancor. Between 1903 and 1909 numerous southern states sought to disfranchise blacks. Maryland was the most northerly state to make the attempt, and its efforts received national attention. The drive was headed by two leaders of Baltimore's Jewish community, who urged the city's white population to protect itself from what it saw as Negro depravity by depriving blacks of the vote.[67]

Not all Jews in Maryland approved of this racist initiative. Rabbi Benjamin Szold of Baltimore—the father of Henrietta Szold, who founded Hadassah—believed that newly emancipated slaves needed schooling and became a leader in the Baltimore Association for the Education and Moral Improvement of the Colored People. For his efforts he was vilified and labeled the Rabbi of Timbuctoo.[68] Another Jew who spoke out against the disfranchisement of blacks was Louis Marshall, the noted New York lawyer. Invited in 1907 to participate in a debate on the issue sponsored by the Educational Alliance, a Jewish settlement house in New York, Marshall angrily wrote back that a body of Jews who had just themselves emerged from virtual slavery and were seeking the franchise denied to their ancestors should never for a moment argue in favor of disfranchising any citizen of this country.[69]

It is clear that varying Jewish attitudes toward blacks existed at this time, some of them overtly racist. And black resentment toward Jews was not necessarily based on anti-Semitism. David J. Hellwig has written of blacks of that epoch that when Jews discriminated against them, they were sharply criticized, because blacks expected more of a group that itself had been a victim of bigotry.[70]

In the post–Civil War years impoverished blacks from rural areas of the South moved north in steadily increasing numbers. Historian Gilbert Osofsky has noted that as the northern black population grew, so did segregation and racial antagonism. Jobs that had been open to blacks—such as cooks, waiters, butlers, cabmen, janitors, barbers, and bootblacks—were now closed. Blacks were refused service in bars and restaurants, and a movement was launched to restore the state law in New York banning interracial marriages. Antiblack rioting in New York City broke out in 1900, the worst disturbances since the Civil War draft riots. In one of the bloodiest of the episodes, beginning on August 13 and lasting for several days, a number of blacks were killed and many injured.[71]

Jews far outnumbered blacks in New York at the close of the nineteenth century. In 1892 alone, 66,544 Jewish immigrants arrived at Ellis Island; there were at that time only 60,000 blacks in the entire city! Most were employed as servants and lived on the city's west side, although some were beginning to move into Harlem. Most of the newly arrived Jews, on the other hand, lived in a densely populated ghetto on the Lower East Side, which ran from the southern tip of Manhattan to 14th Street and from the East River to the Bowery. Many immigrant Jews worked in the garment industry. Only a few Jewish peddlers ventured into black neighborhoods, and there was very little interaction between the poor and working-class Jews and the blacks, although each group was certainly aware of the other's existence.[72]

By the 1880s, however, a web of relationships was already beginning to form between New York City's black and Jewish social and intellectual elites.[73] Jews had been effective in business but not in politics or social activism. Some now saw an outlet for their energies and talents in the Progressive movement, which had been organized to combat such excesses of rampaging capitalism as child labor, slum housing and the seven-day work week, along with other social ills. Members of New York's German-Jewish elite, such as Isaac W. Seligman, Joseph S. Auerbach, and Samuel A. Lewisohn, involved themselves in efforts to improve black housing. The Henry Street Settlement, established on the Lower East Side in 1893 by Lillian Wald with the financial assistance of Jacob Schiff, provided a way for upper-class Jews to assist not only Russian Jews but blacks as well.[74] In 1906 the Henry Street Settlement opened a branch in the black ghetto in San Juan Hill. Other Jewish philanthropists supported the Free Kindergarten for Colored Children, which offered preschool help previously unavailable to blacks. The White Rose Mission, which sought to protect "unsuspecting [black] girls desiring to come North" was supported by prominent Jews, including Paul M. Warburg, a member of Kuhn, Loeb & Company, the Wall Street investment banking firm, and later the vice-governor of the Federal Reserve Bank.[75]

Such support was not always greeted with universal approval. While serving on New York's board of education in 1882, Jacob Schiff called for abolition of the city's segregated school system and the closing of its "colored schools." Besides being needlessly expensive, separate schools for black and white pupils reinforced social and race prejudice contributing to the underlying crisis in education.

Schiff's resolution divided the black community. Although a number of its leaders denounced the colored schools as relics of barbarism, others opposed the closing out of fear that black teachers might lose their jobs. In the end Schiff won: the dual system was abolished and job protection was given black teachers.[76] However, de facto school segregation continued in New York and other northern cities until well into the twentieth century.

Meanwhile, leaders of the black community, particularly Booker T. Washington, sought financial and other ties with the Jewish community. In this he was quite successful, not only among his Jewish neighbors in Alabama but also among affluent Jews in northern cities. Soon Jews constituted the majority of whites at Tuskegee commencement exercises. In 1904 Washington created a "Jewish seat" on Tuskegee's board and persuaded Paul M. Warburg to take it.[77]

Recognizing that New York was the nation's financial capital, Washington soon moved his northern fund-raising headquarters there from Boston. Among the wealthy Jews who were subsequently to contribute to Tuskegee were Jacob and Mortimer Schiff, James Loeb, and Felix Warburg (all members of Kuhn, Loeb), as well as the Seligmans, the Lehmans, Joseph Pulitzer, Jacob Billikopf, and Julian Mack. Jacob Schiff developed so much confidence in Washington that in 1909 he placed three thousand dollars at his disposal—a third for Tuskegee, smaller amounts for four other black schools, and the remainder to be distributed to schools of Washington's choice. Schiff continued this arrangement annually until Washington's death in 1915, by which time his yearly contributions had grown threefold. Even Joel Spingarn, later an ardent critic of Washington, contributed to Tuskegee in 1909.

Although Paul Warburg resigned from Tuskegee's board in 1909, Julius Rosenwald, who had been moved by Washington's autobiography, *Up from Slavery*, to more active concern with black welfare, soon became one of the school's most energetic trustees. Rosenwald had previously subsidized construction of black YMCAs in a number of major cities;* now, on behalf of Tuskegee, he persuaded other Chicago businessmen to become involved and transported out-of-state visitors to the school in his private railroad car. Each year Rosenwald sent Washington a list of wealthy men, many of them Jews, whom he thought should be solicited for contributions. He convinced George Eastman, the inventor and industrialist, to give a million dollars to Tuskegee and large sums to other black institutions.[78]

---

*A recent essay by Nina Mjagkij explores the extraordinary role Rosenwald played beginning in 1910 in creating some twenty-four black YMCAs in Washington, Chicago, Philadelphia, Atlanta, and other cities when such facilities were unavailable to blacks. While it was a controversial move even at that time—they were segregated—W. E. B. Du Bois in 1925 as well as Mjagkij described them as playing a critical role in black leadership training and cultural development.[79]

It is clear that Washington benefited from and admired his Jewish supporters, a number of whom were themselves or were descended from self-made men. He was wary, however, of letting Tuskegee become too closely identified with them. He once urged his business manager to purchase supplies from Gentiles whenever possible, since he thought the Jewish connection could adversely affect public sentiment towards his institution. That Washington was not motivated by personal animus against Jews is evident, however, from later instructions, as when he directed that favorable consideration be given a "Mr. J. Loeb . . . who paid no attention to our want of money and threatened boycott in town and stood by us and sold us goods at wholesale prices."[80]

Jewish philanthropists associated with Washington sometimes drew criticism from more militant blacks who opposed his accommodationist tactics. Such criticism was scattered, however. In his lifetime, Booker T. Washington was honored as a great American, and his emphasis on self-help garnered him attention, admiration, and a respect that has been recently renewed with the emphasis shifting once more toward strong black families and communities. Finally, Washington and the Jewish philanthropists like Schiff, Rosenwald, and Warburg who supported him with money, time, and effort established the first organized ties between the black and Jewish communities.[81]

It is clear that these early ties were tentative and abstract. Elite Jews were meeting and dealing with their black counterparts largely in symbolic terms. Still, it was also evident that some tensions that would later acquire a sharper edge were already present: Old Testament metaphors provided both positive and negative sources of identification, and black leaders who formed ties with Jewish leaders did so with some hesitation and sometimes suspicion. Significantly Jews, while recognized as suffering from certain disabilities not unlike those of blacks, were nevertheless seen as a relatively successful group with access to power that blacks did not have: Identification mingled with a degree of jealousy. The strains evident even then would find later embodiment in such opposed groupings as Washington/King versus Garvey/Malcolm/Farrakhan as well as in personalities involved in the more recent issues associated with black empowerment.

2

ORIGINS OF THE BLACK–JEWISH ALLIANCE

The black-Jewish alliance may be said to have taken institutional shape with the formation of the NAACP in 1909. The participants in this project were a group of upper-class German Jews and WASP reformers inspired by the philanthropic and political ideals of the Progressive Era and a black group led by W. E. B. Du Bois. The NAACP was to become the most important vehicle for racial progress for the next fifty years and more. That it became so was a direct result of Jews and blacks working together for common ends.

This early partnership has become a controversial subject recently because within the NAACP, at least in the early years, blacks did not have equal standing with Jews and other whites. As blacks came increasingly to take over direct control of their fight, the underlying integrationist premise of the alliance came under attack by black nationalists, who argued that the premise was and is dysfunctional. Group power based on economic and political solidarity has come to be seen by many as the primary if not the only means of obtaining full entry into American society. Such a view has given rise to revisionist complaints about Jewish paternalism and even to changes of self-interested hypocrisy. Lost or played down in the revisionist critique is the fact that for more than half a century, the NAACP (along with the Urban League and other similar organizations) pursued the only means available for dealing with the violence and discrimination blacks then faced.

In 1908, a race riot in Springfield, Illinois, sparked by police attempts to protect a black man falsely accused of rape, set off two nights of rioting that took the lives of two blacks and four whites and injured more than seventy persons in all. The tragedy angered and saddened many people, including William English Walling, a southern writer and settlement house worker, and his wife Anna Strunsky, a Russian-Jewish immigrant who as a young woman had been imprisoned for revolutionary activities against the czar. They decided to investigate the situation personally. Their findings were subsequently published in an article in the *Independent* entitled "The Race War in the North." In it Walling warned of a racial holocaust if the suppression of blacks continued. In New York Mary White Ovington, a Protestant social worker, was moved by the piece and discussed it with Henry Moscowitz, also a social worker; together they persuaded Oswald Garrison Villard, editor of the *Evening Post* and the *Nation* magazine, to help bring the issue to the forefront of the American conscience.[1]

On February 12, 1909, the centenary of Lincoln's birth, Villard—who was a grandson of the noted abolitionist William Lloyd Garrison—took the issue to the people. "We call upon all believers in democracy," he wrote, "to join in a national conference for the discussion of present evils, the voicing of protests, and the renewal of the struggle for civil and political liberty." Jewish signers of his statement included Rabbis Stephen S. Wise and Emil Hirsch, settlement house worker Lillian Wald, and Moscowitz. Ovington later remarked upon the diversity of the group: "One [Villard] was a descendant of an old-time abolitionist, the second [Moscowitz] a Jew and the third [Walling] a southerner."[2]

A man who, next to Booker T. Washington, was perhaps the most influential black leader in the country was also present with his followers at the conference held in New York. His views would be vastly influential for decades.

William Edward Burghardt Du Bois was born a free man in Great Barrington, Massachusetts, and educated at Harvard and abroad. A sociologist and author of the pioneering study *The Philadelphia Negro*, Du Bois rejected accommodationism and argued for a more radical approach, including a higher degree of political activism by blacks. While Washington favored the agricultural and mechanical trades for black youth, Du Bois urged quality education for the "talented tenth," who, he said, should compete with the brightest whites at the best colleges.

Du Bois's opinions of Jews are not easy to categorize. Like Washington, he marveled at their capacity for organization in this country. He urged blacks to share his admiration and to emulate them.[3] Yet he was also suspicious of their motives. While crossing the ocean by steamer in 1895, Du Bois confided in his diary that, while two Jewish fellow passengers were congenial, other Jews he had encountered displayed "all that slyness, that lack of straightforward openheartedness that goes straight against me."[4] He was unhappy with the increased influence of Jews in the emerging new South. In 1901 he wrote that he considered them the "shrewd and unscrupulous" partners of the Yankees and the sons of poor whites, all of whom thirsted for wealth and power and were replacing the old antebellum aristocracy.[5] In his classic 1903 study, *The Souls of Black Folk*, Du Bois opined that the "defense of deception and flattery, or cajoling and lying which the Jews of the Middle Ages used left its stamp on their character for centuries." He further wrote that Jews were concerned only with their own problems and indifferent to those of others, especially those of poor blacks.[6]

This characterization drew protests from Jewish financier and philanthropist Jacob Schiff, Rabbi Stephen Wise, and other Jewish leaders. But Du Bois let the comments stand until he revised the book in 1953, when he was eighty-five years old. He then deleted the references and apologized for his own insensitivity. Until the "horrible massacre of German Jews," Du Bois wrote in the revised edition,* he had failed to realize "how even unconscious repeti-

*He also made significant changes in the wording of the original text. In the earlier edition he had written that "the Jew is heir to the slave-baron." In the revised edition the passage read "immigrants are the heirs." The phrase "enterprising Jew" was changed to "enterprising American," and "Jews of the Middle Ages" became "peasants of the Middle Ages." "I am not at all sure," Du Bois admitted, "that the foreign exploiters to whom I referred in my study of the Black Belt were in fact Jews."[8]

tion of current folklore, such as the concept of Jews more guilty of exploitation than others, had helped the Hitlers of the world."[7]

The conferees in New York voted to set up a permanent organization to work for the abolition of enforced segregation, equal education for black and white children, complete enfranchisement of blacks, and enforcement of the Fourteenth and Fifteenth Amendments. Villard was named chairman of the board. There were seven Jews among the forty-five members of the NAACP's first general committee and four on the thirty-member executive committee. (Through the 1930s, Jews made up nearly half of the NAACP's legal committee).[9] Du Bois, the organization's only black officer, served as director of publicity and research. White domination would lead to increasing difficulty for the NAACP in later years, but Du Bois played an important role from the outset. With Villard he ran the organization during its infancy while editing its highly influential magazine, *Crisis*. For blacks and whites alike, he came to symbolize the contrast between the NAACP's drive for racial equality and Washington's conservatism.[10] The NAACP, prodded by Du Bois, would provide activist leadership until the protest movement of the 1960s carried the struggle to a new level; then, ironically, the organization came to be seen as the "conservative" organization.

In 1911 another civil rights group was founded: the National League on Urban Conditions (later shortened to the National Urban League). The Urban League evolved out of a committee to improve industrial life for blacks, a group that had been organized in New York in 1906 with support from Jewish philanthropists Felix Warburg and Isaac N. Seligman, among others. The Urban League's initial focus was on improving social and economic conditions for those blacks moving from southern farms to northern cities. Its board, unlike the NAACP's, was integrated. Several blacks served as executive officers under Seligman, a Columbia University economist, who was its first chairman.[11]

In this same period Jewish "defense agencies" also were organized. The first of these groups, the American Jewish Committee, was formed in 1906, three years after Russia's infamous Kishinev massacre. A number of upper-class German Jews, some of whom would later become active in the NAACP, founded the AJC to mobilize public opinion against such atrocities. In 1913 the Anti-

Defamation League was launched by the Jewish fraternal order B'nai B'rith to combat anti-Semitism within the United States. Later the AJC and ADL were joined by the American Jewish Congress and the Jewish Labor Committee. Starting in the 1940s, local Jewish community-relations councils sprang up in cities across the country.

It was no coincidence that several of these organizations came into existence during the early years of the century. It was no longer accepted during the Progressive Era that corrupt politics, control by giant corporations, and exploitation of workers and immigrants had to be tolerated. A new era was being born, though hardly anyone could predict its future form.

During the first two decades of the twentieth century, the United States was being transformed from an agrarian to an industrial economy and from a rural to an urban society. For countless American workers the transition was a painful one. Even in the best of times, they put up with harsh and often dangerous labor conditions in mills, mines, and manufacturing plants. When the economy went sour (as it often did), they faced extended periods of joblessness without the safety net of public assistance programs. Many lived in overcrowded and unsanitary tenement districts. Added to this explosive urban mix were countless "outsiders"—peasants from Italy and eastern Europe and impoverished southern blacks.

To stem the flow of such "undesirables," Congress enacted immigration laws and other statutes favoring the lighter-skinned and fairer-haired peoples of northern Europe, who were considered culturally more congruent with the existing population. Legislation in some states barred Roman Catholics from attending parochial schools, while the teaching of evolution was still seen as un-American in parts of the country during the 1920s. Such responses were a reflection of a Kulturkampf of American Protestantism (as historian Richard Hofstadter called it), when "rural and small-town America made its most determined stand against ethnic outsiders."[12]

In this transitional period even previously well-established German Jews felt threatened. Colleges and universities that had once welcomed affluent Jews started limiting their numbers or, in the case of elite clubs, banning them altogether.[13]

But if the position of Jews and other ethnic outsiders was difficult, that of blacks was far worse. Between 1890 and 1910 their voting privileges and other civil rights were systematically stripped away throughout the South. Many were hunted down and killed almost at random. Mississippi's Governor Vardaman warned that if it were necessary, every Negro in the state would be lynched to maintain white supremacy. From 1889 to 1916, the NAACP later reported, 3,244 black men and women were lynched and countless others simply disappeared. By the 1920s the antiblack and anti-Jewish Ku Klux Klan claimed a membership of nearly four million people, with operations not only in the South but in the Middle West and other parts of the country as well.

The Progressive party, formed in 1912 under the leadership of Theodore Roosevelt, set out to deal with the excesses of industrial growth through such measures as popular control of government, direct primaries, the initiative, the referendum, and woman suffrage, but the so-called progressive elements seemed uninterested in the sufferings of blacks. Between 1901 and 1918 the Socialist party, enjoying its golden age under the leadership of Eugene V. Debs, passed not a single resolution supporting black Americans at any of its conventions, nor did the Socialists agitate at all against a system that made black people second-class citizens. They simply did not acknowledge the problem.

It was the failure of these reformers and activists to effectively challenge white supremacy that made the work of the NAACP so important. For a time it was virtually the only institutional voice speaking out against racism, and its militant approach stood in stark contrast with Booker T. Washington's accommodationist strategy. Its early initiatives took the form of legal attacks on institutional segregation and race-related violence. Trained lawyers were needed, and few blacks had legal training. Volunteer attorneys included Moorefield Storey, a former head of the American Bar Association; Clarence Darrow, the celebrated criminal lawyer; and later Louis Marshall, the American Jewish Committee's second president. Arthur Spingarn, Joel Spingarn's younger brother (see below), became head of the NAACP's legal committee soon after it was formed and held the post without compensation until 1940.

Other Jews helped in different ways. When Felix Frankfurter, a Harvard law professor who later served on the Supreme Court, learned that Howard University's law library was badly out of date, he and Julian Mack, a federal judge and Zionist leader on the board of the NAACP, persuaded Julius Rosenwald to make a matching grant. Du Bois turned to Joel Spingarn for aid in getting a civil rights plank inserted into the Progressive party's 1912 platform. Joined by Moscowitz and Jane Addams, the settlement house pioneer, Spingarn managed to get the issue before the delegates, but they turned it down.

The NAACP, however, was rife with conflict from the outset. Du Bois, a brilliant and lonely intellectual, and Villard, a man of prickly ego, never got along. Du Bois believed that Villard's unconscious race prejudice fostered paternalism rather than true cooperation between whites and blacks. It was true that in his personal relations Villard—like many other members of the Protestant establishment—kept his distance from ethnic outsiders, whether the descendants of slaves or immigrants from eastern Europe.[14] For his part, the proud, irascible Du Bois found it difficult to get along with people no matter what their color, nationality, or faith.

One of the few white exceptions to this rule was Joel Elias Spingarn. A member of New York's German Jewish elite, Spingarn had earlier gained recognition as a scholar with a doctoral dissertation on the history of Renaissance literary criticism. He taught comparative literature at Columbia University and had been among the first to introduce the work of Benedetto Croce and other important European figures into this country.

Joel served as intermediary between Du Bois and his foes in the NAACP's hierarchy. When the effort at reconciliation between Du Bois and Villard failed, Joel and his brother Arthur openly sided with Du Bois. They argued that he should be allowed to edit the *Crisis* without Villard or anyone else looking over his shoulder. By 1913 Villard had wearied of the wrangling, and he asked Joel to succeed him as the NAACP's chairman. In 1914, Joel Spingarn did, and a few years later Villard dropped completely out of the organization.[15]

Spingarn and Du Bois went on to dominate the NAACP and shape the direction of the civil rights struggle for the next twenty years, giving it a decidedly more militant tone. Though allies, they had sharp disagreements from time to time, and Spingarn did not hesitate to criticize his colleague. Du Bois was willing to wreck the cause, Spingarn believed, rather than concede even a minor point, and Spingarn often felt that Du Bois mistook obstinacy for strength of character.[16]

Between the two men, however, there existed a bond of affection and respect, a shared commitment to the struggle against racism that transcended their occasional quarrels. Both men were Ph.D.'s, and they spoke a common language. In 1940 DuBois dedicated his memoirs, *Dusk of Dawn*, to Joel Spingarn, "scholar and knight."[17]

Besides holding major leadership posts within the NAACP, Joel Spingarn initiated much of its policy, devised many of its tactics, and spoke out passionately on behalf of racial justice. The NAACP achieved important victories during the period, including the beginnings of voting-rights access through court action and reduced racial stereotyping. Spingarn and Du Bois were at the forefront of these efforts. Spingarn was, according to one historian, the most important white in the NAACP and a pivotal figure in the early history of the black movement, yet he is today remembered primarily for establishing the yearly NAACP award, a gold medal, to honor "the highest and noblest achievement of an American Negro."[18] Arthur Spingarn who headed the NAACP's legal committee for many years and succeeded Joel as president upon his death, is far better known.

Joel Spingarn's background as a professor of comparative literature seems an odd preparation for civil rights activism. Off campus, however, he developed a strong social conscience. His biographer, B. Joyce Ross, has described his passionate desire to advance the ideal of justice and equality in the larger community. In an effort to realize this desire, Spingarn ran unsuccessfully for Congress as a Republican in 1908.

His involvement with the NAACP began when a newspaper item caught his eye. The NAACP was seeking funds to represent an illiterate black tenant farmer in Arkansas who had slain his former landlord in what the NAACP said was self-defense. Spingarn sent a small donation to the NAACP's defense fund. The gift attracted Villard's attention, and he persuaded Spingarn to become active. This he did with a passion, becoming in 1910 a member of the NAACP's executive committee.

The following year, Spingarn was abruptly dismissed from his position at Columbia for criticizing the invasion of university affairs by nouveau riche business leaders.[19] Thus freed from his teaching duties, Spingarn took on many new responsibilities, becoming chairman of a newly formed local chapter of the NAACP later that year. His brother and his brother's law partner joined as well, occupying themselves with legal issues while Joel built up the NAACP's internal organization. When Joel Spingarn assumed leadership of the NAACP following Villard's departure in 1914, the organization had no executive director, virtually no visibility, and not much support from blacks or whites.

Spingarn had already begun to question whether race relations could be improved through normal political processes. His apprehension grew when the Progressive party not only failed to adopt the civil rights plank but also refused to seat black delegates. The last straw for Spingarn was when he learned that Theodore Roosevelt believed Du Bois was dangerous. Disillusioned with politics and politicians, Spingarn left the Republican party, observing that reformers and prophets were out of place in such company.[20]

Convinced that white America had no intention of working to improve the lot of blacks, Spingarn felt it was necessary to arouse black awareness and aspirations. On assuming the NAACP's chairmanship, he traveled west at his own expense in 1914 and 1915 to stump for what he termed the new abolitionism. He did so with a fervor that rivaled that of nineteenth-century firebrands like W. L. Garrison and Wendell Phillips, imploring black audiences to demand their rights in language that was sometimes so harsh that some thought he was advocating violence.

Taking a stronger position than any of his white colleagues, Spingarn openly declared that Booker T. Washington's accommodationist stance and popularity within the black community posed the single greatest threat to black advancement and the growth of the NAACP. Villard, too, had differed sharply with Washington, but he did so in private, avoiding public controversy. Spingarn did the opposite; his public attacks on Washington became "a virtual passion." He urged his listeners to reject Washington's gradualism and to shift their loyalties to Du Bois's militancy and to the NAACP.[21] Privately Spingarn agreed with Du Bois's recommendation that the NAACP's Chicago branch cut itself off from such people as Julius Rosenwald, who, Du Bois told him, "do not agree with us and will not whole-heartedly support our aims."[22]

Black newspapers allied with Washington, such as the *New York Age*, attacked Spingarn, but many blacks cheered the militant tone of his speeches. The radical Monroe Trotter, overwhelmed by the NAACP leader's fighting spirit, wrote an ecstatic letter of congratulation. Novelist Jessie Fauset urged Spingarn to "prod us, prick us, goad us by unpleasant truths to ease off this terrible outer self of sloth and acceptance."[23]

Upon Washington's death in 1915, however, the way was opened for unity talks between the several civil rights factions. At Du Bois's suggestion, Spingarn in 1916 called a meeting of leaders of all the large black organizations at Troutbeck, his estate in Amenia, New York. The delegates adopted resolutions supporting all forms of education for blacks—not just Washington's emphasis on industrial arts—demanded political freedom, and called for an end to factional disputes. The event itself, however, was more important than the resolutions adopted. The gathering of so many civil rights leaders with different backgrounds and points of view was, the *New York Age* reported, a significant breakthrough, marking a fresh spirit of united purpose and effort.[24]

In 1917, as America stood at the brink of World War I, a controversial issue arose: How could blacks participate? The military services at this point were totally segregated, and the segregation would continue. Spingarn believed, as did many students at Howard, Fisk, Atlanta, Tuskegee, and other black colleges, that it was absolutely essential that young black men be trained for military leadership. Three months before America entered the war, Spingarn learned of an army plan to train two hundred black officers at a special camp in Iowa to lead black troops. The Army would foot the cost of training the new officers, of course, but they, like other officers, would be expected to pay for their own uniforms.

Spingarn endorsed the army plan, offered to pay for the uniforms of one hundred Howard University students, and began a recruitment campaign. A number of black newspapers opposed the plan because the army was then segregated; some black leaders opposed it too. But Spingarn pressed on. He helped to persuade his Dutchess County neighbor, Franklin D. Roosevelt, then assistant secretary of the navy, to support the scheme and traveled across the country seeking volunteers. Spingarn proved to be an extremely effective army recruiter. By April 1917, when the United States declared war, he had lined up some 350 candidates for black officer training, two thirds of them college graduates. Shortly thereafter, the army announced that the training camp would open in June at Des Moines, Iowa.

By this time black opposition had intensified. The usually decisive Du Bois was in a quandary. In a sense the army plan seemed to be an outgrowth of his own idea for educating and training the brightest blacks, but it would also blatantly perpetuate racial segregation, which the NAACP opposed in all forms. Finally, just a few days before the camp was to open, Du Bois threw his support behind the training, but he did so without fanfare, pleased that the army would have black officers. Thereafter, he enthusiastically defended the commissioning of black officers, whatever the circumstances, attacking hasty editorial critics hostile to Spingarn and the camp.[25] On October 15, 1917, 639 blacks were commissioned at Fort Des Moines, Iowa—106 captains, 329 first lieutenants, and 204 second lieutenants.

The fact is that blacks eagerly sought service in the military. Before the end of the war, according to John Hope Franklin, over fifty thousand—more than a third of the entire expeditionary force—served in 115 different outfits overseas. While some were limited to supply functions, many took part in combat. In the Ninety-second Division alone, 248 enlisted men perished, and 551 were wounded. Despite these sacrifices, there were many incidents at home involving black soldiers, making it clear that blacks were still very far from being full citizens in American society.

While Du Bois remained at the *Crisis*, which served as his podium from 1914 to 1934, Spingarn was chairman of the NAACP for all but three years. Spingarn ruled autocratically and was apparently unruffled by frequent criticism that a white man should play such a role. When the black nationalist leader Marcus Garvey visited

Du Bois at the NAACP's headquarters in 1917, he was dumbfounded to see so many white faces. The only blacks on the premises, said Garvey, were Du Bois, another man, and the office boy. He complained that he could not tell whether he was in a white office or that of the National Association for the Advancement of Colored People.[26] Spingarn himself frequently spoke of his hope for more black participation in the civil rights struggle. "I am tired of the philanthropy of rich white men toward your race," he declared in one of his early speeches to blacks. "I want to see you fight your own battles with your own leaders and your own money." In 1914 he told a black audience: "We white men of whatever creed or faith cannot fight your battles for you. We will stand shoulder to shoulder with you until you can fight as generals all by yourselves."[27]

However, it was clear that Spingarn himself loved the power and excitement of generalship. Twice—in 1915 and again in 1933—he quit as chairman following the NAACP board's rejection of his views on certain issues. In each case he believed it was his race, not his policy positions, that the board was objecting to. Each time he recommended that a black officer succeed him. But each time he was returned to office and stubbornly clung to his leadership post except during illness. Not until 1934, when the NAACP's traditional white leadership came under sharpest attack from militants, did a black man become its chairman.

Throughout this time Du Bois was for all practical purposes the public face of the NAACP. It is true that the organization was dominated by white liberals, but the *Crisis*, whose circulation he built in eight years to 100,000, became the vehicle for the expression of his ideas about lynching, peonage, police brutality, and every aspect of discrimination, segregation, and social injustice faced by his people. From his pen came a torrent of books and articles. *The Souls of Black Folk* would go through twenty-two editions in thirty-five years in addition to several reprints of the origiinal 1903 edition. Works of his have been translated into thirteen foreign languages. He attended pan-African conferences, planned encyclopedias of Africa, and embarked upon an ambitious effort to launch a hundred-year study of black people.

Given this extraordinary output and his very long career, Du Bois sometimes appears to have been on all sides of all questions.

He began as an admirer of Booker T. Washington, congratulating him on his Atlanta Exposition speech. Though Du Bois fought segregation, he simultaneously supported it in cases like that of the black officers episode, which he felt would prepare his people for the struggle. At the heart of his beliefs was his notion of the "talented tenth"—the recruitment and education of an elite group of self-conscious black leaders. Hardly a grass-roots figure to begin with, given his crusty and distant manner, he was not popular with either the black masses or black intellectuals, many of whom respected but disliked him. With Spingarn, however, there was always a special bond. Thus, Spingarn backed Du Bois's postwar efforts to convene a pan-African congress at the Paris peace conference and Spingarn himself addressed congress delegates in 1919.

In contrast to Du Bois, Spingarn was a careful builder. He skillfully integrated the forces allied with Booker T. Washington into the NAACP and arranged at one point for Washington's successor at Tuskegee, Robert R. Moton, to receive the prestigious Spingarn Medal. Under Spingarn the NAACP began to undergo a transformation in the 1920s. His selection in 1920 of the writer and diplomat James Weldon Johnson as executive secretary signaled the beginning of the end of complete white leadership and control.

Although Jews continued to serve as chairman, president, and head of the legal committee throughout the decade, day-to-day operations were increasingly placed in the hands of black professionals and the predominantly black executive committee. Under Johnson's aggressive leadership, the NAACP became truly national with some three hundred branches stretching from coast to coast, most of which were run by blacks. Welcoming these signs of black empowerment, Joel Spingarn claimed that he discerned a new sense of dignity among black Americans. Spingarn knew that, rather than end prejudice, this early manifestation of black power might temporarily increase it. But so much the better, he said, since in the end it would force both races to seek and find some form of compromise or adjustment by which they could live peacefully together.

Modest at first, Jewish involvement in civil rights activities increased significantly after the murder of Leo Frank in Georgia in 1915 and mounting anti-Semitism in eastern Europe, exemplified by the Mendel Beliss "blood libel" episode in Russia. These events strengthened the resolve of such young organizations as the American Jewish Committee and the Anti-Defamation League. It is significant, however, that Jews did not just organize for their own defense; they also rallied to the defense of blacks, who faced even greater terrors. Why did Jews do so? Possibly it was because, as a pariah people themselves, they easily identified with another group of even more oppressed outsiders. They were no doubt also encouraged by the implicit moral imperatives of Judaism.

Revisionist writers have their own answer: Jews became involved mainly for selfish or even ignoble reasons. These writers take as their starting point (but go considerably beyond) the work of Hasia Diner, the Jewish historian of the early days of the black-Jewish alliance. Diner believes that many of the upper-class German Jews acted out of a variety of motives. Despite their wealth and achievements, she argued, some were still not totally adjusted and comfortable in America; they did not feel fully accepted. For a number, she believes, "black issues provided an attractive forum to work out certain tensions of acculturation."

She furthermore suggested that many affluent Jews, though deeply resentful of the establishment's tolerance of anti-Semitism, hesitated to protest for fear of stirring up more. Elite Jews, she continued, may have entered the battle for black rights in some measure as a means of broadening the attack on prejudice and discrimination. In Diner's view, then, Jewishness in all of its social and psychological dimensions drew Jews into activist roles on behalf of blacks.

Revisionism generally ignores or dismisses that idealism motivated people such as Jacob Schiff, Julius Rosenwald, and the Spingarn brothers. In truth, David Levering Lewis argues, the elites of both groups were embarrassed by the huge influx of impoverished blacks and Jews into northern cities and formed parallel organizations like the Urban League and Jewish settlement houses, which were intended to "clean up" the poor and make them more acceptable to mainstream Americans.[28]

For Lewis the black-Jewish partnership, both at its formation and in later years, was not a true alliance but "a misconceived ethnic propinquity." He sees it as a means by which affluent Jews and better-positioned blacks set themselves up as advocates for poor black people, even though they had few ties and little real interest in their own masses. He concedes that in the short term the collaboration was minimally beneficial to black Americans, but he argues that it ultimately "gave rise to an unworkable paradigm of success."[29] He believes with Harold Cruse that the active involvement of Jewish and black assimilationists and the direction they imparted to the liberation struggle deflected blacks from more important economic and political activities. In the process, the two men argue, the Jewish elite used the movement to fight anti-Semitism by remote control.*

It is of course true that class differences separated the early Jewish and black reformers from those they sought to lead. The gulf that divided them was real, and it would remain a problem well into the future. Jewish and black leaders did, in fact, suffer varying degrees of social discomfort with their respective underclasses, even as they sought to raise them up. And it is fair to say that the recipients of such aid often felt resentful of their self-annointed leaders, be they Jewish or black.

There was also almost certainly an element of self-interest in Jewish support for blacks. A decline in racial discrimination, many believed, could lead to a society in which anti-Semitism would also be banished. But acknowledging a degree of enlightened self-interest should not be seen as vitiating the moral conviction or sincerity of many of these Jews. Diner was on solid ground when she wrote that the Jewish involvement sprang from a special sympathy for and a unique ability to understand the suffering of blacks.

This sympathy was perhaps best exemplified in the Jewish labor movement. During World War I, when southern blacks streamed north in search of jobs, a number of affiliates of the American Federation of Labor excluded them from membership. The two leading Jewish unions, the International Ladies' Garment Workers and the Amalgamated Clothing Workers, as well as the organizers of the United Hebrew Trades, took sharp issue with these unions, however. Jewish unions were virtually alone in admitting black members and promoting them. (The mother of Kenneth Clark,

---

*In his Pulitzer-prize winning *W.E.B. Du Bois: Biography of a Race*, published in 1993, however, Lewis appears to back off these characterizations, finding now in many of these uptown Jews "genuine compassion combined with sage self-interest."

the noted psychologist, was one of the first black shop stewards in the ILGWU.) Their interest was not merely economically motivated, that is, to counteract the use of black strikebreakers to undercut wage rates. Many of their leaders as well as the rank and file were also deeply interested in advancing all progressive causes. As Alex Rose, head of the United Hatters, Cap and Millinery Workers said in 1927, "The Jewish unions looked upon their union as an instrument for social advancement, not only for their members but for society."[30]

The Yiddish press was also supportive of blacks. The *Jewish Daily Forward*, the *Morning Journal* and the *Jewish Daily News* were widely read by the Jewish working class in New York. Although these newspapers could agree upon very little else, they were as one in their opposition to racial discrimination and violence. The *Forward* compared the East St. Louis race riot of 1917 with the Kishinev pogrom of 1903. It gave front-page coverage to antilynching legislation and, with the *Morning Journal*, ran lengthy pieces on the history of the slave trade and slavery. The Yiddish papers regularly published statistics on lynching and each year reprinted the Tuskegee Institute's report on the subject.[31] In different ways Jews from many walks of life identified early on with the black struggle for freedom. Their support was especially important in this period when, for much of white America, blacks were at best invisible and most often objects of intense persecution.

While there was doubtless considerable paternalism on the part of the Jewish leadership in civil rights organizations at this time, this leadership was nonetheless critical. It came at a time when few whites, except a handful of descendants of the old abolitionists, took any interest in the plight of blacks. It came, too, when poor blacks whose problems the NAACP sought to support took little interest in the legal battles and casework efforts that were the NAACP's and Urban League's primary activities. Their concerns were far more basic matters of day-to-day survival. In later years the expansion of the black middle class and the drama of some of the court tests, along with broadening white opposition, helped enlarge the constituencies of these early civil rights organizations until a new level of action opened up in the early 1960s.

Jewish motives were indeed complex—as are all peoples' goals and purposes. But revisionists notwithstanding, a belief that the

Jewish cause and the black cause were essentially the same underlay those motives. This belief was to guide the attitudes and actions of most Jews in succeeding years until the race revolution that began in the second half of the 1960s introduced an important new dynamic that would fundamentally transform the relationship of the two groups.

3

THE TWENTIES

The Early Assault on Inequality

A defining moment in the partnership between blacks and Jews occurred with the Leo Frank case, an episode whose painful ambivalence symbolizes the complexity of this alliance from its outset to the present day. A Jew convicted by a black man's testimony set blacks and Jews against each other; yet paradoxically, the lynching of Leo Frank caused the two groups to identify more closely with one another.

Saturday, April 26, 1913—Confederate Memorial Day—was a holiday throughout the South. But Leo Frank, manager of the National Pencil Company's plant in Atlanta, had gone to work anyway. The factory was closed, and save for an office boy and janitor, Frank was alone when an employee named Mary Phagan, a white southern girl of humble parentage, came in to pick up her wages. She was just thirteen years old, young for a factory worker even then, but she would get no older. At three o'clock the next morning, her bludgeoned body was found facedown on a slag heap in the plant's basement.

One day later, Atlanta police arrested Leo Frank for the murder of Mary Phagan. His accuser was the janitor, James Conley, who said Frank had ordered him to conceal the girl's body in the basement after admitting he had killed her when she resisted his advances.

Frank denied the charges. It was his word against Conley's, the word of a white supervisor against a poor black laborer who had previously served time in prison for petty thievery. In the South of 1913, there was no precedent for a conviction under such circumstances. But Leo Frank was not a white Southerner. He was a Brooklyn Jew, a northern transplant who had married into a prominent Jewish family in Atlanta, and president of the city's B'nai B'rith lodge.

The conflicting emotions, the ugliness and bigotry aroused by the controversy surrounding the Frank case mirrored the national mood in microcosm. The South's recurring seizures of anti-Semitism and the North's racist hysteria were embodied in this one case, and it emerged as a watershed event in the history of black-Jewish relations. Its impact had some of the qualities of the Sacco-Vanzetti case of the 1920s and the Scottsboro boys case of the 1930s.

The trial was a mob scene, as angry cries of "death to the Jew!" from white militants outside the courthouse reverberated within earshot of the judge and jury.[1] In this explosive atmosphere Leo Frank's lawyers responded to the intemperate outbursts of Georgia's powerful populist leader Tom Watson (who in his weekly *Jeffersonian Magazine* repeatedly demanded the execution of the "filthy, perverted Jew of New York") with attacks of their own on the key prosecution witness. "Who is this man James Conley?" one of Frank's attorneys rhetorically asked. "He was a dirty, filthy, black, drunken, lying nigger." Frank also wondered how the "testimony of Southern white women of unimpeachable character" who spoke on his behalf could be disbelieved while the "perjured vaporings of a black brute alone [could be] accepted as the whole truth."[2]

On August 23, 1913, Leo Frank was convicted of killing Mary Phagan. In the trial's aftermath Watson, exploiting local distrust and dislike of both Jews and capitalists, continued to denounce Leo Frank as a member of the "Jewish aristocracy," and he accused "rich Jews" of determining that "no aristocrat of their race should die for the death of a working-class Gentile." Worried by the hysteria being generated, the nation's Jewish community mobilized behind the condemned man, hoping to upset the verdict on appeal. By his own account, Albert Lasker, the noted advertising executive, spent $100,000 in personal funds and took a year away from his agency to rally support for Frank. The William Burns Detective Agency was retained to search for leads that might clear him.

As Frank's attorney in the appeal effort, Louis Marshall, president of the American Jewish Committee, attacked James Conley's credibility and argued that rabble-rousing prosecution tactics in Atlanta had deprived his client of a fair trial. Marshall brought the case to the attention of Adolph Ochs, publisher of the *New York Times*, which editorialized in favor of Frank and labeled Conley a "black monster." Without naming the janitor, the *Washington Post* went even further, declaring that the brutal murder appeared to be "characteristic of a drunken, ignorant Negro." The *Post* was convinced that "no intelligent white man would do such a thing."[3]

The Frank episode initially threatened the fledgling partnership between blacks and Jews. The *New York Age* was critical of Frank supporters who sought to place the blame for Mary Phagan's murder on the black handyman. The black-owned *Chicago Defender*—in a manner reminiscent of the *Amsterdam News* headline "Many Blacks, No Jews Arrested in Crown Heights" of almost eighty years later—declared: "Jews Raise Millions to Free Frank and Put Blame on Innocent Man." More restrained, the NAACP's *Crisis* and its executive secretary James Weldon Johnson expressed resentment at what they saw as an organized effort to implicate Conley simply because he was black.[4]

In the two years following the Frank trial, Marshall carried his appeals all the way to the Supreme Court. With Justices Oliver Wendell Holmes and Charles Evans Hughes dissenting, the Court denied a writ of error requested by Frank's lawyers, and his execution was subsequently scheduled for June 1915. Final appeals were made to Georgia's governor, John Slaton. Tom Watson, exercising his political muscle, pressured the governor to let the hanging proceed. Yet at the last minute, in an act of courage that would destroy his career, Slaton commuted the sentence to life imprisonment. Frank's victory was short-lived, however. Two months later, he was taken by angry whites from the prison where he was being held, carried to a field some miles away, and hanged.

Some months after the hanging, on a mountaintop outside Atlanta, the second Ku Klux Klan was founded by the Knights of

Mary Phagan, an organization that Watson had sponsored to make sure Frank was put to death for the girl's murder.

Leo Frank did not kill Mary Phagan. His innocence was finally established in 1982 when Alonzo Mann, who had been Frank's office boy, admitted after sixty-nine years of silence that he had seen Conley with the body of Mary Phagan in his arms on that day in April 1913. Mann, who was eighty-three when he finally cleared his conscience, said the janitor had threatened him with death, and so he had said nothing. With Mann's belated admission the state of Georgia pardoned Leo Frank, and the case was declared closed.[5]

Frank's trial, conviction, and lynching shook the whole Jewish community. If a respected company manager and civic leader who happened to be Jewish could be sent to his death by an angry mob, what about Jews of lower status and fewer means of defense? Even the most emancipated Jews began to wonder if anti-Semitism was not about to supersede racism throughout the country. Would European-style persecution of Jews now be imported into American life? Out of these concerns arose renewed interest and involvement in racial conciliation efforts. In a footnote to the case indicative of its effects, Louis Marshall joined the board of the NAACP and served on its legal defense committee. Some years later, in a letter to the association's president, he wrote that he was glad thereby to make amends for any previous neglect.[6]

Working together in the NAACP, blacks and Jews launched a series of attacks on the widespread violations of black people's rights. Lynching was a special target. This was, perhaps, not coincidental, for Leo Frank's death had focused Jewish attention on this monstrous form of socially tolerated homicide. As the *Baltimore Afro-American* had noted at the time, lynching was an outrage customarily reserved for those of the black race. The *Philadelphia Tribune* observed that Frank's widow and other survivors were now better positioned to sympathize with the relatives of the many black victims of mob violence in Georgia.[7]

With a new Jewish director of publicity, Herbert Seligman, the NAACP campaigned relentlessly against lynching, which took the lives of over thirty-two hundred Negroes between 1889 and 1918. Seligman personally investigated lynchings in Mississippi and placed articles on the subject in the *New Republic, Current Opinion*, and the *Nation*. The campaign helped to awaken the nation's conscience, so that in time this form of murder all but disappeared.

Among other activities in this period, Jews joined in fighting against the stereotyping of blacks in movies. A special target was D. W. Griffith's *Birth of a Nation*, which told a distorted story of black emancipation, enfranchisement, and debauchery of white women. The film, based on Thomas Dixon's novel *The Clansman*, "virtually assassinated" the character of ten million Negroes, Joel Spingarn charged. Acting for the NAACP, Spingarn, Lillian Wald, and Jacob Schiff urged the National Board of Censorship in Moving Pictures to withdraw its approval of the movie. The board initially agreed to do so but later reversed itself. Rabbi Stephen Wise was among those who publicly denounced the decision. Lillian Wald organized a march of five hundred protesters to the office of New York's mayor, John P. Mitchell, who agreed to seek the elimination of some of the film's most offensive scenes. In Boston Ernest Gruening led a similar and equally successful public appeal to Mayor James Curley. But *The Birth of a Nation* continued to be shown elsewhere around the country.[8]

It was in the field of law, however, that the early black-Jewish alliance carried out its most effective work. As late as 1920 there were only one thousand black attorneys in the country, and few of them had time for civil rights efforts. To fill the vacuum, white Protestant progressives like Clarence Darrow and increasing numbers of Jewish lawyers, including Arthur Spingarn and his law partner, Charles Studin, entered the field as volunteers. After joining the NAACP, Spingarn accepted several early cases for the New York branch, and in 1913 he assumed full responsibility for the association's legal work on a pro bono basis.

Spingarn played a major role in *Guinn v. United States*, a 1915 Supreme Court decision that struck down grandfather clauses in the state constitutions of Maryland and Oklahoma, clauses that prevented blacks from voting. Two years later he headed the legal team in *Buchanan v. Warley*, which overturned a residential segregation law.[9] He and his partner gradually became involved in most of the NAACP's cases. In contrast to his highly emotional brother, Arthur Spingarn seemed cool and detached.[10] When blacks sought legal aid, however, he was quick to respond. It became a standing joke between him and Walter White, who succeeded James Weldon Johnson as the NAACP's executive head, that Spingarn carried on his private law practice only in the brief periods when he was not working for the NAACP. He continued as chairman of the legal committee until 1936, when Charles Houston, a black lawyer, took over what was ultimately to become a staff of full-time professionals.

Walter White had gained notice in the NAACP because his light complexion permitted him to visit the scenes of lynchings and secure as much data as possible. His reports were published by the association and widely distributed. In 1929 he published *Rope and Faggot*, a biography of Judge Charles Lynch (after whom lynching was named), which dealt with his findings over a ten-year period. Initially he served as assistant secretary of the association and then as secretary from 1931 to 1935, when he was succeeded by Roy Wilkins.

Some of the greatest Jewish legal minds of the day participated in these early civil rights cases. Though not a member of the NAACP, Louis Brandeis consulted with its lawyers in their campaign against Jim Crow railroad accommodations. Brandeis directed strategy in the case and would have argued it before the Interstate Commerce Commission had not President Wilson appointed him to the Supreme Court. Felix Frankfurter, Harvard's noted legal scholar, served on the NAACP's legal committee and worked quietly behind the scenes in its behalf before succeeding Brandeis on the Court. As a law professor, Frankfurter was ever on the lookout for legal talent for the NAACP. One of the young men he recommended to White was William Hastie, whom Frankfurter described as "one of the finest students who ever studied at Harvard." Hastie joined the NAACP and was named head of its legal committee in 1939, from which post he played a pivotal role in the attack on segregation. He was later appointed to the circuit court of appeals by President Franklin D. Roosevelt and went on to become governor of the Virgin Islands. Other civil rights protégés of Frankfurter included Charles Houston, Nathan Margold, and Joseph Rauh.

Perhaps the most active and effective NAACP lawyer in the 1920s was New Yorker Louis Marshall. The undisputed leader of

American Jewry—he had led the battle against Henry Ford's distribution of the vicious Protocols of the Elders of Zion in the *Dearborn Independent*, had secured Ford's apology, and was involved in every major issue in Jewish life—Marshall was a one-man civil rights movement. While his main focus was defending Jewish rights, his activities were far broader. Whether the case involved Pueblo Indians, Roman Catholics, or Japanese Americans, whether it concerned illiterate immigrants or suspected Communist sympathizers, Marshall was ready to act in defense of individual liberties. Year after year, for example, he opposed the use of literacy tests to restrict immigration. Immigration authorities finally agreed to offer the tests in Yiddish and to exempt victims of religious persecution from taking the exams, thus easing the way for foreign-born Jews to gain entrance. But Marshall refused to accept the compromise because it would do nothing for non-Jewish immigrants.

Without fee Marshall defended the Pueblo nations against incursions on their land in the Rio Grande Conservancy District. He argued against the constitutionality of California laws limiting the property rights of citizens of Japanese descent. And in opposing social discrimination against Jews, he, with the help of B'nai B'rith and the Anti-Defamation League, pushed through laws in New York, Pennsylvania, and Illinois that helped establish the legal principles underlying the modern civil rights movement.[11]

Marshall's critics argue that some of his other legal positions discouraged federal action on matters of great national importance. A political conservative, he opposed federal antilynching legislation. He favored giving states a free hand to deal with the problem as they saw fit, even though he must have known that many of the state legislatures, especially in the deep South, winked at lynchers and would do nothing to stop them. As a defender of states' rights, he also opposed federal child-labor and minimum-wage legislation on the grounds that these, too, were matters best left to the states.

But in the 1920s the NAACP was eager to enlist him in its legal efforts. What initially attracted him was the case of Moore against Dempsey. Twelve black farmers had been convicted of murder and given death sentences after a riot in Arkansas. The NAACP's lawyers, headed by Moorefield Storey, argued that courtroom disturbances by racist mobs had made a fair trial impossible. This was similar to the argument that Marshall had made—and lost—in appealing the conviction of Leo Frank. When the Supreme Court ruled in favor of the black farmers in 1923, Marshall sent a congratulatory letter to Walter White. "The stone the builder rejected," he wrote in reference to the Frank case, "has become the cornerstone of the temple." Marshall enclosed a check as a "thank offering," volunteered his services, and subsequently plunged into the association's work with great energy and enthusiasm. How could one protest the treatment of Jews in Russia, he asked a correspondent in Louisiana, without speaking up on behalf of Negroes in the South?[12]

In one of his first appearances for the NAACP, Marshall argued a restrictive covenant case in the Supreme Court. A white woman had sold property in Washington, D.C., to a black man, despite a deed restriction barring sale "to any person of the negro race or blood." Marshall wrote Storey that he didn't believe the Court could uphold a covenant that discriminated against black persons and thereby abet segregation. He argued that the black purchaser had been deprived of due process. The "moment that there is a differentiation in our courts between white and black, Catholic and Protestant, Jew and non-Jew," said Marshall, "hatreds and passions will inevitably be aroused and that which has been most noble and exalted and humane in American life will have been shattered." He lost the battle when the high court ruled that the prohibitions of the Fourteenth Amendment refer to state action only and not to any action by private individuals. But in a somewhat different context, he won the war. For although his appeal was rejected, the Court later ruled—in *Shelley v. Kraemer* in 1948—that restrictive covenants could not be judicially enforced.[13]

In 1927 Marshall gained a temporary victory for the emerging civil rights movement after a black Texan had been barred from voting in his state's Democratic primary. In the one-party South of that time, the action was tantamount to disfranchisement. Marshall took the position that, by turning away the voter, the Democrats had violated clauses in the Fourteenth and Fifteenth Amendments guaranteeing equal protection of the laws. The Court upheld his position. Writing for the majority, Justice Benjamin Cardozo declared that agencies of the state must act in "submission to the mandates of equality and liberty that bind officials everywhere." Marshall's victory did not last long, however. Texas soon enacted a new primary law circumventing the decision. When the black voter sued once more, Marshall resumed the battle. His health deteriorating, Marshall resisted his family's urgings to take a vacation. "I am working on a very important brief for the National Association for the Advancement of Colored People involving the constitutionality of one of the most important matters that has been brought to the Supreme Court in years," he explained. Marshall died in 1929, before the case could be adjudicated. His son James replaced him, but it was not until 1944 that the Supreme Court, in *Smith v. Allwright*, fully upheld Louis Marshall's position.[14]

Marshall's efforts are described at some length here not only because of the significance of his role but because of the recent attacks against him by a revisionist historian. In *Plural but Equal*, published in 1987, Harold Cruse joined David Levering Lewis in criticizing the motives and activities of upper-class German-Jewish leaders engaged in racial justice efforts. He accused Marshall in particular of using the NAACP to "salve the bitter defeat he had experienced in the Leo Frank case."[15]

This subjective psychological argument, of course, can neither be proved or disproved. But Cruse also charged Marshall with hypocrisy. As Frank's lawyer, Marshall had appealed the murder verdict to federal courts on the grounds that Atlanta's lynch-mob mentality deprived the defendant of a fair trial. But at the same time, Cruse noted, the lawyer declined to support a federal law against lynching. Put another way, Marshall, while favoring intervention by federal courts on behalf of his Jewish client, opposed intervention by Congress on behalf of southern blacks, the prime targets of lynchers.[16]

As a states' rights supporter, Marshall believed that lynching, like other forms of murder, was a crime against the state and should accordingly be policed by the states themselves rather than the federal government. He thus opposed the Dyer Anti-Lynching Bill, which the NAACP vainly supported. Whenever a state failed to protect its citizens, of course, he felt it appropriate and even necessary for the federal courts to intervene. However, while his constitutional argument may have made sense on strict constructionist grounds, in the harsh racist reality of the deep South, where lynching of blacks by white terrorists was virtually a state-sanctioned activity, it did not. Marshall seems clearly remiss on this point.

With less justification but just as bitterly, Cruse (expressing his Marxist assumptions) also attacked Marshall for his associations with the rich and powerful and caustically suggested that a split personality was required of one who championed the rights of the underprivileged while lending legal aid to corporations.[17] He characterized German-Jewish reformers like Marshall, Julius Rosenwald, and Joel Spingarn as people who, while thoroughly practical themselves, desperately sought recognition as champions of social justice and democracy. They and other wealthy Jews, wrote Cruse, would pay any price to enhance their social position.[18]

Cruse further observed that the white liberals never took a position that ran counter to their own interests, and in this regard Jews were especially culpable. "At no time or place, on no issue or circumstance, in the duration of this [black-Jewish] alliance were Jews of any parochial persuasion ever called upon to sacrifice Jewish interests on behalf of civil rights," he wrote.[19]

The fact is, however, that despite group circumstances within American society that differed significantly, the civil rights interests of Jews and blacks in the 1920s and 1930s were virtually identical. Both groups faced discrimination and together opposed it. Marshall himself understood very well that in battling for blacks, he was also battling for Jews and other outsiders. Thus, in a letter to Senator William E. Borah on April 19, 1920, he observed that Washington's restrictive covenant case "affects not only colored people but those of every race and of every nationality or origin."[20] That Jews also benefited from Marshall's civil rights litigation did not minimize its usefulness for blacks.

It was only much later, in the 1970s, with the emergence of such issues as university enrollment quotas for black students and ethnic succession struggles in schools and other arenas, that black and Jewish interests began to diverge. In these instances most Jewish groups, which had historically supported black causes, opposed them. In situations like the Bakke case, where Jewish groups went into the courts to challenge a racial quota system at the University of California–Davis medical school, they *did* decline to sacrifice Jewish interests on behalf of black interests, and their refusal to do so was to become a critical element in the subsequent breakup of the black-Jewish alliance.

In the view of Harold Cruse and other revisionist scholars, the upper-class Jewish and black allies who directed strategy for the early civil rights effort were guilty of limited vision. They failed to involve the black masses in the movement, and because they placed their emphasis on integration, they also failed to work for the development of black identity and group cohesiveness. Marshall (who, of course, was not an assimilationist) and the others were active in building Jewish communal strength, Cruse observed, but not in doing the same for blacks. Jews, in other words, were supporting the wrong kind of black leadership for the wrong reasons, and their participation in the movement actually weakened blacks.

Cruse thus faulted Jews and other white liberals for rejecting on principle any economic development program such as the creation of black businesses. "White liberalism was conditioned," he charged, "not to sanction any effort by blacks toward autonomous self-preservation."

What Cruse, writing when many of the desegregation and voting rights struggles were over, evidently fails to realize was that blacks themselves were not conditioned to initiate such efforts. As they faced direct threats to life and safety and confronted legally enforced barriers, such as state-sponsored segregation, that affected virtually every aspect of their life, the majority of blacks doubtless understood the need for autonomy but settled for first things first, that is, personal safety and the lowering or elimination of barriers—full acceptance as citizens in American society with all of the attendant rights and privileges. In the 1920s the civil rights focus was therefore on urgent questions of political rights rather than community building. Civil rights activists could hardly be faulted for trying to meet these needs.

Moreover, Marshall, the Spingarns, and other Jews could not have taken responsibility for black autonomy even if they had wanted to. Black leaders themselves disagreed over the means of achieving self-sufficiency, and such differences persist to this day. (Marcus Garvey understood autonomy as the paramount goal of black political activity, but he had already given up on America and launched a back-to-Africa movement.) "So long as segregation was legal," Howard Brotz has written, "the struggle for integration was primarily a struggle against political humiliation of the Negro people as a whole—against the equivalent of the yellow badge."[21]

The charge of elitism made against black and Jewish leaders has truth in it, of course. Until the 1920s there was very little interaction among the masses of Jews and blacks. They had largely dealt with one another as abstractions to this point. But all of that would change dramatically with the vast migrations of both Jews and blacks to many northern cities, especially New York.

In the years before the Civil War, New York City had grown in importance as both a mercantile hub and a key business link between North and South. It also became the center of the still very small American Jewry of the period. During this time New York was viewed by some as a virtual annex of the South. Long before cotton became king in the nineteenth century, New York businessmen, Jews and Gentiles alike, cultivated the good will and patronage of West Indian sugar barons, who were central figures in the "triangular" trade of slaves for molasses and rum.

Even those New York-based merchants who may have had compunctions about slavery were drawn into the economic system that connected New York to the South. Often these ties were made closer by marriages that linked elite Sephardic and German-Jewish families in New York with those of Charleston and other southern cities.[22] Many northern Jews also agreed with Abraham Lincoln that saving the Union was more important than destroying slavery, and in the months before the outbreak of hostilities, their worst fears had been realized. The South's economy collapsed, and its northern creditors suffered.[23]

Very early on, therefore, New York presented a setting in which issues affecting blacks and Jews were played out in special ways, an aspect of the black-Jewish story seldom found in other cities. It was in New York that Jews and blacks would work together effectively against discrimination in the coming years. But it was also in New York that many of their bitterest quarrels began, some of which have lasted to the present time. Harlem would become the site of many of the closest associations, as well as the worst of the quarrels.

Harlem, which became the capital of black America in the twenties, had previously been a Jewish preserve. It represented upward mobility for Jewish tradesmen, carpenters, painters, and small businessmen, who there began investing their modest savings in housing before the turn of the century. Sections of Harlem came to be known as Little Russia due to the influx of east European immigrants.[24]

Blacks began moving into Harlem around 1905, though at first the migration was slow. Prior to World War I the number of Harlem's Jews in one census tract actually increased as the black population also rose. But during the war blacks poured into New York for defense and other jobs, and the migration continued after the armistice, gradually causing Harlem's racial balance to shift. In 1920 about seventy-five thousand blacks, 70 percent of Manhattan's black population, lived in the area between the Hudson and Harlem rivers from 118th Street to 144th Street. In the twenties, however, blacks moved to Harlem at the rate of twenty-five thousand a year, and by 1930, 328,000 blacks were living in Harlem—more than four times those in the previous decade. As blacks moved in, Jews moved out to other sections of the city in the Bronx and Brooklyn, leaving the more densely packed neighborhoods behind as part of their upward climb.[25]

Some Jews stayed behind, however, sustaining Harlem's economic infrastructure as landlords, shopkeepers, and merchants. These Jews, rather than the Schiffs, Spingarns, and Warburgs, became the real-life Jewish presence for tens of thousands of blacks in Harlem. Similar transitions would occur in formerly Jewish sections of Philadelphia, Chicago, Detroit, Boston, and other cities.

The pattern of this transformation was the same everywhere. When a white family left, it would be replaced by one or more black families. Blacks would often double up or take in lodgers; family houses would be converted into apartments. The flight of white residents would accelerate; rents would rise; black overcrowding would worsen. Living conditions would decline, and the neighborhoods would become virtually all-black slums. Nevertheless, many Jewish merchants remained in the neighborhoods and continued to do business there.[26]

Jews who resented the influx of blacks sometimes formed neighborhood protective associations to halt or limit the immigration before it became overwhelming. One such group was the West Side Improvement Association. According to the *New York Age*, it was directed mainly by Jews and vainly sought to evict blacks in the area from 90th to 110th Streets out of concern that their presence would cause a decline in property values. At the same time, however, Jewish publications condemned the protective associations. The *Yiddishe Tageblatt* applauded the efforts of the Anglo-American Realty Company, which bought unoccupied apartment houses and rented to blacks. "For the persecuted Jew to enhearten the persecutors of the Negro," the *Tageblatt* said, "is indeed despicable."[27]

While some elements of the Jewish community reacted selfishly, other Jews made efforts to assist blacks in various ways, most notably Jewish teachers who chose to go into Harlem. Some blacks did well in the Jewish cultural environment they found there, and Jews sometimes served as role models for black youth. (Gen. Colin L. Powell's family migrated in the twenties from Jamaica to Harlem, where he was born. They later moved to the South Bronx. Though not an idyllic place to grow up, Harlem was nevertheless a solid working-class district where Jews, Italians, blacks, and Hispanics coexisted. Powell, like many first- and second-generation Jews, went to City College of New York and even picked up a little Yiddish. Years later, when asked whether he had used that language to speak to Israeli prime minister Yitzhak Shamir, Powell answered, "Well, maybe a bissel [a little].")[28]

At the street level, increased contacts with Jews led some blacks to convert to Judaism. From 1915 to 1931, at least eight congregations of black Jews were organized in Philadelphia, New York, Washington, and other eastern cities. Like the conventional synagogues, they emphasized hard work and family values, and several of the black rabbis took Jewish names. In adopting the Jewish religion, they gained a new conception of themselves. According to Howard Brotz in *The Black Jews of Harlem*, they were no longer outcasts but "chosen people, with a proud past and a triumphant future."[29]

The most prominent black Jew, Arnold Ford, studied Hebrew with an immigrant teacher in New York and helped transmit talmudic Judaism to his black followers. Ford soon left New York, however, and his later whereabouts were shrouded in mystery. Legend has it that he emigrated to Africa. Brotz speculates that he went instead to Detroit and there, under the name Fard, Ford, or Farrad, founded the Nation of Islam. Under the leadership of Elijah Muhammad, Malcolm X, and Louis Farrakhan, the Black Muslims would become a potent and divisive force in black-white relations in later years.[30]

Just as Judaism never appealed greatly to most blacks as a religion, so neither did Booker T. Washington's exhortations to emulate Jews and thereby find success yield fruit for those living now in large urban centers. Frustrated by such disappointed hopes, an abiding sense of anger and frustration began to emerge that provided the setting for the rise of one of the most fascinating figures in American black history, Marcus Garvey.

Following the convulsions of World War I, Garvey rose to prominence with a message that attracted a huge following. Washington had spoken for blacks in the rural South before the war. Du Bois's intellect was respected by white and black middle-class reformers. But Garvey's appeal was strongest for the masses of native-born and West Indian blacks in northern slums. The first man of color to develop and lead a mass movement among blacks in this country, Garvey had organized the Universal Negro Improvement Association (UNIA) in his native Jamaica in 1914. Two years later he moved to New York, and with Harlem as its base, the UNIA grew rapidly. By 1919 its leaders claimed thirty branches and two million members.[31]

Garvey delivered a message of economic self-sufficiency that would prove to be of enduring importance to blacks. The UNIA under Garvey's leadership developed a black shipping line, black cooperative housing, black restaurants, and black laundries. He gave millions of blacks a sense of dignity and self-worth. It was no accident that Garvey's biographer, Edmond D. Cronin, gave his book the title *Black Moses*.

In stronger terms than anyone before him, Garvey preached black pride and black power. He told blacks who were ashamed of their color that black was beautiful. Indeed, he argued not for black equality but black superiority.[32]

Accordingly, Garvey coupled an emphasis on racial purity with attacks on miscegenation. He even claimed to see some merit in the Ku Klux Klan. Since Garvey considered the situation for American blacks to be hopeless, the hooded lynch mobs of the South could serve a purpose, he contended, by convincing blacks that there was no room for them in this country and that they should return to their African homeland. Garvey once went to Atlanta and conferred with Klan officials about his back-to-Africa movement, which the Klansmen certainly favored. But Garvey's tactics drew strong criticism from the black labor leader A. Philip Randolph, as well as from the NAACP and the Urban League.

Like Washington and some other black figures, Garvey seemed preoccupied with Jews and Judaism. His call for an African exodus bore a striking similarity to the ideas of Jewish thinkers like Pinsker and Herzl, as well as to those of earlier black figures.[33] In July 1920 Garvey told a UNIA meeting: "A new spirit, a new courage, has come to us simultaneously as it has come to other peoples of the world. It came to us at the same time as it came to the Jew. When the Jew said, 'We shall have Palestine!' the same sentiment came to us when we said, 'We shall have Africa.'"[34]

But Garvey also believed that Jews blocked black progress. He quarreled frequently with the NAACP, and more often than not, his grievances concerned the leadership roles of Jews in what he believed should have been an all-black organization. Thus, where Washington had called upon blacks to emulate Jewish thrift and discipline, Garvey urged them to boycott Jewish businesses. For blacks to create their own enterprises, Garvey believed, they needed to replace existing Jewish ones. For some his argument became an article of faith.[35] Over time, the "buy black" campaigns he sparked in Harlem and elsewhere took on an overtly anti-Semitic tone.

Garvey's anti-Semitism intensified in 1922 after his conviction for mail fraud in a case involving the Black Star Steamship Line, an enterprise he had founded. Presiding judge Julian Mack was a member of the German-Jewish aristocracy who also served on the board of the NAACP. Judge Mack rejected Garvey's plea for a mistrial, fined him, sentenced him to five years in prison, and denied him bail. Not surprisingly, Garvey's subsequent denunciations of Jews were as vitriolic as Tom Watson's had been in the Leo Frank trial.

Citing an "international frameup," Garvey declared: "I am being punished for the crime of the Jew Silverstone [an agent for the line]. I was prosecuted by Maxwell Mattuck, another Jew, and I am to be sentenced by Judge Julian Mack, the eminent Jewish jurist. Truly I may say 'I was going to Jericho and fell among thieves.'" His second wife, Amy Jacques, bitterly assailed Jews in the April 28, 1923, issue of *Negro World*. Her article was entitled "Who Is to Be Blamed?" She blamed the Jews.[36] Meanwhile, Garvey's other followers continued their attack on what they termed the parasitical presence of Jews in black ghettos.

After serving two years, Garvey was deported in 1927. In London he launched a new publication to promote his views on Negro separatism, *The Blackman*, which gave him an outlet for his rage against Jews, particularly those engaged in international finance. During these years Garvey also became an avowed admirer of Adolph Hitler, likening the charismatic Führer's intense nationalism and dream of a greater Germany to his own call for a greater Africa. *The Blackman* wrote, "Hitler's ways could make the Negro the man he ought to be." Garvey warned in 1935—before the Nazis' persecution of Jews had gained widespread public notice—that the Jews would ultimately destroy Germany as they had already destroyed Russia. On the other hand, he frequently complimented Jews for their strong attachment to Zionism and their efforts to obtain a Jewish state.[37]

It should be noted that some Jews were initially attracted to Garvey, not least for his philo-Zionism. Millenarian sentiments involving a Jewish-controlled Palestine and a Negro-controlled Africa were expressed by at least one enthusiastic Jewish supporter in a telegram to the UNIA in 1920.[38] At first the pro-Zionist Yiddish press, including the *Morgen Journal* and *Tageblatt*, took a similar position, describing Garvey as a kindred spirit who sought a homeland for Negroes as they did for Jews. Garvey's anthem, "Ethiopia: Thou Land of Our Fathers" (composed by Arnold Ford, the black rabbi), was dubbed "the Negro Hatikvah," a reference to the Zionist anthem. After Garvey's arrest and conviction, however, the Yiddish papers, concluding he was a fraud, lost interest.

Historian Henry Feingold has suggested that in Marcus Garvey's movement one can see the beginnings of a broader-based anti-Semitism among the black masses. Until Garvey such anti-Semitism as existed in black communities was inchoate and spasmodic rather than pervasive. Most blacks looked on Jews less as exploiters than as fellow victims of discrimination and abuse. Playing on populist notions going back to Andrew Jackson, Feingold argues, Garvey created a "home-grown anti-Semitism" that would reverberate among blacks in later years. But other historians disagree. Robert G. Weisbord and Richard Kazarian, Jr., believe it is a gross exaggeration to label Garvey an anti-Semite. They acknowledge his attacks on Jews but point out that in the *Blackman* Garvey often expressed sympathy for Jews as a despised and oppressed minority and praised Jewish efforts to rebuild Zion in Jerusalem.[39]

It should not be surprising that Garvey, as the leader of a mass movement, reflected or embodied the ambivalence felt toward Jews by many blacks.[40] But however one sees Garvey, he clearly played an important role in shaping black thought, and his admirers may properly claim that he was the most representative black figure of the 1920s. Bursting onto the scene with radical ideas that were ahead of their time, Garvey forced blacks trapped in urban slums to think of themselves in global terms, and he quickly gained a huge following. After being prosecuted and deported for relatively minor indiscretions, Garvey's influence waned, and he died in near obscurity in 1940. Yet his emphasis on black pride in the 1920s found an echo in the American civil rights movement of the 1960s, 1970s, and 1980s.

Garvey's downfall resulted from a combination of personal flaws and organizational weaknesses, as well as the hysteria against radicalism that gripped the nation in the twenties. One young zealot who made his reputation in this period working for the newly formed Federal Bureau of Investigation was J. Edgar Hoover, who pursued Marcus Garvey—to the point of incarceration—with the same relentless intensity he would later display in seeking to destroy the Rev. Martin Luther King.

With Garvey gone, the leaderless black underclass struggled for survival in a society that was too busy coping with the effects of a depression to concern itself about their problems. Anger at this societal abandonment built up in the slums and often turned against blacks' closest allies and neighbors, the Jews. Racial jealousy increased. The experience of Jews had promised so much, yet the reality for blacks was starkly different. Since Jews were seen to profit from black patronage of Jewish stores and businesses in Harlem, the idea took hold among some blacks that Jews were responsible for their problems in the first place and only posed as friends. "Jews and others are the captains of Harlem's industries which Negroes patronize," the *Age* declared in 1924. According to one black estimate, 90 percent of the cabarets and speakeasies were controlled by Jews. Accusations of rent gouging by Jewish landlords became more common. Even A. Philip Randolph's *Messenger* sometimes vented its exasperation on this score, and one can find in its pages various statements complaining that Jews were pushing Negroes out of business in real estate, restaurants, amusements, and small manufacturing. Randolph had wanted to make his paper the black counterpart of the *Jewish Daily Forward*, the voice of the Jewish working class. But the lack of essential financial support from Jews and other whites was to dash his hopes. The *Messenger* limped along for several years, finally suspending operations in 1927.[41]

Jewish philanthropy and support also came under criticism in the black press. While the Jew "sympathizes with and helps us" in many ways, a Norfolk *Virginia Journal and Guide* editorialist wrote in 1926, he also "gets his pound of flesh for doing it [as is] his due and the due of everyone who takes as well as he gives." In the same vein but less charitable was the *Atlanta Independent*'s remark that "the Jew never gives his time and talent for his health." The paper reported that rich Jews owned, directed, and controlled the major civil rights organizations, and it hinted at political machinations within the NAACP.[42]

Despite these accusations (which were little noticed anyway) and at a time when they were also assisting some two million Jewish immigrants in their adjustment to America, Jewish philanthropists helped blacks score many concrete advances. One of the most committed of these philanthropists was Julius Rosenwald, whose support of black schooling in the South had a lasting impact and has long been remembered by blacks. When Rosenwald's fund began pouring money into black schools in 1914, the southern white authorities had virtually ignored black education for decades. The South needed agricultural laborers, and the prevailing view was that educated blacks would refuse to work in the fields. Thus, nearly all public funds for education went to all-white schools, which blacks were barred by law from attending. Between 1914 and 1932 the Rosenwald Fund gave $4,364,869 for black education in fifteen states. This infusion of money went to black schools throughout the South; to schools in 95 percent of the counties in South Carolina, 90 percent of those in Alabama, 86 percent of those in Louisiana, Maryland, and North Carolina, and 75 percent of those in Virginia. By the time the program ended, more than one-fourth of all the black children in the South had been educated in Rosenwald schools.[43]

To qualify for Rosenwald support, blacks were required to raise funds of their own on a matching basis. Given their straitened finances, the task was excruciatingly difficult. But sharecroppers, tenant farmers, and other blacks overcame hardships and banded together to do what had to be done. In a truly heroic example of self-help, they actually raised slightly more money for the schools than the Rosenwald Fund put in. In many cases they contributed their own labor to the school building projects as well, promoting a stronger sense of community among blacks as a beneficial side effect. It was partly for these reasons that Horace Mann Bond, the father of civil rights activist Julian Bond and author of a classic study of black education in the 1930s, credited the Rosenwald school campaign with energizing the collective will and educational ambitions of blacks in the rural South.

Critics have charged that the segregated schools supported by the Rosenwald Fund trained blacks for work which whites did not want and thereby left them unprepared for leadership in business and politics. Perhaps so, but Rosenwald's efforts were bitterly resented by southern whites for whom *any* assistance to blacks was already too much. Taking note of such criticism, a historian of black education suggests that the pattern of southern racism made it necessary to adopt Rosenwald's alternative.[44]

Black public opinion in this period was not, furthermore, universally anti-Jewish. Far from it. The *Chicago Defender*, which had condemned Jewish efforts to exonerate Leo Frank, had also called for blacks and Jews to ally themselves in the coming confrontation over bigotry and racism.[45] Now, a decade later, it sympathized with a Jewish traveling salesman who had been mutilated by a mob in North Carolina for allegedly mistreating a young Gentile girl.[46] Blacks criticized the influx of Jewish immigrants from eastern Europe, but on the other hand, Harlem mothers gathered layettes for Jewish refugees fleeing pogroms in Poland. The explanation offered by the *Amsterdam News* for such sympathetic responses was that "only these two knew what it meant to drink the bitter dregs of race prejudice."[47]

Indeed, for Jews there were constant reminders in this period of their continuing outsider status. Immigration restrictions and university enrollment quotas were aimed in part at limiting their numbers and educational opportunities. The Ku Klux Klan expanded, and pioneer automaker Henry Ford conducted a seven-year war against Jews in his bitterly anti-Semitic *Dearborn Independent*. Racism existed among Jews, just as anti-Semitism did among blacks. But other forces, which appeared far more threatening, helped draw blacks and Jews together. When neighborhood conflicts arose, the Yiddish newspapers noted that Jewish merchants accused of exploiting blacks had often been barred from employment opportunities in other sections and were, like their customers, trapped in poor Negro districts. After one anti-Semitic incident in Harlem in 1929, the *Morgen Journal* advised its readers: "We cannot blame it on the Negroes for acting this way." The newspaper, appealing to socialist sentiments in the Jewish community, placed responsibility on a harsh, repressive economic system that violated the rights of blacks and Jews alike.[48]

In the late 1920s blacks and Jews working together made a number of concrete strides forward. The largely Jewish Amalgamated Clothing Workers' Union formed a housing cooperative that, with state assistance, built cooperative apartments in the Bronx for black families moving from Harlem. Jewish attorneys and legislators, including New Yorkers Judge Samuel Rosenman and Congressman Abraham Grenthal, advised black tenants of their rights in regard to rent gouging and overdue building repairs. Julius Rosenwald built a block of low-rent housing units on Michigan Avenue in Chicago for black teachers, postal workers, and librarians. When the apartments were completed, the city's black leadership honored him at a banquet.[49]

One of the most remarkable and enduring black-Jewish relationships was that between Jewish labor and socialist leaders and A. Philip Randolph, the black founder and longtime head of the Brotherhood of Sleeping Car Porters. After arriving in Harlem from Florida in 1911, Randolph had enrolled in the evening division of City College. A history and economics professor named J. Salwyn Shapiro got him interested in socialist literature and European working-class movements. Randolph later described this discovery as so exciting that he began reading Marx as enthusiastically as a child might read *Alice in Wonderland*. Randolph was also influenced by Morris R. Cohen, a young professor of philosophy and politics who provoked in him more intellectual restlessness than any other teacher at City College.[50]

Jewish union leaders helped Randolph organize the sleeping car porters, which very quickly became the spearhead and principal support for black mass politics until the emergence of the modern civil rights movement. Randolph and his partner, Chandler Owens, co-editors of the *Messenger*, took a leading role in the 1917 mayoralty campaign of Morris Hillquit, a Jewish socialist, terming him the only candidate that "any self-respecting Negro would vote for." Hillquit lost, but in return Jewish congressmen from New York provided crucial votes for antilynching legislation and other black causes.[51]

When Randolph began organizing the nation's Pullman porters in 1925, he turned to Congressman Emanuel Celler for help. Celler, who represented a predominantly Jewish constituency in Brooklyn, became Randolph's spokesman on Capitol Hill. He introduced a resolution calling upon the House labor committee to investigate the wages, hours, and conditions of employment of Pullman porters. When the resolution was killed, Celler solicited the aid of influential Jews like Samuel Untermyer, Louis Waldman, and Morris Ernst. Eventually the Pullman Company was forced to recognize the Brotherhood of Sleeping Car Porters, and Randolph became one of the nation's most important labor leaders. He forged close ties with numerous Jewish trade unionists, including Morris Hillquit and Joseph Schlossberg of the Amalgamated Clothing Workers, Rose Schneiderman of the ILGWU, and I. A. Shiplacoff of the International Pocketbook Workers. He also received financial support from such uptown Jews as Herbert Lehman, as well as advice and help from Rabbi Stephen Wise.[52]

For nearly half a century, he and his protégé Bayard Rustin served as keystones of the black-Jewish labor alliance. Randolph cited two reasons for the intensity of Jewish interest in black labor. First, Jews possessed "a deeper and more fundamental understanding of the class struggle." Second, Jewish workers shared with blacks a "history that is complete with unspeakable outrages . . . they have drunk the bitter dregs of the cup of persecution."

Throughout his long and extraordinarily productive career, which stretched into the period of the civil rights revolution and the years of conflict and tensions that followed, Randolph never lost faith in the belief that Jews and blacks had to progress together. Such a unified effort stood at the core of his philosophy. The close links he established, especially with Jewish labor, provided an underpinning for the black-Jewish-labor alliance during these years. Moreover, as we shall see, the organizational models, ideology, and protest tactics of the Jewish labor movement would be built into the civil rights movement of the late 1950s and 1960s. Many later black leaders gained their first civil rights experience working with Randolph and the Jewish left. If Joel Spingarn and W. E. B. Du Bois were the major figures in the alliance's first years, Randolph and Louis Marshall became its personification in the 1920s.

4

THE THIRTIES

The Tensions Grow

Kate Simon's family emigrated from Poland to New York City in the 1920s, living first on Second Avenue, then in East Harlem, and finally in the Bronx, where she grew up. Before coming to America, her father had been a "princeling in his mother's household in a small Polish town," she writes in a memoir of her teenage years. He imagined himself a "grand seigneur." Alas, in New York in the Great Depression, he became "a factory slave, a Jew slave in a city that rubbed wops and niggers and micks against his singularity." He hated the place.

Simon, who grew up to become a respected author, recalls how difficult life was for so many New Yorkers, Jews and non-Jews alike.

> To earn little, to do with little, to give up one pleasure for another, was the atmosphere we breathed, our natural climate. Many of our houses held as prisoners unabashed, unemployed fathers. A number of girls, though fairly well dressed, lived in apartments almost empty of furniture, the few sticks frequently moved from apartment to apartment to avoid paying rent or being shoved on the street. Some of the fathers went to distant boroughs, where they were not known, to sell apples; some continued sitting with vacant eyes.[1]

Amid all this suffering, however, the sight that made the deepest impression on adolescent Kate was that of black women—"schvartzes" was the Yiddish term used by an older generation of Jews to identify blacks—competing frantically for jobs as day servants in the Bronx at a few pennies an hour. The bidders for their labor were white women, many of them Jewish. The gathering places were called "slave markets." Simon remembers:

> The one experience of profoundest poverty that infuriated me, made me painfully sorrowful and ashamed that I could not alter anything, nor scream and yell and protest effectively, was the slave markets that were held in front of Woolworth stores in several neighborhoods, black women facing white women who wanted a few hours of household work at the lowest possible cost. It was dreadful to watch black women outbid each other downward for the jobs: "I'll take twenty-five cents an hour." "Hey, missus, I'll work for twenty cents." Another offered herself for eighteen cents. I don't know if the bidding ever went lower; after a few moments I would run from the shameful scene.[2]

The slave markets were a common part of depression-era life for black Americans. "All the submerged prejudices of people were exposed in the raw as the scraping poverty rubbed away at their psychological devices, leaving their real selves exposed," wrote Harold Cruse, who was living in Harlem at the time.[3] By 1935 every second black adult in Harlem was jobless. And although New Deal social programs eased the pain for millions of impoverished families, only a few of Franklin D. Roosevelt's initiatives benefited blacks. Farm workers and most domestic servants—job categories that included numerous blacks—were not covered by the new Social Security Act.

Jews suffered as well. Besides being hurt economically, they faced a rising tide of anti-Semitism. Inspired by events in Hitler's Germany, more than one hundred Nazi-type organizations sprang up on home soil. A Roman Catholic priest, the Rev. Charles E. Coughlin, attracted a wide radio audience during the thirties with his weekly tirades against the Jews.

At this time, too, many of the nation's best colleges and universities limited Jewish enrollments. Some, like Yale and Dartmouth, had quotas. In law, banking, insurance, and other fields, Jews were often barred from employment or advancement. They were excluded from social clubs, and in numerous other ways their outsider status, like that of blacks, was reinforced.

Although not much was made of it at the time, black-Jewish relations in the slums worsened during the Great Depression. One who recognized this fact was Ralph J. Bunche, then chairman of Howard University's political science department and later a top official at the United Nations. In his foreword to a graduate paper by Lunabelle Wedlock, "The Reaction of Negro Publications and Organizations to German Anti-Semitism," Bunche wrote that as was well known, there was all too much mutual dislike and mistrust between the two communities. "Many Jews exhibit the same prejudiced, stereotyped attitudes toward Negroes that are characteristic of so many members of the dominant Gentile population. Likewise, many Negroes embrace enthusiastically the anti-Jewish concepts which have attained wide currency, and adapt them." He noted an undercurrent of apparent black resentment of the relatively greater social, political, and economic success enjoyed by Jews, who did not suffer the injustice and misery of Jim Crow.[4]

That black-Jewish antagonisms flared into the open in the 1930s hardly seems surprising, given the collapse of the nation's economy and the lower classes' struggle for survival. What is perhaps more puzzling is why the eruption of these tensions during the depression has so rarely been acknowledged.

It is widely believed—perhaps more so today by Jews than blacks—that the two groups were as one through most of American history, united in their common fight for justice and civil rights until the rupturing of the alliance in the mid-1960s. That is a lovely story—not without important elements of truth—but it is incomplete. As we have seen, there were differences, disputes, and bad feelings on both sides from the first, and they continued almost without interruption even as the black-Jewish alliance was taking shape and making its first gains. Mutual distrust was always present alongside the sense of a common experience and a willingness to cooperate in overcoming prejudice and discrimination. For a long time, the alliance withstood these strains and stresses remarkably well. That side of the story—the account of disparate outsiders forging a lasting coalition—has already been told and retold. But for whatever reason, the underlying conflicts and animosities of the black-Jewish relationship have been overlooked.

To some extent the clashes of the 1930s may have been obscured by the more urgent tragedy of the Great Depression. Yet there also appears to have been a reluctance on the part of those seeking to improve the conditions of both groups to grapple with the uncomfortable fact that blacks and Jews were often in conflict. It was frequently a case of underdogs fighting each other instead of the top dog. One of the unlikely battlegrounds in this conflict was Harlem Hospital.

In the early 1930s many of the nation's most prestigious medical schools limited Jewish admissions, and many prominent hospitals discouraged Jewish doctors from applying for positions on their staffs. As a result, Jews often found themselves competing with blacks for places at predominantly black medical schools and hospitals. At Harlem Hospital most of the patients were black, but most of the doctors were Jewish. Charging discrimination in hiring, black groups led by Adam Clayton Powell, Jr.—then pastor of the Abyssinian Baptist Church in Harlem—initiated a campaign demanding that more blacks be added to the hospital's medical staff. Black newspapers took up the cause, running stories about blacks refused emergency treatment at Harlem Hospital and black patients dying because of white doctors' malpractice.

The tensions at Harlem Hospital gained citywide attention and became a sensitive political issue. Mayor Jimmy Walker ordered a reorganization of the hospital's medical staff. Five physicians were ousted without cause, and nineteen black doctors were appointed, with more added later. The NAACP praised the reorganization for recognizing the competence of Negro physicians. But that was not the end of it. The dismissed staff members sought reinstatement, charging that some of the new black staff were unready to assume their responsibilities. A public fight erupted. To make matters worse, a small group of black physicians employed by the hospital before the dismissals actually sided with the dismissed doctors, arguing that they were needed to assist and train junior staff.[5]

At this point Jewish philanthropist Julius Rosenwald proposed a solution. Based on a medical survey of Harlem, his foundation, the Rosenwald Fund, recommended the establishment there of a private black hospital to meet community needs. Rosenwald had helped set up such a hospital in Chicago, and a number of New York's black leaders thought that a new community hospital might represent for blacks what Mount Sinai did, and still does, for Jews. Other blacks, however, opposed the plan, fearing that it would undermine efforts then underway with the Anti-Defamation League to tamp down conflicts by seeking more jobs for blacks. To some blacks Rosenwald's proposal smacked of racism pure and simple. His foundation (which had also financed all-black schools in the South) was charged with encouraging and advancing segregation, and the hospital was viewed as another example of this. The plan was soon abandoned, and by the time of his death in 1932, Rosenwald's positive image, based on his efforts for black education, had been severely tarnished. The *Amsterdam News* declared that his gifts constituted a disservice to Negroes. But as an Urban League official noted insightfully, the real issue was not Jewish money or Jewish doctors but the inability of an impoverished community to create enough hospitals to support its black physicians.[6]

As the Harlem Hospital crisis abated, other black-Jewish tensions worsened. As white clientele left the area, department store merchants H. C. F. Koch and L. M. Blumstein treated black customers discourteously and refused to hire blacks except for menial positions. However, most of Harlem's businesses then were mom-and-pop operations, few of which, given their character and the disastrous business slump, were hiring anyone, white or black. In the 1920s Marcus Garvey and others had encouraged blacks to start their own businesses, and this movement continued into the thirties. For the most part, however, Harlem's black entrepreneurs lacked the capital and experience needed to stock their shelves adequately and build inventories and clientele. More often than not, their marginal businesses failed. By contrast, the Jewish merchants, while often poor immigrants, were aided by a long business tradition and usually stronger financing—a result of Hebrew free-loan societies and other communal supports—and they were able to offer their customers a wider selection of goods.[7] Not being as dependent on quick cash turnover as the black merchants were, they developed customer-credit arrangements that further increased sales, although this hardly improved relations between the two groups. Thus in 1932 it was reported that black-owned stores in Harlem got less than 10 percent of the black trade.

The Harlem Colored Merchants Association began efforts to improve the performance of black businessmen. These were encouraged by prominent Jews, but to little effect. At one point Julius Rosenwald urged President Herbert Hoover to hold a national conference on strengthening black entrepreneurship, but nothing came of this proposal either. The times were too difficult for many white businesses, to say nothing of minority-run shops and stores.

For many blacks, however, the Jews symbolized the power of an oppressive white world they could not reach, and their resentment took the form of rent strikes, business boycotts, and other forms of economic pressure. Some of these actions were modeled after successful Jewish efforts to block American trade with Nazi Germany. But not all blacks shared Jewish loathing for the German chancellor; Ralph Bunche described those who didn't as adopting an only slightly refined version of white anti-Semitism.[8] Some even saw justification for Hitler's attitude. "If the Jewish merchants in Germany treated the German workers as Blumstein's [a Jewish-owned department store] is treating the people of Harlem," the *New York Age* declared on June 2, 1934, "then Hitler is right!"[9]

Not all blacks felt this way, of course, and there were many criticisms of Hitler's treatment of Jews, often in black newspapers that were otherwise highly critical of Jewish behavior toward blacks. For example, in Harlem's tenement districts there were constant reports of rent gouging. The *New York Times* reported that apartment rentals in Harlem in 1935 ranged from forty to one hundred dollars per month, in contrast with rents of thirty to fifty dollars elsewhere in the city. Stereotypes of the "fiendish Jewish landlord" and the "Shylock" were taken up by blacks in the slums of Chicago, Detroit, Philadelphia, and Pittsburgh as well as New York, even though many tenement owners were not Jewish. Indeed, Leonard Dinnerstein has shown that blacks owned 75 percent of Harlem real estate in 1936 and that "Daddy" Browning, John D. Rockefeller, and the estate of John J. Astor were among the largest single property owners in the area.[10]

Early in 1933 Harlem tenement dwellers threatened to continue a rent strike until increases were rescinded and janitorial services improved. When a judge ruled in favor of the strikers the following year, the strikes spread, and a number of landlords were forced out of business because of rising costs. In the spring Harlem's street corners began to resound to the rhetoric of a series of anti-Semitic soapbox orators. One of the most radical was a turbaned Muslim from Chicago named Sufi Abdul Hamid. In Chicago Sufi's exotic dress and his claim to have been divinely ordained by Muhammad to redeem the city's south side from Jewish merchants gained him a certain notoriety. In New York his racist message lost none of its punch. Identifying himself as the black Hitler and a man that the Jews were terrified of, he urged his listeners to run Jews out of Harlem. In a manner Louis Farrakhan would make familiar many years later, Sufi attacked what he termed Zionist colonialists and the Jews in Washington who rule everything. The black writer Roi Ottley wrote that, as a result of street-corner agitators like Sufi and Arthur Reid (a former youth leader in Garvey's back-to-Africa movement), Harlem staggered under a torrent of propaganda.[11]

An admirer of Haj Amin el-Husseini, an Arab ally of Hitler and grand mufti of Jerusalem, Sufi openly courted the German-American Bund and the Nazi-like Christian Front. Sufi was one of Harlem's most influential figures in this period and an effective demagogue. Hundreds of white businessmen joined his Negro Industrial and Clerical Alliance, which he founded to organize all black labor. In effect, they paid protection money to avoid violence and to deflect the threat of anti-Jewish boycotts. As a result of such boycotts led by Sufi and others, owners of a number of stores in Harlem, including Blumstein's Department Store and the new lessee of Koch's, Morris Weinstein, agreed to hire black sales personnel.[12]

Ultimately, however, Sufi's anti-Semitism backfired. A group of black ministers, supported by Harlem's leading newspapers, sharply attacked him and called for reconciliation with Harlem's Jews. The Rev. Adam Clayton Powell, Jr., the Harlem preacher who would later become a controversial congressman, organized a joint committee to find more jobs for unemployed blacks and defuse the anti-Semitic atmosphere.[13] The Harlem Merchants Association also spoke out against Sufi and produced witnesses to corroborate his anti-Jewish statements.

After Mayor Fiorello LaGuardia strongly criticized Sufi, the agitator was arrested on charges of inciting to violence. Although a magistrate dismissed the case for lack of evidence, Sufi discontinued his efforts. Rumor had it that the merchants bought him off.[14] He told Ottley that with his newly acquired money he purchased an airplane, hired a white female secretary, and got an Asian mistress. He erected a gaudy temple and became Bishop Amiru Al-Mu-Minin Sufi A. Hamid, head of the Universal Holy Temple of Tranquillity. His mysterious career was cut short when he was killed in an airplane accident.[15]

Rabble-rousing demagogues like Sufi and Reid and wide-scale unemployment and overcrowded living conditions were a volatile mixture. Only a spark was needed to set off an explosion in Harlem.

On March 19, 1935, a young Puerto Rican was caught stealing a ten-cent penknife in a store on 125th Street. Soon after the youth's arrest a false rumor spread that he had been beaten to death. Black crowds gathered and shouted accusations of police brutality and discrimination by merchants. Then the mob began to smash store windows and raid shelves. The rioting continued through most of the night. Three blacks were killed and two hundred stores were looted, with two million dollars in damages. Although Mayor LaGuardia denied that Jewish stores had been singled out, it was clear that they had. A reporter for the *Amsterdam News* even dubbed the riot, "Moses' coming-out party."[16]

Contemporary observers as well as black and Jewish leaders either did not recognize the anti-Semitic aspects of the rioting or chose to ignore them. The hesitation of blacks and even Jews to deal with this subject is a continuing curiosity. The reason for the Jews to hesitate may have something to do with the investment Jews have had in the liberal agenda and the central role improving the lot of blacks has played in their universalist creed. But more recently, in a period of heightened ethnic identification as well as greater public candor, historian Hasia Diner has concluded: "It was in 1935 that the seeds of the disintegration of the black-Jewish alliance were sown."[17]

Faced with the rising tide of anger against Jews, Adam Clayton Powell, Jr., and other black leaders sought to shift the target of black anger to white Christians. The influential Harlem minister was one of the organizers of the Citizens League for Fair Play, which had begun picketing and boycotting Blumstein's in 1934.

Powell now suggested that, while Jews might be chiselers, Christians were worse. "One group might cut the change a little or pad the bill," he said at one point, in an apparent reference to Jewish merchants, but "it is the so-called good white Christian that is giving us the most hell right now."[18]

This shift did not mean that Powell's view of Jews had changed. As others had done, he complained that American Jews seemed more concerned about Hitler's anti-Semitism than about the rampant racism and oppression of blacks in this country. He challenged Jewish Americans to worry less about German Jews and do more about passing an antilynching law in the United States. Langston Hughes also declared in 1935 that blacks did not have to be told about fascism: They knew all about being driven off the streets, having their women beaten, and being pursued by bloodthirsty mobs; yet the world paid no attention to their problems. Roy Wilkins, the NAACP assistant secretary who had been named editor of the *Crisis* when Du Bois stepped down in 1933 and who had advocated a strong stand against Hitler, nevertheless questioned what blacks were getting from Jews in return. In his view, Jews were paying too much attention to exaggerated charges of Nazi persecution and not enough to the realities of black persecution.[19]

The black ambivalence toward Hitler in the 1930s was one of the strangest aspects of the entire black-Jewish relationship. On the one hand, black writers and civic leaders denounced Nazism almost without exception, and many expressed their sympathy for German Jews; but at the same time, many black writers who formally denounced German anti-Semitism inadvertently revealed either some admiration for Hitler or at least some dislike for the Jews.[20]

In a personal memoir of his youth in 1930s' Harlem, a memoir written from the black power perspective of the late 1960s, Harold Cruse explained that he could not be sure which side to favor in the war, the Axis powers or the Allies, since from the Communist press and his black nationalist associates he had gained the impression that Great Britain, as the key colonial power in the world, was the chief imperialist criminal, especially in Africa. The Communist party at the time—initially under pressure from Soviet leaders who had found much support for the Revolution among the nationalities within the Russian empire—emphasized black issues. While Communism failed to make real inroads among the black masses, this current of anti-Americanism has played a role in past and present black thought.[21]

The flirtation of some blacks with Hitler—if such it was—clearly stemmed from a sense of powerlessness.[22] For the same reason apparently, some blacks were attracted to Japan. Addressing the prestigious Pan-Pacific Club in Tokyo in 1933, Langston Hughes hailed the Japanese as the world's only large group of free and independent dark-skinned people. According to Hughes, blacks needed the psychological assurance that there existed some dark people that had not been victimized and oppressed.[23] It is curious that today Japanese and Asians are no longer considered dark-skinned peoples.

Even Du Bois, who had frequently criticized Nazi Germany for its treatment of Jews, took a perverse delight in needling the *New York Times* over its selective concern about oppressed peoples. "Nothing has filled us with such unholy glee as Hitler and the Nordics," Du Bois wrote in the *Crisis* shortly after the Nazis took power. "When the only 'inferior' peoples were 'niggers' it was hard to get the attention of the *Times* for little matters of race, lynchings and mobs. But now that the damned include the owner of the *Times*, moral indignation is perking up."

Roy Wilkins was also to condemn the *New York Times*. Writing in his weekly column in the *Amsterdam News* a week before Pearl Harbor, Wilkins charged that the *Times*'s news coverage reflected its southern and Jewish roots. The newspaper regarded criminal acts of blacks against whites, he said, as more serious than crimes of whites against whites. "Rich, powerful, international in scope, with a Jewish ownership, which should temper its racial stories, the *Times* makes irresponsible references to the racial identity of criminal offenders [and] stoops to petty color sniping to batter a community that can fight back only feebly," Wilkins wrote.

Others also attacked the *Times*. "That defender of democracy (for Jews), that sterling and relentless foe of Hitlerism (in Berlin)," a Harlem spokesman sarcastically commented at a neighborhood meeting, "has branded 200,000 blacks as criminals. Is the *Times* trying to lead a pogrom against the Negroes of New York?" The cause of crime, he argued, was that 117,000 New Yorkers were unemployed and at least 40 percent of Harlem was on welfare, while Harlem businessmen discriminated against Negroes.[24]

At the time of the Olympic Games in Berlin in 1936, Jews urged a boycott by American athletes. A number of black leaders, including Powell, who was then a New York City councilman and news columnist as well as Harlem's most prominent preacher, supported the Jewish position, as did the NAACP. But others, proud of the accomplishments of black athletes, did not want them to boycott the games. The *Amsterdam News* considered it wrong to allow a purely Jewish problem to thwart this black achievement. Lacking support from the Roosevelt administration and from most Americans, the boycott effort failed.

As Europe moved closer to war, intergroup tensions in America worsened. Anti-Semitic propaganda was widespread as a result of the efforts of Nazi sympathizers and Klan members as well as black nationalists. Between 1938 and 1941 Detroit suffered recurrent episodes of anti-Jewish violence, especially along Hastings Street, as youths assaulted merchants and their stores.[25] Some Chicago blacks mounted an effort to drive Jewish businessmen out of their community. In May 1938 a radical black magazine in Chicago called *Dynamite* published an inflammatory story under the headline "What the Black Belt Needs Is a Hitler to Fight for Our Race and Purge Us of the Exploiting Jews."[26] In response to Jewish appeals that they speak out against such extremism, Roy Wilkins and Powell equivocated. Indeed, Powell agreed with *Dynamite* that Jews had exploited blacks and were therefore to blame for the resultant black hostility.[27]

In Harlem Sufi Abdul Hamid's successors continued to stir up trouble. In pressing for jobs for blacks, they employed Nazi-style harangues and dismissed "Roosevelt's Jew-Deal" as a program to deceive blacks.[28] Meetings called to protest high rents or job discrimination often turned into anti-Semitic demonstrations, and at least one speaker said that blacks, like Hitler, were trying to rid themselves of Jewish oppression. There were even suspicions (but no proof) that the Nazis and Japanese had provided money to foment anti-Semitism. Whatever role they may have played was exploitative rather than causative.[29]

Also causing strains in black-Jewish relations were newly arrived Jewish refugees from Nazi Germany, many of whom were seeking and finding employment in this country at a time when very large numbers of blacks were being forced to place themselves on public relief. In fact, the number of Jewish immigrants was limited by law, and only a few were admitted. Nevertheless, when Works Progress Administration (WPA) employment was cut back in 1939, some Harlemites lost their jobs. The *Amsterdam News* declared that all of the aliens should have been dismissed before one American black was laid off, adding that the immigrants should also have been dropped from the relief rolls. *Crisis* editorials in 1938 and 1939 noted that blacks in the United States had suffered longer than the Jews in Germany, while the bishop of the A.M.E. Church insisted that blacks in Harlem were far worse off than Germany's Jews.[30]

Leonard Dinnerstein has suggested that economic depression and the social barriers blacks faced in the 1930s unsurprisingly led them to draw comfort from the persecution of another minority group. Lunabelle Wedlock found, in her survey of the black press's response to German anti-Semitism just after America's entry into the war, that most of the writers viewed the spectacle favorably. She added that many blacks seemed to accept the larger white society's view of Jews, to the point of adopting the same stereotypes. In short, black anti-Semitism apparently was one of the few ways blacks could identify with the majority culture.[31]

These sentiments were fed by a fierce propaganda campaign by the Axis powers and such American Nazi sympathizers as Gerald L. K. Smith, whose newspaper, the *Cross and The Flag*, charged that the conflict in Europe was a Jewish war. Blacks were told it would be foolish to fight for the Jewish landlords and merchants who actively discriminated against them. From London, in the pages of his monthly publication, the *Blackman*, Marcus Garvey also continued to attack Jews and express his admiration for Hitler as a fervent nationalist.[32]

On August 4, 1938, after four months of conferences, Powell's biracial Uptown Chamber of Commerce and the Negro Coordinating Committee founded by Sufi reached an agreement on expanded black employment. In it blacks were guaranteed at least one third of all white-collar jobs in Harlem's retail establishments. Thereafter, attacks on Jews appeared to level off. And when Fritz Kuhn, the German-American Bund leader, told a gathering in Harlem that, as Christians, blacks were also Aryans and that blacks and Nazis were brothers in the struggle against the Jews, police had to be summoned to hold back the hecklers.

A number of black leaders declared that the jobs compact had helped to quiet unrest, but Wilkins was skeptical, noting that even if every business in Harlem were completely staffed by blacks, the community would still face an acute employment problem. Black anti-Semitism, however, disturbed not only Wilkins but Walter White of the NAACP, Adam Clayton Powell, and other black leaders as well. Powell underscored his concern by warning that if fascism came to this country, fifteen million blacks would join the Jews as scapegoats.

As America moved closer to war, conditions for blacks showed little improvement. Joblessness remained very high, and much of the minority population was still ill housed and fed. Throughout the nation blacks were routinely barred from better hotels and restaurants. Baseball, the national pastime, still had not admitted its first black major league player, and in a celebrated incident Marian Anderson, the great contralto, was not allowed to sing at Constitution Hall in Washington, D.C. The southern states still legally deprived blacks of basic human rights, and the North segregated them in housing, schools, and employment. Ralph Ellison's term for the typical American black became the title of his novel: *The Invisible Man*.

In spite of all this, on another level the relationship between blacks and Jews was strong and supportive. Thus, during the Great Depression, when the NAACP came close to shutting down for lack of operating funds, a group of Jewish philanthropists, including Julius Rosenwald, Felix Warburg, Mary Fels, Herbert Lehman, and Harold Guinzberg, came to its rescue. Theirs was a textbook example of wealthy Jews looking beyond daily antagonisms to support an important mainstream black organization.[33] In turn, the NAACP and Urban League spoke out against Hitler's persecution of the Jews.

Another issue involving judicial callousness toward blacks that aroused wider segments of the Jewish community was the Scottsboro case. On the flimsiest of evidence, nine black youths were arrested in Scottsboro, Alabama, in 1931 and charged with raping two white women in a freight car. Eight were sentenced to death, and the ninth to life imprisonment. No issue in race relations so aroused the Jewish community as the campaign to free the Scottsboro boys, which stretched from the summer of 1931 through the spring of 1935. The case of these unfairly accused black men captured the attention of Jews because it coincided with the growing threat to Jews developing in Germany, and two Jewish attorneys—Joseph Brodsky and Samuel Liebowitz—were centrally involved in their defense.

The sentencing outraged much of the nation, setting off court appeals and demonstrations against "southern justice." Jews provided shock troops for Harlem protests, and the Yiddish press rallied in support of the Scottsboro boys. In the five years it took to free the youths, a total of 104 articles appeared on the case in the *Forward* and the *Morgen Journal*. The *Forward* supported them unstintingly, arguing that the trial was a mockery and that the young men stood in danger of losing their lives only because they were Negroes. Samuel Liebowitz took his life in his hands by arguing the case and was vilified as a meddling New York Jew. Working closely with the NAACP, he fought the case through the appellate courts and eventually won acquittal.[34]

America's entry into the war after Pearl Harbor brought a temporary end to black-Jewish clashes as mobilization created a sense of national unity. Blacks and Jews were now joined in the common cause of defeating the Axis powers. "We are Americans all," a black leader announced. Powell brought Jews to their feet by declaring at a rally that the nation could not fight Nazism abroad while permitting anti-Semites "to spew their hate on the streets of New York."[35] Army enlistments jumped in Harlem, which took special pride in its own 369th National Guard unit. Moreover, the war effort meant jobs in defense industries, jobs that blacks could apply for. A. Philip Randolph saw to that. His threat to bring thousands of blacks to Washington forced President Roosevelt to sign Executive Order 8802 in June 1941, which barred employment discrimination in defense industries or government because of race, creed, color, or national origin.

Early in 1942, the *Amsterdam News* sounded a call for every Jew to form an alliance with every colored American. "The Black man must realize," the newspaper said, "that his natural ally is the Jewish race which has not only suffered elsewhere but who inevitably will be the next victim in America." That summer a new journal, the *Negro Quarterly*, featured two articles that candidly explored black anti-Semitism and Jewish antiblack feeling. In one, Dr. L. D. Reddick, curator of the Schomberg collection of Negro literature, examined black admiration for Hitler. He believed that such feelings were stimulated by unscrupulous blacks and Axis agents, both white and black, who sought to exploit the community's legitimate grievances, particularly in their attacks on Jewish landlords. Reddick saw whatever support existed for the German dictator as reflecting ignorance of his racial policies. There was no organized movement to promote such views, and he felt that the problems could be worked out. The *Jewish Daily Forward* and *Jewish Review* agreed, demanding that Jews begin by backing Negroes in their battle against discrimination and eliminating anti-Negro feeling among themselves.[36] Meanwhile Roy Wilkins attacked the anti-Semitic soapbox orators as the most sinister and mortal threat to every black man. In the spring of 1942, cracking down on what Harlem newspapers termed a Nazi spy ring there, the government jailed a number of blacks for violation of the Alien Registration Act. Several were subsequently indicted on conspiracy charges. The arrests broke up what the *New York Times* considered a move in an Axis plan to use domestic upheaval to help it establish world dominance.[37]

The war brought blacks into closer involvement in American life. Approximately half a million blacks saw service in the U.S. military, and in January 1945 it was announced that black troops would be integrated with white troops in a unit to fight on German soil. Twenty-two black combat units were active in the ground operations in the European theater. Meanwhile, despite criticism of the operations of the new Fair Employment Practices Commission set up by Roosevelt, more than one hundred thousand blacks found employment in the iron and steel industries. Although the problem of promoting them remained difficult, there were increased indications that industries were beginning to lift employment barriers. Black involvement in labor unions set the stage, during the war and after, for larger roles in the United Automobile Workers, the United Steel Workers, and other organizations.

Although the war effort reduced joblessness for some and helped unify the nation, its overall impact on employment proved limited. While joblessness became less of a problem for blacks because of the military buildup and conscription, harsh discriminatory experiences on the home front during the war demonstrated that blacks battling for democracy abroad were still second-class citizens at home; they remained essentially powerless. Before long, morale tumbled to a new low and resentments grew.

Some of this spilled over once again on American Jews. Despite some gains by blacks, the *Amsterdam News* reported ruefully in February 1942, there was an unprecedented amount of anti-Semitic sentiment in Harlem. A year later the newspaper noted editorially that compared with the Jews, blacks had little to lose from an unsuccessful outcome to the war. By the spring of 1943, the same newspaper noted that Harlem was ready to explode. A similar situation prevailed in Philadelphia.[38]

The explosion came first in Detroit, on June 20, 1943. In the previous three years, close to half a million workers had poured into Detroit factories humming with defense work. Scarcity of housing, the activities of race-baiters and demagogues, the difficult adjustments of newly arrived workers, and government disinterest created the circumstances for a riot.[39]

The disturbance began with a fight at Belle Isle between one white man and one black man and soon erupted into a brawl. Within hours it had escalated into a full-scale, citywide race war. The blacks were badly outnumbered. When Michigan's governor hesitated to declare martial law and call out the troops, masses of whites began roaming the streets, assaulting blacks and burning their cars. After President Roosevelt proclaimed a state of emergency, six thousand troops were sent in to restore order. In some thirty hours of emergency, twenty-five blacks and nine whites had been killed.[40]

From Detroit the rioting spread to Harlem. The immediate cause was the shooting of a black soldier by a white policeman after the soldier had sought to prevent the arrest of a black woman. The soldier's wounds were minor, but newspapers, both black and white, had been filled for some time with stories of lynchings and mistreatment of black soldiers on domestic duty or leave. As in the case of the 1935 Harlem rioting, word quickly spread that the soldier had been killed.[41] Before long, gangs of young people were throwing milk bottles and stones at passing cars. They then turned their attention to shops and stores. In a twenty-four-hour period five persons were killed and several hundred arrested. Along 125th Street alone, display windows of four hundred stores were smashed. Many of the shopkeepers—especially grocers, haberdashers, and proprietors of liquor stores and pawnshops—lost everything. A few stores managed to reopen, but 125th Street looked as if it had been hit by an armored division.[42]

At first, anti-Semitism had seemed not to be a factor in the Detroit rioting. But when blacks heard of the attacks by whites at Belle Isle, they descended on the Jewish business area along Hastings Street and demolished it. According to one report the rioters' loot ranged from guns to sides of beef and vintage port wine. Left untouched, however, were black-owned and friendly white businesses. A black journalist reported that the rioters attacked only Jewish stores in Paradise Valley's three-mile corridor. A rival reporter pointed out that they did so systematically and with a passion seldom witnessed even in southern riots against blacks. Another white journalist agreed, noting that Gerald L. K. Smith had been recruiting blacks for the isolationist America First Committee by playing on their anti-Semitic tendencies. Smith himself agreed with some government investigators that the looting along Hastings Street reflected anti-Semitism. The rioting sparked a movement of Jews from their old neighborhoods to northwest Detroit; it would be vividly recalled by them years later when violence broke out against Jews in Crown Heights in Brooklyn.[43]

Several months later Adam Clayton Powell wrote that there were few Jews who did not deserve the hatred of Negroes. Isabel Boyko Price concluded that black-Jewish relations had sunk to their lowest point. "To Harlem," she observed, "it had become a way of life to blame the Jew for discrimination and abuse."[44]

That these ill feelings threatened to destroy the black-Jewish ties that had been forged before the war is evident from the extraordinary steps taken by both groups to heal the breach. Black publicist Chandler Owen wrote a widely reprinted article in the *Chicago Defender*, "Should the Negro Hate the Jew?" which expressed surprise and dismay that despite Nazi contempt for the whole

Negro race, their anti-Semitism program had probably been more successful among Negroes than any other group in the nation. Owen went on to praise Jewish leaders for their support of black causes.[45] Further support for maintaining the ties between the two groups came from the Urban League's magazine *Opportunity* and the NAACP's *Crisis*.*

Before America's entry into the war, the Anti-Defamation League had dispatched prominent personalities to describe Jewish efforts on behalf of poor blacks. Arthur Spingarn had appealed to blacks in New York not to be won over by Nazi propaganda. Rabbi Joshua Roth Liebman had taken the same message to Boston. The Jewish press had begun placing special emphasis on the Jewish commitment to civil rights. The death of Joel Spingarn in 1939 and the retirement a few months later of Supreme Court justice Louis Brandeis, the first Jew on the Court, had provided the opportunity for glowing accounts of this commitment. Three Jewish newspapers, the *Forward*, the *Jewish Morning Journal*, and the *Day*, had published in 1939 a dozen articles on blacks, Harlem, and anti-Semitism, and several had suggested ways in which Jews could improve relations with blacks. Seeking solutions, Jewish leaders had met with black leaders and Harlem newspapermen for candid talks about the problem.

After the destructive Detroit rioting in 1943, leaders of the local NAACP chapter and Jewish community center financed a study of the disturbances. Although some observers had viewed the destruction of Jewish property as related to black-Jewish conflict, Wayne State University sociologists did not agree. Instead, they described the rioting as the kind of black-white clash that could have occurred in any densely populated section of the city, and they traced its origins to socioeconomic problems that were unrelated to "the factor of racial ownership."[46] From a present-

*Dr. Winston C. McDowell of Rhodes College in Memphis has kindly shared with me his recent research on the jobs campaign in Harlem, noting that despite the harsh and ugly rhetoric, it was Sufi and other racial agitators who focused the issue rather than the black elite and their Jewish allies. He argues further that in their rush to stamp out the strains that had arisen, they tended to blind themselves to a problem that needed to be addressed.

day perspective it is difficult to know, but there seems little doubt that the tendency existed, then as later, to ignore or underplay black-Jewish conflict in the interest of the common assault against the widespread prejudice and discrimination faced by both groups. Only in recent years and as the alliance has deteriorated has there been a greater willingness to acknowledge some of the underlying tensions that often existed simultaneously.

In 1941 Randolph's Brotherhood of Sleeping Car Porters and the Jewish Labor Committee cosponsored a conference at Columbia University to examine racial tensions in Harlem. Speakers argued that anti-Semitism among blacks was a defense mechanism against the racial prejudice they faced. The solution was thought to lie in improved economic opportunities.[47] Certainly there was much truth in such a judgment, since black anger against Jews has always paralleled the deterioration of the condition of the black underclass. It is not the entire answer to the problem, however; the growth of anti-Jewish feeling among younger, better-educated, and presumably more successful blacks is probably the result of political and ideological changes associated with the growth of black nationalism and the race revolution evidenced in the latter part of the 1960s.

In any case, the period prior to and during World War II marked a watershed in black-Jewish relations. Black perspectives and expectations had grown. Black soldiers were among the liberators of Dachau and Buchenwald. They saw the stacks of emaciated corpses and the laboratories where German "doctors" had experimented on humans. This sight would not be easily forgotten, and PBS reminded Americans of the experiences of the black soldiers when it aired its controversial program "Liberators—Fighting on Two Fronts in World War II" late in 1992, although it misidentified the army units involved.[48]

During this time, too, Howard University in Washington, D.C., was transformed under its president, Mordecai W. Johnson, into a center for black militancy. This new energy proved to be attractive to young students, like future psychologist Kenneth Clark, who wished to sustain a sense of black responsibility and consequently chose Howard over other schools.[49]

One of the areas of this new militancy was Howard's law school, where Johnson appointed Charles Houston, a bright young protégé of Felix Frankfurter and Roscoe Pound of Harvard, as dean. For the law faculty Houston recruited his brilliant cousin Bill Hastie as well as James Madison Nabrit, a brilliant lawyer working in a black law firm in Houston, and he converted the school into a training ground for black lawyers.

A number of organizational changes that would give the NAACP a new burst of energy had also taken place. With the resignation of Du Bois and Joel Spingarn (Arthur had now retired as chairman of the legal committee and moved up to the largely ceremonial post of president) an opportunity was presented for new—black—leadership to emerge. For the first time the organization had a black chairman.

As late as 1933 the NAACP did not have a single black lawyer on its staff. Arthur Spingarn's advice was required on a day-to-day basis. When big cases came up, the organization would scramble to take them on as best it could. Shortly after Houston revitalized Howard's law faculty, the NAACP, in a landmark move, chose Houston to head its legal program. Henceforth it would no longer be dependent on volunteer lawyers, Jewish or otherwise, but be represented by talented black lawyers in its most important cases. (Jewish attorneys, however, would always remain a part of its legal staff, most notably Jack Greenberg, who joined in 1949.) Men like Houston, Hastie, and Thurgood Marshall (who began working for the NAACP in 1938) would become the architects of the coming revolution in civil rights law.

In the mid thirties the NAACP also changed its legal tactics in the civil rights struggle. Until this point, it had litigated civil rights cases on an ad hoc basis: When a particularly outrageous abuse occurred, the NAACP would enter the case and seek relief. As a result, its lawyers were often effective, but their work lacked focus. A grant from the American Fund for Public Service (the Garland Fund) offered an opportunity to broaden the strategy to one founded on the principle of equality. The Garland Fund also proposed that taxpayers' suits be brought to enforce equal (albeit separate) accommodations.

At Frankfurter's suggestion Nathan R. Margold, solicitor in the Interior Department, was retained to map the new approach. Margold, a Romanian Jewish immigrant with a burning social conscience, proved to be the perfect choice. Margold, who had grown up in Brooklyn, attended City College and Harvard Law School, and taken a job in FDR's Interior Department (one of the few employers of Jewish attorneys in the 1930s), provided the clear-eyed vision of an outsider, one who could pinpoint problems and offer brilliant and daring solutions. Unsatisfied with the Garland Fund's limited goals, Margold proposed (in 218 legal-size pages turned over to NAACP executive Walter White in May 1931) an unprecedented all-out attack on segregation itself. The report's central passage declared that it would be a great mistake to fritter away a limited budget on sporadic attempts to force the equal division of school funds in those few instances where such attempts might be expected to succeed, especially as no new principles would be established. The NAACP would be leaving untouched "the very essence of the existing evils."

Soon after receiving Margold's report, the NAACP launched its campaign. Rather than attack segregation in elementary and secondary schools, however, it first filed a suit against southern graduate and professional schools. They were the most vulnerable segments of the education system because of the difficulties of setting up dual and equal programs. Victories in these cases led to pivotal public school rulings two decades later. Under Houston and Thurgood Marshall (who succeeded him in 1938) the association also fought restrictive covenants, segregation in public accommodations and interstate travel, voting restrictions, and other discriminatory activities as part of a coordinated effort to create a body of civil rights precedents in the courts.

It was Margold's pathfinding report, according to Jerold S. Auerbach, that set in motion the series of decisions resulting in the Supreme Court's eventual overthrow of segregation. Margold's approach to civil rights legislation proved surprisingly effective, and Walter White said that Margold's research and legal skills enabled the NAACP to launch an across-the-board attack on the root causes of discrimination. Hastie said that Margold's report became the bible of the NAACP, and Marshall described him as a man ahead of his time.[50]

Alongside this broadened NAACP push, World War II heightened the sense among Jews that their fate, the fate of blacks, and that of the nation itself were all inextricably linked. Accordingly, magazines like B'nai B'rith's *National Jewish Monthly* called for greater Jewish involvement in social justice campaigns. Increasing numbers of Jews would respond to such calls in the postwar years, as efforts to relieve the suffering of blacks became part of the broader Jewish social agenda to build a new and better world.

5

BLACKS AND JEWS AS ALLIES IN THE ARTS AND SOCIAL SCIENCES

In his 1990 film *Mo' Better Blues*, Spike Lee portrayed two Jewish nightclub operators, Moe and Josh Flatbush, as cynical exploiters of black talent. When he was criticized by the Anti-Defamation League and other Jewish groups for stereotyping Jewish characters, Lee responded that the characterizations were inspired by "the many, many, many, many Jewish club owners throughout the years, whom every great jazz musician had to fight for the couple of pennies they got."[1]

As the film made the rounds of movie houses, the NAACP was holding its national convention in Los Angeles. During a panel discussion on barriers to blacks in the movie industry, several panelists criticized what they termed a century of Jewish racism in Hollywood.[2]

As the controversy grew, Lee became more combative. "Let's compare their ten minutes of screen time with one hundred years of Hollywood cinema," he told the *New York Times*. "I've gotten more press for being a 'racist' and an 'anti-Semitic' filmmaker for the ten minutes of Moe and Josh than a slew of really racist, anti-Semitic filmmakers."

The charge that Jews exploited blacks in the arts was, of course, not new. In *The Crisis of the Negro Intellectual*, Harold Cruse went further than Lee, arguing that Jews on the left, who he felt enforced cultural (as well as political) standards, "retarded and smothered" Negro artists and writers and kept them from grappling creatively with the as yet undeveloped cultural status of blacks. Indeed, these ideas were smoldering tinder waiting to be ignited as the race revolution took shape, according to Neal Gabler, author of *An Empire of Their Own: How the Jews Invented Hollywood.*[3] City College professor Leonard Jeffries—whose widely publicized allegations ranged from Jewish financing of the eighteenth-century slaves ships to the Jewish-dominated Hollywood studios' conscious degradation of blacks—ignited the tinder in his 1991 Albany speech. He charged that an agenda of white supremacy was "planned and plotted and programmed out of Hollywood, where people called Greenberg and Weisberg and Trigliani . . . put together a system of destruction of black people." His calumnies set off a fresh round of name-calling and ill will.

Certainly, the intersection of blacks and Jews in the arts encompasses all of the ambiguities of their relationship. But how much truth was there to these charges? No doubt there *were* some Jewish nightclub owners who, as Spike Lee alleged, exploited black musicians, just as there were some Jews who owned and sold slaves in the nineteenth century. No one should deny these assumptions. The question is, how many and to what extent? Unfortunately, when we look for historical evidence pertaining to any special or unique Jewish role, almost nothing comes to light. There is therefore very little factual basis for concluding, as Lee does, that this relationship was unbalanced and largely detrimental to black artists.

The story of Hollywood is more complex and is put in context by Neal Gabler. There can be little doubt that Hollywood, especially before World War II, served up stereotypical images of blacks as savages, slaves, or servants, even as it presented simultaneously an unflattering picture of Italian gangsters and vulgar and crude Jews. Certainly, too, Jews have played a dominant role in Hollywood, as Gabler notes, although the role has been considerably diminished in recent years as major conglomerates (including some from overseas) have entered the filmmaking business.

However, the charges of a nefarious role played by Jews in the field of popular culture is quite an old one, antedating both Cruse and Lee. Insofar as films are concerned, it goes back to the 1920s if not before, when old-line Protestant leaders decried the movies as dangerous instruments of social subversion—in the hands of the devil and five hundred un-Christian Jews, according to one fundamentalist group. The idea, too, that Jews today, as earlier, run the Hollywood power structure grew out of an obvious truth—the early film moguls were at the margins of American society, were under constant threat of being pushed out, and therefore favored their own. While acknowledging that it is pointless to deny that blacks have been kept out of decision making in Hollywood, Gabler does dispute the notion that this is exclusively a black-Jewish problem.

> Instead, the friction in Hollywood reflects, as Hollywood so often does, the social realities and dynamics of modern America generally, where the ideology of pluralism pulls one way and the muscle of the implacable market pulls the other, where cronyism resembles racism, and where inertia may be the most powerful force of all.

In the new climate created by the civil rights and race revolutions and under the impact of contemporaneous social and economic developments, this situation would change radically. The emergence of Lee himself is symbolic of this change. (Indeed, in films like Columbia's *Legion of Terror* in 1936 and Warner Brothers' *Black Legion* in the following year, Hollywood had already begun to attack religious and racial extremism, an effort that would intensify after the war.)[4] At worst (as Gabler concludes), Hollywood Jewish moguls of an earlier era did little better than Gentile executives. This may not be much to boast about, but it is a far cry from the kind of racism and exploitive behavior that critics like Spike Lee and Leonard Jeffries see at the heart of the black-Jewish relationship.

Since there is little to justify these charges, since Lee cites them without evidence, and since many contemporary blacks presumably share them, where do they come from? The answer can only be that they are based on anecdotal evidence passed on within black society, particularly within elements of the black intelligentsia, perhaps reflecting a psychological proclivity to hold the Jews responsible for certain problems faced by blacks today. If this is so, then there is little prospect of persuading Spike Lee and others like him to adopt a different view, even though the actual historical record shows Jews, in relation to other whites, in a more positive light. This record offers a more balanced picture of wealthy and not so wealthy Jews as the primary advocates and supporters of black American literary, artistic, and intellectual achievement throughout the century.

Among the first to recognize black literary talent was Amy Spingarn, the wife of Joel Spingarn. When the poet Langston Hughes, a key figure in the Harlem Renaissance, who enjoyed a special relationship with her, encountered hostility while still a student at Columbia University, Amy encouraged him to transfer to the nation's oldest black college, Lincoln University in Pennsylvania, and helped him with loans and grants.[5]

Hughes felt especially close to both Spingarns. He dedicated his novel *Not without Laughter* to them, expressing his sincere appreciation for their interest in helping black people and his great pleasure in their friendship. Later, Blanche Knopf, the wife of publisher Alfred Knopf, also befriended Hughes, helping him get some of his stories published in magazines and his first book of poetry published by Knopf.[6]

Right through the forties the Rosenwald Fund (created in 1917 for the "well-being of mankind") subsidized many black artists and writers with grants and fellowships. The recipients included Ralph J. Bunche in political science, Marian Anderson in music, John Hope Franklin in history, Kenneth Clark in psychology, and Gordon Parks in photography. Among the writers Rosenwald assisted were Ralph Ellison, James Baldwin, and William Motley, as well as Hughes. Grants also went to such white liberal Southerners as journalist Ralph McGill, historian C. Vann Woodward, and sociologist Rupert Vance. Such assistance drew angry cries from segregationists. Governor Eugene Talmadge of Georgia rightly considered Rosenwald "a menace to the Southern way of life."[7]

While affluent Jews provided financial backing, Jewish radicals like Warsaw-born Max Lieber reached out to the black literati in other ways. Lieber became Hughes's literary agent. His profitable production of Erskine Caldwell's play *Tobacco Road* permitted him to indulge his social passions. He kept reminding Hughes and the other writers he represented of their leftist political obligations while representing them in negotiations with bourgeois publishers.

Blanche Knopf passed along to Lieber some stories that resulted from a trip Hughes had taken to the Soviet Union. To Hughes's surprise Lieber sold one of them, "Slave on the Block," to the venerable *Scribner's* magazine. Other stories he placed in *Esquire* won their author critical acclaim greater than that of any black writer of fiction.[8]

James Baldwin was another black writer whose talent was first recognized and nurtured by Jewish editors of small but influential magazines: Elliot Cohen and Robert Warshaw at *Commentary*, Saul Levitas at the *New Leader*, and Philip Rahv at the *Partisan Review*. In 1946 Levitas gave Baldwin his first book review assignment, an act the grateful author never forgot; indeed, in 1961 he told his biographer that these editors had helped save his life.

In 1948, after Baldwin's first important piece, "The Harlem Ghetto," appeared in *Commentary* (the magazine of the American Jewish Committee), Nathan Glazer, then a member of *Commentary*'s editorial board, wrote of the board's pleasure that a remarkable young black writer—"how remarkable we didn't yet know"—had come to the magazine.[9] The editors of *Commentary* (then much more a Jewish magazine than today) suggested that Baldwin write something about blacks and Jews, and Baldwin agreed to do so. The young writer found it difficult to deal with anti-Semitism in Harlem, but Warshaw forced him to confront the issue squarely. Baldwin found Warshaw an extraordinary editor, who taught him "you had to force from your experience the last drop, sweet or bitter, it could possibly give."[10]

Baldwin's piece on Harlem was one of the first serious explorations of black-Jewish relations. He wrote with deep empathy for both groups: "The Negro identifies himself almost wholly with the Jew. The image of the suffering Christ and the suffering Jew are wedded with the image of the suffering slave." But then Baldwin turned to the harsh reality of life in Harlem. There, Jews were "small tradesmen, rent collectors, real estate agents, and pawnbrokers." They followed the American tradition of exploiting Negroes, and becoming identified with oppression, they were hated for it. "[J]ust as society must have a scapegoat, so hatred must have a symbol. Georgia has the Negro and Harlem has the Jews."[11]

During the sixties Norman Podhoretz, the editor of *Commentary*, prodded Baldwin to write his most famous essay, although to Podhoretz's consternation the resulting article, "Letter from a Region in My Mind." first appeared in the *New Yorker*, presumably because *The New Yorker* paid more and offered a larger audience. The essay was later published in book form as *The Fire Next Time*. It remained on the best-seller list for forty-four weeks, helping to make Baldwin America's most widely read black author.

Baldwin had moved beyond Jewish tutelage and the little magazines edited by Jews. In some respects, the experience of black writers like Baldwin paralleled that of blacks in the civil rights movement. Needing Jews as intermediaries with the broader culture, they initially welcomed assistance; but once blacks had achieved leadership positions, Jews could be safely charged with paternalism.

Baldwin also abandoned his earlier view that Jews and blacks were both victims of an oppressive society. *The Fire Next Time* represented black rage against white America and pioneered a genre that other black writers would adopt. Black power advocates would later honor Baldwin by repeating his retort to white liberals, "Do I really want to be integrated into a burning house?"[12]

The relationship of Jewish philanthropists and sponsors to Hughes, Baldwin, and other black artists and writers was openly paternalistic—necessarily so, given their disparity in social position and blacks' lack of access to the broader culture—and it exacted some cost as black artists struggled to be true to their gift and their message while simultaneously bending to the views of their sponsors. Was Baldwin's strong but generally sympathetic treatment of Jews in "The Harlem Ghetto" a true reflection of his feelings, a response to his editor (who most certainly would have wanted a more nuanced treatment of the controversial role of Jews), or a little of both? Did the Jewish editors at *Commentary* see in Baldwin only a new and gifted black writer (as Nathan Glazer writes) or a black writer who could be trusted to deal with an inflammatory subject with compassion and sympathy as well as realism? These are interesting questions without clear answers.

As they gained greater success and in some cases adopted a more militant stance, some black writers and artists broke with their white patrons, wishing to avoid even the appearance of dependence. Since so many of the patrons were Jews, it was often Jews from whom they grew estranged. As early as 1932, Langston Hughes denounced the cowardice of educated blacks. Fear, he felt, had silenced their mouths—the tossed scraps of white philanthropy had bribed their leaders. To an extent, however, Hughes was indicting himself. He always felt a tension between his desire to please his sponsors and his need to expose racial prejudice and poverty. When his flirtation with Communism irritated Blanche Knopf, he pulled back fifty pages from the Harlem section of his autobiography. There was too much Harlem in it for her, he felt. For the same reason, he decided not to include in the book a radical poem contrasting the opulence of the newly opened Waldorf Astoria Hotel in Manhattan with the aching poverty of so many New Yorkers. Although grateful, Hughes remained suspicious of rich Jews (and rich blacks), who could always buy their way out of trouble.

From the race-conscious perspective of later decades, the role of black leaders and their Jewish partners at the time of the Harlem Renaissance appears ambiguous at best. To the revisionist historian David Levering Lewis, black-Jewish cultural cooperation, besides reflecting a general urge to mobilize the arts on behalf of civil rights, was a diversionary track intended to keep blacks away from Garveyism in favor of the milder legalism of the NAACP. In a conference paper delivered at the University of the District of Columbia in 1985, Lewis expressed particular bitterness towards "white philanthropy, much of it Jewish," which encouraged blacks to enter careers in entertainment, blacks who, in the normal course of events, would have gravitated to teaching, lawyering, and business.

What is missed or downplayed in the current atmosphere of racial assertiveness is the extraordinarily important role Jews played as intermediaries between black artists and writers and the general public. They also helped facilitate the assimilation of black culture into the American mainstream, a contribution not often recognized. That Jews were a group that had experienced forced displacement certainly made them better able to identify with the similar experience of another racial group.

By the 1920s Jewish composers, writers, and entertainers had won cultural recognition, and some of them set out consciously to bridge the white and black worlds. George and Ira Gershwin began to use black music in their work in a manner not seen since the ballads of Stephen Foster. Al Jolson donned blackface to sing "Mammy," a performance as popular then as it would be repugnant today. Manhattan's social set frequented Harlem nightclubs for booze and blues such as could be heard nowhere else.

For a time, Langston Hughes toiled in Hollywood as a scriptwriter, where he was troubled by the trivialization of his work, a frequent complaint of film writers. As a black writer, however, Hughes encountered an additional problem: the stereotypical presentation of blacks by most movie moguls, many of them Jewish. But apart from Hughes, blacks were still virtually invisible in Hollywood, nor would they gain serious recognition there until after World War II.

Many black intellectuals also resented what they took to be white usurpation of their cultural heritage on the stage and in the ballrooms of America. In their view, black music, especially jazz, had been taken over by white (often Jewish) composers. Jazz—which had been born in the turn-of-the-century South—became popular in the interwar period with a wider, largely white audience. It was played from Broadway to the Hollywood Bowl, Hughes complained in his poem "Notes on Commercial Theater."[13]

In his biography of George Gershwin, Charles Schwartz essentially agreed, dismissing the musical arrangements of Gershwin and other white musicians. "What they had to offer the public as 'jazz' was slickly and skillfully orchestrated," Schwartz wrote, "but it was really only a bland version of the real thing."[14]

In 1935 Gershwin transformed DuBose Heyward's tragic tale of a crippled black beggar into the folk opera *Porgy and Bess*, which became a long-running hit on Broadway. But while audiences loved it, others (including Duke Ellington) found fault with the "white" musical treatment. "The times are here to debunk Gershwin's lampblack Negroism," Duke Ellington declared. The great composer and band leader accused Gershwin of having borrowed from everyone, from "Liszt to Dickie Wells' kazoo." The white composer and music critic Virgil Thomson weighed in with an even sharper attack. Thomson described Gershwin's show as a "libretto that should never have been accepted on a subject that should never have been chosen [by] a man who should never have attempted it. Folklore subjects recounted by an outsider are only valid as long as the folk in question is unable to speak for itself, which is certainly not true of the American Negro in 1935."[15]

Since its premiere *Porgy and Bess* has attained the status of an American classic and is frequently revived, but opinions about it remain divided. "What was a Jewish man doing after all," asked Edward Rothstein in a *New Republic* article of March 18, 1985, summarizing the negative sentiment about a recent revival, "writing an opera about southern blacks that included two murders, widespread cocaine use, ersatz jazz and African music, spirituals, and a wildly promiscuous heroine?"*

However, what was actually involved here (as Schwartz and Rothstein have noted) was that Jews like Gershwin, in the self-assumed role of cultural intermediaries, were combining their own experience with the traditions of another group to create something new. The same pattern, Rothstein notes, can be seen in *Guys and Dolls*, a "distant descendant" of *Porgy and Bess*, in which black spirituals become prayer meetings of the Salvation Army and the black low-life characters, with all their virtues and vices, move to Broadway.[16]

Revisionist historians see much wrong and almost nothing right with the Jewish role in mediating black cultural expression. Harold Cruse blames Jews for degrading an authentic cultural

---

*Much the same sort of controversy developed around the recent revival of the 1927 Jerome Kern and Oscar Hammerstein musical, "Showboat," in Toronto. Blacks complained about dated language (including the word "niggers") and scenes of black workers loading cotton. The controversy escalated when in a television interview, a black school trustee declared that whites, "usually Jews," were anxious to stage plays that mock blacks.

movement into a commercialized cultural fashion.[17] And David Levering Lewis, as we have seen, deplores the diversion of the "talented tenth" into cultural activities when they might better have served their communities in other fields of work.[18]

Whatever the merits of these arguments—and it is not the present purpose to resolve them—Jews *did* open opportunities for talented black artists, writers, and entertainers long before other white Americans were prepared to do so. And though assimilating Jewish producers and writers often reflected the culture to which they, as recent immigrants, wished to belong, in at least one sense they were pioneers in racial progress. Nightclub owners such as Max Gordon and Barney Josephson opened their doors to blacks when no other establishments would. Josephson's Cafe Society, which opened in a basement room in Greenwich Village in December 1938, broke new ground for the entire industry. It was the first nightclub where blacks and whites worked out front together, performing before white audiences. There was probably no place like it in New York or elsewhere in the country. Cafe Society proved so successful that Josephson opened a second club uptown two years later. For a decade his places showcased promising black performers, some of whom became legends in the entertainment business. Billie Holiday starred in Cafe Society's opening-night show. Lena Horne, Sarah Vaughan, Hazel Scott, Josh White, Nellie Lutcher, Sister Rosetta Sharpe—all sang to Josephson's hushed audiences.[19]

In 1935 Benny Goodman became the first band leader to integrate his orchestra. Artie Shaw, also Jewish, went out of his way to take Billie Holiday on tour with him to segregated cities, places where blacks were not allowed to drink at "white" water fountains! Impresario Sol Hurok meanwhile persuaded the great contralto Marian Anderson to return from Europe, where she had gone on a Rosenwald scholarship because she saw no future in the United States. On her return Hurok managed the tour that launched her American career. When the chairman of the Howard University concert series applied to the Daughters of the American Revolution for the use of its facility, Constitution Hall, for a performance by her and was told it was booked, Hurok asked another artist's representative to apply on behalf of the pianist Ignaz Paderewski for several of the dates that had been requested for Miss Anderson. They were open. Hurok then applied for them again and was told the hall was not available. Anderson was also turned away from appearing at Central High School's auditorium by the school board. Following this, Hurok released the entire file of correspondence to the press, precipitating one of the major events in the history of American race relations. Anderson ultimately sang in front of the Lincoln Memorial.[20]

Paul Robeson, the world-acclaimed singer and actor, perhaps best personified black-Jewish cultural ties in this period. His compassionate concern for other people had been taught him by his father, a Methodist minister in Princeton, New Jersey, who had been born into slavery. At college he won twelve athletic letters and became an all-American football end. After graduating from Columbia Law School, he found legal work unsatisfactory and began a career as a performer. His dominating presence and extraordinary bass voice brought him fame in such shows as *The Emperor Jones* and *Show Boat*. His stock-in-trade as an artist was black spirituals, which he probably heard first in his father's church. One of Robeson's favorite songs was "The Kaddish of Rebbe Levi-Yitzhok of Berditchev," which takes God to task for the agelong suffering of Jews. In Robeson's version the song became an outcry against oppression everywhere.[21]

Robeson was one of a number of black artists and intellectuals that included Richard Wright and Langston Hughes who were attracted to communism before the crimes of Stalin became well known and generally acknowledged. Though he was probably never a member of the Communist party, Robeson made numerous friendly statements about the Soviet Union, where in 1949 he traveled and was feted by Soviet leaders at a time when Jewish writers and intellectuals—among them some of Robeson's personal friends—were being secretly arrested and purged. Later, even after these events became generally known, Robeson never publicly criticized the USSR.

Murray Kempton has speculated that Robeson's unwavering fealty to the Soviet Union may have represented a transfer of allegiance from the uncompromising Old Testament Jehovah, whose spirit infused the Negro spirituals of his youth, to a new and equally uncomproming Communist god, "the ark of another covenant."[22] Be that as it may, however, Hasia Diner believed that men like Robeson provided ample evidence that a genuine emotive and cultural bond linked the hearts of blacks and Jews. Few artists of any race were more beloved by Jews than Robeson.[23]

In the last twenty-five years historians have begun to reevaluate the role of Communists in the movement for black equality. During the period of the Cold War, the tendency was to describe American Communists as tools of Moscow utilizing the grievances of blacks for party interests alone. Wilson Record's two books, *The Negro and the Communist Party* (1951) and *Race and Radicalism: The NAACP and the Communist Party in Conflict* (1964) dealt with them almost exclusively as naïfs or as "fronts for the expansion of world Communism." Though frequently true, Communists (Jewish or otherwise) and those connected with them were often at the cutting edge of efforts for racial equality.

One such effort was led by New York's Local 1199, which represented hospital and retail drug workers and had a largely black membership and Jewish leadership. The radical and controversial union's roots were in the rough-and-tumble thirties, when a small group of left-wing Jewish pharmacists and drug clerks set out to organize workers in New York's huge private and nonprofit hospital system even as they toed the Moscow party line. (The 1935 Wagner Act, which had legitimized union organizing in many industries, had left hospitals untouched.) The twenty-year effort to unionize hospital workers was led by Jewish pharmacists, many of whom had earlier been denied admission to medical schools because of anti-Jewish quotas. Though Jews dispensed prescriptions, most other drugstore workers were black. The union's pattern of interracial and interethnic unionizing thus became an organizational necessity. Under Elliott Godoff and Leon Davis, Local 1199 became the driving force of hospital unionism in the postwar period.

In the twenties and thirties, Communists also ran the only racially integrated social clubs in Harlem. The party members, many of them Jewish intellectuals disillusioned by failings of America's capitalist system in the Great Depression, warmly welcomed blacks when few other whites were reaching out to them. Bayard Rustin, a black Quaker who would become one of the

In pre–Civil War America, Jewish views generally paralleled those of the local populace in various parts of the country; some southern Jews held slaves. However, a number of Jews — especially veterans of revolutionary movements in central Europe — did become involved in abolitionist causes. August Bondi was among the three Jews who assisted John Brown during one of his raids. *(American Jewish Archives)*

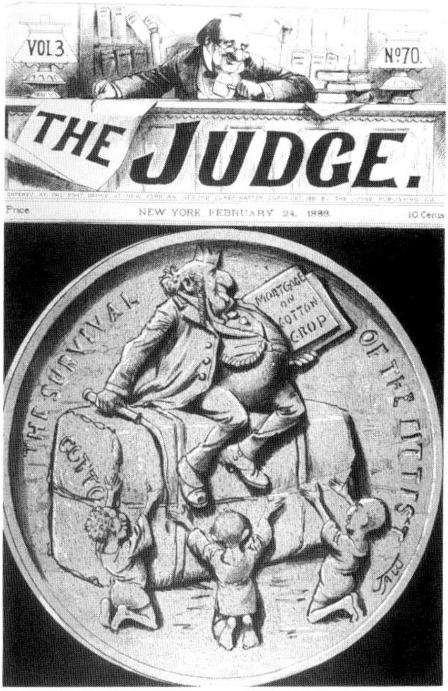

In the post-war South, Jewish peddlers were among the few to do business with newly freed black sharecroppers. Anti-Semitism, as evidenced by this cover of *Judge* magazine, intensified greatly among white southerners because Jews were perceived as agents of the northern victor. *(American Jewish Archives)*

One of the beneficiaries of early Jewish efforts on behalf of blacks was Booker T. Washington, who was one of the two preeminent black spokesmen of his day. Of J. Loeb, a Jewish merchant, he wrote: "When other merchants refused to deal with us, Loeb paid no attention to our want of money and sold us goods. We owe him a great deal for helping us out this way in the early days." *(Library of Congress)*

Alongside Washington, Harvard-educated sociologist W.E.B. Du Bois emerged as a powerful voice for black Americans. Du Bois' message of racial equality stood in contrast to Washington's "accommodationist" philosophy and became the guiding principle behind the National Association for the Advancement of Colored People, which he helped found. The dichotomy between the radical and moderate views of racial justice were to inform much of the subsequent history of relations between blacks and whites, and especially blacks and Jews. *(NAACP)*

One of Du Bois' few confidants during the NAACP's early years was Joel Spingarn, member of New York's German Jewish elite and former professor of literature at Columbia. Spingarn, a critic of Booker T. Washington, staunchly defended Du Bois' right to edit *The Crisis*, the NAACP journal, without outside interference. Together, Spingarn and Du Bois guided NAACP policy and tactics for three decades. *(NAACP)*

'Pretty Words, Ugly Deeds'

As poor blacks moved from the rural South to the urban North, they encountered populations of equally poor immigrant Jews. Among many Jews there was a growing awareness that the fight against racial discrimination should involve both groups; this anti-lynching cartoon, published in the *Jewish Daily Forward* of July 4, 1917, powerfully manifests their antiracist impulse. *(Jewish Daily Forward)*

A scene is shown from D.W. Griffith's *Birth of a Nation.* The film came under censure in the aftermath of the imprisonment and lynching of southern Jewish businessman Leo Frank for the rape-murder of a young white girl. Louis Marshall (below), an early president of the American Jewish Committee, launched campaigns against the Klan and against racial bias in the film industry.

Marshall, who had battled against Henry Ford's distribution of *The Protocols of the Elders of Zion* and unsuccessfully defended Leo Frank before the Supreme Court, was a major volunteer and legal voice for the NAACP until his death in 1927. *(American Jewish Committee)*

Two of the foremost leaders of the black community during the teens and twenties had diverging attitudes about Jews as well as diverging racial strategies. Marcus Garvey (above), founder of the "Back to Africa" movement, admired efforts of Jews to create a Jewish state even as he promoted "buy black" campaigns — often directed against Jewish merchants — in newly emerging black slums. A. Philip Randolph (shown at right in 1911 or 1912), organizer of the Brotherhood of Sleeping Car Porters and giant of civil rights for nearly fifty years, actively courted the support of Jewish labor leaders throughout his life. *(UPI/Bettmann; Library of Congress)*

During the depression, ethnic tensions were greatly exacerbated within cities across the nation. Adam Clayton Powell, controversial city councilman — later, U.S. representative — from Harlem, tried to calm tensions in New York City, but was unable to prevent a riot in 1935 that left three blacks dead and hundreds of stores looted, many of them Jewish-owned. *(UPI/Bettmann)*

Thousands of blacks migrated to northern cities for factory jobs during World War II, creating new tensions. In Detroit, a race riot took place in 1943; here, a black man is surrounded by his attackers. Many of those injured were black, and many Jewish-owned shops and businesses were destroyed by blacks in response. In the aftermath, a considerable number of Detroit Jews moved across town to the northwestern part of the city. *(UPI/Bettmann)*

Protest against white, and especially Jewish, coopting of black musical idioms such as jazz and gospel was fairly widespread in the 1930s and 1940s, but many blacks and Jews did work together. Benny Goodman's was the first integrated swing band — and one of the first to perform for integrated audiences. *(Bettmann)*

Jewish impresario Sol Hurok persuaded the great contralto Marian Anderson to return from her exile in Europe to perform in the United States. In one of the most memorable moments in the history of American performance, she sang in front of the Lincoln Memorial after being turned away from Washington's Constitution Hall by the Daughters of the American Revolution. *(UPI/Bettmann)*

Among the many legal victories that united black and Jewish interests and paved the way for the civil rights movement was the Scottsboro case, in which attorney Samuel Leibowitz won the acquittal of nine black youths falsely charged with the rape of two white women. *(UPI/Bettmann)*

Another major victory for blacks was the decision resulting from *Brown v. Board of Education* (1954). The legal team is shown below. Thurgood Marshall is fourth from the right, and fifth from right is Jack Greenberg, who later succeeded him at the NAACP's Legal Defense Fund. *(NAACP)*

While the emerging black southern protest movement of the late 1950s coalesced around Martin Luther King, Jr., A. Philip Randolph's protégé, Bayard Rustin (at right, with Randolph), became the prime intermediary between King and various progressive groups, including Jewish and other labor groups. *(UPI/Bettmann)*

King's other "right hand" was Stanley Levison (shown with Coretta Scott King in the 1970s), whose earlier radical background led to FBI surveillance of King and himself. Unlike Rustin, however, Levison worked mostly behind the scenes, raising money and forging connections, and yielding the spotlight to King and others. Along with Rustin and Ella Baker, Levison first helped bring King's protests to nationwide attention and created the organizational structure of the Southern Christian Leadership Conference. *(Courtesy of Mrs. Stanley Levison)*

E DRIVING TO US

As sit-ins and other nonviolent protests on behalf of racial equality proliferated throughout the South, thousands of freedom riders, many of whom were Jewish, were recruited to the South to stage integrated bus rides in 1961. They initially met stiff resistance, as in the photo above, taken at Anniston, Alabama: White southerners set fire to the bus and attacked passengers as they left it. *(UPI/Bettmann)*

In 1964, the Mississippi summer brought thousands of white activists, including many Jews, to the South to demonstrate and be arrested, with the aim of paralyzing the Southern penal system. In late June, three activists, James Earl Chaney, who was black, and Andrew Goodman and Michael Schwerner, who were both Jewish, were killed by segregationists. This event, more than any other, brought home the reality of racial violence to white Americans. *(UPI/Bettmann)*

MISSING
CALL FBI
THE FBI IS SEEKING INFORMATION CONCERNING THE DISAPPEARANCE AT PHILADELPHIA, MISSISSIPPI, OF THESE THREE INDIVIDUALS ON JUNE 21, 1964. EXTENSIVE INVESTIGATION IS BEING CONDUCTED TO LOCATE GOODMAN, CHANEY, AND SCHWERNER, WHO ARE DESCRIBED AS FOLLOWS:
ANDREW GOODMAN
JAMES EARL CHANEY
MICHAEL HENRY SCHWERNER

Two great spiritual leaders, Martin Luther King, Jr. (right) and Abraham Heschel (center), attend a memorial service in 1965. Heschel, a refugee from Nazi Germany, was a fervent antiracist who galvanized the entire spectrum of activists, Jews and non-Jews alike. *(American Jewish Archives)*

In the mid-1960s, the civil rights movement and the black-Jewish alliance reached their zeniths. Below, the march on Washington, August 29, 1963. King is at the center of the photo. On his left are Rabbi Joachim Prinz and Joe Rauh, and next to them are Whitney Young of the Urban League and Roy Wilkins of the NAACP. *(UPI/Bettmann)*

Stokely Carmichael, who became chairman of the Student Nonviolent Coordinating Committee (SNCC) in 1966, was King's polar opposite. Flamboyantly radical and controversial, Carmichael advocated black power and later railed against Israel, angering many in the Jewish community. *(UPI/Bettmann)*

Malcolm X, shown below at a New York City rally in 1963, spearheaded a new radical black consciousness in America. His view of Jews as "colonialist exploiters" signaled the beginning of a new, turbulent era of black-Jewish relations. *(UPI/Bettmann)*

Toward the end of Martin Luther King's life, Rev. Andrew Young (shown here with Martin Luther King in Chicago in 1967) was among the advisers pushing him in a more radical direction. Young would later become ambassador to the United Nations — where he became embroiled in controversy following his meeting with a PLO official — and still later he was elected mayor of Atlanta. *(UPI/Bettmann)*

Resurrection City, a tent city erected by the Poor People's Marchers who massed in Washington after King's assassination, was ill-fated. Violence, infighting, and mud conspired to turn the event into a fiasco. *(UPI/Bettmann)*

Jesse Jackson, "mayor" for a time of Resurrection City and founder of Operation Breadbasket in Chicago, was the most charismatic black leader to appear in the wake of King's assassination. His resignation from the Southern Christian Leadership Conference in 1971 coincided with the decline of that organization's effectiveness. *(AP/Wide World Photos)*

Rabbi Meir Kahane headed the Jewish Defense League, a radical, occasionally violent group that gave voice to the anxieties of embattled inner city Jews. Kahane ultimately fled to Israel after being indicted on conspiracy charges. He was assassinated in 1990. *(AP/Wide World Photos)*

Albert Shanker (center), president of the American Federation of Teachers, is accompanied by Bayard Rustin (at right). Shanker, a long-time civil rights activist, fought bitterly with the black leadership of the Ocean Hill–Brownsville school district after that district was opened to community control in 1968. He is shown here at a demonstration of 15,000 teachers at City Hall in New York in September of that year. *(UPI/Bettmann)*

The vitriolic antiwhite and anti-Jewish orations of Louis Farrakhan, head of the Nation of Islam, aroused controversy on college campuses and in cities throughout America during the 1980s and early 1990s. Here Rev. Al Sharpton is at the extreme right. *(AP/Wide World Photos)*

In Crown Heights, August 1991, a Hasidic Jewish automobile driver struck and killed 7-year-old Gavin Cato, who was black. Four days of rioting erupted. Jews living in the area were attacked by blacks, and a visiting rabbinical scholar from Australia was murdered, bringing black–Jewish relations to an all-time low. Here, Hasidic Jews demonstrate against the violence. *(Reuters/Bettmann)*

In another episode, Isaac Britton, who was coming home from work with his 12-year-old son, was struck by a brick. In this photo, Britton has fallen to the ground, and the distressed boy looks on helplessly. *(©New York Post)*

nation's most prominent civil rights activists, joined the Young Communist League in New York. Richard Wright, whose autobiography, *Black Boy*, would become an American classic, was drawn to the party in Chicago. Both Wright and Ralph Ellison explored the role of Jewish Communists in the black rights movement as central subjects in their work.[24]

In *The God That Failed*, Wright described the presence of so many Jewish artists and writers in the movement as exhilarating. A Jewish writer invited him to a meeting of the John Reed Club on Chicago's south side, where he was introduced to a group of young men and women who were to become leading painters, composers, novelists, and filmmakers. These men and women—all Jewish—formed with him the first sustained relationships of his life, and although he looked hard, he found no condescension in them. Wright, who twice married Jewish women,* has a Jewish Communist, Boris Max, defend his black protagonist in *Native Son*. When the protagonist refuses to cooperate in a police investigation because police "hate black folks," Wright has Max reply, "They hate others too. They hate me because I'm trying to help you. They're writing me letters calling me a 'dirty Jew.' "[25]

The Communist leadership made a conscious point of dispatching Jewish party members to Harlem, where they operated under Comintern discipline. In certain respects their mission was analogous to that of the nineteenth-century revolutionaries who had sought to radicalize the Russian peasantry. One historian has observed that their Jewish ancestry may have inclined these radical missionaries to manifest a strong emotional response to black oppression. Certainly the rise of Nazism in Germany and of anti-Semitism at home made even the most assimilated American Jewish Communists aware of their own vulnerability.[26]

Of course, Communist leaders had their own reasons for courting blacks. The party saw a political vacuum in the ghettos of America and sought to exploit it. They also sought to counteract the pull of black nationalism. Yet there was nothing phony or contrived about the commitment of most Jewish Communists to

---

*Lorraine Hansberry, John Wideman, LeRoy Jones, and Alice Walker, among others, also married Jews. Some of them were left-wingers.

black civil rights. Most were sincere in their desire to improve the lot of the downtrodden generally.[27]

Those whom the Communist party sent to Harlem did not initially provoke stereotypical anti-Semitic reactions there, probably because their Jewishness was set aside in favor of a broader class appeal. With the rise of Hitlerism in the late 1930s, however, the American Communist party changed its tactics and sought to form a "popular front" with other groups in support of the Soviet Union. It stepped up its attacks on anti-Semitism, encouraged Jewish Communists to identify themselves as Jews, and tried to mobilize the broader Jewish community against fascism. These moves gave greater prominence to Jewish Communists in Harlem and elsewhere, with the unintended result that there was a resurgence of the festering hostility towards Jews, especially among black nationalists. This hostility was reinforced by white party members who sometimes bemoaned the backwardness of blacks. According to historian Mark Naison, the Jewish Communists came to be seen less as poor or working-class people who had identified with the cause of blacks and more the representative of a new kind of establishment preying on blacks for their own advantage. Never popular among the black masses, Communism was therefore added to the catalog of black grievances against Jews. And black Communists themselves, of whom there were never very many, resented what they saw as Jews arrogating power for themselves within the party. Small clouds on the horizon at the time, these differences would later intensify and became more divisive with the emergence of the black power movement in the 1960s. Revisionist critics of Jews—Harold Cruse, for example—are particularly harsh on what they deem the inordinate involvement of Jewish Communists in black affairs.

Meanwhile, however, such party-affiliated Jewish scholars as Philip Foner and Herbert Aptheker began to rewrite black history. Aptheker's role was especially important. He had made friends with Carter Woodson—the dean of black historians and founder of the Association for the Study of Negro Life and History—and often met him in Washington for dinner at the Union Station restaurant, the only one outside the black section of town that welcomed white and black customers.[28] Aptheker's research into black abolitionism and slave uprisings challenged widely held assumptions concerning black slaves and field hands. Conventional histories pictured them as meek and submissive, never resisting the iron rule of their white masters. But in *American Negro Slave Revolts* Aptheker showed, as one white historian later noted, that "many not-so-docile 'old Black Joes' tucked numerous exploiting 'massas' in the cold, cold ground."[29]

In 1937 Philip Foner successfully agitated for the introduction at New York's City College of what was probably the first black history course offered at a predominantly white university. The course was taught by Max Yergan, a leading Communist spokesman in Harlem, who became City College's first black faculty member.

Thus Foner, Aptheker, Harvey Wish, and Melville J. Herskovits, all from Jewish backgrounds, along with Woodson and (earlier) Du Bois, set the stage for what would come to be known in the sixties and seventies as the "new" black history.

During the same period, a number of prominent Jewish social and natural scientists assumed leading roles in other important civil rights battles. The scientific attack on racism, though rarely in the headlines, proved enormously significant within the academy at a time when it was still widely accepted by white Americans that blacks were genetically inferior and therefore undeserving of full citizenship rights. The attack began abroad with the work of British scholars Edward Burnett Taylor, Wallace Galton, Julian Huxley, and Sir James Frazier and the sociologists Max Weber and Ferdinand Tönnies in Germany and Emile Durkheim in France. It was continued in this country by the Chicago School of sociologists, led in the twenties by Robert E. Park and Louis Wirth.[30]

The two U.S. leaders of this movement early in the century were Du Bois, the black intellectual, and Franz Boas, a German-Jewish anthropologist. Du Bois attributed his own early interest in Africa to a lecture delivered by Boas at Atlanta University. He was so impressed by the anthropologist's presentation, Du Bois said later, that he began to study Africa himself.

The light-skinned Du Bois had grown up in Great Barrington, Massachusetts, far from the ghetto blacks he would ultimately elect to speak for. As a child he had played with white youngsters and knew little of racial rejection. With a doctorate from Harvard and postdoctoral study in Germany, he was hired by the University of Pennsylvania in the fall of 1896 to study criminality in a heavily black section of Philadelphia. At Penn he first encountered discrimination. The university created a new faculty position just for him—assistant instructor, one rung below the lowest existing academic rank. Du Bois was paid $800 for one year, a demeaning sum even then. He had no office, no assistants, and no contact with other students. As he wrote later, all he had were legs and a notepad.[31]

They were enough as it turned out. *The Philadelphia Negro*, published in 1899, was the first important sociological study of American blacks. In a field dominated by white academics, Du Bois displayed extraordinary thoroughness, developing an ecological map of black population groups by social condition. He provided extensive data on typical members of each class of blacks—who their friends were, how much schooling they had, what sorts of jobs they held, what their goals were, how the broader society impacted on their lives. Du Bois demonstrated that, like whites, individual blacks were the product of wide-ranging class distinctions and environmental forces. The effect of his study was to challenge the concept of innate disabilities. The fact that talented blacks had risen from the humblest of circumstances, just as many whites had done, refuted racist theory.

Du Bois's book broke new ground. In its emphasis on environmental factors rather than genetics as the primary cause of black poverty and crime, it showed the way for a vast body of subsequent research that would describe the appalling condition of blacks and immigrants in the slums of American cities and stimulate calls for reform. But Du Bois remained an outsider in the world of scholarship. (The *American Historical Review*, while commenting favorably on his book, noted that he had failed to analyze the effects of racial mixing and the possible absorption of "inferior" into "superior" groups of mankind.) Eventually, frustrated by his lack of professional acceptance, Du Bois abandoned sociology and became a black activist and writer.[32]

A group of white social scientists centering around Boas also attacked the dominant racist thinking of the time. Isaiah Berlin has pointed out that Jews, being peripheral outsiders, studied the majority cultures in which they lived with special care and came to know more about them than the majority groups themselves. It may not be surprising, therefore, that Jewish scholars played a leading role in this radical effort.

Boas was born in Minden, Westphalia, and grew up in a home where notions of liberty and equality—the ideals of the 1848 revolution in Germany—were still a living force. At school he earned a doctorate as well as, by some accounts, dueling scars acquired in fights with anti-Semitic fellow students. Afterwards Boas emigrated to the United States and began teaching at Columbia in 1899, the same year that Du Bois published *The Philadelphia Negro*. He taught there for four decades and almost single-handedly established the field of anthropology.

In his most influential work, *The Mind of Primitive Man*, published in 1911, Boas laid out his central proposition:

> We have found that the unproved assumption of identity of cultural achievement and of mental ability is founded on an error of judgment; that the variations in cultural development can as well be explained by a consideration of the general course of historical events without recourse to the theory of material differences of mental faculty in different races . . . a similar error underlies the common assumption that the white race represents physically the highest type of man . . . anatomical and physiological considerations do not support these views.[33]

The concept of race was inherently ambiguous, Boas believed. It denoted major groupings of mankind, each distinguished by its own genetic characteristics reaching far back into antiquity. Race was certainly one element to be analyzed in the study of human societies but, in his view, hardly the most important one. He was more interested in the permutation of races resulting from their integration with other cultures. In an article entitled "What Is Race?" published in the *Nation* in 1925, Boas rejected the idea that race consciousness and racial hatred reflected instinctual drives in human nature. Each race contained so many variations, he argued, that it was impossible to generalize about them.

Boas's books, speeches, and articles, together with his four decades at Columbia, gave him a dominant place in the field of anthropology. From his lofty position he trained a small army of followers, including such prominent figures as Alexander Goldenweiser, Ruth Benedict, A. L. Kroeber, Margaret Mead, Melville J. Herskovits, Edward Sapir, and Robert H. Lowie. Mead later likened Boas to a general who had only a handful of troops to save an entire country. He was a frail man with a large head and one eye that drooped from partial facial paralysis, but he spoke with compelling authority. In 1910 Boas became active in the NAACP, and even when engaged in field work, he kept in close touch with the organization, writing one of its pamphlets, "The Real Race Problem from the Point of View of Anthropology." Afterwards, when a newspaper article assumed the inferiority of blacks, James Weldon Johnson, the executive head of the NAACP, was able to note in an angry letter to the editor that Professor Boas, Goldenweiser, and others had effectively disposed of this idea.[34]

Boas was not active in Jewish affairs, nor were a number of the Jewish scholars he trained. But their background made them acutely aware of the irrationality of racism. Goldenweiser, a Jewish community participant, made the point in an article in the *Menorah Journal*. Since Jews were separated from the rest of society, he declared, they were not only unaffected by existing biases but better able to understand the irrationality of racism than those who were not outsiders.[35] Certainly, Jews had good reason for challenging racial theories that were as theatening to them as to blacks.

Thus, by the 1920s the attack on "scientific racism" was well underway. E. B. Reuter spoke for many social scientists when he declared in *The American Race Problem* that Negroes trailed whites on IQ tests, not because of inborn inferiority, but because of inferior educational opportunities. Gunnar Myrdal, the Swedish sociologist, would later put his considerable influence behind the egalitarian ideas of Boas and his associates. "The gradual destruction of the popular theory behind race prejudice," Myrdal wrote, "is the most important of all social trends in the field of race relations."[36]

In the fall of 1933, Boas summoned a group of intellectuals to "devise ways and means for effectively counterattacking Nazi propaganda in the United States, and particularly Nazi racial theories." He urged his colleagues not to deal only with the "surface symptoms of Nazi propaganda but to plan a truly educational effort based on scientific data."[37]

Boas, Goldenweiser, and other scholars were acutely conscious of the link between Jewish identity and the broader problems of prejudice and discrimination. As of the 1930s, the bulk of the psychological and anthropological research on race had been done by Jewish students and scholars. Indeed, the scholarly critique of society that evolved into sociology had, like psychoanalysis, earned the reputation of being a Jewish science. But as interest in the subject grew, participation broadened. Historians began to focus on the harmful effects of nationalism. Psychologists began to state—as Margaret Mead had argued so persuasively in *Coming of Age in Samoa*—that racist thought was not innate in human beings but was perpetuated by each generation.[38]

The first college courses on race and nationality were offered at the University of Chicago in the 1930s, and over the course of the decade, as such courses caught on elsewhere, teachers consciously sought to change attitudes about race.

There was a market for their work. *Patterns of Culture* by Ruth Benedict, another Boas protégée, sold more than a million copies in paperback. Benedict concluded that people are by nature suspicious of outsiders and that racism was a manifestation of this natural suspicion. Otto Klineberg and M. F. Ashley-Montague, in a flood of books and articles in the thirties and forties, stirred controversy by producing evidence that the intelligence quotient of northern blacks consistently exceeded that of southern whites. Thus, from modest beginnings in the Progressive period, John Higham has written, the repudiation of race-based thinking had grown to become, in the 1930s, almost the hallmark of a civilized man.[39]

The movement reached its virtual apotheosis with the publication of Gunnar Myrdal's *An American Dilemma* in 1944. Myrdal was neither Jewish nor American, yet this Swedish sociologist's examination of race relations in the United States quickly established itself as a landmark work on the subject.

With a grant from the Carnegie Corporation, Myrdal assembled a team of sociologists, historians, economists, political scientists, anthropologists, and other experts and began the project in 1938. The goal was to synthesize several decades of research into a broad assault on racial prejudice and misunderstanding. Myrdal's book appeared at a critical time. Madison Grant, perhaps the most widely known apostle of scientific racism, had just died. Boas himself had passed away in 1942, fighting to the very last the "false philosophy" of racism.[40] (He was expounding on this theme at a luncheon at the Columbia University Faculty Club when he fell over dead.) Robert Park, the Chicago School's mainstay, also died in 1944.

The field was left to Myrdal and his collaborators, chief among whom were his Swedish associate, Richard Sterner; Samuel A. Stauffer, a University of Chicago professor; and Arnold Rose, a graduate student in sociology. Rose's role was especially important. During his wartime absence Myrdal entrusted Rose with preserving the integrity of the manuscript. Rose subsequently wrote portions of it under the loose plan laid out by his mentor and filled in gaps in the research. With his future wife, Caroline, Rose also handled the many details required to prepare for publication a manuscript with 1,024 pages of text and another 526 pages of introduction, footnotes, appendices, and bibliography. When Harper recommended paring the book down, Rose resisted; the publisher eventually backed off. Myrdal later insisted that the names of Rose and Sterner appear on the volume's title page.

The dilemma referred to in the title was what Myrdal and his collaborators perceived as the discrepancy between the professed American creed and American conduct. While Americans had paid lip service to the notion of human equality since the founding of the republic, Myrdal said, they had practiced racism, often of a most virulent strain, equally as long. Myrdal's team concluded optimistically, however, that times were changing at last, now that scientific racism was discredited. "The gradual destruction of the popular theory behind race prejudice is the most important of all social trends in the field of interracial relations," they wrote.

For the next generation *An American Dilemma* dominated public discussion of race relations. Of course, the day-to-day struggle against racial and religious prejudice and discrimination was far from over. It would be (and remains) a long and difficult battle that would encounter major obstacles. However, the social sciences were clearly causing a shift in public attitudes and casting a critical light upon racist thought and behavior. In the 1930s and 1940s, Senator Theodore Bilbo and Representative John Rankin of Alabama openly castigated Jews and blacks on the floor of Congress, but with racist ideas now on the defensive, they and their views ceased to be respectable.

However, coupled with the idea of racial equality was a notion that bore the seeds of future conflict between blacks and Jews. This was the idea of assimilation. As one intellectual would put it: "I should like to live in a world in which all people regarded men as individuals, good or bad, able or mediocre, interesting or dull, but not as New Englanders, or Middle Westerners, or Irish or German or Italian or Jews, except for the bland interest in origins that men have always had."[41]

This view had been shared by many. Back in 1782 Crèvecoeur had written that America was a place where individuals of all nations were melting into a new race of men. Jewish playwright Israel Zangwill echoed this sentiment in 1908: "America is God's Crucible, the great Melting Pot where all races of Europe are merging and reforming Germans and Frenchmen, Irishmen and Englishmen, Jews and Russians—into the Crucible with you all! God is making the Americans."

From the beginning, those who endorsed the melting pot idea assumed that, in shedding their ethnic identities and cultures, the new Americans would adopt the ways of thinking and doing of the majority group. This assumption continued unchallenged into the 1940s, when the melting pot theory crossed the color line, encompassing not just Europeans but Africans as well, although it is worth noting that the unwitting arrogance of some assimilationists was typified by Kenneth Stampp's comment that Negroes were "innately only white men with black skins."[42]

Myrdal accepted neither this "environmentalist" idea nor the thesis of Melville Herskovits that over the centuries American blacks had preserved a distinctive African heritage that they should cherish and perpetuate. Instead, Myrdal embraced the contrary findings of Robert S. Park and his illustrious student, the black sociologist E. Franklin Frazier. Frazier argued that Negroes in this country retained few relics of their African past and were, in effect, made in America.[43]

In the more race-conscious 1960s and 1970s black nationalists and some revisionist historians attacked such assimilationist concepts. Preaching black power and black pride as a means of building strong, cohesive black communities, they totally opposed white involvement in these activities. And since Jews were often central to such efforts, they were frequently seen as propagandists of assimilation and ultimate obstacles to progress.

6

THE ORIGINS OF THE CIVIL RIGHTS REVOLUTION

The Niggers and Jews of New York are working hand in hand.
—Senator Theodore Bilbo

World War II was America's most popular war. Never had the nation seemed so resolute, so strong, so united—or so successful. Hollywood added to this image with a spate of films showing Protestants, Catholics, and Jews fighting and dying together, battling a common enemy. Broadway did its part by bringing James Michener's *Tales of the South Pacific* to the stage (minus its first three words).

The vaunted unity of these disparate ethnic groups in combating the Axis powers was more apparent than real, however. Thousands of Japanese Americans were interned on the West Coast. The armed forces were strictly segregated. Black workers flocking to defense jobs in northern cities faced frequent harassment, and anti-Semitism lingered throughout the country. A survey of 1942 employment advertisements in the *New York Times* and elsewhere showed that nearly a third of the businesses seeking workers desired only Christian applicants. Shortly after Germany's surrender a national poll asked Americans whether they thought Jews had too much power in the United States. Fifty-eight percent responded yes. In postwar America qualified Jews were still being excluded from the nation's most prestigious medical and law schools. Jewish quotas kept their numbers down.[1]

Though Jews may have feared renewed outbreaks of anti-Semitism, blacks had even more cause for alarm, as the example of an especially heinous crime that occurred in a small Georgia town in 1946 quickly demonstrated. Two black war veterans and their wives were set upon by a mob of whites, who lynched the ex-servicemen and then killed the women, who had witnessed the hangings. The murderers were not prosecuted. Emboldened by the lack of police response to these atrocities, racists terrorized blacks in other parts of the South and in some northern communities as well.

The effect of such developments was to bring blacks and Jews closer together. "Weren't Blacks in the United States hated as much as the Jews in Germany," the black-owned *Chicago Defender* asked its readers. The *Defender* and the *Amsterdam News* in New York repeatedly urged blacks and Jews to unite in the face of the reactionary tide threatening both groups. The *Amsterdam News* warned that black anti-Semitism endangered their alliance, and it defended Jews who were experiencing discrimination.[2]

Despite the harshness of continuing racism and anti-Semitism, the postwar years marked the beginning of a golden age of American Jewry. Many Jews were beginning to move up and out of older, immigrant areas of settlement. The end of the war had seen the creation of the State of Israel and put in place a United Nations to guard the peace. All of this engendered high hopes among Jews that racial hostility and even poverty itself could be ended once and for all. (I recall personally the optimism that impelled many poor Jews of my generation into leftist causes, even as the Cold War began, convinced that in these efforts lay the path to a brave new world.) Jews came to be driven by what Stephen D. Isaacs described as "a religio-cultural obsession with the equalitarian ideal" for all people.[3]

To combat bigotry and develop greater tolerance for racial and religious differences, Jews began strengthening their "defense" agencies in this period. A measure of their broadened interests was the use then and in subsequent years of the term "community relations organizations" to describe them. A network of Jewish community relations councils, organized in wartime, became more active in many cities and joined together in the National Jewish Community Relations Council, which coordinated and augmented the work of national groups like the American Jewish Committee and other local bodies.[4]

Some Jewish leaders initially opposed joining forces with blacks in fighting bigotry. Arnold Aronson soon to become Washington representative of the NCRAC (later the NJCRAC), recalled a plenary session of the National Community Relations Advisory Council in 1946 or 1947 at which the Washington representative of B'nai B'rith had argued strongly against direct relations with blacks. The speaker feared, said Aronson, that the affiliation would drag Jews down, since the identity of the Jewish cause would be lost in that of blacks. He favored going it alone. Another attendee, Rabbi Stephen S. Wise, the president of the American Jewish Congress and perhaps the best-known Jew in America, was, Aronson says, vehement in denouncing the B'nai B'rith representative. The go-it-alone approach was ultimately rejected, and it was agreed that the Jewish cause and the black cause were to be joined in some respects, especially in the quest for legislation and related efforts.[5]

At this time, too, the national agencies themselves underwent a significant change in leadership. Gone from top posts were such German-Jewish patricians as Jacob Schiff, Louis Marshall, Julius Rosenwald, and Joel Spingarn. Although concerned and committed, often ahead of their times, these men were basically conservative in their politics and social relations. Marshall, a legal giant and a key figure in the American Jewish Committee, rejected the notion (advanced by some of his colleagues) that the committee should represent only the higher classes of Jews in America. Yet he would have been miscast as a postwar civil rights leader.[6]

Except for their Jewishness, the new agency leaders had little in common with the old. Their predecessors were men of means who mingled easily in upper-class circles and whose business success enabled them to give considerable time and money to civic work and charitable activities. However, such endeavors were never more than a sideline, albeit a serious one, for those men. By contrast, many of the newcomers were professionally trained social workers and what today would be called public interest attorneys, devoted full-time to civic activism. Whereas the earlier leaders were largely affluent Republicans, the new men (there were few women) came primarily from socialist-labor backgrounds. Having grown up poor in eastern Europe or in families of recent immigrants, they could relate directly to the poverty they encountered in the black and Jewish ghettos of big American cities.

John Slawson, who assumed the leadership of the American Jewish Committee in 1943, had emigrated from Poltavia in the Ukraine as a boy of seven. Although his family lived in extreme poverty in the Middle West, Slawson won admission to Columbia University in 1918 under what he later described as President Nicholas Murray Butler's religious quota system. A superior student, he excelled in clinical psychology and wanted to teach. A friendly professor informed him, however, that he could never get a faculty position. "Slawson, I wish you weren't a Jew" was the professor's not-so-subtle way of putting it. Slawson returned to the Middle West, where he became associated with Jewish welfare federations in Cleveland and Detroit. He published *The Delinquent Boy*, a treatise on juvenile delinquency, in 1926. Later he returned to New York to head the Jewish Board of Guardians, a children's agency, where he introduced principles of modern psychiatry into casework. He then became leader of the American Jewish Committee.[7]

Will Maslow's background as a socialist, a Zionist, a lawyer, and a nephew of David Ben-Gurion, Israel's first prime minister, prepared him for the posts of counsel and, later, executive head of the American Jewish Congress. Like Slawson, Maslow was an immigrant, coming to this country at the age of three from Russia. He studied economics at Cornell and planned a career in teaching but switched to law on discovering, again like Slawson, that universities were not hiring Jewish professors. Most big law firms also discriminated against Jews in hiring, but certain New Deal agencies did not. They were virtually alone in looking for bright lawyers, regardless of their religious preference. So Maslow went to Washington and took a post with the National Labor Relations Board, working there from 1937 to 1943 as a trial attorney and administrative law judge. Later he supervised the regional offices of the Fair Employment Practices Commission. In this position he was among the first to appoint blacks to his staff.[8]

Another immigrant intellectual who made his mark on the American Jewish Congress was Alexander H. Pekelis, described by Rabbi Stephen S. Wise as "one of the most brilliant and creative men I have met in my lifetime." Born in Russia and educated in

Italy and Germany, Pekelis fled the Nazis in 1940. In America he studied law and edited the law review at Columbia while serving as a teacher at the New School for Social Research. He later joined the American Jewish Congress; in 1945 he was named chief consultant to its commission of law and social action. In that capacity he developed many of the arguments that helped topple segregation. Pekelis died in an airplane crash in 1946, but his influence was profound for years thereafter.[9]

Out of personal experience with Jewish and black poverty, a sense of themselves as outsiders, and the social democratic tradition in which they had grown up, the new group of Jewish activists and thinkers forged a philosophy of economic radicalism, utopian humanitarianism, and—for some, like Maslow—Zionism. These personal political and intellectual commitments impelled them to reach out beyond the parochial needs of the Jewish community and to strive for broader social goals, ultimately winning a central place in the civil rights movement.

Since many of the new young Jewish leaders were ardent New Dealers, they tended to favor an enhanced role for government in ending bigotry and discrimination. Their political liberalism drew them naturally to social justice efforts and to closer ties with blacks. To end black anti-Semitism, which they were aware of but only rarely acknowledged publicly, it was necessary, they believed, to make blacks and black organizations aware that they could count upon finding Jews on the side of social justice.[10]

The American Jewish Committee, American Jewish Congress, Anti-Defamation League, Jewish Labor Committee, and the newly formed community relations councils all played their part in the assault on racial and religious inequality. With professionally trained personnel, fully equipped offices, and public relations know-how, they had the resources to make a difference. Most important, they were strongly motivated, and their timing was propitious: World War II and the opening of Hitler's death camps had made Americans aware of the end product of racism and discrimination. Coming out of the Great Depression, many Americans had also become increasingly conscious of inequities in their society and were anxious to correct them. Nevertheless, the role of the Jewish agencies in nurturing the national mood and making it more receptive to change was critical. Arguably, the period from just before the end of World War II to the mid-1950s, when the black-led protest movement got underway, may be said to have been the Jewish phase of the civil rights revolution.

In 1948 the American Jewish Committee set up the National Labor Service to help finance civil rights programs within both the American Federation of Labor (AFL) and its smaller but feistier rival, the Congress of Industrial Organizations (CIO). "It was a pump-priming approach," Slawson wrote later, "an expression of a universalistic concern with civil rights for the benefit of the entire American community." Over the next two years, in a series of actions never made public, NLS funds were used to engage civil rights workers in the educational departments of each labor organization. With the subsequent merger of the AFL and CIO, machinery was established for fighting bigotry in the union movement, and civil rights work became a regular part of the AFL-CIO's activities, both on a national level and in its dealings with affiliates.[11]

While seeking to deal with bigotry on a day-to-day basis, the Jewish organizations also promoted and popularized the social-scientific attack on racism that was then under way. In this long-range initiative they mobilized eminent scholars to argue that racial prejudice and religious discrimination were the products of twisted minds and character defects in the human personality. Slawson and his colleagues were aided by the flight from Hitler's Germany of numerous scientists and writers, many of them Jewish, with firsthand knowledge of racist murderers running amok. The list included Albert Einstein, Thomas Mann, Hannah Arendt, Herbert Marcuse, Erich Fromm, Erik Erikson, Theodor W. Adorno, Max Horkheimer, and Kurt Lewin.

Working in the relatively new disciplines of psychology, sociology, and anthropology, the refugee social scientists developed fresh methods of examining totalitarianism and other aberrations of modern industrial society. In two books, *Escape from Freedom* (1941) and *Man for Himself* (1947), Erich Fromm advanced a novel character typology, contrasting the exploitive, hoarding, "authoritarian" personality and the loving, gentle, "humanitarian" one. American society had no shortage of authoritarians, and Fromm's great fear (and that of the other emigré German scholars) was of "thinking with the blood," whereby the authoritarian type would gain dominance in mass society and crush the humanitarians who were working for social betterment.[12]

In 1944 the American Jewish Congress organized a Commission on Community Interrelations (CCI) under the leadership of Kurt Lewin, who recruited a distinguished group of social scientists—Isidor Chein, Kenneth B. Clark, Morton Deutsch, Marie Jahoda, Ronald Lippitt, Marion Radke—to study group identity, group tension, and racial attitudes. With their help Lewin became a leading strategist for social change. In contrast to the milder, reformist approach of the American Jewish Committee, Lewin's methods—like those of the American Jewish Congress—were confrontational, intending to break through the complacency and self-righteousness that seemed to typify American society. Lewin's ideas were institutionalized at the Research Center for Group Dynamics at the Massachusetts Institute of Technology and the National Training Laboratory in Bethel, Maine, both of which he helped establish. Lewin's early advocacy of strong group identity for minorities seeking to survive in a hostile world would later influence both the black power and black pride movements of the sixties and seventies.

The American Jewish Committee, however, was the primary organizer of the social science–based attack on religious and racial discrimination. With Hitler's rise, the committee had shifted its tactics from apologetics—that is, arguing that Jews were not as bad as some people thought—to a full-scale assault on Nazism and prejudice. More important than stressing Jewish accomplishments and denouncing anti-Semitic canards, said Cyrus Adler, the agency's third president, was the refutation of so-called racial science. Adler thought it was essential to mobilize public opinion in the United States against Hitler and his party without any reference to Jews at all. His views were shared by the group's other German-Jewish leaders, who had helped to subsidize the work of Boas and related social scientists in the interest of demolishing the Nazis' master-race mythology.[13]

John Slawson, who knew Fromm and some of the other German exiles from his work at the Jewish Board of Guardians, refined this effort, making it more comprehensive and systematic. On taking the reins at the American Jewish Committee in 1943, he enlisted their help in searching out the causes of anti-Semitism and of prejudice in general. "In this endeavor," he later explained, "science performs an essential function, uncovering the hidden causes of tension and outbreaks, and thus making it possible to tackle prejudice at its source."[14]

In May 1944 Slawson convened a conference on anti-Semitism at the Biltmore Hotel in New York. The participants included Adorno, Horkheimer, and Lewin, as well as such prominent scholars as Gordon Allport, John Dollard, Paul Lazarsfeld, Talcott Parsons, and Lloyd Warner. The conferees identified anti-Semitism as a central element in the antidemocratic personality. But they also felt that studies of this phenomenon should be linked to broader research into antilabor and antiliberal views and into other more general manifestations of antidemocratic tendencies. Viewing notions of another group's inferiority as an aggressive personality mechanism, they emphasized the need for understanding the bigoted individual and finding ways to deal with him. Following the conference, Slawson placed Horkheimer in charge of the American Jewish Committee's division of scientific research, where he was joined for a while by the young sociologist Nathan Glazer.[15]

Slawson's efforts culminated in 1949 and 1950 with the publication by Harper and Row of the Studies in Prejudice series. These enormously influential books were sponsored and paid for by the American Jewish Committee. The series central volume, *The Authoritarian Personality*, extended and strengthened Fromm's ideas. Through thousands of questionnaires and numerous in-depth interviews, the team of authors, headed by Adorno and R. Nevitt Sanford, explored more comprehensively than ever before the psychological forces predisposing individuals to group hostility.

The authors argued in effect that authoritarian tendencies develop in small children as a result of parental upbringing. Such individuals become rigidly conformist in their views, somewhat self-righteous, and deferential to those they consider superior. They lack introspection and cannot tolerate life's ambiguities. They are often prejudiced and are likely candidates for totalitarian movements.[16]

Widely praised for focusing on emotional disorders in the bigot, the book stimulated a variety of similarly oriented studies (some three hundred by 1962). Earlier in the century many social scientists had believed that anti-Semitism and racism were more or less natural results of the misbehavior and innate inferiority of these minority groups. The scientific reassessment, however, seemed to demonstrate that bigotry in all its forms was a mental abnormality, while tolerance and liberalism were not only morally right but gave evidence of a well-developed personality.[17] As it happened, the volume was published in 1950, just as Senator Joseph R. McCarthy launched his highly publicized campaign against alleged Communists in the State Department and other key sectors of American society. To his critics McCarthy was a dangerous demagogue, who perfectly epitomized the authoritarian personality described in the classic study. His notoriety vastly increased the book's impact.

The body of thought slowly accumulating since the turn of the century in the works of Du Bois, Boas, Slawson, Adorno, and others intersected with the widespread shock and horror of World War II to help improve the climate for tolerance and understanding in the United States. One reflection of this change could be seen in the way public schools now dealt with different cultures. A half century earlier, when immigration tides were at their peak, the nation's schools had relentlessly transmitted the values and styles of a single ethic, that of Protestant America. Black children and the children of Catholic and Jewish immigrants were forced to learn and expected to conform to these standards, no matter how sharply they differed from their own backgrounds. In the postwar period the acculturation process was turned on its head, and schools overhauled their curriculums to emphasize the strengths of all groups. Nathan Glazer wrote later that if any one group was principally involved, it was the Jews frightened at the rise of anti-Semitism.[18] However, many other social groups took part, and numerous organizations were formed to drive home the message, one in which two themes predominated. The first was that children should be proud, not ashamed, of their ethnic heritage. The second was that racial, religious, and cultural differences should be understood and tolerated instead of stigmatized.

In subsequent years cultural pluralism came to be generally recognized as an organizing principle of American society. It was only in the eighties and early nineties that the concept was challenged by some elements of the multiculturalist movement, which claim that American society is Eurocentric and argue that children from minority backgrounds can do well in school only if addressed in terms of their own ancestral culture. Arthur Schlesinger, Jr., Diane Ravitch, and others have argued that what was meant to be a practical recognition of a healthy diversity in American life would, when pressed too far, create a danger of increasing fragmentation, resegregation, and tribalization.[19]

In the postwar period the Anti-Defamation League utilized radio and television spots, clever jingles, filmstrips and other media efforts to promote cross-cultural understanding. One typical postcard depicted a black youngster wiping away tears because he wasn't allowed to play baseball with white children. The caption read: "What difference does it make what his race or religion is? He can pitch, can't he?" The league enlisted Hollywood stars in its effort, and Bess Myerson, the first Jewish Miss America, joined its roster of speakers. In schools and auditoriums around the country, she insisted that "you can't be beautiful, and hate."[20]

Even film producers, who had often displayed insensitivity to the problems of minorities (including those of the immigrant Jewish minority), now got involved. Following an appeal by the NAACP's Walter White, Wendell L. Willkie, attorney and spokesman for the movie industry, convened a meeting of its leaders in Los Angeles. Willkie, who had been the Republican candidate for president in 1940, bluntly observed that many of the people responsible for Hollywood films belonged to the group that had been the target of Hitler. Noting that the movies often demeaned Jews and other minorities with hurtful clichés and stereotypes, Willkie told the producers that they should be the last ones to inflict the same indignities on another minority group.[21]

Whether as a result of Willkie's lecture or the more benign social atmosphere now developing, Hollywood soon became a major instrument for racial and religious understanding. In 1945 Frank Sinatra appeared in *The House I Live In*, based on a popular song that referred to "neighbors white and black." The film won a special Academy Award. Two years later RKO's *Crossfire*, based on Richard Brooks's novel *The Brick Foxhole*, dealt with a demented redneck's anti-Semitism. Twentieth Century–Fox's film version of Laura Z. Hobson's novel *Gentlemen's Agreement* threw the spotlight on respectable white Protestants who engaged in employment and housing discrimination against Jews and supported anti-Semitic covenants and agreements. Critic John Mason Brown wrote in the *Saturday Review of Literature* that the exciting thing about these films was that they dared to speak publicly on a subject long kept private.[22]

This new egalitarianism reached deep into American culture. In one five-month period in 1947, national magazines with a combined circulation of sixteen million readers published waves of articles about bettering human relations. *Collier's* presented "The Outcasts," by B. J. Chute, an indictment of anti-Semitic covenants in real estate. The *Saturday Evening Post* described the color line in medicine in an article by Henry and Katherine Pringle. *Harper's* analyzed moves against job discrimination by fair employment practices commissions in New York, New Jersey, Connecticut, and Massachusetts. In *Better Homes and Gardens*, Hodding Carter, the liberal southern editor, described "How to Stop Hatemongers in Your Town," while Bruce Bliven, in a seven-part series in the *New Republic*, discussed the causes of anti-Semitism and possible ways to end it.[23]

Far more attention and applause, however, was accorded the Rodgers and Hammerstein musical *South Pacific*. The musical—later a Hollywood film—featured a romance between a Frenchman and a Little Rock nurse initially repelled by his earlier interracial marriage. It underlined the message that bigotry does not come naturally to humans. Its show-stopping song "Carefully Taught," stating that children had to be taught to hate, made the point in a way that Theodor Adorno and his colleagues at the American Jewish Committee could never have dreamed possible.

It was in this postwar period that the modern civil rights movement began to take shape. Besides the Jewish agencies, early participants included the NAACP, the American Civil Liberties Union, the Japanese-American Citizens League, and the National Lawyers Guild, as well as the AFL, the CIO, and affiliated unions like the United Automobile Workers.

Towering over all of them was the soft-spoken, iron-willed founder-president of the Brotherhood of Sleeping Car Porters, A.

Philip Randolph. It was Randolph's threatened march on Washington in 1941 that had forced FDR to form the President's Committee on Fair Employment Practices, later known as the FEPC, to curb job discrimination against blacks and other minorities in war industries. (Jewish lawyer Joseph Rauh at the Justice Department, one of Felix Frankfurter's "happy hot dogs," actually wrote the executive order.) By 1944, however, Randolph had grown increasingly skeptical of Roosevelt. He knew the agency was merely a wartime expedient that would be abolished with the end of hostilities, and he feared that the nation would thereafter revert to past discriminatory practices in dealing with blacks. Randolph accordingly took the lead again in organizing a National Council for a Permanent FEPC. Jewish groups were focused almost entirely on the struggle against Nazism, however, and gave low priority to Randolph's initiative. Their seeming disinterest drew criticism from black newspapers like the *Pittsburgh Courier*, which charged that "foxy Jews" had never helped set up the FEPC and had only swung into line after seeing that it might be useful. (Even so, this same newspaper editorially deplored what it saw as anti-Semitism among the Negro masses.)[24]

With the FEPC's demise Randolph's council vainly lobbied Congress to revive it through legislation. In 1946 Roy Wilkins was named chairman of the council's executive committee, and Randolph asked Arnold Aronson, a member of the staff of the National Jewish Community Relations Council, to serve as the group's secretary. Most of the funding came from Jewish agencies and the labor movement, particularly the UAW.[25]

Aronson's relationship with Randolph went back to the projected 1941 march on Washington when the two men first met. Aronson, then in Illinois, had sought to get people from Chicago to join the march. Aronson saw Randolph as the father of the civil rights movement. Randolph, in turn, trusted Aronson implicitly. He once told Bayard Rustin that if Rustin wanted to go forward with a project and Randolph was not around to okay it, Rustin could get approval from Aronson and Norman Thomas, the longtime socialist leader.

From 1946 on, while Randolph remained active as council chairman, Wilkins and Aronson ran the organization and directed its civil rights forces in Washington.[26] In some respects these two men personified the black-Jewish alliance at its best. Wilkins, the grandson of Mississippi slaves, was a former newspaper editor, a versatile and politically astute man. He had a gift for words and was often visible as the movement's spokesman. Aronson, quiet and self-effacing, functioned as the inside man. The two became good friends, so much so that when Wilkins died, his widow asked Aronson to deliver the eulogy.[27]

Wilkins and Aronson spearheaded the continuing battle for a permanent FEPC. In January 1950 the National Emergency Civil Rights Mobilization of which Wilkins was chairman and Arnold Aronson secretary convened in Washington. Between four and five thousand delegates from thirty-five states showed up—the largest mobilization yet organized—to demand a permanent FEPC and a stronger civil rights agenda. Though the effort failed, the Mobilization and the National Council for a Permanent FEPC merged later that year to form the Leadership Conference on Civil Rights. The two men headed the merged organization. In subsequent years the Leadership Conference became the nation's broadest-based civil rights organization, with 186 national groups as members. The Leadership Conference, a coordinating body, led major campaigns for the civil rights acts of 1957, 1960, and 1964, the voting rights bill of 1965, and the fair housing act of 1968. It remains a powerful force in Washington today with a broadened agenda that includes education and housing as well as employment.[28] Although blacks were the primary beneficiaries of the resulting legislation, all minorities gained. Randolph, Wilkins, and Aronson always considered discrimination of all kinds indivisible and felt that equal rights and opportunities had to be dealt with accordingly.[29]

During the struggle to create a national FEPC, there was also much activity at the city and state level. Here the Jewish agencies, with their well-established local and regional structures, made their influence felt. The American Jewish Congress was particularly effective. A grass roots organization politically left of center, the congress scorned the "brotherhood" sloganeering employed by the Anti-Defamation League and other bodies in favor of direct assaults on discrimination. (Before long, groups like the ADL and American Jewish Committee became active in legislative efforts as well.) Kurt Lewin, whom many hailed as the Albert Einstein of social psychology, led the charge for the American Jewish Congress, based in some measure on the earlier work of Pekelis.

Lewin and his associates at the CCI were pioneers at developing a comprehensive rationale for human rights legislation that brought government authority into the battle against discrimination for the first time since the Civil War. Lewin disagreed with social scientists who believed that antisocial behavior could be changed by altering social attitudes through a propaganda blitz lauding "fellowship." He reasoned that the best way to alter antisocial behavior was through legislation. Laws banning discrimination could create a psychological climate that would make it difficult for prejudice to thrive. In taking this position, of course, Lewin challenged William Graham Sumner's nineteenth-century aphorism (which remained widely accepted) that stateways cannot change folkways. Lewin was convinced, however, that laws firmly enforced and supplemented by broad programs of community education could prove effective in creating new social norms.[30]

The American Jewish Congress established in 1945 the Commission of Law and Social Action (CLSA) under Will Maslow and Alexander Pekelis. In an essay that year, "Full Equality in a Free Society," Pekelis wrote that "American Jews will find more reasons for taking an affirmative attitude toward being Jews if they are part and parcel of a great American and human force working for a better world whether or not the individual issues involved touch directly upon so-called Jewish interests. The tradition and fate of Israel are indissolubly bound to those of the forces of liberalism."[31]

Pekelis was eager to prove that legal and legislative campaigns were the most effective means of public instruction, that the drama of a lawsuit or a legislative drive would attract attention and educate the wider community.[32] CLSA employed seven civil rights lawyers at a time when there was no civil rights division in the U.S. Justice Department, and it quickly became what the *Yale Law Journal* described as the "private attorney general" acting on behalf of all minorities.

Pekelis also believed that anti-Semitism in the United States, unlike that in czarist Russia, had its roots in private governments, by which he meant the aggregations of power in giant corporations, large universities, real estate boards, and professional associations. Accordingly, in 1945, the American Jewish Congress opened fire on

Columbia University. It seemed an unlikely target since Rabbi Wise, the congress's head, was a Columbia graduate. But the university's tax-exempt status was challenged on grounds that its medical school limited Jewish enrollment. Concurrently, CLSA attacked the quota system limiting the enrollment of Jews at all of New York State's nine medical schools. It helped organize a statewide committee to push for passage of fair employment and educational-practices laws drafted by the American Jewish Congress and supported by other Jewish agencies. The educational-practices legislation was enacted after a two-year effort, and New York became the first state in the nation to provide such protection.

Through court tests and legislative lobbying the American Jewish Congress fought housing discrimination resulting from racial and religious covenants, "gentlemen's agreements," and conspiracies of realty boards. CLSA sued the $100 million Stuyvesant Town housing project in New York City for its refusal to rent to blacks. While the suit was dismissed, a state committee against discrimination in housing, created largely by Jewish groups in 1949, gained passage of four major state laws and two antidiscrimination ordinances in New York City.[33]

Regional branches of ADL, the American Jewish Committee, and the Jewish Labor Committee and various local Jewish community relations councils were also extremely active then and in succeeding years, forming or participating in coalitions of church, labor, and civic groups to lobby for fair employment, fair education, and fair housing laws and spearheading drives to create local human relations commissions to implement the legislation. Indeed, many of the laws, from first draft to final enactment, owed their existence to Jewish legal staff, lobbyists, and legislators.[34]

By the early sixties, when the civil rights movement entered a new, more militant stage, some twenty states and forty cities had enacted fair employment practices laws covering 60 percent of the nation's population and about 50 percent of minorities. New York State's 1958 ban on discrimination in housing sales and rentals led the nation, but by 1963 seventeen states and cities had similar legislation on their books. Of course, these laws did not end prejudice and discrimination, but they did make bigotry appear immoral and un-American to many people, as Lewin and Pekelis had predicted, even when such behavior continued surreptitiously.

Revisionist writers have begun to question in recent years the motivation of Jewish civil rights activists. Adolph L. Reed, Jr., has argued that the push for civil rights was undertaken to mobilize black support to advance a Jewish agenda. David Levering Lewis declared that the formation of the NAACP and other racial justice efforts earlier in the century was an effort by a German-Jewish elite to curry favor with upper-class liberal WASPs as well as to fight anti-Semitism by remote control. Conceding the black-Jewish relationship was a defensive alliance against the common enemy of bigotry, he believed it gave rise to a "mystique" of some special racial bond, when it was, in fact an "apparent rather than real soul fellowship." In his view, it was and presumably remains today a "misconceived ethnic propinquity."

Clayborne Carson has argued that most Jews (except for a small number of highly assimilated left-wingers) have been uninvolved and uninterested in liberal causes which he claimed to be outside the Jewish tradition. But even Harold Cruse, perhaps the sharpist critic of the black-Jewish alliance, was forced to admit, "The truth was (and is) that the American Jewish Committee and its intellectual adherents pioneered in ways never equaled by their white liberal Protestant allies."[35]

Although Jews were certainly motivated in part by self-interest, they were not the only ones who gained from the opening to ethnic outsiders of hitherto closed areas of American life. Blacks, Asians, and women benefited, as did all those excluded. Racial extremists recognized this right away. Outraged at the challenge to white supremacy, Senator Bilbo declared, "The niggers and the Jews of New York are working hand in hand."[36]

What transformed the civil rights cause from a moral issue at the periphery of the nation's consciousness into a movement that would revolutionize American society was the emergence of blacks as a political force. Between 1910 and 1940, New York City's black population grew from 60,000 to 250,000; Philadelphia's grew from 84,000 to 250,000; and Chicago's from 30,000 to 277,000. In the next decade, with southern workers drawn north by the wartime industrial boom, the black population outside the old Confederacy doubled, rising from 2.4 million in 1940 to 4.6 million in 1950. In some northern cities the numbers of blacks increased at a rate five to ten times that of whites.

Franklin D. Roosevelt had taken steps toward recognizing the growing strength of black voters by securing black specialists and advisers in various departments and by the vigor of his economic reforms, but his moves were halting and limited. He had to be virtually coerced by Randolph to issue the executive order banning discrimination in defense industries; the work of his wife, Eleanor, and Secretary of Commerce Harold L. Ickes was more aggressive. It thus remained for Missourian Harry S. Truman to launch the first presidential initiative on behalf of civil rights.

Truman, a World War I veteran, had been deeply affected upon returning home by the growth of the Ku Klux Klan in his community. "It scared the shit out of me," he later told Morris Ernst, the civil liberties attorney. He had been elected to the Senate with the help of black and Catholic votes and as president was conscious of postwar changes in the nation's social climate and demography. In the off-year elections of 1946, the Democrats were stung by losses in the House and Senate. A month later, after prodding by a delegation led by Walter White and at the suggestion of presidential assistant David K. Niles, who was Jewish, Truman created the President's Committee on Civil Rights. Its mission was to assess civil rights law and, where necessary, strengthen and improve it.

Truman picked a panel of distinguished whites and blacks for the new committee, including Morris Ernst, Rabbi Roland B. Gittelson, and Charles E. Wilson, president of General Electric, who became chairman. As a mark of the importance he attached to his precedent-setting move, the president directed committee members to meet in the cabinet room of the White House. Following a series of hearings, the committee laid out its recommendations in a document entitled "To Secure These Rights." According to Will Maslow, the document was based in part on his own testimony and on an article that he and Joseph Robison of the American Jewish Congress had written in the *Lawyers Guild Review*. The proposals went beyond anything Truman had expected. They called for a permanent commission on civil rights, a fair employment practices act, federal antilynching legislation, elimination of the poll tax, and actions to end segregation in education, the armed forces, housing, health care, and public services.[37]

In effect, Truman's committee set forth a civil rights agenda for the coming years, an agenda dramatically illustrated by the difference in the number of bills before Congress prior to and after Truman took office. Only ten such bills were introduced in the Seventy-Fifth Congress (1937–1938), but the number rose steadily until seventy-two such bills were presented in the Eighty-First Congress (1949–1950).[38]

The Democratic convention of 1948 saw the nation's first important political battle over the issue of civil rights. The young mayor of Minneapolis, Hubert H. Humphrey, called for the party to include in its platform the recommendations of Truman's committee. Humphrey's impassioned plea resulted in the adoption of a strong civil rights plank that led to a walkout by Senator Strom Thurmond of South Carolina, police chief Eugene "Bull" Connor of Birmingham, Alabama, and a young alternate delegate from Alabama named George Wallace. The angry Southerners then formed the short-lived Dixiecrat party. But Truman, to the surprise of many, was reelected.

In this more favorable national climate for civil rights, the NAACP and its legal defense fund, led by Marshall and his colleagues, moved to strike down public school segregation. Among those involved in this initiative were Robert Carter, the battlefield commander, who was black, and Jack Greenberg, his junior colleague. Carter sold Marshall on the idea of blending psychological and social scientific data with the straight legal approach to desegregation. Greenberg drew the assignment to find experts in the Midwest for the landmark case *Brown v. Board of Education of Topeka, Kansas*.

Although many civil rights gains were made by blacks and Jews working together at the professional or organizational level, blacks and Jews acting as individuals also contributed. For some of them, the NAACP was not aggressive enough. For example, a pretty, hazel-eyed, thirty-year-old white Jewish woman, Esther Brown, played a central role in pushing the local chapter of the NAACP in Topeka into the Brown case (Oliver Brown was the name of the black plaintiff). Local black leaders hesitated out of fear that some black teachers would lose their jobs if the schools were desegregated. Over a period of years in which she actively pressed local school issues, Esther Brown was threatened and insulted, a cross was burned on her lawn, her husband was fired from his job, her father-in-law called her a Communist, and she suffered a miscarriage. The local NAACP secretary later said the task could hardly have been accomplished without her, although opposition to segregated schools had been in the air for years.[39]

A Jewish judge and a black psychologist also played important roles in this and other school segregation cases. Their backgrounds could hardly have been more dissimilar. Felix Frankfurter, born in Vienna in 1882, immigrated to New York City at the age of twelve and won distinction while still a young man. With degrees from City College and Harvard Law School, he joined Harvard's law faculty in 1914 and over the next quarter century became one of the nation's best-known legal scholars. He was elevated to the Supreme Court in 1939 just as the NAACP, using tactics advocated by Nathan Margold and others, began stepping up its campaign against segregated schools.

Frankfurter took an intense interest in this litigation. His centrist and reformist stance—similar to that of the moderate Jewish agencies and the NAACP—would draw heavy criticism as the school segregation issue unfolded. Earlier, he had served on the NAACP's legal committee, but he resigned from this and other outside positions when Roosevelt named him to the Court.[40] Frankfurter clearly recognized the importance of bringing excluded minorities into the system, but he felt it should be done without disrupting society. On the Court he made no secret of his commitment to civil liberties. In a controversial dissent in a Jehovah's Witness case, he had explained his position by saying of himself, "One who belongs to the most vilified and persecuted minority in history is not likely to be insensitive to the freedoms guaranteed by the Constitution." He went on to observe, however, that justices should not allow their personal emotions to affect their legal judgment.[41]

Nonetheless, Frankfurter's Jewishness sometimes did become an issue on the Court. In 1944 he had been assigned to write the majority opinion in *Smith v. Allwright*, reversing a 1935 decision upholding the South's all-white primary system, which excluded blacks from Democratic primaries, in effect barring them from elections in that part of the country. The assignment troubled Justice Robert H. Jackson, who wrote Chief Justice Harlan Fiske Stone that a unanimous decision challenging southern sensitivities should be written by another justice. Frankfurter, he said, "united in a rare degree factors which may unhappily excite prejudice." Jackson observed bluntly: "In the first place, he is a Jew." On Jackson's recommendation the assignment was shifted to Justice Stanley Reed.[42]

Kenneth B. Clark was a product of the very segregated schools that were being challenged in the Brown litigation. Born in the Panama Canal Zone in 1914, he did his undergraduate work at Howard University and earned both master's and doctoral degrees at Columbia. City College appointed him to its psychology department in 1942. Two years later, when the American Jewish Congress formed its commission on community interrelations, Clark and his wife, Mamie, a psychologist at Columbia, began the research into racial attitudes and group tensions that were to become his life's work. In 1950—the year *The Authoritarian Personality* was published—Clark completed a six-month study for the American Jewish Committee, on the impact of discrimination on the personalities of young children. Clark's paper, based in part on data developed in the Studies in Prejudice series, argued that legally enforced school segregation damaged black children psychologically. As proof he cited the results of a test conducted with black children, in which he had given them white dolls and colored dolls and asked which they preferred; a statistically significant majority viewed the white dolls as "nice" and the colored dolls as "bad." This led him to the view that the average black American has been scarred by self-hatred.

The Supreme Court, meanwhile, was inching toward a ruling in *Brown v. Board of Education*. Starting in the 1930s, a series of suits had been launched by the NAACP against segregation in graduate and professional schools—the so-called soft underbelly of Jim Crow. Those opposed to the "separate but equal" doctrine at the graduate level won their first victory in the law school of the University of Missouri in 1938. By 1950 blacks had been ordered admitted to the law school of the University of Texas as well and to the Ph.D. program at the University of Oklahoma. The constitutionality of public school segregation, however, had been repeatedly upheld.

One of the NAACP cases that reached the Supreme Court concerned school segregation in South Carolina, and Clark became a witness. The NAACP turned to Clark for help in planning with its attorneys how social psychologists and other social scientists could best be used in the school cases. With two colleagues Clark drafted a summary document that was endorsed by thirty-two social scientists; it was presented to the court as an appendix to the NAACP's briefs. It argued that segregation was inseparably linked with discrimination against black children and inflicted vast psychic damage on both white and black children. The statement was silent, however, on the subject of school segregation that existed, not because of government action, but because of residential patterns in neighborhoods in which whites and blacks lived apart. One was de jure segregation, the other de facto. To many activists this was a distinction without a difference—the kind of segregation found in the North was just as damaging as that in the South.[43]

Chief Justice Earl Warren could have based his decision in *Brown* solely on John Marshall Harlan's eloquent dissent in *Plessy v. Ferguson*, the 1894 decision upholding racial segregation "The arbitrary separation of citizens on the basis of race," Harlan wrote, "is a badge of servitude wholly inconsistent with the civil freedom and equality before the law established by the Constitution." There seemed sufficient ground to strike down enforced segregation solely on legal grounds—violation of the "equal protection" clause of the Fourteenth Amendment.

Warren's decision of May 17, 1954, noted this, but it went on to cite the findings of Clark, Myrdal, and other noted social scientists, writing that racial segregation generated a "feeling of inferiority [among black children] as to their status in the community." In developing the argument, Warren cited, in a now famous footnote, seven works that the NAACP had introduced earlier in the litigation. First on the list was the analysis prepared by Clark for the American Jewish Committee in 1950; two others were psychological studies prepared by the American Jewish Congress. Footnote 11 ended with references to "[E. Franklin] Frazier, *The Negro in the United States* (1949)" and "See generally Myrdal."[44]

Clark's research, however, was flawed. His sampling of children in the dolls test was too small to be scientifically accurate. Moreover, one of his earlier studies had shown a less pronounced preference for the white dolls among young black children in the South. The finding seemed to contradict his main point, but it was ignored, although Clark himself, to his credit, recognized the limitations of his research. At one point he told an NAACP lawyer that, in assessing the psychological impact of prejudice and discrimination on black children generally, he did not think it possible to isolate the effect of school segregation alone. Amid the efforts of politicians and social scientists in what they considered a good cause, however, Clark's own reservations were put aside.[45]*

The Court's May 17, 1954, decision in Brown was one of the most important it had ever rendered. It would spur the civil rights revolution that followed and move toward closing the gap Myrdal and his associates had noted between America's promise and its racial reality. Much of the controversy over desegregation in subsequent years, however, stemmed from Warren's use of social science data and the subsequent politicization of the issue. Though Clark's statement for the thirty-two scientists had spoken of de jure, not de facto, segregation, activists in the NAACP and elsewhere concluded that, given the harm done, there was no real distinction between the two forms. The effect of segregation by either method was equivalent. This conclusion would give rise to efforts to achieve racial balance wherever imbalance existed, even

---

*The idea that blacks have been damaged by self-hatred was first brought forward as a "scientific" finding by a clinical psychologist, Ruth Horowitz, in 1939, but her work was overshadowed by that of the Clarks. In her exploratory study of seventeen white and seven black children two to five years of age, she asked them "to show me which one is you" among various photographs or drawings. From their response to this and other questions, she concluded that black children engaged in "wishful thinking" about being white, in spite of the fact that the white boys in her study were more inconsistent than blacks in their choices. Nonetheless, her interpretation, according to William E. Cross, Jr., an associate professor at Cornell University's African Studies and Research Centers, set the tone for research on black self-hatred for thirty years. In his book *Shades of Black* (Temple Press, 1991), Dr. Cross describes this movement, one which he deplores. The goal of his book, he told a reporter for the *Chronicle of Higher Education* (May 8, 1991), was to "purge black psychology" of overly pejorative and romantic tendencies and replace them with discussion centered around diversity and complexity in black psychological responses.

where no governmental action was involved.[46] The ground was now ready for major battles as the issue of school segregation moved to the implementation stage.

As the debate within the Court proceeded, Frankfurter's role expanded. He was acutely aware of how upsetting the decision would be to millions in the South and elsewhere, and he recognized that deeply entrenched patterns of life would be overthrown. Perhaps as a Jewish immigrant, conscious of his people's historical experience, he thought orderly reform, not social disruption, was the safest way to proceed. In a memorandum to his fellow justices on May 27, 1953, he expressed the view that psychological adjustment to the unfamiliar and unpleasant would be the biggest problem for American society.[47]

Frankfurter then suggested a timetable for implementing the decision. Borrowing a phrase from his old idol, Oliver Wendell Holmes, he recommended that the decision should promote "a process of racial betterment, not social deterioration." The Court could not correct a deplorable situation overnight. It would do its duty, he wrote, if it ordered the end of school segregation "with deliberate speed." Warren's implementation decision in 1955 amended this slightly to "with all deliberate speed," making clear that a start had to be made.[48]

To much of the South, the Court's desegregation timetable was an excuse for procrastination. Ten years after the ruling not a single school in Mississippi had been desegregated. And yet the long-range effect may have been salutary. Thurgood Marshall, the NAACP's chief counsel, who shepherded the case all the way to the Supreme Court (and later became the Court's first black justice), thought it was. Separate but equal facilities were unlawful. The laws of the states had to yield to the Constitution. Southern resisters, Marshall said, would grow "tired of having Negro lawyers beating 'em every day in court."[49]

From 1945 to 1953, large numbers of black families moved into formerly Jewish sections of northern cities, renewing frictions that had earlier marred black-Jewish relations. Jews had been less resistant to black move-ins than other ethnic groups, who often responded with violence directed against the newcomers. But

Jews were not entirely free of prejudice, nor of the fear—often the reality—of declining property values fueled by opportunistic brokers and mortgage lenders. (Hillel Levine and Lawrence Harmon, in their study of the Boston neighborhood of Dorchester, *The Death of an American Jewish Community*, make this abundantly clear.) In the 1940s black writers like James Baldwin and Kenneth Clark wrote openly and candidly about some of these neighborhood tensions in the pages of *Commentary*.

Even within civil rights coalitions, there was sometimes among blacks an undercurrent of suspicion and resentment in the postwar years about the predominant role played by Jews in black affairs. Some blacks felt they saw hypocrisy in the Jewish help, even when they gave Jews credit for it. A black Chicago alderman, for example, introduced a resolution outlawing racial discrimination in public housing, and a housing expert from New York testified in favor of the measure. But such was the climate of hostility that blacks who backed the legislation distrusted the expert, who was Jewish. The measure was derided as a Jewish ordinance, and much suspicion and skepticism were expressed about the real motives behind it. When the Leadership Conference on Civil Rights reluctantly accepted the weak civil rights bill enacted by Congress in 1957, Richard Parrish, secretary of the American Negro Labor Council, excoriated NAACP leaders for caving in to phony Jewish liberals.[50]

Strains between blacks and Jews were also developing in the labor movement. One issue was what some blacks perceived as the glacial pace of integration. A. Philip Randolph found himself increasingly in conflict with AFL-CIO head George Meany on this issue in the late fifties. While Randolph recognized that Meany was not a racist, he felt Meany lacked a sufficient sense of urgency about bringing blacks into unions. Meany's reliance on moral pressure was not enough; every international affiliate with local unions that engaged in race discrimination should be suspended or expelled.

In December 1959 the *Pittsburgh Courier*, a black newspaper, declared that the failure of the AFL-CIO's civil rights committee to move more aggressively was due to the Jewish Labor Committee's paternalism toward blacks. It singled out Charles Zimmerman, the chairman of the JLC, a vice-president of the

International Ladies' Garment Workers' Union, and chairman of the AFL-CIO civil rights committee. Founded in 1934 as a rescue-relief operation to aid Jewish trade unionists and socialists in escaping from Nazism and Stalinism, the JLC had become active after World War II in the field of civil rights. However, only blacks should speak for blacks, the *Courier* wrote. It also charged that the ILGWU had moved too slowly in elevating blacks to leadership positions.[51] A few years later Herbert Hill, an official of the NAACP of Jewish background, testified before a House committee investigating discrimination in the garment industry, charging that the all-white and Jewish leadership of the ILGWU had sought to maintain their control of the organization in the face of rising numbers of black and Puerto Rican workers. When the NAACP supported Hill, Zimmerman resigned.

Randolph himself was sometimes distressed by dominance over black affairs exercised by groups like the American Jewish Committee's National Labor Service and the Jewish Labor Committee, as well as certain Jewish unions. He was particularly annoyed by the appointment of Zimmerman as chairman of the civil rights committee. In July 1959 Randolph summoned seventy-five black trade unionists and formed the Negro American Labor Committee to speak more directly for organized black workers. But Randolph was also aware that preserving the black-Jewish-labor alliance was critical if progress was to be made. He therefore released a carefully worded statement implying that the *Courier* article was anti-Semitic, noting that Jews had always stood with blacks in progressive efforts for racial justice. So long as he lived, Randolph remained a powerful force keeping blacks and Jews from being pulled apart.[52]

7

THE CIVIL RIGHTS REVOLUTION AND THE CRISIS OF THE LEFT

In 1955 the civil rights battleground shifted dramatically from the courts to the streets. Before, the struggle against racism had been waged largely by white liberal lawyers and social scientists, most of them Northerners, many of them Jews. In courts and classrooms they had led the intellectual assault against discrimination, seeking to establish the principle of equality before the law. In spite of their many achievements, however, the pace of change was slow. Southern blacks continued to encounter racism in schools, in public accommodations, and in their daily lives.

Starting with Rosa Parks's historic refusal to move to the back of the bus in Montgomery, Alabama, in December 1955, local blacks took matters into their own hands. Under the leadership of a little-known black minister, Rev. Martin Luther King, Jr., a bus boycott was begun in that city. Black churches and their members became the focal point of protest activities.

The Montgomery campaign was not the first black-only attempt to develop a southern boycott. In June 1953, even before the Supreme Court handed down its momentous decision in *Brown*, a mass bus boycott had been undertaken in Baton Rouge, Louisiana, by blacks impatient with the slow-moving legal actions of the NAACP. The white establishment in Baton Rouge ultimately worked out a compromise in which two front seats were reserved for whites, the rear seats for blacks, and every seat in between would be occupied on a first-come, first-served basis. This was accepted by local black leadership as a temporary measure. King and Ralph Abernathy, another Montgomery minister, were well aware of the partly successful Baton Rouge model and consulted with the leadership there. Where Montgomery differed was that there, for the first time, large numbers of blacks directly confronted and effectively disrupted the system felt to be responsible for their oppression—and won.[1]

Still, before Montgomery, King had had very little experience as a civil rights leader, and the movement he led only gradually gained national attention.[2] Historian J. Mills Thornton has pointed out that the protest, like that in Baton Rouge, attracted surprisingly little notice. Not until it became linked with what Clayborne Carson has termed the Afro-American–Jewish radical community and the remnants of the organized Left did the southern protest movement burn itself into the conscience of Americans from coast to coast.[3]

As it happened, the American left was greatly in need of a cause at this time. Whether liberals or labor leaders, pacifists or socialists, Communists or fellow travelers, the left had played an important role in helping to shape the welfare state under Presidents Roosevelt and Truman. But by the 1950s, with its influence diminished and its numbers reduced by congressional witch hunts and intramural antagonisms, the left was in almost total disarray. Liberals and leftists who testified before the House Un-American Activities Committee and other investigative bodies often found themselves ostracized by their friends and neighbors. Former *Washington Post* reporter Carl Bernstein has written poignantly about his father, an official of the United Public Workers of America and a Communist, who along with his wife was called to testify before HUAC in the summer of 1954.[4] Many accused of Communist affiliations or sympathies were driven from jobs in government, universities, and public schools. Over one hundred Communist party leaders were convicted under the Smith Act, which made it a crime to teach or advocate the overthrow of the government by force. Others were indicted under state sedition laws. Meanwhile, Democratic socialists Walter Reuther and Philip Murray spearheaded a campaign against a number of Communist-controlled unions, including the United Public Workers of America.[5]

Many disillusioned Jewish leftists became depoliticized. Some responded as if they had been cast adrift. David Horowitz, a principal figure in the New Left and an active supporter of the Black Panthers in the 1960s, wrote that his own parents never spoke out publicly. Like thousands of other former Communists, they had left the party but could not leave the faith.[6]

The Montgomery bus boycott also coincided with Nikita Khrushchev's widely publicized 1956 denunciation of the crimes of Stalin and Khrushchev's own deployment of Soviet tanks and troops to crush the Hungarian democratic revolution. These events depleted the ranks of the American Communist party even further. So great was its loss of membership, Taylor Branch suggests, that J. Edgar Hoover entertained the idea of using informers to gain control of the party at its convention in February 1957. Debates raged among the shrinking core of party regulars as to how to face these devastating developments.[7]

The badly discredited Stalinist left, led by William Z. Foster, ordered party leaders and other stalwarts underground to escape prosecution. Another faction, while retaining its Marxist perspective, sought to "Americanize" the party. Early in 1956 leaders of the latter faction, many of them Jewish like John Gates, editor of the *Daily Worker*, and Joseph Starobin, its former foreign editor, as well as Eugene Dennis, suggested taking a new look at the causes of the party's failures. In the ensuing struggle the Foster faction won out.

According to Irving Howe, the Americanizers stayed in touch with one another, forming a kind of reserve apparatus ready to go into action at the first hint of social ferment. They were present in the civil rights movement and the peace groups as a powerful though informal organizational presence.[8] Maurice Isserman has written that the most influential adult radical group in the 1960s was probably this party of ex-Communists—"a party that could do almost everything that a more formally organized radical group could do in the same situation: everything, that is, except recruit new members."[9]

What was vaguely envisioned at the time of the Montgomery bus boycott was a new Left, though not necessarily the New Left that would emerge so forcefully in the sixties. Thus, the socialist (and bitter anti-Communist) Michael Harrington has written that he and his colleagues set out in search of the black masses. While they did not know much about average blacks and were sometimes guilty of condescending and manipulative impulses, Harrington insisted that he and his colleagues were ultimately good for the movement and for black people.[10] This Afro-American–Jewish radical community in New York and elsewhere became the "seedbed for civil rights activism" in the 1960s.[11]

The figure who now emerged as the critical link between the embattled left and the newly emerging southern black protest movement was Bayard Rustin. A West Indian, Rustin had been raised by his grandparents in West Chester, Pennsylvania, where, as he later recalled, blacks could not walk safely through the streets.[12] When the Great Depression forced him out of college, Rustin, a Quaker, moved in with relatives in Harlem, joining his Quaker background with the nonviolent strain in the civil rights movement. The model was Mohandas Gandhi, the martyred Indian leader who preached a form of pacifist defense against the evil in society. Rustin attended the tuition-free City College of New York at night while earning a living as a backup vocalist for folksingers Leadbelly and Josh White. During this time he joined the Young Communist League.

In 1939 Rustin met A. Philip Randolph and established a lifelong friendship with him. Rustin was impressed, he later said, by "this man of great dignity and inner beauty." Randolph became Rustin's mentor, perhaps representing the father he had never had. Arnold Aronson, who knew both men, remarked on the tenderness of their relationship, recalling that when Randolph became physically helpless late in life, Rustin would patiently spoon-feed him.[13]

When the Communist party ordered Rustin to toe the party line following Germany's June 1941 invasion of the Soviet Union, he quit the party and helped Randolph organize the March on Washington, which forced President Roosevelt to ban discrimination in defense industries.[14] Under Randolph's tutelage Rustin learned important lessons in the theory and practice of building mass movements by combining the themes of racial and economic justice. Randolph arranged for him to meet A. J. Muste. Muste headed the Fellowship of Reconciliation, which had been organized in England in 1914 to seek social change through the "confrontation of ideas." The organization came to the United States one year later and quickly grew into the nation's leading exponent of pacifism. Rustin so impressed the British activist that Muste appointed him FOR's youth secretary, and Rustin traveled widely as the organization's "itinerant Gandhian." In that capacity he helped James Farmer organize the Congress of Racial Equality (CORE) in New York in 1942.[15]

Tall, angular, animated, and full of ideas, Rustin was a popular figure on the left in the forties and fifties. Harrington recalled how he, Muste, David Dellinger, and others seeking the "beloved community" often gathered at parties in Rustin's Greenwich Village apartment, where their host would play the harpsichord and sing Elizabethan songs and old spirituals.[16]

Howell Raines tells that, shortly after the start of the Montgomery bus boycott, Rustin received a telegram from the writer Lillian Smith, a member of FOR, urging him to meet with Martin Luther King, Jr., who had agreed to help organize the effort. Rustin discussed the idea with Randolph, Farmer, and John Morsell of the NAACP; they agreed that he should go. Randolph raised the money for the trip.

On his first visit to King's house, Rustin was stunned to find armed guards stationed outside and a gun on a chair inside. King explained that the firearms were to be used only in self-defense, but Rustin was struck by the presence of such weaponry, which ran totally counter to the concepts of nonviolence that the Fellowship of Reconciliation espoused. Glenn Smiley, an alumnus of the organization, had already started instructing the boycott leaders in the tactics of nonviolence. Soon the message got through; within six weeks Rustin was able to report that there were no more armed guards and that King had dissociated himself from all forms of violence.[17]

Rustin found King an odd and appealing mixture of determination and vulnerability. "I need your help," King told entertainer Harry Belafonte, who had also joined King's entourage. "I have no idea where this movement is going." After several lengthy conferences, King and Rustin reached agreement on how supporters in the North could assist the Montgomery Improvement Association, the central vehicle of the bus boycott. King knew that Communists and other radicals, in seeking to alleviate working conditions in the South, had worked alongside blacks in textile mills and union shops. But he himself opposed Communism and recognized the perils that lay ahead if his actions appeared to be influenced or controlled by leftists. The Improvement Association, which was in fact a grass roots organization, must give the appearance of developing all the ideas and strategies used in the struggle, King told Rustin.[18]

With this remark King unknowingly laid out the future agenda of the black-Jewish alliance. Until Montgomery, Jews had dominated the alliance; after Montgomery, blacks would do so. It would remain a symbiotic relationship from which both sides would draw strength, but no longer would Jewish leaders and other outsiders call the shots. They would work behind the scenes, providing money and advice to King and his lieutenants, who would head the movement, win the headlines, and take the arrests and jail sentences. Later, large numbers of Jews would join in protest activities in the South and expose themselves to some of these dangers but only as a part of the new black thrust and subordinate to its direction. The black masses now became the shock troops and the central force in the civil rights revolution.

Following King's instructions, Rustin worked quietly in the background as an all-purpose aide. He helped set up mass meetings; he did chores; he helped King answer the mail, write speeches, and plan for meetings. He telephoned key people all over the country to drum up support. When things got tough and people needed to be fed, Rustin and King cosigned letters asking for money.

Taylor Branch, King's biographer, saw Rustin as filling a far more significant role than that of a mere factotum. Rustin opened up the movement to the outside world by virtue of a range of experience and influences that reached far beyond the black church spirit that had thus far sustained the yearlong boycott. Harris Wofford, also an early supporter (later President Kennedy's special assistant for civil rights and now a senator from Pennsylvania), viewed the relationship less charitably. He considered Rustin a sinister, manipulative influence on King, who was treated like a puppet performing symbolic actions planned by a

"Gandhian high command."[19] Rustin prepared the way for Stanley David Levison, who now entered the scene.

In the summer of 1956, with the boycott gaining momentum, Rustin introduced King to Levison, who would become King's closest white friend and most reliable colleague for the remainder of his life, according to Coretta King.[20] Levison would epitomize the black-Jewish alliance's new look, just as Louis Marshall had typified the relationship in the 1920s. Although both men were lawyers active in civil rights organizations—Marshall as head of the American Jewish Committee and Levison as an unsalaried official of the American Jewish Congress—they exhibited far more differences than similarities, differences that reflected the changes that had swept the civil rights movement (and the black-Jewish relationship) in the intervening years.

As we have seen, Marshall was an establishment figure, one of the nation's most honored Jews. Levison was a political radical who had worked on behalf of the convicted atom spies Ethel and Julius Rosenberg (who were executed in 1955) and in efforts to abolish the McCarran Act and other limitations on political expression. He was also a financial pillar of the Communist party and other radical causes. Though Levison won no honors in his lifetime, he was enormously influential behind the scenes and throughout King's career.

Born in New York in 1912, Stanley Levison grew up in modest circumstances on Long Island. The son of an accountant, he was radicalized by the poverty he saw in the Great Depression. He attended the University of Michigan—his identical twin, Roy, studied at Ohio State—and earned a law degree as a night student from St. John's University in 1938 and a Master of Laws the following year. Instead of practicing law, however, he invested in real estate and other business ventures and quickly made a great deal of money. His success in the business world did not at all dampen his radicalism.

While Roosevelt was in the White House, both Levison and his brother, a journalist (who later changed his name to Bennett), were active in Democratic politics. When Congress hounded American Communists after World War II and passed laws to restrict their activities, Levison sprang to their defense. According to his brother, he raised money for party leaders who had gone underground to elude Smith Act prosecution. Roy described Stanley and himself at this time as fellow travelers, violently opposed to McCarthyite tactics. He recalled that Stanley had a talent for raising funds from left-wing contributors who preferred giving money to him personally to giving it directly to the Communist party.[21] He lived frugally; causes rather than people mattered most to him, according to his close friend and business associate Joseph Filner.[22]

Levison's opposition to the McCarran Act, which required the registration of officers of the Communist party, and his support of Julius and Ethel Rosenberg brought him under surveillance by the Federal Bureau of Investigation. In June 1953, FBI files listed Levison as a Communist, and throughout his involvement with King and even after King's death, the bureau watched him closely—so closely, indeed, that one early report passed along the intelligence that Levison "allegedly had a hemorrhoid condition."[23]*

Numerous American liberals and leftists were attracted to Communism in the thirties and forties, before the crimes of Stalin were fully unveiled and the failures of the Soviet system became widely known. Many joined cells or lent their names to party causes. However, Levison's involvement was much deeper, according to historian and King biographer David J. Garrow, who bases his account in part on information obtained from former FBI agents, who in turn relied on FBI informants high up in the party. Garrow believes Levison's role as a financial angel for the Communist party began in 1945 or 1946.[26] The bureau was informed that Levison, in 1953 or early 1954, began assisting in the management of Communist party finances. When the party's national treasurer, William Weiner, died in 1954, Levison became the interim chief administrator of its highly secret funds. In this connection, according to Garrow, he is said to have created business fronts to earn or launder money for the party.[27]

---

*In this period the FBI also suspected Communist infiltration of the American Jewish Congress and other left-liberal organizations. Levison was a leader of the congress's West Side Manhattan branch.[24] (Communists did in fact seek to take over the congress after World War II, according to longtime official Will Maslow. They were rebuffed, however.)[25]

Was Levison acting under Communist discipline when he entered the King movement? The FBI, and especially J. Edgar Hoover, believed that he was. For years the Bureau listened in on Levison's phone conversations. It did the same with King after he emerged as the most powerful black leader in the United States. This surveillance remained in place throughout the sixties. A result of this spying was that the FBI subsequently circulated rumors of King's extramarital affairs in an effort to undermine him. But Levison, it would appear, was the initial target of this shocking investigation.

Although he would remain a man of the left throughout his life, Levison (according to Branch) was a fiercely independent thinker, and as the fifties wore on, he did not automatically accede to every twist and wrinkle in the party line. The party, for example, initially derided the Supreme Court's 1954 school desegregation decision as running counter to Moscow's stated goal of "separate national development" for American blacks. But Levison worked with Rustin, Randolph, and others to help implement the historic ruling. For the same reason, U.S. Communists opposed the Montgomery bus boycott, which Levison strongly supported.[28]

Possibly because of these differences, late in 1955 Levison began to cut back on his party work, and the FBI's interest in his activities subsequently slackened for a time. The break was not abrupt, however, suggesting that, as with so many on the left, his radical friendships and associations were not so easily cast aside. Even after beginning his association with King in 1956, Levison continued to make pro forma contributions to the party. He continued, also, to keep in touch with Communist leaders, or as his brother put it, they kept in touch with him.[29]

In February 1956, before joining King's inner circle, Levison, working with Rustin and Ella Baker, a former field secretary of the NAACP, formed an organization called In Friendship to help victims of segregationist vigilantism. Randolph was persuaded to serve as chairman. The group drew heavily from broad elements of the black-Jewish-labor alliance and the Left generally. Levison served as the AJCongress liaison with the group, which operated from a building that he partly owned on 57th Street in New York. The new organization collected money for, among other causes, the Alabama bus boycotters in a May 1956 Madison Square Garden rally.[30]

Ella Baker, the least known of the three, had come of age during the depression. She was raised in North Carolina and moved to New York in 1927, working with the Young Negro Cooperative and Works Progress Administration. Just before World War II she joined the staff of the NAACP and as director of branches worked especially to strengthen the organization in the South. During these years she became friendly with members of the Communist party and other leftists bent on provoking mass action. While president of an NAACP branch, Baker had also been associated with Levison in fighting the McCarran Act. Together with Rustin, they had talked about the need for developing a mass force in the South that could counterbalance the NAACP, whose leadership, for them, was too tame. The three were, in short, authentic products of the New York Afro-American–Jewish radical community; working together they became a strong triumvirate supporting King when he most needed that support.[31]

One of the Jewish leftists who worked on behalf of In Friendship was Arthur Kinoy. In his autobiography Kinoy told of being shaped by the drive, latent in those who have experienced discrimination and exclusion, to seize the tools of knowledge and learning normally reserved for a society's elite. At Harvard he joined the leftist John Reed Society and in his subsequent law practice spent much of his time backing Communists, real or suspected. He defended leaders of the United Electrical, Radio, and Machine Workers of America when their union was thrown out of the organized labor federation for alleged Communist front activities, and he assisted in the defense of the Rosenbergs and of Communist party members tried under the Smith Act. Later he would gain notoriety with William Kunstler in representing the Chicago Seven at their trial for violently opposing the Vietnam war.[32]

When Ella Baker, soon to be In Friendship's executive director, returned from Montgomery and recruited Kinoy to support the boycott, he jumped at the chance to get back into the fray. He felt instinctively that this new struggle would lead him again down friendly and familiar paths. In Friendship, he wrote, "brought those of us who had been so immersed in the Cold War tensions into a close relationship with an exploding new social force."[33]

However, the NAACP and other civil rights groups committed to more conventional tactics were not entirely comfortable at first with the kind of mass action that had occurred in Montgomery. Not long after the boycott ended, Levison recalled a meeting at Randolph's office with John Morsell, Wilkins's second in command, at which the veteran socialist leader Norman Thomas was also present. Morsell recounted a discussion with Wilkins in which the latter claimed that mass action had been discredited by Hitler. Hitler had pulled out hundreds of thousands in public squares, and as a consequence the average peson looked with suspicion on such gatherings. Thomas exploded. The day of mass action had just begun, he said. Roy Wilkins also believed that the NAACP's paramount position had been usurped, and he was worried finally about the possibility of Communist infiltration.[34]

What helped unite the movement's various strands—King's demonstrators, In Friendship leaders, the NAACP, the black-Jewish-labor alliance—was a Prayer Pilgrimage for Freedom, held in Washington on May 17, 1957, the third anniversary of the *Brown* decision. The Prayer Pilgrimage helped bring together the older northern black leadership and the new breed of more militant southern blacks spurred by the success of the boycott led by King. Medgar Evers, the NAACP's Mississippi representative, was elected secretary of the pilgrimage, and Bayard Rustin became chief of staff. While the event was very consciously planned by an all-black organizing committee, according to Coretta King, its leaders relied heavily on In Friendship's racially integrated members. Levison worried about funding; Rustin drafted strategy memos; the NAACP's Wilkins worked the Washington end through his man there, Clarence Mitchell, and two of Rustin's young aides, Rachelle Horowitz and Tom Kahn, helped organize busloads of students from Brooklyn College and other nearby schools to join the black ministers coming up from the South.[35]

As the Prayer Pilgrimage date drew near, Wilkins grew increasingly anxious. Fearing that the White House might interpret the event as a militant power play, he issued a statement disclaiming any intent to exert pressure on the executive branch. In Kinoy's view, however, that is exactly what the pilgrimage was designed to do. He saw it as the first large-scale attempt to secure positive social action in Washington since the advent of McCarthyism. In this he was undoubtedly correct.[36]

The event in front of the Lincoln Memorial was a forerunner of the more famous August 28, 1963, March on Washington. It gave

King his first major audience outside the South, and he made the most of it. The theme of his speech was the crucial importance of the franchise for all Americans, regardless of creed, color, or social class. Both Levison and Rustin had prepared working papers for him, but the speech was basically his own. "I'm better at words than you are," he had told them. A crowd estimated at between fifteen to thirty thousand heard King speak that day. His remarks, though brief, were delivered in the soaring cadences that years later would electrify huge throngs and galvanize an entire nation. "Give us the ballot," he said, "and we will no longer plead—we will write the proper laws on the books." Michael Harrington, who was there, wrote later that people were stirred because King touched a level deeper than speech.[37]

As its New York backers had hoped, that one event helped the protest movement break out of its small-town southern setting and into the national spotlight. The press started covering King's activities in greater depth. President Eisenhower sent word that he wanted to meet with him. Vice President Richard Nixon did, in fact, meet with him. (King asked Levison and Rustin to draw up a list of requests to submit to the Vice President; they coached him in minute detail.)

In the months that followed, a series of Youth Marches for Integrated Schools initiated by Randolph, were organized. They set the pattern for later demonstrations. A number of young activists—Bob Moses, Eleanor Holmes Norton, Norman Hill, Tom Kahn, and Rachelle Horowitz—gained their earliest experiences in protest demonstrations here, as did Wyatt Tee Walker, a northern-born preacher occupying a Virginia pulpit.[38] Walker would later become the executive director of the Southern Christian Leadership Conference.

More than ten thousand young people took part in the first youth march, and thirty thousand in the second. Suddenly the left was out of the lofts and on the streets in the thousands, as Harrington enthusiastically recalled. Beyond the struggle against Jim Crow statutes, he saw a bitter battle against the entrenched economic and

---

*A recent biographer of Randolph, however, is less enthusiastic. She sees the breakdown of the solid black front created by Randolph's black-generated 1941 March on Washington and a return to greater dependence on white support.[40]

social elements underlying the society's racism.[39]* The normally reserved Levison was elated too. The demonstrations reminded him of thirties student activism in support of trade unions. He wrote King that if America's young were stirred from their lethargy, the results would be felt throughout society. The demonstrations were in fact precursors of the later and larger demonstrations of the 1960s and provided experience to many who would later take on leadership roles in the New Left.[41]

Learning that Randolph had thanked Levison for his help in the second march, J. Edgar Hoover stepped up surveillance on him.* Hoover believed that Levison was orchestrating the Washington marches and King himself (that was certainly not the case). However, though Levison was not calling the signals, he became increasingly influential as he and King became better friends.

At first King was guarded but over time grew fond of Levison and his family and came to trust him completely. The two men would talk for hours on the phone, usually late at night, discussing fund-raising, speech making, and civil rights strategy. Andrew Young, later one of King's key aides and President Carter's ambassador to the United Nations, said that Levison was one of the few with whom King could let his hair down and also one of the few who felt free to criticize King to his face. According to King's biographer, David J. Garrow, the secret of their relationship was very simple: Levison wanted nothing for himself, and King knew it.

Rachelle Horowitz, Rustin's aide, saw Levison as a good organizer, fund-raiser, and writer but also as more of a plodder than the charismatic Bayard Rustin. She saw Rustin as the idea man, Levison as the man who put the ideas into words.[43]

In subsequent years, although King would travel widely with his "road buddies"—Ralph Abernathy, Wyatt T. Walker, Clarence Jones, Bernard Lee, and Andrew Young—it was only with Levison that he formed a separate inner circle. On the big questions agreement was assumed and largely unspoken. However, King, the Bap-

---

*Though Levison had retained ties to Communist associates for some years, he finally broke off financial support to the party at a luncheon meeting in March 1963, believing the party to be irrelevant. The next day he told his twin brother that he had been tough and had taken a firm position.[42]

tist minister, refused to accept Levison's agnosticism. "You don't know it, Stan," King told Levison, "but you believe in God."[44]

When King was stabbed and nearly killed by a deranged woman in a Harlem department store in September 1958, Levison, Rustin, and Ella Baker met Coretta King at the airport. While King slowly recovered from his wounds, Levison watched over the cash contributions flooding in in response to King's successes. Several times King offered to pay him, but Levison refused. In a letter to King, he self-depreciatingly referred to the "abhorrent" skills he had acquired in the commercial jungle and declared that by using them in the liberation struggle was as positive a reward as anyone could ask.[45]

King's great strength was oratory, and his New York adviser sought to exploit this talent, even going so far as to seek a sponsor for a weekly half hour on the radio. Although King never got a radio program, Levison negotiated and obtained for him a book contract with Harper Brothers. The book that resulted was *Stride toward Freedom* (1958), an autobiographical account of the Montgomery action. Levison supervised the project, contributed sections (as did Rustin and Wofford), and did not hesitate to criticize King's writing. He told King that his account of the Montgomery protest sounded egotistical. There were also serious omissions and misinterpretations, Levison told him, concerning voting and registration, black self-improvement, and pursuit of social goals. With the final chapter unfinished and the deadline approaching, Levison, Rustin, and Wofford each drafted passages that were integrated into the published text.

Though hurriedly put together, *Stride toward Freedom* was nevertheless well received. It was critical of black Montgomery prior to the boycott, noting especially the crippling factionalism and lack of unity. Its central message, however, came through loud and clear: In effecting social change, street protests by ordinary black folks were as important as NAACP law suits, perhaps more so.[46]

Although King welcomed the assistance of Levison, Rustin, and other advisers, he was far from a puppet in their hands. The twenty-eight-year-old civil rights leader, still inexperienced in many projects, needed their help; but they needed him, too, as an instrument of their social vision. King skillfully integrated their ideas and others' into often brilliant plans of action. He displayed an extraordinary instinct for knowing where to strike next and how to move. In a conversation after King's murder (transcribed by the ubiquitous FBI), Rustin and Levison spoke freely of themselves as having guided not so much King's direction as his mode of pursuing that end. They saw themselves as vehicles for the expression of ideals he either had or would accept.[47]

The Levison-Rustin-Baker team was a remarkable alliance that bore little resemblance to the black-Jewish linkages of the past. Rustin was not accepted in the black middle-class establishment; nor was Levison, despite his American Jewish Congress connections, a part of the organized Jewish community. His Communist associations were known among civil rights insiders, and a number of Jewish civil rights activists, no doubt spurred by FBI warnings, kept their distance from him. Baker, a woman in King's heavily masculine world, felt even more strongly than her two partners that the leadership of the movement must come from below. (In time this conviction would bring her into conflict with King who, she came to feel, like Moses, seemed unaware that it was the movement that made him rather than the reverse.)[48]

In casting about for a means to extend the Montgomery protest movement throughout the South, King considered many options. Like Rustin, Levison, and Baker, King understood that the new thrust in civil rights could not be dominated by whites. Blacks had to run their own independent church-based organization. With this in mind, Rustin and Levison drafted a memorandum that was the genesis of the Southern Christian Leadership Conference. King agreed with their suggestions, and while Rustin drew up an agenda, King contacted other southern ministers and arranged for a meeting. SCLC was to be an umbrella organization that affiliates—mostly ministers and their churches—could join in loose confederation. It did not have individuals as members and therefore would not invade the turf of the NAACP or other groups.[49]

Ella Baker later suggested that the idea was conceived in the North, not in Montgomery. After the boycott victory there was a complete letdown and not much was happening.[50] Levison also noted that the talent for organization came from New York (which is where Rustin, Baker, and he came from), but he added that the impetus for SCLC came from blacks and the genius of King. He found it very difficult to single out one individual as the originator of the SCLC idea but named many other contributors besides Dr. King: Fred Shuttlesworth, C. K. Steele, Ralph Abernathy, Mrs. King, A. Philip Randolph, Bayard Rustin, Ella Baker, and himself. In brief, the SCLC was the result of much collective discussion, though unquestionably the one who clarified and organized the discussion was Dr. King.[51]

With King's approval Rustin, Levison, and Baker drew up a list of prominent southern black ministers and activists who could serve as a nucleus for a coordinating group and sent them a letter. King called them all together for SCLC's founding meeting early in 1957. SCLC was structured to capitalize on King's growing prestige. To finance a central office in Atlanta with a full-time executive director and a paid staff of field workers, SCLC would need an annual budget of $200,000.[52] The operating methods of the organization were quickly established: Whites would be encouraged to support SCLC in various ways, but it would be led by blacks. Indeed, many of King's southern supporters were barely aware of the role of Levison in the development of the organization.[53]

Once SCLC was launched—In Friendship was now dissolved—Rustin and Levison labored behind the scenes in New York to assist King with fund-raising and coalition building.[54] They connected him not merely with the pacifist fringe but with such major figures of labor and the left as Randolph, Norman Thomas, and Ralph Helstein, the Jewish head of the Packinghouse Workers, who brought in SCLC's first big contribution of $27,000.[55] They helped him draw on Walter Reuther for funds and Chester Bowles for political influence. They were also able to guide him in distinguishing between the rhetoric appropriate to an audience of black trade unionists and the etiquette of an immediate thank-you note for a generous contribution from Corliss and Margaret Lamont.

Early in 1957 Levison and Rustin persuaded King to launch a voter-registration campaign. They sent Ella Baker to Atlanta to set up SCLC's office for the effort and to organize Crusade for Citizenship rallies. Levison drafted a letter that went out over King's signature seeking to enlist the support of blacks and sympathetic whites in the registration drive. The campaign would not conflict with NAACP efforts, the letter made clear, but would instead implement the legal advances of that organization. The registration of black voters quickly gained momentum. The Kennedy administration later joined numerous liberal groups in rallying to the cause, and the Council of Federated Organizations (COFO) coordinated the drive in the South. But at the outset, the idea was Levison's and Rustin's.

King had originally planned to name Rustin SCLC's first executive director. He chose not to, however. The Rev. John L. Tilley was appointed to the position; Ella Baker was to replace him a year later, and she in turn was succeeded by the Rev. Wyatt T. Walker. As the protest movement intensified, King came under increasing pressure from Harlem congressman Adam Clayton Powell and from AFL-CIO officials to remove Rustin from his inner circle. King's followers in the South also feared that Rustin's early Communist associations, coupled with his well-known homosexuality, would hurt SCLC. Earlier, Levison himself had advised King against sending Rustin south to work on the Crusade for Citizenship. Now, at a critical moment, Levison did not speak up for his friend. Horowitz describes him as joining the pack of those opposed to broadening Rustin's role.[56]

Ironically it had been Bayard Rustin who brought Stanley Levison into King's entourage in the first place. Moreover, Levison's own earlier Communist ties would ultimately damage King far more seriously than Rustin's undergraduate link to the Young Communist League. Perhaps Rustin, with his flamboyant personality and background, seemed more threatening to King's southern supporters than Levison, who shunned the spotlight. In any case Rustin was deeply hurt by Levison's lack of support. From 1960 until the March on Washington in 1963, he had little to do with King. Levison, however, remained King's key northern adviser. In spite of mounting pressure from the FBI, King resisted severing his ties with the radical New Yorker until President Kennedy himself intervened in 1963 and persuaded him to do so for the sake of then pending civil rights legislation.

In mapping strategy and weighing major decisions, King looked time and again to Levison for guidance or to evaluate individuals, such as Andrew Young, who wished to join King's campaign. (Levison found the young clergyman unfocused but competent and recommended that King accept him, which King did.)[57] Levison also recruited Jack O'Dell, a young black radical he had met working with Rustin on the youth marches. O'Dell was particularly helpful in fund-raising.

This particular appointment set off alarm bells at the FBI, which knew of O'Dell's suspected Communist associations. Levison was aware of this, yet he chose to put King at risk, possibly out of high regard for O'Dell as an administrator but more likely out of hostility to red-baiting tactics. King kept O'Dell on SCLC's payroll and asked him to run its two-person office in New York, where O'Dell spent 90 percent of his time raising money. By intensive direct-mail efforts O'Dell and Levison developed a list of nine thousand people who would contribute twice a year to SCLC. Thus did these two men from radical backgrounds, in another illustration of the black-Jewish alliance in microcosm, muster much of the financial backing for King's efforts in the South. "There is no way to calculate what Stanley Levison and Jack O'Dell have meant to SCLC in this regard," Wyatt T. Walker told its 1960 convention.[58]

In this period another Jewish figure, Harry Wachtel, joined King's movement. Wachtel's credentials were similar to Levison's: a successful left-wing New York lawyer and businessman seeking to use his skills (as Levison had said of himself) for socially constructive ends. Wachtel, who was counsel and executive vice president of the McCrory Corporation, was troubled by his company's segregated work force. He obtained an introduction to King and asked his advice: Should he stay with McCrory or resign? King advised him to stay and fight segregation in the company. Wachtel did so, but he began giving much of his personal time to King, setting up a tax-exempt foundation for him and enlarging his connections among some of New York's wealthiest Jews. The fact was, as Levison later told Young, that only some 10 percent of SCLC's money came from Jews because Jews understandably found it difficult to contribute to Christian organizations. Yet so important was Jewish support that King's advisers considered dropping the word "Christian" from the organization's title. Rustin never failed to remind King to mention the *Judeo*-Christian tradition in his speeches.

Whereas Levison's friends were generally limited to leftists and labor union leaders, Wachtel had contacts in many fields and cities. In Washington, for example, he knew Abe Fortas, one of the capital's top lawyers (later named by Lyndon Johnson to the Supreme Court). Wachtel and his wife joined the Kings on the trip to Oslo in 1964, when King received the Nobel Peace Prize. After King's assassination Wachtel handled his estate and negotiated the contract for Coretta King's reminiscences.[59]

In 1962 Wachtel set up the Gandhi Society with the help of Levison, Theodore Kheel, Clarence Jones, and William Kunstler. Kunstler envisaged the organization as a provider of emergency legal assistance, analogous to the NAACP's Legal Defense Fund; but Levison, Wachtel, and Jones saw it as a fund-raising vehicle, and eventually this is what it became. Within SCLC itself, rivalries over control and for King's favor would soon develop between his New York and southern supporters. There was a certain amount of resentment against Levison among some of the latter, possibly because he was Jewish. Others who knew of Levison's role chose to ignore it.

As the organization began to take shape, King asked Wyatt Walker to head up the Atlanta operation. Walker, a man of abrasive personality, demanded to have complete authority inside the organization even as he agreed to promote the charismatic King. This brought him into direct collision with the New York group. King asked him to meet privately with Levison and Rustin in New York before assuming the post. Walker balked. He saw no reason to do so since the two men were not even on SCLC's board. Nevertheless, they met and reached a compromise at the Sheraton Atlantic hotel. Walker felt he had established his primacy; Levison and Rustin believed they had blocked Walker's attempt to seize power—he wanted to abolish all of King's support organizations in New York and control all fund-raising out of Atlanta. There would, in effect, be two operations backing King.[60]

Despite these power plays King kept the team alive and effective. In 1960 SCLC was still a blueprint; by 1962 it had acquired professional fund-raisers, recruited full-time organizers, and absorbed a healthy dose of administrative talent.

Sociologist Doug McAdam has noted that activism requires not only idealism but also formal organization and informal social networks to structure and sustain collective action. It was the black-Jewish-labor network in New York that helped the collective action in the South. The network provided the organizational skills, funding, connections with the media and publishing, and broader political contacts in Washington and elsewhere needed to sustain the movement. Thanks in part to that remarkable alliance, what had begun as a protest by local blacks against intolerable conditions in one Alabama city evolved under the leadership of King into a massive civil rights effort that would change America forever.[61]

8

THE JEWS WHO WENT SOUTH

Early in February 1960 four black students demanded service at a whites-only lunch counter in a Woolworth department store in Greensboro, North Carolina. What happened next surprised everybody, including the students, who had expected to be ejected. Instead, Woolworth officials vacillated, and their inaction encouraged the demonstrators there in support of the students to stage a sit-in. By the third day the sit-in had attracted more than eighty protesters, and before the week was out, four hundred.

The sit-in movement spread rapidly across the South, and by the end of February, demonstrations were underway in thirty-one cities and eight states. The demonstrations were local spontaneous, and black-led. However, according to Clayborne Carson,
89

the sit-ins were to some extent modeled on tactics developed earlier by black and Jewish radicals in the labor movement. Carson believed that the sit-in leaders learned the use of protest and propaganda techniques from these radicals. They also learned that through hard work and dedication a relative handful of activists could make a significant difference.[1]

The sit-in movement won wide support in the country, especially among Jews. An important question, in light of revisionist and black militant discussion of the subject, is the role of Jews in this new movement. What was the motivation of the large number of Jews who went South?

The Congress of Racial Equality (CORE), revived under James Farmer, sponsored "sit-ins on wheels" to desegregate interstate bus terminals in the South. Riders on CORE's buses—a number of whom were from socialist or pacifist backgrounds and had taken part in the youth marches for integration—were often beaten. Though their assailants were rarely prosecuted, the movement steadily gained momentum.[2]

Farmer was a product of many forces—his family, his resentment of Jim Crow in his native South, and his religious and philosophical training as a disciple of Ghandi through the Fellowship of Reconciliation. But he was also linked to New York's black-Jewish culture. His close associate had been (and would remain) Morris Milgram of the Workers' Defense League and the Young People's Socialist League.[3] Farmer recruited Jews for top posts in CORE, which from its very beginnings was interracial. (CORE's key speech writer and fund-raiser was Marvin Rich, a Jew from St. Louis. Rich was succeeded by another Jewish activist, Alan Gartner. Two of CORE's Jewish civil rights workers, Andrew Goodman and Mickey Schwerner, would later be martyred with James Chaney in Neshoba County, Mississippi.) In his speeches Farmer endlessly repeated what Rich called "the quote"—the centuries-old teaching of Hillel, the great Jewish religious leader: "If I am not for myself, who will be for me? But if I am only for myself, what am I? And if not now, when?"[4]

The success of the sit-in movement spearheaded by CORE stunned the White House. President Kennedy, who took office in January 1961, had hoped and expected that the emphasis would be placed on black voter registration instead of sit-ins and freedom rides. Besides being less controversial, voter registration would increase Democratic strength in the South. Also caught off guard was the older civil rights establishment, which was unprepared both for the ad hoc demonstrations themselves and for the demonstrators' tactic of "jail without bail." This tactic made no sense to Thurgood Marshall, head of the NAACP's Legal Defense Fund, which initially declined to defend students arrested in the sit-ins. Marshall thought a lawyer's job was to gain freedom for his clients, not let them languish in prison. But civil rights leaders believed that by filling the jails with people of all ages and backgrounds, they would totally disrupt the southern justice system while bringing the region's racist laws and regulations into national disgrace.

Some in the protest movement feared that Farmer's resurgent CORE would take the spotlight and funding from Martin Luther King's SCLC. Levison, always pragmatic, sought to play both sides of the issue. Working closely with singer Harry Belafonte, he encouraged the Kennedy voter-registration drive while simultaneously raising money for the freedom riders. He also ghostwrote for King a *New York Times* article linking the freedom riders to the Montgomery bus boycotters.[5]

Meanwhile, another direct-action group emerged, the Student Nonviolent Coordinating Committee. An outgrowth of the Greensboro sit-ins, SNCC was organized in Raleigh, North Carolina, in April 1960. A key element in this initiative was the fifty-five-year-old Ella Baker, who, while serving as executive director of SCLC, sought to facilitate it. Baker had cooled to King's leadership, viewing him as too cautious and self-centered. To encourage more militant activities, she wrote to student activists, praising what they had done and inviting them to her alma mater, Shaw University, to plan future action. Some three hundred students from fifty-eight black colleges showed up. King and others spoke at the meeting, but it was Baker who pressed the students to assert their independence by forming SNCC. They elected a twenty-two-year-old native of Mississippi, Marion Barry—later the controversial mayor of the District of Columbia—as chairman.

The differences between SNCC and SCLC or the NAACP were both generational and philosophical. The earlier groups were built top-down in traditional hierarchical fashion; SNCC started at the grass roots and built up. Most of its founding members were well-educated students from the privileged stratum of black society, according to historian Robert Weisbrot. They had strong job prospects and at the outset did not challenge the basic tenets of American capitalism.

SNCC was nevertheless heavily dependent on the established civil rights groups, and its founding statement linked King's ideal of nonviolence with the Judeo-Christian traditions. The students believed integration should begin in their own ranks, and Jews and other whites did take part in its activities in significant numbers some years later.[6]

Though King could have included SNCC as a youth branch within SCLC, he chose not to. He let it go its own way.[7] Ella Baker persuaded King to advance eight hundred dollars for the new group at a time when his own legal expenses were draining the SCLC treasury. SNCC's first office was in a corner of the SCLC's headquarters in Atlanta. (It later moved across the street.) Initially there was a natural affinity between King and the student activists. At rallies the young people often carried banners exhorting observers to remember the teachings of Gandhi and King. Before long, however, strains developed over the pace of change. SNCC's leaders would come to see the SCLC as too conservative. SNCC's growing radicalism in turn troubled SCLC, which remained the protest movement's mainspring and focus.

In the spring of 1961, Farmer and CORE called for a series of interracial "freedom rides" on public buses throughout the South. The program's purpose was to pressure the federal government to protect black rights more vigorously by showing up the lack of law enforcement. Early in May, seven black and six white volunteers departed from Washington with Alabama and then Mississippi as their destination. Among them was future congressman John Lewis, who told his fellow passengers that human dignity was the most important thing in his life. When he sought to enter a white restroom in Rock Hill, South Carolina, he was beaten by a group of young toughs. Another busload of passengers received similar treatment at a stopover in Birmingham. FBI files disclosed that Birmingham Public Safety Commissioner Theophilus Eugene "Bull" Connor granted Ku Klux Klan members fifteen minutes to beat the riders "until it looked [in Connor's words] like a bulldog got a hold of them."

It is sometimes believed today that as blacks took control of the protest movement, resentful Jews withdrew. There is reason to question this belief. Jews like Michael Walzer, a distinguished political scientist, then a student at Brandeis, became involved in support activities by helping to coordinate the picketing of Woolworth stores in Boston. Likewise, Andrew Goodman, who later met his death in Mississippi, marched in CORE demonstrations in support of blacks both at a New York City Woolworth's and at the 1964 New York World's Fair.[8] Jews probably made up two thirds of the white Freedom Riders going into the South in the summer of 1961 and about one third to one half of the Mississippi summer volunteers three years later.[9]

Satirist Allen Sherman captured their mood when he wrote a parody to the tune of "Frère Jacques": "And how's your sister Ida?/She's a Freedom Rida."[10] Some of the young volunteers doubtless went south for the sheer excitement of participating in a crucial period in history. For others it was a kind of romantic interlude before seeking jobs in business, on Wall Street, or in law offices. Eli Evans, a southern Jewish writer and historian, found that few had experienced poverty or deprivation themselves. Even so, as Evans wrote, they were ready to dedicate themselves to the concept of equality for blacks.[11] Social critic Arthur Liebman saw this civil rights volunteerism as especially attractive to white middle-class students, who could act out their liberal values without endangering their socioeconomic status. Several, however, risked and even lost their lives for the cause.[12]

Older people joined the movement, too, among them the now octogenarian Arthur Spingarn, who sought to express solidarity with the Freedom Riders. Scores of schoolteachers, clergymen, and lawyers participated. The heavily Jewish United Federation of Teachers set up "freedom schools" in Virginia to replace those that had been closed as part of the state's program of massive resistance to *Brown*.[13]

Radical attorneys from the National Lawyers Guild and the American Civil Liberties Union provided legal assistance for those who became entangled in the region's laws and customs. By the 1960s the guild's roster of Jewish activist lawyers included Arthur Kinoy, Victor Rabinowitz, William Kunstler, Morton Stavis, and Michael Stander.[14] Stavis and others had bitter memories of anti-Semitism in the big Wall Street firms.*

---

*Jonathan Kaufman reports that as late as 1956 Columbia law professors hesitated to recommend Jewish law students, no matter how bright, to the prestigious New York firms.

The guild lawyers formed close ties with SNCC, which, unlike the SCLC, did not bar Communists from membership. The guild opened an office in Jackson, Mississippi, where civil rights protesters were continually being arrested for violating injunctions and ordinances. Kunstler and another white attorney unearthed an old Reconstructionist statute that allowed many of the cases to be transferred to federal courts, where emotions and prejudices were less likely to sway the verdicts. In the Fifth District Court in New Orleans, Kinoy won an important decision permitting the use of out-of-state counsel during the critical Mississippi summer project in 1964. Kunstler quipped, "Have writ, will travel."[15]

But the radicals' participation proved troubling to some in both the South and North. Southern conservatives denounced the Jewish lawyers as Communists plotting to subvert the social order; in the North the Kennedy administration and mainstream civil rights groups viewed their activities with some disdain. Among these critics were Jack Greenberg, now head of the NAACP's Legal Defense Fund (replacing Thurgood Marshall), and labor lawyer Joe Rauh. Kunstler in particular was seen by some SNCC volunteers as a self-promoter and troublemaker.[16] At one point Carl Rachlin, CORE's chief counsel, Edward J. Lukas, general counsel of the American Jewish Committee, and Leo Pfeffer, general counsel for the American Jewish Congress, met with an FBI official to discuss Communist infiltration of the National Lawyers Guild. Many of the younger attorneys, they told him, had no experience in combating Communism in the course of their careers.[17]

To encourage greater participation by establishment attorneys, the Lawyers Committee for Civil Rights under Law was organized in May 1964 after a White House meeting. Its initial cochairmen were Bernard G. Segal, a prominent Philadelphia lawyer and later national president of the American Bar Association, and Harrison Tweed of New York. Jerome Shestack of Philadelphia served as the committee's first executive director. He was succeeded by David Stahl of Pittsburgh.

Henry Schwartzchild, a veteran of the Freedom Rides, a former ADL staff member, and an escapee from Nazi Germany, helped form the Lawyers Constitutional Defense Committee, which also provided legal support to civil rights protesters. With names provided by the American Jewish Committee, it sent additional lawyers into the South during the "freedom summer" of 1964.

Through these various groups hundreds of lawyers were recruited on a rotating basis to represent civil rights workers in court and to perform a range of other chores. More than half of them, according to Kaufman, were Jews. In cluttered offices of the NAACP's Legal Defense Fund, the American Civil Liberties Union, and the Lawyers Committee, the volunteers schooled themselves in southern welfare standards, arrest and bail procedures, and justice of the peace rulings. One moment they might be racing up to Greenwood, Mississippi, to seek a parade permit, the next dashing over to Tupelo to gather evidence for a complaint to the Justice Department on jail beatings.[18]

For Kinoy, Kunstler, Stavis, and other leftist attorneys establishment lawyers like Jack Greenberg moved too slowly. Greenberg was in fact more sympathetic to direct action than his predecessor, Thurgood Marshall, but there was constant friction between him and the National Lawyers Guild. For King, however, despite differences of opinion over tactics, the NAACP and Greenberg were indispensable elements in his campaign.

Among the young Jewish lawyers who went south to demonstrate was a New Yorker named Edward I. Koch. Told to go to Tennessee, he chose Mississippi instead because he wanted danger and involvement. Soon Koch found himself defending a group of black and white youngsters who had been assaulted after demanding service at a whites-only soda fountain in Laurel, Mississippi. Leaving the courtroom after one session, Koch sensed that he was being followed. He escaped his pursuers by dodging back into the courthouse and fleeing out a side door, but the incident left a strong impression. "The state of Mississippi is a police state rivaling Nazi Germany," wrote the man who would later serve three terms as the mayor of New York.[19]

Another volunteer lawyer, Allard K. Lowenstein, freed himself from the law's clutches through pure chutzpah. With troopers standing next to him after his arrest on trumped-up charges of motor vehicle violations, Lowenstein bluffed a person-to-person call to Franklin Delano Roosevelt III. The call was actually placed to a friend of Lowenstein's in Manhattan. When the friend picked up the phone, Lowenstein loudly informed him that he had been arrested by police in McComb, Mississippi; he suggested, however, that Roosevelt postpone calling Attorney General Bobby Kennedy at the Justice Department until Lowenstein called again the next morning. Twenty minutes later the police released him.[20]

In these perilous times close ties were often forged between northern Jews and militant blacks. Allard Lowenstein recalled a harrowing night in SNCC headquarters with Stokely Carmichael while angry segregationists circled the building and fired shots in the air. Those inside feared an assault that might cost them their lives. As it turned out, there were no casualties, but the night of terror was ingrained in Lowenstein's memory. It forged a bond, he wrote later, between him and Carmichael, with whom he shared a deep sense of mutual affection and respect.[21] One wonders what his reaction might be today to the spectacle of Carmichael, now known as Kwame Touré, touring college campuses and attacking Zionist Jews in the bitterest terms.

Born into a socialist-oriented family in Newark, Lowenstein at thirty-one was typical of many Jews who went south at this time. With his boyish haircut, thick eyeglasses, and a permanently rumpled suit he seemed the very embodiment of commitment to a higher ideal. In a career that was to end tragically with his murder in Washington in March 1980, Lowenstein would agitate against fascism in Spain, try to clean up Democratic politics in Manhattan, serve as national chairman of Americans for Democratic Action, win election to Congress, and help organize the Dump Lyndon Johnson movement. Hendrik Hertzberg would later refer to him as "a restless samurai of American liberalism."[22]

By the summer of 1963, the voting rights drive in Mississippi had ground to a halt. All available money was tied up in bail bonds. Police hounded the few civil rights workers who dared to set foot in the state. At this point Lowenstein, who had led a drive to integrate Raleigh while teaching at North Carolina State, appeared on the scene, and Robert Moses, the SNCC leader who was seeking a new strategy, formed an alliance with him. Unlike Carmichael, whose inflammatory rhetoric would soon outrage many Americans and terrify others, the soft-spoken Moses was a man of deeds, not words. The subsequent relationship of Lowenstein and Moses would become another example of the black-Jewish alliance in microcosm.[23]

Before being banished from SCLC, Bayard Rustin recommended to Ella Baker that Bob Moses, then a young black volunteer in the New York office of SCLC, work with King in Atlanta. Moses had observed the Atlanta office's disorganization and had alerted King to the problem. Born and raised in Harlem, he had attended Stuyvesant High School, a school for gifted children. Moses went on to Harvard and later taught mathematics at the Horace Mann School in New York. He was a product of the black-Jewish radical culture, having attended a Jewish socialist camp as a child and become friends with Jewish young people from similar radical backgrounds.[24]

While working with King in Atlanta, Moses joined a picket line thrown up by the Southern Conference Education Fund (SCEF), a left-wing group that had been investigated by a Senate committee in 1954. Although King remained noncommittal about the group's alleged Communist ties, he advised Moses against taking part in any more demonstrations.[25] Shortly thereafter, Moses left Atlanta and the SCLC but returned in 1961 to work, like his mentor Ella Baker, with SNCC. Before long he became the charismatic leader of its Mississippi Summer Project. In that capacity he skillfully included Jewish and other volunteer whites and blacks in local protest efforts and quickly won recognition as a major player in the southern protest movement.[26] Bob Moses probably contributed more than any other leader, save King himself, to holding together the alliance of blacks and Jews in the South at that time.

In Mississippi Moses and Lowenstein faced the greatest challenges of their lives. Both men recognized they needed help from outside the state, help that they could only get by drawing national attention to Mississippi. Lowenstein saw Washington officials as being neither interested nor informed about the true situation. He set out to shake some people up.[27]

What he and Moses devised first were mock local elections at which blacks, still disfranchised by the white majority, were urged to cast "freedom votes" for black candidates of their choice. Moses had previously used this tactic in the Delta. It succeeded in focusing attention on the Mississippi civil rights struggle for the first time, while simultaneously raising the political consciousness of Mississippi's black population. All of the major elements in the civil rights leadership supported the effort.

Next came the remarkable "freedom summer" project, which attracted students from all over the United States. From the outset this project was controversial. It was feared that hundreds of white volunteers flocking to Mississippi would overwhelm what had been a predominantly black movement. At first a quota system was considered: ten black workers for each white. This plan was abandoned out of concern that, if word leaked out, white financial backing would dry up. Moderates like Fannie Lou Hamer, a black sharecropper, came to favor broader involvement of whites, since if the movement's aim was to break down the barrier of segregation, blacks should not segregate themselves. Moses told black field workers that whites toiling at their sides would strengthen their cause. Aaron Henry, who had won the freedom election, agreed. He argued that outsiders coming down to Mississippi would have the ear of important people all over the country. At one point SNCC deadlocked on the issue, but Lowenstein pushed hard for it and Moses broke the deadlock in his favor. Moses was then named project director.[28]

Lowenstein traveled from coast to coast, recruiting students through the National Students Association, which he had headed. Addressing small groups, exhorting students and organizing them, Lowenstein was indefatigable. At Yale he worked closely with his friend William Sloane Coffin, the university's leftist chaplain. Barney Frank, later a Democratic congressman from Massachusetts, helped to direct the effort in Boston. At Stanford Lowenstein made a speech entitled "Mississippi: A Foreign Country in Our Midst." It was after hearing Lowenstein in New York that Andrew Goodman decided to go south.

On October 27, 1963, the first contingent of Stanford students arrived in Mississippi.[29] The students kept coming and coming. As many as one thousand made their way to Mississippi in the summer of 1964. They came from little-known colleges and from the best ones, too. Jerry Brown, the son of the governor of California (later governor himself), was one of those recruited by Lowenstein. Another was New Yorker Paul Cowan, who described Lowenstein as acting out the fantasies of his more repressed contemporaries and devising practical modes of expression for the more courageous generation that followed.

In his diary Lowenstein jotted down cryptic notes of events that summer: "Yalies jailed in Clarksdale for violating Curfew; Bond posted, Arrests near 50—NAACP fights curfew—Intimidation general and growing. Yale reinforcements arriving, car due from Stanford." To his parents he wrote: "We are under a reign of terror and it is not pleasant. . . . We've been in touch with the White House, Justice Department, Senator [Wayne] Morse, etc."

Danger was everywhere present. John Lewis recalled that he and Lowenstein were riding in a car outside Greenwood, Mississippi, when snipers opened fire on them. Lowenstein covered Lewis with his body. "It didn't matter to him if he got killed," one activist wrote of Lowenstein.

Such was Lowenstein's towering reputation that Hertzberg, later an editor at the *New Republic*, credited him with hastening the end of black disfranchisement in the Deep South. In *The Pied Piper*, his biography of Lowenstein, Richard Cummings expressed the view that many of the preppie recruits would never have become involved had it not been for their extraordinary and persuasive leader. He endeared himself to them through his wit, his rumpled appearance, and even his Jewishness. He brought the children of the upper-middle-class WASP culture into the world of social conflict and gave them a cause.[30]

Among those inspired by Lowenstein was Andrew Goodman. Goodman spent only one night in Mississippi before meeting his death, along with Michael Schwerner and James Chaney, in the slayings that shocked the nation and galvanized the civil rights movement. The young men were three of the hundreds of black and white civil rights workers who had come South for the massive voter registration drive. The twenty-year-old Goodman had been a college student from an upper-middle-class New York family before deciding to go south. Schwerner and his wife had been there since early in the year, responding to the television coverage of the violence perpetrated on blacks registering to vote in Birmingham. The twenty-one-year-old James Chaney was a black from Meridian, Mississippi, who had become friends with the Schwerners and worked closely with them on the voting campaign.

Goodman, Schwerner, and Chaney—two Jews and a black.

Goodman's parents had been Communist sympathizers and in the 1950s held fund-raisers in their large Manhattan apartment for professors accused of Communist ties. Alger Hiss had been a visitor in their home.

Schwerner, however, was the primary target of the killers, because of his longer involvement with civil rights workers in Mississippi. Formerly a social worker in New York, Schwerner joined the movement when four black children were murdered in a dynamite explosion in a Birmingham church on September 15, 1963. He and his wife first applied to SNCC but were rejected because in Mississippi Schwerner, who sported a beard, would be conspicuous and his wife, a school teacher in Queens, would be a liability. The Schwerners then applied to CORE, and it was as CORE volunteers that they traveled to Mississippi. Schwerner soon earned the hatred of many local whites for investigating violence directed toward protesters and organizing a voter registration drive in Meridian. He was jailed once but continued his activities. The decision was made by Klan members or sympathizers to "exterminate" him, and the execution was carried out on a dark, lonely road near Philadelphia, Mississippi, during the "freedom summer" of 1964. Goodman and Chaney were killed because they happened to be with Schwerner.

When the bodies of Schwerner and Goodman were returned to their families, Aaron Henry accompanied them. His gesture reflected the affection of many southern blacks for the Jewish volunteers. Eli Evans termed the volunteers ubiquitous and talented. He said that in southern civil rights circles, a reference to "Jew federal lawyer," rather than being a term of opprobrium, meant a sympathetic, hard-headed man who knew how to help.

In later years there would be considerable discussion of how Jewish the Jews were who went south. Charles Silberman, author and social critic, did not think they were Jewish enough. He saw those involved in the racial struggle as lacking a commitment to Judaism and those committed to Judaism as rarely involved in the fight for civil rights. He noted that Jewish activists often received training not from Jewish organizations but from such groups as the National Council of Churches. Significantly, funeral services for Goodman were held at the Ethical Culture Hall without the rituals of organized religion, and those for Schwerner, at the Community

Church in New York. Judith Weinstein Klein, a clinical social psychologist who counseled numerous Jewish civil rights workers, found that they seemed far more involved in others' search for identity than in their own relationship to Judaism.[31]

Many of the young Jewish activists were children of affluence in a society of vast economic disparities. Emotionally committed to the leftist positions of their parents, they were uneasy with their own advantages while millions of blacks were living in poverty. One young leftist, discussing her feelings about her Jewishness at a symposium, spoke of the "sickness" in the Jewish communities of New York's Westchester County. She saw people with standards based mainly on money and a very shallow understanding of success. She found nothing to be proud of in this kind of Judaism, whereas in going to Mississippi she found a great deal to be proud of, as well as a very different kind of community of young people.[32] Schwerner similarly often identified himself as an atheist who believed in all men rather than in one God. His parents had begun the shift away from Judaism, and he continued it, deciding at thirteen not to be bar mitzvah. He would later declare that he was not Jewish but rather only a man.

William Bradford Huie, who studied the murders of the three civil rights workers, remarked that it was because Schwerner had no hope of heaven that he held such extravagant hopes here on earth.[33] And for many the pursuit of racial justice became a kind of secular religion. Twenty years after Goodman's death his mother declared that it had never occurred to her that her son had gone south as a Jew; he went simply because at that moment it was the most important thing that he could do.[34]

This argument that "real Jews"—more orthodox or traditional Jews—were not involved in the protest movement has been given particular emphasis by Clayborne Carson. He stresses the role of blacks in their own liberation struggle and suggests that Jewish involvement was peripheral, arguing that there was little in Jewish tradition and ethics to impel Jews to engage in civil rights work or liberal reform generally and much that mitigated against such engagement. The fact of the matter, of course, is that an extremely high proportion of whites involved in the freedom rides and other protest activities were Jews, undoubtedly because of the egalitarian strains within Judaism, as well as the entire Jewish historical experience as an oppressed minority group. There was, in short, nothing that prevented "real Jews" from participating in the civil rights movement.[35]

In the same vein, some historians and black militants have criticized moderate blacks for working with whites and continuing to emphasize the importance of integration in a period of racial realignment. In a biography of A. Philip Randolph, Paula F. Pfeffer criticized his role in the Youth Marches for Integrated Schools as a breakdown of the solid black front created (by him!) in the 1941 March on Washington. This criticism fails to take time and circumstances into account. During the period of the civil rights movement, blacks needed to strip away the barriers that stood in the way of their acceptance at all levels of society. There was also a need for economic and political empowerment, but this need could hardly be met at a time when whites, particularly in the South, could and did engage in physical violence to maintain the segregated institutional structure. The civil rights tactics employed then clearly served the first priority. Only when society began to open up to blacks after the successes of the civil rights revolution could the next stage of the struggle proceed.

It is true that some Jewish religious and organizational leaders were slow to join the new phase of the movement. Their tardiness was due, in part, to their reliance on the technical expertise and primacy of the American Jewish Committee, the American Jewish Congress, and other Jewish civic agencies. Jews have traditionally looked to these agencies to lead the battle against prejudice and discrimination.

But the methods of the protest movement and the radicalism of National Lawyers Guild activists and others proved worrisome to mainline Jewish organizations who remembered only too well how groups and individuals were destroyed during the McCarthy era. Henry Schwartzchild recalls that in 1961 he telephoned an official of the Union of American Hebrew Congregations to ask whether he could use the organization's name in his efforts to recruit lawyers to go south. The official wished him godspeed but categorically refused permission.[36] Ironically, this official would later become a dedicated civil rights activist.

Moreover, even some religiously indifferent Jewish activists may be said to have operated within the Jewish tradition. Rabbi

Philip Bernstein made the point that the Jewish radical who ignored his Jewishness was still the product of messianic fervor: Though he might not be aware of it, he was spiritually wearing his yarmulke as he headed South.[37]

Eventually, virtually every segment of the Jewish community enlisted in the civil rights struggle. The 1963 National Conference on Religion and Race in Chicago, commemorating the centennial of Lincoln's Emancipation Proclamation, helped precipitate broader Jewish involvement. More than 650 delegates from all parts of the country heard Dr. King describe religious leaders as the principal moral guardians of the community and chide them for failing to be true to their prophetic vision.

Abraham Joshua Heschel, a refugee from Nazi Germany and professor of Jewish ethics and mysticism at the Jewish Theological Seminary, became the chief spiritual spokesman for American Judaism. In opening the Chicago meeting, he electrified his audience by naming the participants in what he called the world's first conference on religion and race: Pharaoh and Moses. He described racism as man's greatest threat to man and wondered how many disasters had to be endured before people realized that all humanity has a stake in the liberty of each person.

Heschel's argument was rooted in existential Jewish theology, where the struggle for human rights begins with an encounter with God. He linked the injustice done to black people with the profanation of God's name and accused all who had been silent or neglectful of being accessories to this great injustice. He spoke dismissively of those who cared only for prosperity, calling them complacent, vapid, and foolish, and challenged his listeners to reach for new heights.[38]

The rabbi suited action to words. In the famous 1965 voting rights march from Selma to Montgomery, Alabama, Heschel was a prominent figure—"Father Abraham," they called him—walking alongside King and Ralph Bunche at the head of the procession.[39]

Heschel stirred not only the Jewish religious community but Jews young and old into direct action, galvanizing the whole spectrum of activists from fund-raisers to lawyers. The democratic moralism of the civil rights movement, Taylor Branch noted, touched every corner of the Jewish tradition and experience—from Isaiah to Marx, from Einstein to Schwerner and Goodman and thence to Heschel.[40] Even segments of Orthodoxy, the most isolated wing of American Judaism, were caught up in the fervor. In an address to a Young Israel meeting in New York, Rabbi Aaron Soloveichik, a leading Talmudic authority, discussed the support for civil rights from the perspective of halakah (Jewish law). During the Selma demonstrations, an Orthodox rabbi from Berkeley was arrested on the Fast Day of Esther. Continuing to fast in jail, he read the megillah (Book of Esther), with its recitation of the persecution of Jews by Haman, to a captive audience of two students from Berkeley. In countless demonstrations rabbis were heckled, arrested, and sometimes physically assaulted. A photograph of Rabbi Arthur J. Lelyveld of Cleveland, with blood streaming down his face after a beating in Hattiesburg, Mississippi, was reprinted in newspapers throughout the country.

Martin Luther King was aware of the similarities of his own social gospel and the Jewish religious tradition, and he made special efforts to reach Jews, declaring at one point that it would be impossible to record the contributions made by the Jewish people to the black struggle for freedom because they were so numerous. In a speech at the 1963 convention of the Union of American Hebrew Congregations, he linked his dream to the demonstrated ability of Jews to transcend discouragement and despair. When the Central Conference of American Rabbis met in Atlantic City the following year, King was in St. Augustine, Florida, challenging the city's segregated public accommodations. He met fierce opposition and, knowing the rabbinic conference was in session, sent a telegram asking for support. Within hours, sixteen rabbis and a member of the conference staff, Albert Vorspan, were on their way to St. Augustine. On their arrival they received a briefing from King and attended services in a crowded black church. Leaving the church, the rabbis walked through a gauntlet of menacing state troopers, who "protected" them from an equally menacing mob. In violation of St. Augustine's laws, Vorspan and one of the rabbis sat down in a local restaurant with two blacks. Ordered to leave, they refused and were immediately arrested and placed in a cell with other demonstrating rabbis from other parts of the country. They were jailed for two days before being freed on bail. The case against them was subsequently dismissed by a federal court.

Before leaving St. Augustine, the rabbis, emulating King's famous letter from the Birmingham jail, issued one of their own, asking forgiveness for not having acted sooner and citing silence as the great unpardonable sin of the time. They came, they said, in the hope that God would accept their small involvement as partial atonement for the many things they ought to have done before, mindful of the millions who stood quietly by and watched the smoke rise from Hitler's crematoria.[41]

By the early 1960s some 930 demonstrations had been held in 115 cities in eleven southern states; in 1963 alone, more than twenty thousand people were arrested. King had been seized time and again, as had his deputy Ralph Abernathy, CORE's James Farmer, and SNCC's John Lewis. By marching together and risking injury, even death, at the hands of racist police and civilians, tens of thousands of demonstrators—blacks and whites, men and women, rich and poor—had won the world's attention. Nothing would be the same again in the South, for a true revolution was under way. Blacks supplied the preponderance of workers, the motive force, and the emotional fervor that made the astonishing events possible. But for Jews allied with them, there were new possibilities offered by an aroused and courageous black community.

During the first marches and demonstrations Roy Wilkins and Arthur Spingarn attended the NAACP convention in St. Paul. At one point they visited five hundred representatives from NAACP youth councils, many of whom had been involved in demonstrations or other forms of protest. Wilkins brought word that, as a result of the latest efforts, a number of stores in northern Virginia had been integrated. Following the announcement a great cheer filled the air. Wilkins was lifted on to the shoulders of the young people and carried around the room. Then the room grew silent as the old man who had begun his work with the NAACP almost half a century earlier rose to speak. Recognizing the changing of the guard, Arthur Spingarn, blinking back tears, said that in all of his years with the NAACP, nothing had moved him more than the intelligence and courage and the resolution they had shown. "Don't stop," he continued. "Don't delay. The time for advance is always now."[42]

9

THE ALLIANCE PEAKS AND SPLITS

The black-Jewish alliance was a key element in bringing the civil rights revolution to arguably its highest point, the 1963 March on Washington. But in only a year, as black leadership became radicalized, the movement had split. Yet in the spring and summer of 1963, prospects for the movement and the relations of blacks and Jews never looked better.

On June 22, 1963, King was summoned to the White House to help plan the drive for passage of major civil rights legislation. His mood was buoyant. In April and May he had taken a daring gamble in the Deep South and he had won, leading a tense, traumatic, but ultimately successful boycott of businesses in Birmingham, Alabama. Not only had he and the other boycott leaders forced Birmingham firms to desegregate lunch counters and hire blacks for jobs other than the most menial, but in standing up against Police Commissioner Eugene "Bull" Connor's dogs and fire hoses, they had gained support from an American public outraged by scenes of police violence on the nightly television news. Hundreds of demonstrators, King among them, accepted imprisonment rather than yield on their principles in this most formidable bastion of segregation. King's moving, nineteen-page "Letter from a Birmingham Jail," written in response to criticism from local ministers for having brought civil disorder to Birmingham, became one of the most hallowed documents of the civil rights revolution.

Before Birmingham the Kennedy administration's civil rights stance could best be described as cautious. Behind the scenes, Attorney General Robert F. Kennedy had helped raise bail money for the jailed demonstrators, but his brother's reluctance to speak out publicly irked civil rights leaders. King's triumph pushed the president into a more activist posture, however. On June 11 he sent his long awaited civil rights bill to Congress. Thus, when King arrived with other civil rights leaders for lunch at the White House eleven days later, he expected a hero's welcome. Instead, he received stern lectures from the president and the attorney general on the threat of a Communist conspiracy within his own ranks and a demand that he dismiss both Stanley Levison and Jack O'Dell.

Assistant Attorney General Burke Marshall bluntly outlined the danger facing the administration. The president was about to risk his political life on the civil rights bill; the legislation would be opposed by virtually the entire southern leadership of his own party in Congress; he could not afford to have his effort destroyed by King's Communist associations. Marshall further termed Levison a paid Soviet agent.[1]

Marshall next delivered King to Robert Kennedy, who insisted that Levison was acting on Soviet orders to weaken the United States by manipulating the civil rights movement. The attorney general told the startled King that proof of Levison's duplicity came from unimpeachable counterespionage sources.[2] The president himself urged him to get rid of both Levison and O'Dell. Kennedy described O'Dell as the "number five Communist in the United States" and Levison as his handler, and he warned King that their Communist ties could create a scandal that might destroy the civil rights movement.[3] In fact, Kennedy was not exaggerating the peril. The following month Governor Ross Barnett of Mississippi would assail the administration on the issue of subversion. "Barnett Charges Kennedys Assist Red Racial Plan," the *New York Times* reported.[4]

On July 3 King regretfully fired O'Dell. Levison, quiet, efficient, and intensely loyal, was another matter. King relied on him heavily. He was the flip side of King's personality and his closest white adviser. Although always working behind the scenes, he knew all the players and the moves they made.

Seeking to accommodate the administration without giving up his friend, King sent attorney Clarence Jones to Marshall with a compromise offer. King would cease direct contacts with Levison but would not cut off all communications.

The arrangement suited the Kennedys up to a point. The president felt comfortable enough to announce his support of the upcoming March on Washington, and the attorney general declared publicly that Communists had not penetrated the civil rights movement. Privately, however, Robert Kennedy was outraged. He distrusted Jones, who had been brought into the movement by Levison himself and whose left-wing views and fierce opposition to racial discrimination in the army as an enlisted man in the 1950s had not gone unnoticed. The FBI was already eavesdropping on Levison's phone calls. Kennedy now considered extending the wiretaps to King and Jones as well.[5]

With the departure of Levison and O'Dell, SCLC's operations faltered. A visitor to its New York office in November 1963 found the place looking "junky" and disorganized. King sought unsuccessfully to get Rustin, among others, to run it. Early in 1964 Adele Kanter took over, and efficiency was restored.

Despite his promise to President Kennedy, King continued to phone Levison, according to Levison's twin brother, Roy Bennett. Alarmed, Levison reminded King of his pledge to the president. He asked his brother to visit King in Atlanta to urge King to cease contacts. Bennett went to King's house and delivered the message. King responded, "Roy, what difference does it make whether you or Stanley come to see me? You know you look exactly the same."[6]

The ubiquitous FBI learned of King's brash violation of his pledge and persuaded Robert Kennedy to authorize wiretaps on his home and office in Atlanta. Kennedy also permitted bugging of Rustin's phones. In his biography of the attorney general, Arthur Schlesinger, Jr., insists that the Kennedy motives in approving the King wiretaps were benign, designed to protect King, the civil rights movement, and themselves. To protect themselves against the fulminations of J. Edgar Hoover, certainly. But to protect King? This seems disingenuous. The King-Kennedy relationship was always ambivalent.[7]

The King-Levison relationship was a different matter altogether. But how disappointed the FBI must have been with their long phone conversations! Instead of urging his friend to take radical action, Levison almost always counseled moderation. It was as though he had learned from past experience with often hapless Communists that to get things done in this country it was necessary to work within the system. Historian Maurice Isserman has suggested that the exposure of the crimes of Stalinism forced numerous radicals to change their ways of thinking, discard old illusions, and develop new ideas. For the Left the fifties had been a period of discovery.[8] In this period asking whether or not Levison was a Communist was the wrong question. But Hoover failed to note the changes and remained transfixed by notions of American left-wing subservience to Moscow.

Because Levison was probably typical of the radicals described by Isserman, the advice he gave King was tough-minded and pragmatic rather than idealistic or Moscow-oriented. The organization and development of SCLC, for example, reflected his view of what was politically feasible. Recognizing that SCLC could not survive on Sunday-morning collection plates in southern churches, he established an elaborate New York–based fund-raising network that provided a steady flow of money for King. When another SCLC leader recommended before the March on Washington that demonstrators tie up public transportation, Levison was furious. The movement, he said, needed allies and coalitions, not more enemies. He told Jones that King should abandon people "who shoot their mouth off in his name."[9]

According to historian Adam Fairclough, the idea for the March on Washington was conceived by King some ten days before the president announced his support for an omnibus civil rights law. Although A. Philip Randolph was already preparing a march for jobs, his plan had gained little support. Following Birmingham, King took over the idea and transformed it into one of the most memorable events in American civil rights history. Randolph was overall chairman of the event, but he insisted upon bringing Rustin back in to organize, direct, and orchestrate it. Thus, just as Levison was being forced out (as Rustin had been earlier), Rustin returned to become a central figure in the dramatic events unfolding. When King consulted his advisers on June 10 on the purposes and tactics of the march and whether it should be aimed at the president or Congress, Levison argued that at least 100,000 people had to be brought to Washington for it to be a success. King's New York advisers felt that strong support from the New York area was required to meet that figure, which they thought could best be reached by gaining the backing of religious leaders. The goal, they finally agreed, was to target Congress.

Mass demonstrations were rare in Washington in those days, and skeptics questioned whether the march would be successful. There was also fear of violence and of Communist penetration. George Meany, head of the AFL, refused to take part, and the CIO's Walter Reuther substituted for him. Roy Wilkins, who remained hesitant about the march almost to the very end, was especially worried about the role of Rustin. Working with Rustin to turn out labor was the twenty-four-year-old member of the Young People's Socialist League, Rachelle Horowitz, now director of the American Federation of Teachers' political action department.

Isaiah Minkoff, head of the National Jewish Community Relations Council, was scheduled to be the Jewish speaker. His name was listed in the first printing of the program, but at the last moment he was withdrawn by the council. At the suggestion of Arnold Aronson, Rabbi Joachim Prinz, a refugee from Hitler Germany and president of the American Jewish Congress, was substituted.[10]

In the end, the anxiety about turnout was shown to be groundless. Ordinary citizens of various colors and religious persuasions poured into Washington by the tens of thousands, along with a constant stream of teachers, trade unionists, priests, pastors, and rabbis. Countless groups were represented, but Jewish representation was particularly strong. In fact, Horowitz said that after the trade unions, the greatest participation came from Jewish organizations.

At the Religious Action Center in Washington, D.C., created by veteran NAACP leader Kivie Kaplan two years earlier, the Reform branch of Judaism set up a "Jewish headquarters." The United Federation of Teachers and other predominantly Jewish labor unions were also deeply involved in the march. According to Sol Levine, who organized the UFT contingent, recruitment was carried out by word of mouth. When buses were unavailable in New York, he made calls to Connecticut and New Jersey. He finally got some from Pennsylvania. Buses carrying American Federation of

Teachers members came from Cleveland, Chicago, St. Louis, and other midwestern cities.[11]

The organizers had hoped to bring 100,000 people to Washington on August 28, 1963; nearly double that number actually showed up. Prinz eloquently linked the racial struggle to the battle against Nazism. King's inspirational "I have a dream" speech electrified the throng and helped provide impetus for enactment of the omnibus civil rights bill. It also made a national hero of the eloquent preacher from Atlanta.

In the procession Arnold Aronson of the Leadership Conference on Civil Rights marched arm in arm with A. Philip Randolph. Twenty-five years earlier the two men had vainly sought establishment of a permanent national Fair Employment Practices Commission. What they had failed to accomplish then now seemed within reach.

While the jointly run protest movement created the climate for enactment of civil rights legislation, the black-Jewish-labor coalition helped provide the votes in Congress. King himself had little understanding of the legislative process. When Joseph Rauh, vice-chairman of Americans for Democratic Action and of Jewish background, outlined the roadblocks to passage of the legislation prior to the March on Washington, King was surprised and puzzled by the degree of complexity.[12]

What was required for actual legislation were the talents of lawyers and lobbyists, not those of orators. Early in 1963 the Leadership Conference on Civil Rights opened an office in Washington in space provided by Reuther. Its chief negotiators were Rauh, who had drafted the 1941 FEPC order for President Roosevelt, and Clarence Mitchell, then labor secretary and later Washington representative of the NAACP. Rauh and Mitchell personified the lobbying collaboration of blacks and Jews. Glancing at the gallery where they were seated during the Senate debate one day, Harry Byrd, the legendary Virginia Democrat (and opponent of the proposed legislation), scoffed, "There they are, the gold dust twins."[13]

A quintessential liberal, Rauh was resourceful in argument and well versed in the law. He was also stubborn, unwilling to give an inch. Aronson considered Rauh the architect of the legislative lobbying effort. Rauh, however, viewed the mild-mannered Mitchell as the guiding spirit of the enterprise and himself as the junior partner.

Congress was dominated then by Southerners, whose seniority guaranteed them key committee posts (fifteen of twenty-two House chairmanships). A number of their aides, however, were liberal Jews whose technical skills were unquestioned (and needed) but whose civil rights sympathies ran counter to those of the congressmen they served. Benjamin Zelenko, who was general counsel of the important House Judiciary Committee, recalled that one member constantly referred to him as his "New York lawyer." Coming themselves from backgrounds where prejudice had often been experienced personally, they identified thoroughly with civil rights legislation.[14]

An exception to this pattern of southern domination was the Judiciary Committee, whose chairman, Emanuel Celler, a liberal Democrat from Brooklyn and a longtime battler for civil rights, had spent forty-one of his seventy-five years in the House. Shortly after Kennedy's inauguration Celler introduced a bill that won the support of the Leadership Conference on Civil Rights. Although based on the civil rights plank in the Democratic platform, Celler's proposed legislation was stronger than the administration's, and President Kennedy resented it. He believed Celler was unrealistic. Kennedy thought the bill had no chance of passage and did nothing to push it along.

The legislative battle continued through the summer of 1963. Celler, working closely with William McCullough, a conservative Republican from Ohio eager to maintain the party's post–Civil War support for civil rights, rewrote his bill to make it acceptable to the GOP. But liberal Democrats and the Leadership Conference were dissatisfied with this watered-down measure. The conference then turned the tide, according to legislative historians Charles and Barbara Whalen, by bringing intense pressure from religious and labor groups on Attorney General Kennedy, who thereupon supported the stronger bill.

On September 24, 1963, the two amendments to the legislation most eagerly sought by the Leadership Conference were introduced. One permitted the attorney general to initiate suits charging discrimination by state or city officials; the other established an Equal Employment Opportunities Commission with sweeping powers. On

October 17 Aronson sent Kennedy, who was still opposed to the legislation, a telegram warning him that a weakening of the bill might encourage civil unrest and heighten racial tensions.[15]

As the bill was debated on the House floor, members of the Leadership Conference packed the galleries and lobbied recalcitrant congressmen. The conference's pressure influenced many House members, the Whalens believe. When the House finally passed the bill, Celler described it as the greatest accomplishment of his life.

John F. Kennedy's assassination in November 1963 thrust a new leader into the still unresolved civil rights struggle. Lyndon Baines Johnson displayed none of the caution of his predecessor. From his first day in the White House, he poured all of his seemingly boundless energy into the fight. Johnson had few equals as an arm-twister, and as a veteran of both houses, he knew better than any other recent president exactly how to get legislation through Congress. Though LBJ usually prevailed, even so skillful and tenacious a politician sometimes needed help. When he did, the Leadership Conference provided it. One of its lobbyists attended the daily Capitol Hill meetings of leaders guiding the Celler bill through the Senate.

The Leadership Conference's most important contribution, however, may have been in mobilizing religious groups from all parts of the nation, thereby placing the forces opposed to civil rights on the defensive. Under its direction Protestant, Catholic, and Jewish theological students staged a quietly dramatic round-the-clock vigil at the Lincoln Memorial until the Senate enacted the House bill. Georgia Democratic Senator Richard Russell, who opposed the lobbying effort, nevertheless conceded its effectiveness, calling it as strong a lobby as then existed in Washington.

Mainstream leadership and coalition politics also helped put across the vitally needed Voting Rights Act of 1965. Once again, the black-Jewish-labor alliance played its part. Two factors helped get the historic legislation enacted. One was King's decision to hold civil rights demonstrations in Selma, Alabama. Police use of tear gas, whips, and clubs and the deaths of two civil rights workers there attracted worldwide attention. The second factor was the continuing stir over the earlier murders of Schwerner, Chaney, and Goodman in Mississippi.

With much of the nation demanding action, the Leadership Conference sent a telegram to President Johnson, urging the immediate submission of voting rights legislation. It also called for the maximum use of federal power to prevent further violence and to protect constitutional rights in Selma. Even Republican Congressman Gerald R. Ford endorsed the telegram. On August 6, 1965, Johnson signed a bill granting blacks the broadest extension of political rights since the enactment of the Fourteenth and Fifteenth Amendments.

The impact of the new law was rapidly felt. Black voter registration rose from 5 percent in Mississippi in 1965 to more than 60 percent in 1972. In 1965 there were fewer than fifty black elected officials in the entire South. By 1972 there would be more than eleven hundred. By January 1992 the number of blacks holding public offices in towns, counties, cities, and states throughout the nation would exceed seventy-five hundred.

Although the final legislation was far from perfect—blacks could still be refused service by small retail businesses—passage of the Omnibus Civil Rights Act of 1964 and the Voting Rights Bill the following year were historic achievements that completed the civil rights revolution. The legislative branch now joined the executive and judiciary branches in their unwillingness to tolerate further racial discrimination.

Enactment of the legislation marked a milestone as well in the history of black-Jewish relations. It was the culmination of an effort that began at the turn of the century, when American blacks were just emerging from slavery and its aftermath. By working together in courts, in academe, and in the civic arena, black and Jewish leaders—Joel and Arthur Spingarn and W. E. B. Du Bois; James Weldon Johnson and Louis Marshall; Franz Boas, Will Maslow, and John Slawson and A. Philip Randolph, Thurgood Marshall, Kenneth Clark, and Martin Luther King; Arnold Aronson, Stanley Levison, and Joe Rauh and Clarence Mitchell and Bayard Rustin—had mounted a successful challenge to the dominant racist ideology of the time. They helped create a new climate of opinion that was opposed to prejudice and discrimination in all of its forms. The Whalens wrote that this new public climate, reinforced by the black protest movement, had made it possible for the president and Congress to act without fear of electoral retribution.[16]

Today white politicians campaign for black support. In many cases, they can not win without it. By the same token, winning black politicians often must obtain substantial white backing. The lesson of the early civil rights movement and the black-Jewish alliance is that, while black political success today is sometimes based on mobilization of black constituencies, coalition politics remains the key to winning elections in America.

Even as blacks were gaining political strength elsewhere, Mississippi continued to exclude them systematically from the polls. A *Saturday Evening Post* article on the situation was fittingly entitled "The Deep South Says 'Never.'" To end Mississippi's resistance the Student Nonviolent Coordinating Committee moved in.

By late 1961 SNCC had become perhaps the most dynamic force in the southern protest movement.[17] More radical than the middle-of-the-road SCLC, SNCC was at first run largely by indigenous southern blacks with hardly any white participation or financial backing. (A few highly assimilated Jews, however, like publicist Dotty Miller, a graduate of Queens College, and Howard Zinn, a professor at Spelman College in Atlanta, were involved early on.) SNCC would further involve whites and Jews during the "freedom summer." Not surprisingly, given the enthusiasm with which Jews had welcomed the civil rights protest movement, Jewish liberals and leftists responded. Many signed on as volunteers, and much of SNCC's later financing came from Jews.

From 1963 to 1966, SNCC's New York office, by concentrating on Jewish support, raised far more money than any other SNCC unit, according to its historian, Clayborne Carson. Folksinger Theodore Bikel, who was closely allied with the American Jewish Congress, joined Sidney Poitier, Diahann Carroll, Shelley Winters, and other stars in supporting SNCC through concerts and cocktail parties.

Carson contends that a symbiotic relationship developed between SNCC—which, though uncompromising in its militancy, needed financial support—and a small coterie of radical northern Jews who were attracted by SNCC's militancy and by its willingness to take help from sources viewed with suspicion by more moderate civil rights groups.

A number of blacks who assumed leadership roles in SNCC (and later in other radical and separatist black movements) grew up in the black-Jewish radical culture. Robert Moses was one such, and Stokely Carmichael's early political development had been influenced by Jewish students whom he met at the Bronx High School of Science in New York. There he associated with a number of socialist and Communist youth groups and got involved in politics. The first demonstration in which he participated was on behalf of Israel, in response, as he later recalled, to an anti-Semitic incident. He joined Jews on the picket line.[18]

Many of the volunteers, however, were not upper-middle class WASPs but rather radicals from the North and the West; their coming planted the seeds of later conflict. At heart even Allard Lowenstein was not a revolutionary but a prototypical Jewish liberal reformer, who liked to play the role of broker between SNCC and other civil rights groups. He favored sharp confrontation with Mississippi's racist institutions, not as a form of nihilist expressionism, but to spotlight abuses and force federal intervention. To that extent he believed in working within the system. His legalistic approach proved unsatisfactory, however, to some of the rebellious young people who joined him in the "freedom summer" and were totally radicalized by what they saw. For them Mississippi's voting barriers became visible and ugly symbols of a larger problem—America's exploitation and oppression of the masses. It was not just one state's injustices that they wanted to eradicate but the entire social and economic system of American life. And so they broke with Lowenstein.

Lowenstein could never understand how people he had sent into action could be transformed almost beyond recognition. When they spoke of their disgust with the American government, Lowenstein reacted bitterly, accusing them of disloyalty to an admittedly faulty system to which he was nevertheless committed. He wanted the "summer project" in 1963 (which preceded the freedom summer) to be addressed to American opinion makers and voting rights; he objected to students in freedom schools reading radical theorist Frantz Fanon, who wrote of the purifying value of violence in social change, and Lenin's "Essay on Imperialism." In turn, SNCC leader James Forman felt that Lowenstein was too close to Kennedy and (later) Johnson administration officials. Indeed, he suspected that Lowenstein had been sent into the South to bring the movement under the control of "the liberal-labor syndrome." Lowenstein's stand cost him the respect of many of his white recruits as well as that of some southern black activists, who were themselves influenced by their increasingly more radical leadership.

Lowenstein's position was further weakened by the disclosure of links between the Central Intelligence Agency and the National Students Association during the time he had served as NSA president. Lowenstein himself was charged with being a CIA agent between 1962 and 1967. In retrospect such a conspiracy theory seems preposterous. Whatever else he might have been, Lowenstein was no one's lackey. With the McCarthy movement of the 1950s fresh in mind, Lowenstein did not want the civil rights movement tarred with a radical brush, nor did he want the students he had brought in subjected to charges of the sort that liberals earlier had to undergo. But the fact that the rumor gained credibility in some quarters suggests the civil rights movement's leftward drift.[19]

The movement's growing radicalization produced strains within SNCC. SNCC's militant blacks and the handful of whites who worked with them saw themselves as a band of brothers sharing a life of monastic simplicity and commitment. They came to resent the overlay of privileged northern part-timers, many of them Jewish, who, after brief participation in the struggle, returned to the comfort and safety of their homes, leaving SNCC's core membership to deal with the daily violence and harassment. Lowenstein himself, who was writing a novel at this time, often departed on other business. Once, when he returned with Norman Thomas, suspicions arose that he was trying to take over the movement.[20]

Mississippi's generally conservative black population also feared that the radicals were moving too swiftly. Local blacks were often scandalized by the white newcomers' dress and deportment. In a state where interracial contacts were infrequent and interracial sex was against the law, white and black civil rights workers openly flouted both conventions. "The members of that [civil rights] community were expected to be free," Doug McAdam writes, "free from the restraints of racism and consequently free to truly love one another. For many volunteers then, interracial sex became the ultimate expression of this ideology, conclusive proof of their right to membership in the 'beloved community.'"[21]

In the November 1963 issue of *Life* magazine, political analyst Theodore White, in what may have been the first national report on SNCC's increasing radicalization, wrote that SNCC was the target of penetration by unidentified radical elements that had attempted to convert peaceful demonstrations in Jackson and Birmingham into a violent takeover of government offices. When SNCC announced its willingness to work with the National Lawyers Guild, the announcement hit the established civil rights organizations like a thunderbolt, for they considered the guild a Communist front. When Bob Moses wrote to the NAACP's Jack Greenberg that SNCC would accept legal help from any source, including the guild, Greenberg responded that the NAACP's unit would then pull out of Mississippi. He later modified his decision, but his exasperation was evident and liberals generally shared it. Arthur Schlesinger, Jr., for example, found it unpardonable that SNCC would accept help from the Lawyers Guild.

For decades Jews working in concert with blacks in established organizations had striven to improve the civil rights climate. Many of them now feared that the entire movement might be taken over by Communists. They did not want it imperiled by such ties. Nor were they prepared to see an effort into which they had poured so much emotional energy over so many years destroyed by the far Left.

The issue was more complex, however, than the debate over left-wing influences made it out to be. The radicals had a point. James Forman, soon to become the head of SNCC, argued that its leaders had earned the right to chart their own course. People who have dedicated their lives to the cause of moving history a few steps forward did not need to listen to criticism from Greenwich Village or the Upper West Side that they were soft on Communism.[22]

There was also the issue of final authority. SNCC leaders believed decisions should be made locally; the national bodies that had created the Council of Federated Organizations (COFO) in 1962 to coordinate the voting rights drive in the South thought they should be made centrally.

Al Lowenstein, a strong anti-Communist, was disillusioned and deeply disturbed by SNCC's radicalization. According to David Harris, Lowenstein sought to move the headquarters of SNCC from Jackson to New York as a means of combating this leftward movement. Moses's determination to use the National Lawyers Guild angered Lowenstein, who decided to quit SNCC and advised his Stanford recruits of his decision. The murders of the three young civil rights workers in Philadelphia, Mississippi, caused him to change his mind. His response was not unlike that of other Jewish activists. They distrusted the movement's drift and resented personal slights and ingratitude for their past sacrifices, yet they saw the continuing need for a united front against racism. Lowenstein therefore sought to patch up the rift over the NLG with the NAACP and other liberal groups.

What came next, however, was a fissure in the civil rights movement, one that has not yet closed. The movement—and the black-Jewish-labor alliance that had supported it for so many years—split in a bitter battle over Mississippi's delegates to the Democratic National Convention in August of 1964. In retrospect one might wonder why such a relatively minor matter had such cataclysmic repercussions. The convention itself was a mere formality: President Johnson had the nomination sewed up beforehand, and the only question concerned his choice of a running mate. As it turned out, he also had the general election sewed up. In November the president would lose only six states, one of them Mississippi, to Republican Barry Goldwater.

But, of course, none of this was known when the Democrats assembled at Atlantic City. Instead, Johnson appeared to have his hands full, fighting off conservatives in both parties. Showing surprising strength, Goldwater had captured the GOP nomination with the support of the far right wing, defeating liberal Republican Nelson Rockefeller. Meanwhile, George Wallace, the segregationist governor of Alabama, had frightened liberal Democrats with a very creditable showing in the spring primaries. Working-class northern whites, southern segregationists, and other conservative voters thus threatened to create an entirely new political force. It turned out that this was an exaggerated fear, but for some, especially in Jewish, labor, and civil rights circles, the smell of fascism hung in the air.

Into this explosive mix came the Mississippi Freedom Democratic party (MFDP) with a demand that its delegates, rather than party regulars, be seated at the Atlantic City convention. Both Lowenstein and Moses had helped form this splinter group, and Joe Rauh served as its counsel. (It was a measure of continued black dependence on liberal Jewish intermediaries that Rauh was given this role.) A moderate himself, Rauh was a natural bridge linking the radicals in SNCC, who backed the MFDP, to the Democratic leaders in Washington. As the UAW's principal lawyer, he was close to Walter Reuther, who in turn had President Johnson's ear. With Eleanor Holmes Norton, a brilliant young black attorney who would later head the Equal Employment Opportunity Commission, Rauh wrote the legal brief defending the MFDP's position. Rachelle Horowitz prepared a memorandum on Mississippi precinct organization. Michael Harrington sought support for the party on the West Coast. "To all appearances," he wrote in his diary, "our happy family was once more working harmoniously together."

Behind the scenes, however, Reuther bitterly opposed Rauh's representation of the MFDP. According to Todd Gitlin, a former SDS activist and author of *The Sixties*, the union leader phoned Rauh at one point to say that Johnson was very upset with him and, what was more, believed that if the Freedom Democrats were seated, Goldwater would win the presidency. Rauh dismissed this notion; he told Reuther that he was backing the MFDP as a private citizen, and if the union leader did not like it, he could fire him. Reuther was so "fucking mad," Rauh said, "you could fry an egg on his heart."[23]

Rauh continued to represent the Freedom Democrats. Initially Johnson, who had more to fear from his right flank than his left, offered to make the Freedom Democrats guests of the convention without votes. After the Mississippians rejected this gesture, they began to pick up support nationally. The timing was right for them. Two days before Ella Baker, executive director of the MFDP's Washington office, appeared before the credentials committee, the bodies of the three murdered civil rights workers were found. And when Michael Schwerner's widow, Rita, testified, the entire MFDP delegation rose in silent tribute.[24]

Rauh presented his brief describing the discriminatory and exclusionary practices of Mississippi's party regulars, and he arranged for the appearance of Fannie Lou Hamer, a black sharecropper. Her moving televised account of being beaten while seeking to exercise her franchise stirred the nation. If the Freedom Democrats were not seated, she said, "I question America."[25]

Sensing mounting public support for the Mississippi irregulars, Johnson proposed a compromise: two Freedom Democrats could be seated and given the vote. The other members of their delegation would remain voteless. The White House exerted heavy pressure on white and black liberals to accept the compromise. Minnesota Senator Hubert H. Humphrey, whose liberal credentials were impeccable and who desperately wanted the vice presidential nomination, became Johnson's point man. Bayard Rustin helped persuade Martin Luther King to give the deal his blessing. Lowenstein approved it. Meanwhile, according to Gitlin, fifty FBI men were deployed in Atlantic City, ferreting out information on civil rights activists. The rooms of King and Rustin, as well as the headquarters of SNCC, CORE, and the MFDP, were bugged.

With the controversy still unresolved, Johnson modified his proposal. The regular Mississippi delegates would be seated, he decreed, only if they pledged to support the Democratic ticket (that is, Johnson) in November. And starting in 1968, no delegation could represent Mississippi unless black voters were enfranchised. Rauh, Rustin, Lowenstein, Aaron Henry, and King reluctantly backed the compromise. After the agreement King addressed the Freedom Democrats. There were segregationists in the party, he told them, but it was the best they had. He was not going to advise them to accept or reject the offer since this was their decision. He had talked to Hubert Humphrey, who had promised there would be a new day for Mississippi if they accepted the proposal.[26]

Bob Moses opposed the deal, as did James Forman, then SNCC's director. The MFDP delegates voted 64 to 4 against it. Even so, with the support of Humphrey and Reuther, it easily passed the credentials committee. (Despite press reports of a unanimous vote, Rauh insisted that he had voted no.) The Freedom Democrats charged betrayal, but the Mississippi regulars were also outraged. They walked off the floor in protest, and the state was unrepresented when Johnson and Humphrey were nominated by acclamation.

Many of the Freedom Democrats stayed in politics and became official delegates at the Democrats' stormy meeting in Chicago four years later. Rauh later declared that the appearance of an integrated delegation from Mississippi on the floor of the convention was a high point of his life.[27] A number of those disillusioned in Atlantic City would turn up later as leaders in Jesse Jackson's campaigns for the presidency.

Cleveland Sellers, a SNCC activist, wrote that after Atlantic City, "our struggle was not for civil rights but for liberation."[28] The national Democratic party's rejection of the MFDP at the 1964 convention was to the civil rights movement what the Civil War was to American history: an event after which things could never be the same. From then on in the civil rights movement, the term "white liberal," previously used as a neutral or even praiseworthy description of a person's politics, became an epithet.

The issue that split the movement was a crucial one in a democratic society: how to effect social change. Jewish liberals like Lowenstein believed in working through the system. They were convinced that only by building alliances in coalition politics could needed reforms be won in voting rights, employment, education, housing, and medical care. This was the liberal message, and it was the fundamental strategy underlying the black-Jewish-labor connection. Many blacks in the established civil rights movement agreed. After Atlantic City, however, the strategy lost credibility among SNCC radicals, who spoke angrily of having been sold out. Their motto—and that of the New Left generally—became "Don't trust anybody over thirty." The informal grouping of all shades of the left that Rustin, Levison, and Ella Baker brought together after the Montgomery bus boycott in 1956 was thereby shattered.

In Bob Moses's mind the Democratic party was a creature of both the northern industrial complex and the southern power structure, and Moses turned away from it and sharply to the left. He dropped Joe Rauh as SNCC's lawyer and began to rely more heavily on Kunstler and Kinoy from the National Lawyers Guild—whom Rauh had excluded from strategy discussions in Atlantic City—to help expose local conspiracies against civil rights workers and to demand federal protection.[29]

While not recognized at the time in the euphoria resulting from passage of the Omnibus Civil Rights bill in 1964 and the Voting Rights Act the following year, Atlantic City marked a watershed in the civil rights movement and began the decline of the black-Jewish alliance.

Throughout the history of the black-Jewish-labor partnership, there had been considerable tension and conflict over the motives of the partners, the direction of the movement, its tactics and organizational loyalties. But the alliance had been held together by common goals. In Atlantic City the prevailing liberal-reformist thrust was overtaken by a new and more radical dynamic. How radical would be highlighted by a series of racial disorders that shortly broke out in a number of major American cities.

A new group of leaders had now emerged to challenge the authority and tactics of the older civil rights leadership. While the changes that occurred were both generational and philosophic, some of these leaders—including Bob Moses and Stokely Carmichael—were products of the radical-Jewish-labor group that had been at the center of the earlier efforts. As Moses and the others in the Mississippi Freedom Democratic Party cut themselves off from mainstream leadership and coalition politics in 1964, the civil rights revolution began to be transformed into a race revolution. The effects of this change both significantly influenced efforts for social reform in subsequent years and effectively doomed the black-Jewish alliance.

10

THE RACE REVOLUTION

"The streets are going to run with blood," Malcolm X warned in January 1964. "Whole sections of cities will be bright with flame. Black people are going to explode. It'll be like a war."

The anger and resentments had been building in black slums for many years. A tangle of pathologies growing out of unemployment, broken families, racial discrimination, and the widespread feeling that the police were part of the system of brutalizing repression were the generating forces.

In summer 1964 the looting and burning began in Harlem after an altercation with the police; they quickly spread to Jersey City, Rochester, and Philadelphia. Later, even more destructive uprisings in Detroit, Cleveland, Newark, and Los Angeles climaxed in the widespread violence that followed the assassination of Martin Luther King in April 1968.

Between 1964 and 1968 there were 329 riots in 257 cities across the country. In most big cities, however, the pillars of power were left untouched. Instead of torching the major banks, office buildings, and department stores in the affluent downtown districts, the rioters laid waste to the stores and the shopping strips in their own ghetto neighborhoods. They targeted the small shopkeepers, many of them Jews, as near-at-hand symbols of America's racist economic system. In Marcus Garvey's "buy black" campaigns in the 1920s, in the Harlem rioting in 1935, and in the Harlem and Detroit disorders of 1943, the Jewish shopkeepers and landlords who appeared to be the visible presence of economic power in the ghettos had been the targets of black hostility. The degree of anti-Semitism involved was not at all clear, but once again, Jewish businessmen were in the path of the urban storm.

In subsequent years their situation worsened. There were at least twenty-two Jewish merchants killed and twenty-seven shot or beaten in slum areas of Philadelphia from 1968 to 1972. There is good reason to believe that similar tolls were exacted in other cities. For many of the affected Jewish businessmen and their families, the rioting brought back memories of stories of pogroms in czarist Russia.[1]

As in the past, Jews were charged with price and rent gouging. Even in the best of times, running businesses in the slums is difficult. Most stores are cash-and-carry operations. Pilferage is high, violent crime is common, and economies of scale are absent. Under such conditions, what might appear to be exploitive price gouging could actually represent markups necessary for survival. This is not to say that exploitation never occurred. But the point is that the economics of ghetto businesses were and are far more complex than is generally noted.

In this same period slum landlordism was for the most part a losing proposition, simply because there was nothing left to exploit.[2] Blacks who rented shabby tenements and Jews who owned them were both prisoners of economic history. James Baldwin had written words to that effect a generation earlier, in his famous essay for *Commentary*, and it was even truer at the time of the riots. The Jewish owners of marginal retail businesses were just a step or two above the customers they served.[3]

Bayard Rustin ascribed the attacks on the Jewish merchants to the intense frustration in the black neighborhoods. When conditions steadily worsen, he said, and all improvement efforts fail, it is not the Ku Klux Klan or the John Birch Society that is blamed. First, moderate blacks are held responsible, and then all those who have worked over the years for civil rights become the enemy. In short, blame is shifted to those who, though not black, have had faith in the community and a visible stake in its well-being.[4]

Ironically, the Jewish-operated stores that were burned and looted had often been islands of stability in a sea of social torment. Black economist Walter Williams knew this from personal experience. While living in a public housing project in crime-ridden North Philadelphia, he was spurred to make something more of himself by a neighborhood Jewish grocer he worked for who emphasized the importance of education. Comedian and social activist Dick Gregory also remembers the positive (if ambivalent) impact of another Jewish grocer, whom everybody called Mr. Ben, in the St. Louis neighborhood where Gregory grew up. Though his peaches were often rotten and the bread was not fresh, Gregory wrote in *Nigger*, his autobiography, Mr. Ben could be counted on when it came down to the nitty-gritty. At the start of the Jewish holidays, he would remove from his shelves all the food that would spoil and take it to the Gregorys. Before Christmas he would send over meat, well aware that he might never see his money.[5]

In today's climate of racial and ethnic ferment, such reminiscences seem almost quaint. And memories like these are fast receding, as most of the small, Jewish-owned shops and stores of Dick Gregory's day have closed or been sold, many of them to Koreans or other Asians. Following the riots of the 1960s, those Jewish merchants not forced or burned out elected to leave almost en masse. With few exceptions their children chose not to work in neighborhoods that were openly hostile to whites, and by the 1990s hardly any of these small white-owned businesses were left in the urban slums. When the Jews moved out, according to a local black businessman of North Philadelphia, the neighborhood became like a ghost town.[6]*

During the racial disorders of the 1960s, writers both black and Jewish attempted to come to grips with the fear and anxiety that had been aroused. The result was a new phase of open disagreement

*Ironically, as Asians took over or started businesses, the cycle of distrust and hostility was repeated. Nevertheless, the durability of the anti-Jewish stereotype remained. During a recent Southwest Philadelphia demonstration in front of a Korean-owned store, following the shooting and death of a black man who pulled a knife on the owner's son, one black protestor yelled, "Behind every Oriental guy there's a Jew."[7]

between black and Jewish intellectuals. *Commentary* editor Norman Podhoretz, in a remarkable essay written just prior to the urban disorders, cast the black-Jewish relationship in an entirely new light. "My Negro Problem—and Ours," published in July 1963, focused, not on themes of brotherhood or fellowship, but on the cultural chasm separating Jews and blacks. Podhoretz, writing from his own experience of growing up poor in Brooklyn, told of being harassed and robbed by young blacks, and he described his feelings of envy for their undisciplined upbringing, which seemed to embody the free, reckless, masculine, and erotic values of the street.[8] In his version of the black-Jewish relationship, however, Jews were the victims. Ironically, Podhoretz—not yet a neoconservative—suggested that the only way to deal with the race problem in America was through miscegenation. His piece aroused a storm of disapproval and was the occasion for Harold Cruse's sharp response, "My Jewish Problem and Theirs." In his essay Cruse described his mistreatment by Jewish teachers as he grew up in Harlem and the subordination later of black intellectuals to Jewish control.

If Podhoretz accurately gauged emerging Jewish fears and suspicions about blacks, it was James Baldwin who captured the tone of the black struggle in transition. Denouncing the sterility and decay of the racist society of his Harlem youth, Baldwin wrote—at the height of the 1960s racial disorders—"Letter from a Region in My Mind"; it was time, he said, for blacks to control their own destiny, end the racial nightmare, make the country their own, and change the history of the world. "God gave us Noah and the rainbow sign. No more water, the fire next time." Frustrated by the failure of the hope and promise that the civil rights revolution had once offered, Baldwin caught the growing anger and resentments of virtually all segments of the black community.

The Fire Next Time was the title selected for the book that resulted from the expansion of his essay. Baldwin, it is true, struggled to hold onto the dream. To create one nation was difficult enough, he declared; there was no need to create two, one black and one white.[9] But it was not long before militant blacks began repeating one of the essay's most haunting questions: "Do I really want to be integrated into a burning house?"

Podhoretz and Baldwin can be seen as emblematic of the changing interaction between blacks and Jews. Over drinks, each had influenced the other in the writing of their essays. Baldwin had persuaded Podhoretz to write of his youth in Brooklyn, and Podhoretz had convinced Baldwin to write the autobiographical essay that helped to make his reputation. Baldwin's first essay had appeared in *Commentary* in 1948, and three years later, while still in his twenties, Baldwin published his first collection of essays, *Notes of a Native Son*. Joseph Epstein, editor of *The American Scholar*, has written that on the basis of these essays, he thought Baldwin would have been the last to turn to polemics. In "Everybody's Protest Novel" Baldwin had sharply criticized Harriet Beecher Stowe's *Uncle Tom's Cabin*; in "Many Thousands Gone" he was equally critical of Richard Wright's *Native Son*, declaring that it was not the writer's task to propagandize for his people.

By the 1960s, however, Baldwin had advanced far beyond his early Jewish tutelage and the little magazines published by Jews to become America's most widely read black author. Some argued that Baldwin had grown and found his voice; others thought he had traded his nuanced viewpoint—and even talent—for, in Epstein's words, a "pot of message" and refinement of the art of victimization.[10] No longer did he demonstrate sympathy for the sometimes comparable plight of blacks and Jews in the slums. Instead he became the chief spokesman for the new black extremism, and *The Fire Next Time* became the model for a new generation of black writers seeking to vent their rage against white society.

Jewish concerns over deteriorating race relations at home were exacerbated by events in the Middle East, starting with the Six-Day War in June 1967. Six years later, in 1973, even the most assimilated and secular Jews were deeply shaken when Arab armies, striking just as Israelis were observing Yom Kippur, the holiest day of the Jewish year, threatened to drive them into the sea. Novelist Henry Roth later told the readers of *Midstream* that after breaking with Communism, he still adhered to leftist causes as a form of Jewish identity but that the Six-Day War had forced him to recover certain buried tribal loyalties. Simultaneously, the successes scored by Israeli armies, as well as photographs of heavily armed soldiers praying at the Wailing Wall, generated a fresh sense of Jewish group pride.[11]

Occurring at the same time as the rioting in major American cities, the Six-Day War underlined the issue of survival. For many Jews concern over Israel's security became paramount. It would modify (when it did not replace) the political liberalism that had shaped their thinking in the immigrant and postimmigrant generations. Support for Israel, as Nathan Glazer noted, became the "secular religion" of many Jews.[12]

For blacks, too, the decade proved crucial. The failure of the civil rights revolution to reach far enough into the black ghettos to lift its residents into the middle class, along with the intensification of the problems there, caused many to turn their back on integration and look inward, in the manner that black nationalists from Garvey on had urged. For many at all levels the struggle had evolved into a search for black empowerment, identity, and pride—a search that, whatever its similarities to the Jewish experience, could not be shared by Jews and other whites.

Black nationalism was not the philosophy of the ordinary middle-class black. But black solidarity was, and it had enormous appeal. What St. Clair Drake and Horace Cayton had written about Chicago in the 1940s in *Black Metropolis* still held true. "Frustrated in their isolation from the main streams of American life, and in their impotence to control their fate decisively, Negroes tend to admire an aggressive Race Man even when his motives are suspect. They will applaud him, because in the face of the white world, he remains 'proud of his race' and always tries to uphold it whether it is good or bad, right or wrong."

Out of the growing rage and frustration now came a new generation of Race Men, who diverged dramatically from the path set by earlier moderates. The new urban radicals—Stokeley Carmichael, H. Rap Brown, Malcolm X, Eldridge Cleaver, Amiri Baraka (formerly LeRoi Jones), Claude Brown, Julius Lester, Cecil B. Moore, Ron Karenga, and others—consciously sought to represent street-level blacks. They articulated the anger building up in black neighborhoods and transformed the civil rights movement into a race revolution.

Malcolm X, the most important of these figures, sprang to prominence as the disciple of Elijah Muhammad, head of the Nation of

Islam. Elijah Muhammad's extremist outlook was similar to that of Marcus Garvey. The son of a Georgia sharecropper, he bore the name Elijah Poole and was a Detroit autoworker in the 1930s when he met an Arab silk peddler named Wali Farrad.* Farrad introduced him to Muslim texts and told him he (Farrad) was the Mahdi, the Muslim messiah. After Farrad disappeared—his followers said he had gone off to Mecca—Poole assumed the name Muhammad and took the leadership of Farrad's inchoate organization. He taught his followers that white "blue-eyed devils" had imposed Christianity on black people to keep them under heel. His message resounded among disillusioned slum dwellers and those on the edge of society. By the 1960s Muhammad's Lost Found Nation and its neatly dressed adherents had swept across black America, gaining wide appeal by asserting the superiority of blacks and the rejection of all things white.[13]

During this period Malcolm X became a powerful force in his own right, giving voice to the frustrations and despair of blacks in the northern ghettos. He claimed that his father, an admirer of Garvey, had been killed by hostile whites (a recent biography casts doubt on his recollection), and Malcolm's early life was that of a street hustler, pimp, and small-time robber who educated himself in prison. Bright, able, and charismatic, he grew beyond his tawdry environment and by the mid sixties proved himself capable of stirring masses of black men and women. His best-selling autobiography, written with the assistance of Alex Haley—whose own book (and later television series) *Roots* made a major contribution to the development of black pride and identity—was a moving personal account of what it meant to be poor and black in a racist society. The autobiography quickly became an American classic.

After he broke with Elijah Muhammad and made a pilgrimage to Mecca, Malcolm moderated his black nationalist views. His assassination in New York on February 21, 1965, transformed him from a radical of limited appeal into a beloved and inspirational African-American leader. Books, plays, a feature film, and even an opera have celebrated his life.[14] Just before he died, Malcolm indicated that he recognized that he and King had important

---

*He was also known as Fard Muhammad or W. D. Fard.

but different roles in the black liberation struggle, and he told Haley that he hoped his voice would become a force for reconciliation. Throughout most of his public career, though, Malcolm scorned King's philosophy of nonviolent protest and attacked King's tactics in civil rights demonstrations as mealymouthed and worse. "Any Negro who teaches other Negroes to turn the other cheek," he said of King, "is disarming the Negro."

Like Garvey and other black nationalists, Malcolm denounced Jews as exploiters of blacks. At a meeting in 1959, he characterized them as among the worst of the devils. Jews, he wrote in his autobiography, were hypocrites, whose claim to be friends of the black man was intended only to focus the prejudice in America upon the Negro, thereby diverting it from themselves. He called Jewish businessmen in Harlem colonialists and deeply resented them. Two years later he held an off-the-record meeting with Klan leaders in Atlanta, seeking their support for a Muslim effort to create a Muslim enclave in the United States. He told the Klansmen that the Muslims were as anxious to maintain segregation as the Klan, and according to an FBI report, he assured them it was Jews who were behind the integration movement.

Malcolm encouraged his followers to develop linkages with peoples of color in Africa and Asia, joining forces with the world's non-Caucasian majority.[15] He also adopted the Muslim ideological and religious position toward Israel, namely, that the Jews, with the help of American and European Christians, had stolen a centuries-old Muslim homeland and taken it for themselves. He charged that American aid to Israel was taken from the pockets of American blacks. It was Malcolm, as Earl Raab has pointed out, who more than anyone else put together all the Third World pieces, at home and abroad, that would soon take root among the black intelligentsia and elsewhere.[16] Jews, of course, especially those who had worked for civil rights, were furious at finding themselves condemned and indeed consigned to the wrong side of history.

In 1966, after Malcolm's murder, a group of young California militants, inspired by him and headed by Huey P. Newton and Bobby Seale, organized the Black Panther party, which was prepared to defend blacks by force, if necessary. "We've never advocated violence, violence is inflicted upon us," Newton told a reporter in June 1970 after a California court overturned his conviction for killing an Oakland police officer. However, he did advocate self-defense for himself and for black people generally. Eldridge Cleaver was even more confrontational. The choice before the country, he said, was complete freedom for black people or complete destruction for America.

Writing of Malcolm X and Huey Newton in the *Village Voice*, black writer Stanley Crouch has described them as defending the downtrodden against the powerful. Certainly their disaffection was not surprising, given the frequent indifference of the FBI and other law-enforcement authorities to violations of civil rights statutes. But despite self-help breakfast programs of the Black Panthers, the gangster tendencies of these new forces were unmistakable, and their dissolution was well illustrated by the spectacle of Newton some years later sitting in the Great Hall of China, snorting cocaine, and raving unintelligibly.[17]

At the same time, the second half of the 1960s witnessed what historian Robert Weisbrot has called an intellectual and cultural black renaissance not unlike what occurred in the 1920s. Langston Hughes caught the tenor of the earlier period in a poem calling on his people to seize their own identities from white image makers and write and sing about themselves.

Someday somebody'll
Stand up and talk about me,
And write about me,
Black and beautiful—
And sing about me!
I reckon it'll be
Me, myself!
Yes, It'll be me.[18]

Weisbrot believes the later period was more radical. The cultivation of distinct black values often glided into arguments for separate black institutions, denunciations of white liberals, and calls to revolution. The rebellion against integration provided an ideological thoroughfare that linked the realms of cultural nationalism and black power politics.[19]

Many of the black writers and activists who emerged in the sixties coupled calls for black pride with vicious attacks on whites.

Jews were often singled out. Julius Lester, who worked with SNCC in the South and later converted to Judaism, said that neither Jews nor the State of Israel deserved any special sympathy for the six million of their number murdered by the Nazis. Others recalled the black rallying cry: "We got to take Harlem out of Goldberg's pocket." The *Liberator* magazine published a series of articles exposing what it said was Jewish exploitation of Harlemites and Jewish imperialism worldwide. Amiri Baraka spoke of Jews as double-crossers and called for a body of poetry whose topics and focus could become a part of the destruction of Jews.[20]

The publication of Harold Cruse's *The Crisis of the Negro Intellectual* in 1967 gave a degree of respectability to the radicals' cry for racial separation. He urged black intellectuals to break away from the domination of white intellectuals, especially from Jews, who he claimed played a major role in influencing black thought. Some whites were enthralled. Christopher Lasch, for example, wrote that "when all the manifestos of the sixties are forgotten, this book will survive as a monument of historical analysis." The *Kirkus Review* received *The Crisis of the Negro Intellectual* rapturously, sympathizing with its attack against the advocates of integration, who had misdirected blacks from truly radical and creative goals. Before long, Cruse's writings became a source in the burgeoning Afro-American studies programs on college campuses, foreshadowing the revisionism of black intellectuals of the eighties and nineties. Though Jews had mastered the art of playing both ends against the middle, he argued, the average Negro would never buy the line that blacks and Jews were in the same boat.

In the 1960s young blacks began attending predominantly white colleges and universities in unprecedented numbers. Since the civil rights movement had sought to encourage minority enrollment, liberals welcomed the enormous increase. Despite their gains, however, many black students were dissatisfied with the pace of change and resentful of their social isolation on campus. Their dissatisfaction and resentment were often reflected in their dress, speech and deportment.

More significant in the long run, though, were the curricular changes. Prior to the sixties none of the most prestigious schools paid much attention to African-American culture. Black studies programs were unknown, and black literature, as such, could rarely be found in a syllabus. Moreover, few black students were pressing for such a focus. Houston Baker recalls sitting next to Stokely Carmichael in a Howard University literature class taught by novelist Toni Morrison early in the 1960s. Carmichael questioned the relevance of studying the *Odyssey* when the class could be doing a Marxist critique of Western literature; Baker recalled wishing Stokely would shut up so that Morrison could get on with her lecture. Baker, however, soon found a mentor who exposed him to black literature, and as a professor of English at the University of Pennsylvania, Baker later became a major figure in the effort to redefine the literary canon.[21]

Baker's experience was not unusual. More black students gradually got caught up in the movement. Throughout the late sixties and subsequently, they could be seen clutching Eldridge Cleaver's *Soul on Ice*, Malcolm X's autobiography, Cruse's *The Crisis of the Negro Intellectual*, and Frantz Fanon's *The Wretched of the Earth*. College administrators sought to accommodate their black students by setting up black dorms and Afro-American studies programs, usually separate from established history and literature departments. In 1969 Cruse was one of the founders of the Afro-American Studies Program at the University of Michigan. By the early seventies some five hundred colleges and universities had such programs.[22]

The latter half of the 1960s brought the development of a new black history that sought to cast the Afro-American experience in this country in a fresh light. Building on the pioneering work of black historians like Carter Woodson and W. E. B. Du Bois, as well as left-wing Jewish scholars like Herbert Aptheker and Philip Foner, the new black history developed by white and black scholars argued that blacks needed to be studied as healthy subjects who had played significant roles in their own liberation rather than as maimed and passive objects. Further, their contribution needed to be examined in the context of the nation's political history.[23]

The movement was long overdue. Besides teaching important lessons to whites, the new studies gave blacks a fresh understanding of their own past, an awareness that could strengthen their resolve in dealing with contemporary problems. "One must learn how to be black in America," Henry Louis Gates, the black scholar-activist, would later declare.[24]

On many campuses, however, the movement led to bitter faculty infighting over teaching authority and positions. Some blacks insisted that white professors, no matter how well qualified, could not teach black history. Only black professors could understand the black experience and transmit a firm sense of racial pride to the growing number of black students. Since many of the white professors of black history came from Jewish backgrounds—they had entered the academy in the postwar years as part of their commitment to liberal reform—another area of conflict between blacks and Jews opened.*

One beneficiary of this process was Leonard Jeffries, Jr., who in 1991 became embroiled with critics, Jewish and otherwise, for charging that Jews bore a heavy responsibility for slavery in this country and that they had subordinated and exploited blacks in the movie industry. In 1971, as he was finishing his doctoral thesis, City College was organizing departments of ethnic studies. This had been one of the demands of black militants, who had closed down the campus after having taken over its buildings in 1969. The search committee recommended Dr. Jeffries, who, despite modest academic credentials, became the tenured chairman of the black studies department. Although he became a popular campus lecturer, he rarely published. His role, he said, was to disseminate the ideas of others.[26]

Sometimes these collisions spilled over into professional meetings and conventions. Robert Starobin, a Jewish left-wing historian and supporter of the Black Panthers, rose to deliver a paper entitled "Privileged Bondsmen and the Process of Accommodation" at one such meeting; Vincent Harding, a black-nationalist colleague, walked out. Starobin's paper was subjected to merciless

*While formal studies of this friction seem to be lacking, there is reason to believe that a younger generation of Jewish scholars of the black experience either left the field or were forced out. As director of the American Jewish Committee, I handled the complaint of one scholar at a local university. Though I won for him a small monetary settlement, he was not offered the job in question and left the field, never to return.[25]

ridicule. A biography of Starobin said that in the classroom many black students resented him, feeling that the color of his skin disqualified him from teaching the course. They often heckled, jeered, or walked out of his lectures.[27] Gilbert Osofsky, another Jewish scholar and author of a highly regarded book, *Harlem: The Making of a Ghetto*, wanted to write a biography of A. Philip Randolph. He was warned away, according to a colleague, because Randolph was considered "a black topic."

Other left-wing white scholars who had sought to make common cause with blacks were not spared. Herbert Gutman had found a pattern of two-parent households among southern blacks prior to and even after the Civil War. His research took issue with the celebrated Moynihan report on the breakdown of the Negro family. Yet Gutman was shouted down at a meeting of the Association for the Study of Negro Life and History in 1969. Not surprisingly, he was shattered. He told a colleague he could not understand why people would not just forget that he was white and listen to what he was saying, especially since he was lending support to the black liberation movement.

Nevertheless, Gutman continued to teach and write about black history. He and other senior scholars from Jewish backgrounds—for example, Lawrence Levine and Leon Litwack, sometimes described as the "bull elephants"—won praise both for their determination to remain in the field and for the quality of their research and writing. Indeed, Litwack's *Been in the Storm So Long* won a Pulitzer Prize.[28]

Among a number of the newer historians, however, ideology was now put to the use of "group uplift." One of them frankly declared that he wrote subjective history in order to criticize and condemn white America. In his introduction to *There Is a River*, Vincent Harding wrote that his first commitment was not to such ambiguous abstractions as objectivity and scholarship but to the lively hope of a people struggling for a chance to be whole. Harding did not mince words: "We work for control of our own story."

It was a time, too, to settle old scores. In *The Crisis of the Negro Intellectual*, Cruse bitterly attacked Aptheker and other assimilated Jewish Communists for assuming the mantle of spokesman on black affairs, "thus burying the potential for a true black radicalism under a mound of white intellectual paternalism."[29]

Although sympathetic to the new black history, many mainstream white historians had reservations about its exclusivity. At the Organization of American Historians convention in 1969, C. Vann Woodward, an old-fashioned southern white liberal, declared in his presidential address that white historians all too often wrote black history as a record of what white men believed, thought, and did about blacks. A corrective was needed, he said. But he added that radicalism was not a sufficient qualification for the exclusive preemption of the subject. A number of black historians agreed, including John Hope Franklin and Nathan Huggins. While enthusiastic about the new black history, they were also critical of nonobjective methods. They feared the politicization of the field and its segregation from mainstream history.[30]

Similar battles in ethnic succession were waged in the late sixties and subsequent years over leadership of urban school districts, public welfare departments, and human rights organizations where Jews had been dominant figures. Blacks sought now to wrest control of these positions, and very often they succeeded.

Moderates like Bayard Rustin recoiled at many of the developments that made headlines in the 1960s: the ghetto uprisings, the West Coast radicalism, and the spread of black nationalism. He saw these developments as dysfunctional and even dangerous. In speeches and newspaper articles Rustin warned that it was pointless to ignore the harsh realities of American demography and capitalism. The way out of the black dilemma, he said, lay not in adopting colorful hair styles and costumes but in dealing with basic problems of education, employment, and housing. These problems could only be solved, he maintained, in alliance with the liberal white majority.[31]

By mid decade, however, some moderate and integrationist black leaders were beginning to move to left-nationalist positions, their negativism differing only in degree from that of radical blacks. They were not, of course, the only ones moving leftward at this time. So were many Hispanics, white students, and Native Americans. But blacks were the most visible. In the *New York Times* psychologist Kenneth Clark, who had worked closely with the American Jewish Committee and other civil rights groups, charged that what he called the cancer of racism had advanced too far to be cured. At a special conference sponsored by the Academy of Arts and Sciences, Clark, sounding much like James Baldwin, castigated the Myrdalian analysis of race relations. "The American dilemma is one of power," he said. He added that Martin Luther King's appeal to the white conscience had become irrelevant to fundamental social change.[32]

CORE's director, James Farmer, came under heavy pressure at CORE's convention when he sought to name one of his Jewish advisers, Alan Gartner, as president. Ultimately he abandoned the effort to get Gartner elected. Farmer's ties to whites, his calls for interracial unity, and the fact that his wife was white eventually made him suspect as well. At the close of 1965, Farmer left CORE for a position with a federal literacy program.[33]

In February 1966 the city of Mount Vernon, New York, was polarized by a dispute over the use of school busing as a desegregation tool. When the Jewish president of a local PTA spoke against such busing at a public meeting, the local head of CORE denounced him and all Jews, saying that Hitler's mistake was not killing enough of them. The CORE official later resigned, but his widely publicized outburst resulted in the resignation of Will Maslow, longtime American Jewish Congress activist, from CORE's board of directors. Another anti-Semitic episode occurred during Philadelphia's debate over desegregation. Cecil B. Moore, radical head of the city's NAACP, accused the Jewish special counsel for the board of education, Sam Dash (later of Watergate fame), of playing footsie with racial bigots. Moore demanded that Dash and Jews in general leave the fray.[34]

SNCC, however, underwent the most radical shift. In its first phase, from 1960 to 1962, SNCC's members were predominantly middle class and very religious; they were primarily interested in securing integrated public accommodations and basic dignity for blacks. Cleveland Sellers, a SNCC staff member, attributed its success to its reliance on civility and a Gandhian ability to take punishment. In its second phase, from 1962 to 1964, SNCC was dominated by "guerilla organizers," who according to Sellers, regarded nonviolence as nothing more than a tactic. The riots in Philadelphia, Harlem, Watts, and Detroit prompted these organizers to search for ways to mold the discontent in the urban ghettos to revolutionary advantage.[35]

The third phase followed in August 1964. After the Democratic national convention in Atlantic City, Bob Moses, James Forman, John Lewis, Fannie Lou Hamer, and seven other SNCC staff members traveled to Africa on a trip arranged by Harry Belafonte. They met Guinea's leader, Sékou Touré, who related SNCC's work in the United States to the Africans' battle for independence. "The [SNCC] delegates were impressed not only by their warm reception from government officials," wrote Carson, "but also by their observations of daily life in a nation dominated by blacks."[36]

The party returned home from Africa, committed to making SNCC a revolutionary force. At Berkeley in 1965, Moses told his audience that he spoke as a member of the Third World and as a foe of the American buildup in Vietnam. The following year he organized a conference just for field secretaries of SNCC and CORE. Representatives of SCLC, the NAACP, and other civil rights groups were barred from this first-ever segregated meeting, thereby sealing the break with Rustin and the black-Jewish radical community in New York.

Under Forman SNCC broke openly with the SCLC. It ceased dealing with NAACP's team of lawyers, headed by Jack Greenberg, who had been utilized in the SCLC-led demonstration in Selma and staged its own marches and sit-ins, which differed markedly from those of the SCLC. One journalist sympathetic to the civil rights movement termed them "ugly, cop-baiting demonstrations."

In May 1966 Carmichael was elected SNCC's chairman, succeeding Forman, who was seen as too moderate. Carmichael preached black power and flaunted his radicalism. Carson viewed him as a complex man torn between an urban black-nationalist tradition with which he had little personal contact and the radical black-Jewish culture in which he had been formed and which continued to influence his rhetoric.[37]

Although contemptuous of conventional liberalism and middle-class values, Carmichael sought for a while to retain whites and white support in SNCC. But those favoring blacks-only membership put the issue to a vote at a December 1966 SNCC staff meeting in upstate New York. Nineteen staff members backed expulsion of whites, eighteen were opposed. No action was taken, but the days of heavy white participation in southern demonstrations were virtually over.

Carmichael's harsh rhetoric and SNCC's inflammatory action outraged mainstream civil rights organizations. The Leadership Conference on Civil Rights, the lobbying organization under which all the civil rights groups were organized, decided to force a confrontation. It adopted, for the first time in its history, bylaws and a statement of purpose which, if endorsed, would commit the members of each organization to achieving their aims by working together democratically. In March 1967 Carmichael responded to the statement by withdrawing SNCC from the conference, effectively abandoning the force that had led the successful fight for passage of the historic civil rights and voting rights legislation just a few years earlier.[38]

Carmichael then veered even more sharply to the left, traveling to Havana in July to meet with Third World revolutionaries from North Vietnam, South America, and Africa. The trip coincided with racial rioting in Detroit, where President Johnson had called in federal troops. Carmichael told the Havana gathering that they had a common enemy, white Western imperialist society, and a common aim, to overthrow this system. He said that he and his allies were moving into open guerilla warfare in the United States and that he saw no alternative to the use of violence to gain control of the land, houses, and politics of black communities.

The following month, in a visit to North Vietnam, Carmichael told a public meeting in Hanoi that the organization he headed was not reformist but revolutionary. He hoped not for peace but for the defeat of America.

Julius Lester, a SNCC staff member who accompanied Carmichael to Cuba, grew increasingly more uncomfortable as he saw that Carmichael's politics and rhetoric came as much from his ego as from a concern for the welfare of blacks. Lester, who later broke with the movement, confided to his diary, "I sit here with the Mick Jagger of revolution and think about all the people who believe in him, and I am frightened—for him, for them, and for myself."[39]

The following year H. Rap Brown succeeded Carmichael, who had allied himself with the Black Panthers in Oakland. Under Brown SNCC declared itself a "human rights organization for the encouragement and support of worldwide liberation struggles against colonization, racism, and economic exploitation." It proclaimed its willingness to connect with Third World governments and liberation groups.[40] James Forman was named to head its International Affairs Commission.

In seeking to unify blacks by developing a Third World perspective and linking the movement to revolutionary movements abroad, SNCC virtually abandoned its projects in the black community in this country. Indeed, the majority of SNCC's remaining staff members concluded that the new thrust should be extended to include support for the Palestinians in their struggles with Israel.

SNCC's new Third World thrust cut it off from most civil rights supporters. It especially antagonized Jewish activists, who resented being portrayed as racist colonializers. When the Six-Day War broke out in 1967, the editor of SNCC's newsletter published a strongly anti-Israel article, listing thirty-two "documented facts" about the Palestinian problem and asserting that as early as 1897 Zionist imperialists had been active in Palestine and were responsible for the unrest there. It charged that the United States supported Zionism for neocolonial reasons and was using Israel for its own purposes in Africa. Accompanying the allegations were anti-Semitic drawings and cartoons and a photograph purportedly showing Zionists shooting Arabs.[41]

At first, SNCC leadership, reluctant to take such a strong stand against Israel for fear of losing what was left of its Jewish support, was ambivalent. Yet it did not rein in the editor, Ethel Minor. In the fall of 1967, the newsletter declared that SNCC had now associated itself with oppressed peoples and liberation movements; addressing the crucial issue of black-Jewish relations, it suggested that the liberal Jewish community, or certain segments of it, had gone as far as it could go. In a world in revolutionary ferment, few things were worse than being caught on the wrong side of history.[42]

SNCC's posture was a wrenching break with black-Jewish radicalism. The two traditions that have dominated black thought and tactics—the black-Jewish radical and integrationist culture and the black nationalist model symbolized by Marcus Garvey—had always been at war with one another. SNCC and those who followed its ideological direction had chosen Garvey's route.

SNCC's stance against Israel contrasted with the pro-Jewish advocacy of earlier black leftists. Du Bois, while often critical of whites, had written numerous articles strongly supporting the Zionist cause. A. Philip Randolph had drawn parallels between the strivings of blacks and Zionists. Paul Robeson had taken every opportunity to denounce anti-Semitism and support creation of the Jewish state.[43] His son, Paul Robeson, Jr., writing in the eighties in the left-wing, pro-Israel journal *Jewish Currents*, continued to support the black-Jewish alliance, arguing that "the only coalition that would serve the interests of blacks is a coalition between the broad majority of blacks and the broad majority of Jews."[44]

Forman's apostasy brought a storm of protest from outraged Jewish groups and individuals. The American Jewish Congress labeled SNCC's position shocking and viciously anti-Semitic. Folksinger Theodore Bikel, veteran of many civil rights benefits concerts, called it obscene and equivalent to spitting on the graves of Schwerner and Goodman. Harry Golden, editor of the *Carolina Israelite* and a strong civil rights supporter, broke from SNCC because of its increasing anti-Semitism, which he likened to the statements of the Ku Klux Klan. Another SNCC supporter, Rabbi Harold Saperstein, privately warned that he could no longer back an organization that had so eagerly become a mouthpiece for Arab propaganda.

As a result of all this, SNCC's funding declined precipitously. Clayborne Carson concluded that SNCC's failure to galvanize blacks and its success in angering Jews had catalyzed a major disruption of the postwar black-Jewish reform alliance.[45] With this as its last "achievement," SNCC shortly thereafter went out of existence.

These developments within the civil rights movement coincided with a series of broader eruptions in the larger society in the latter half of the 1960s. It was a time of extreme social bifurcation, an abrasive period that saw a rejection of the Protestant establishment's sense of order and stability by people of all ages and interest groups. Families were fractured. Schools and colleges came under attack. Police were reviled as pigs, and leaders were assassinated. The nation embarked on its most unpopular war—one that it would lose in the seventies. With hippies, yippies, radical feminists, antiwar activists, and critics of various stripes assaulting

American institutions, the social fabric of the country was stretched nearly to the breaking point.

What many of the radicals had in common was previous participation in the civil rights movement. Many young people were changed in fundamental ways by their role in the Mississippi Summer project. Abbie Hoffman and Mario Savio were among those whose New Left careers were influenced by their experience in SNCC voter rights demonstrations. In 1961 Tom Hayden, while sitting in a Georgia jail, conceived the idea for the Students for a Democratic Society's Port Huron Statement, the charter of the new youth-oriented protest movement. The civil rights marches had taught an entire generation that nonviolent demonstration was responsible, heroic, and an effective means of protest.[46]

During the Watts rioting in 1967, a small group of Jews—including Marcus Raskin, Arthur Waskow, James Warberg, and Philip Stern—joined a few liberal Republican and Democratic congressmen to plan a way of bringing the various strands of radicalism together into an effective coalition. The group, which had formed the Institute for Policy Studies in 1963, briefly toyed with the idea of creating a third political party, headed by Martin Luther King and pediatrician Benjamin Spock, to challenge President Johnson in 1968.

The vehicle ultimately selected to build this coalition was called the Conference for a New Politics, which was held at Chicago's Palmer House over the Labor Day weekend of 1967.[47] Helping to bankroll the meeting was Martin Peretz, a well-heeled Harvard academic whose second wife, Anne Farnsworth, was an heiress to part of the Singer sewing machine fortune. Along with his friend Michael Walzer, Peretz had funneled hundreds of thousands of dollars into the civil rights and peace movements. Peretz and his wife, according to journalist Jonathan Kaufman, were two of the biggest "angels" in the protest effort. While favoring leftist solutions to societal problems, Peretz was also experiencing a sense of Jewish renewal as a result of Israel's battle for survival.[48]

Peretz and Waskow were antiwar progressives who opposed America's involvement in Vietnam but supported Israel's Six-Day War, which they considered defensive. They viewed SNCC's newsletter as an aberration. Nevertheless, though he was picking up most of the tab for the Chicago convention, Peretz went with foreboding and registered at another hotel. He had doubts about the effectiveness of a radical, multiracial coalition and was seriously troubled by the left-wing anti-Semitism he had personally experienced.

The two thousand conference attendees quickly split into diverse groups. There was a White Radical Caucus, a Black Caucus, a Whites in Support of the Black Caucus, a White Revolutionary Caucus, a Radical Alternatives Caucus, a Poor People's Caucus, a Women Strike for Peace Caucus, and a Labor Caucus, among others. Although the Black Caucus, led by Forman and Brown, never numbered more than fifty, it insisted on getting fifty percent of the votes. Despite being a member of the steering committee, Peretz was not permitted to speak. Martin Luther King, the convention's keynoter, was jeered by black militants shouting "Kill whitey." Surrounded by bodyguards, Forman then seized the microphone and declared SNCC "the victim of the "liberal-labor circle of lies," whose false propaganda had sought to destroy the organization.

King, along with aides Andrew Young and Julian Bond, walked out. So did Peretz and many other whites. Walter Goodman of the *New York Times* suggested that those who remained were deriving a masochistic pleasure from Forman's abuse. Waskow stayed on, emotionally estranged but anxious not to lose contact with elements that he felt he could still work with.

Forman's militants then pushed through thirteen resolutions. For many of the Jews and other whites present, the most troublesome of these condemned the "imperialist Zionist war" in the Middle East. When James Bevel of King's organization sought to speak against it, his life was threatened. Waskow, still hoping for some kind of accommodation, tried to explain that appeals to liberal Jews for funds and support against the war in Vietnam would be permanently soured by the resolution. The Black Caucus later voided the resolution on Israel, but the damage had been done. The Palmer House conference, the last significant effort during the 1960s to forge a national, interracial, radical coalition, was the effective end of an important part of the black-Jewish alliance as it had been known.[49]

11

MARTIN LUTHER KING

A Response to the Race Revolution and the Jews

As the black condition deteriorated and the voices of extremism grew louder, one might have expected Martin Luther King to cut himself off from his Jewish advisers. But that did not happen. On the contrary, while he clearly moved to the left and sought ways to remain in touch with the new and angry forces coming to the fore, he held on tenaciously to the black-Jewish alliance. As long as he lived, the ties between blacks and Jews would not be severed.

Now, deeply in trouble, he turned increasingly to Stanley Levison, Harry Wachtel, and Bayard Rustin—occasionally to Jack Greenberg, Rabbi Heschel, and Allard Lowenstein—for counsel and encouragement. Levinson and Wachtel sometimes competed with each other and with Andrew Young and other black confidants for King's ear. Despite rivalries and jealousies their loyalty to King never wavered.

King's most influential white adviser was clearly still Stanley Levison, even though the FBI and the White House thought him a subversive pulling King to the far left. Curiously his advice, when given, was invariably cautious, even conservative. When the Kennedy brothers demanded in 1963 that King cut off all ties to Levison, King reluctantly did so. The separation ended in April 1965 when, after an encounter at a fund-raising concert in New

York, King sought Levison's advice on a possible economic boycott of Alabama.

Several days later, Levison responded with a remarkable letter setting forth his thoughts on the state of the civil rights movement in general. Although the black-Jewish alliance was by no means the central issue in his letter, he highlighted what lay ahead for that partnership as well. The letter was remarkable for its moderation and keen awareness of the political realities. As a veteran of failed leftist causes, he was totally out of sympathy with the fantasies and infantile narcissism of such groups as SNCC.

Levison cautioned King against staking out a position far to the left of most Americans. He argued that the nation's civil rights groups had worked together, not for radical social change, but for moderate and gradual improvement. Their coalition was broad but shallow. It would be a mistake, a mistake the Communists made in the thirties, he wrote, to call for a revolutionary change that the nation would not answer. Though the American people were no more prepared to push for a transformation of society in the 1960s than they had been in the 1930s, the earlier experience had demonstrated that important reforms could be won within the existing system.

King might consider the civil rights movement revolutionary, Levison wrote, but this was true only within a southern context. In the North it was merely a reform effort, not unlike the union movement of the thirties. Levison acknowledged that King had built stronger support for civil rights than had ever existed before; indeed, he readily admitted that Selma and Montgomery had made King one of the most powerful figures in the country, among blacks and whites both. Even so, the American people were not inclined to make a revolutionary change in their society in order to free the Negro; they might, however, be prepared for reforms, perhaps even major ones.[1]

Shortly afterward King invited Levison back into SCLC's inner circle. Dismissing the possible FBI smear, King said: "I have decided I am going to work completely in the open. There's nothing to hide. And if anybody wanted to make something of it, let them try."[2]

Levison now resumed his earlier role with King, discussing important policy matters in long-distance telephone conversations that were monitored by the FBI. He helped prepare speeches and statements for King, worked on book manuscripts for him, and—

with the FBI continually eavesdropping—made his presence felt at SCLC meetings and retreats. The SCLC's historian, Adam Fairclough, noting that King found writing difficult and welcomed assistance, termed Levison King's most dependable source of help. But despite increasing demands upon King's time, Fairclough insisted that King wrote most of what he published and usually criticized and thoroughly amended what he did not write. No passive mouthpiece, King rarely accepted either advice or written material without subjecting it to critical analysis.[3]

To investigators, Levison was a shadowy figure, and even among friends he was hardly charismatic. With his dour aspect and penchant for detail, he seemed more like a Dickensian bookkeeper than a commanding presence in the America's most significant twentieth-century social movement. But Levison inspired deep affection and respect among some within King's entourage, and his influence was unmistakable. Andrew Young later described Levison as perhaps the most important of all the unknown supporters of the civil rights movement, a man who never pushed his views on black leaders but was always willing to offer critical assistance and to think through ideas with them.[4] Roy Wilkins's nephew, Roger, a Justice Department official and King associate, said that when "sibling rivalry" developed between himself and Andrew Young, they turned to Levison as peacemaker. When Levison died, he left his watch to Roger Wilkins, who later wrote that the one alliance of honor and decency in America was the one that existed between Jews and blacks. Should others deny this, he added, "I will scratch at their eyes with the watch of the Jew, the watch of my father Stanley, strapped around my wrist."[5]

Alarmed by Levison's renewed ties with King, the FBI tightened its surveillance of his New York apartment in May 1965. The bureau had persuaded President Johnson that King was controlled by the wily Levison, operating under Communist discipline, as well as by the Communist sympathizers Harry Wachtel and Clarence Jones. Bureau headquarters viewed Levison as the undisputed number-one adviser to Martin Luther King.[6]

Levison's advice, however, was hardly aimed at undermining the republic. In conversations recorded by the FBI, he urged King not to worry about either SNCC's radicalism or its criticism. SNCC made a lot of noise, he said, but this was only a death rattle. On other tapes Levison—sounding much like the mainstream Jewish organizations—expressed both his unhappiness with King's participation in the New Left conference in Chicago and his joy at the meeting's abortive outcome. King had attended the conference, despite Levison's opposition, in the hope of unifying the factions; as Levison had predicted, the effort failed. He hoped and believed that as a result of that fiasco, King would never again be lured into the clutches of the New Left.

Although the FBI did not draw fine distinctions between Old and New Left radicals—it considered both abhorrent and dangerous—there were significant class differences between the groups. The New Left drew adherents from young people from affluent families, many of whom were headstrong, impatient, arrogant, and sometimes prone to use violence. By and large, the Old Left radicals had come from lower-middle-class or working-class backgrounds, and having survived the Great Depression and the traumas of Stalinism, McCarthyism, and the like, they were more pragmatic, less inclined to cut themselves off from the rest of society. It might be added that by the late 1960s greater affluence and increasing social acceptance made many formerly leftist Jews like Levison, Wachtel, and others less alienated from society and less willing to challenge its fundamental underpinnings.

In short, in a period of radical turmoil, the advice King received from his Jewish advisers was often conservative and never extreme. In opposing the Alabama boycott, Levison argued that community education and political action were the next logical steps after the struggle for voting rights. Bayard Rustin agreed. According to David Garrow, Levison convinced King to take a public position against black power sloganeering. King approved a Levison draft of a statement that appeared as a paid advertisement under King's name in the *New York Times* on July 25, 1966. The ad declared that "black power" was an unfortunate phrase that had provoked substantial confusion and alarm and had proven disruptive and harmful to the movement. King predicted that the phrase and the idea it represented would ultimately lose ground.[7] Here, of course, both Levison and King had misjudged the growing mass appeal of black nationalism.

Earlier, in March 1965, when a federal judge issued an injunction against the planned civil rights march from Selma to Montgomery, King's advisers had split on the question of what to do next. James Forman and others had argued for going ahead anyway. Jack Greenberg and Harry Wachtel recommended that King obey the court order. Siding with the latter, King postponed the march pending an agreement with federal officials. So as not to defy the injunction, the march was shortened to carry it only to the Pettus Bridge, where the historic confrontation with the police took place.

King's advisers split again over whether King should go beyond civil rights issues to press for broader social reforms. For several years, Rustin had been saying that the movement should go beyond race relations to economic relations. Lyndon Johnson's landslide victory over Barry Goldwater in the 1964 presidential election proved, said Rustin, that there existed a national liberal consensus that would support major changes. He urged King to join major labor unions in organizing mass demonstrations of the nation's thirty-five million poor to demand a guaranteed annual income. What finally emerged was the badly run and ineffective Poor People's Campaign of 1968.

In his April 1965 letter to King, Levison expressed strong doubt that Rustin, who had likewise reentered King's circle of advisers, was reading current opinion accurately. When King was invited to appear before the Senate Government Operations Committee on December 15, 1966, Levison prepared a forty-four-page statement identifying the Vietnam War as the major obstacle to adequate funding for social welfare programs. This statement formed the basis of King's last book, *Where Do We Go from Here?*.

A few days after rioting in Newark took twenty-six lives, King told Levison that the nation faced more Newarks. He confided that he had been trying to think of a way to make a major statement about the riots and where the country was going but had not yet settled on the right approach. He knew that he had to condemn both the riots themselves and the intolerable conditions that had led to them. It had to be made clear that not enough was being done.

Levison replied that King should go further. He reminded King that when the country was bankrupt in the thirties, the WPA was started with the sole purpose of employing the jobless. The approach had been, not to train people for jobs, but to tailor jobs for people. Since this had been done at a time when the nation was nearly broke, said Levison, why could it not be done now when the nation was rich?

King liked the idea but deliberated whether he should make the statement at a press conference or on television. When Detroit went up in flames a few days later, Randolph and Wilkins jumped the gun. Without consulting King, they issued a statement condemning the rioting and affixed his name to it. King was affronted. He did not want to be associated with a condemnation solely of the black rioters, nor did he want to break publicly with the black establishment leaders. He called Levison, who suggested that he write a letter to the *New York Times* to refocus attention on the cause of the rioting: the plight of poor blacks trapped in awful slums. King asked Levison to draft the letter.

"The rioters have behaved irrationally," the Levison letter read, "but are they more irrational than those who expect injustice eternally to be endured? To put an Asian war of dubious national interest far above domestic needs and to pit it against reforms that were delayed a century is a provocative policy." King believed the letter—which did not dissociate him from Randolph and Wilkins—would help him with the radicalized sectors of the black community. He signed it, and without changing a word, he sent it off to the *Times*, which published it. After President Johnson condemned the outbreak of lawlessness in Detroit, Levison also dictated a draft of a telegram calling for major federal action to deal with the basic causes of the rioting. King sent the telegram with only minor changes.[8]

Levison, of course, was only putting into words what King himself felt. It was a measure of King's independence, however, that while he listened closely to his advisers, he always made up his own mind.

Late in 1965 he decided to take the civil rights movement up north. Chicago, where there were more black people than in the entire state of Mississippi, was to be his first target. Rustin and other New York advisers sensed disaster. The movement had originated in the South and had proved its effectiveness there. They questioned the wisdom of exporting it. Levison, too, was dubious.

Ever practical, he worried about the new campaign's effect on fund-raising. Rioting in Watts had hurt SCLC in the pocketbook; a northern drive might damage it further. Levison sought to restrain his friend but failed to do so.[9]

In January 1966 King moved into a tenement apartment on Chicago's west side and announced that he would lead a rent strike unless the city's landlords improved their properties immediately. In high spirits he phoned Levison and Rustin, urging them to join him. He said that for the campaign to work, they had to live in the slums, not in a bourgeois hotel.[10]

As his New York advisers had feared, however, the campaign soon foundered. Rioting by working-class whites and artful maneuvering by Chicago Mayor Richard Daley handed King one of his most humiliating defeats. In a postmortem with Levison the following year, King conceded his mistakes. He had promised too much too soon. Levison believed King's approach was too leftist. Instead of pressuring landlords to surrender the buildings, King should have organized the tenants to obtain needed changes.[11]

Throughout this period King faced challenges from right and left. On one side was the FBI, closely watching all of his activities and associations. On the other was the black separatist movement, which distrusted him and resented his close relationships with whites, whether Gentiles or Jews. The militants derided and mocked his coalitional style and kept their distance from him, just as Malcolm X had refused to participate in the 1963 March on Washington, saying that he and his followers would not join in a pilgrimage to a dead man's statue.

In 1966, after the shooting of black activist James Meredith in Mississippi, Stokely Carmichael sharply denounced King's doctrine of nonviolence. And King's revisionist biographer, David Levering Lewis, deplored a few years later the "inherently exploitable limitations of compromise and gradualism" imposed on his subject's philosophy.

King understood the impatience of the black separatists but knew that, with blacks comprising just 10 percent of the American population, they were doomed to fail. Only through coalitions with other groups would their goals be achieved. "They have a strange kind of dream of a black nation within the larger nation," he told Kivie Kaplan of the NAACP; often their public expressions "bordered on a new kind of race hatred and an unconscious advocacy of violence."[12]

But King also recognized that without measurable improvement in the living conditions of angry and frustrated blacks, millions might be radicalized. In the letter from the Birmingham jail, he had warned that lack of progress "would inevitably lead to a frightening nightmare." As his fortunes waned and his frustrations grew, King came to feel that his movement had made only superficial changes in American life.

Somewhere around this time, King began to move out beyond his circle of northern Jewish advisers and establishment black leaders. His rise had been something of a roller coaster and, following Selma, he was moving into the downside of the ride. Several months after the March on Washington in 1963, a *Newsweek* poll showed that 88 percent of blacks saw him as their top leader and that he was also popular among broader groupings of Americans. But by spring 1967 King's numbers had dropped significantly. White Americans no longer ranked him among the top ten national leaders. SCLC had become immobilized. Fund-raising was proving more difficult, and the war in Vietnam was blunting his message.

King began to believe that only the black middle class or those able to enter it had benefited from his civil rights triumphs; for the black masses life remained desperately difficult. He now began to find more and more things wrong with the American free-enterprise system. He challenged the economic organization of society, calling it manifestly unfair. In a speech before A. Philip Randolph's Negro American Labor Council, he said that whether it was called democracy or democratic socialism, there had to be a more equitable distribution of wealth in this country.[13]

C. Vann Woodward believes that in King's last years he moved closer to Stokely Carmichael's concept of collectivist egalitarianism. However, King renounced Carmichael's appeals to revolution and violence and would have been appalled by his later anti-Semitism. Both King and Levison considered Carmichael a destructive force. (Levison told his brother Roy that though confident that Carmichael would destroy both himself and his movement, he and King feared that in the process Carmichael would kill a lot of the Negro youth that followed him.) By this time King was even critical of Jesse Jackson's Operation Breadbasket in Chicago, the forerunner of PUSH. The program to have business open up jobs for blacks was a palliative, King believed, not a solution.[14]

David Halberstam, who traveled with King for ten days in the spring of 1967, observed the political shift. He noted that Andrew Young was among the advisers pressing King to move in a more radical direction. "We see the ghettos now as a form of domestic colonialism," Young told Halberstam. "The preachers are like the civil servants in Ghana, doing the white man's work for them. King has decided to represent the ghettos." According to Halberstam, King acknowledged that he was becoming a more radical critic of society. He agreed that the term "domestic colonialism" reflected his view of the North's treatment of blacks.[15]

In October King took his message of a major federal initiative to rebuild the black slums to the commission President Johnson had formed to study the urban disorders. King also told the group, headed by Illinois governor Otto Kerner, that since the government had failed to act, SCLC planned a massive campaign of civil disobedience by thousands of poor people in Washington. He was prepared, he said, to disrupt the city. Initially dubious about moving from nonviolent direct protest to massive civil disobedience, he was persuaded to do so by Levison and Andrew Young. According to Fairclough, he had tried out this idea (albeit tentatively) the previous August in a speech drafted by Levison for the SCLC convention. The idea for the Poor People's Campaign is generally credited to a young black attorney, Marian Wright Edelman, but Levison's son believes it came from his father. Recalling the "bonus march" of World War I veterans in 1932, Levison recommended that a tent city be erected in the heart of Washington for the army of the poor. The FBI monitored a King-Levison phone conversation on August 22, 1967, in which the campaign was discussed. "King," the tape reported, "agrees on Washington, D.C."[16]

King's move to the left is more clearly seen in his evolving position on Vietnam. If his call for restructuring American society caused little controversy, his opposition to the war brought a storm of criticism, some of it from his own friends and supporters. After receiving the Nobel Peace Prize in 1964, he saw himself as a moral leader for the entire world rather than merely an American activist fighting for civil rights. His nation's role in Vietnam appalled him, and his conscience would not permit him to keep silent. He described the Viet Cong insurgency as a nationalist revolt against a corrupt and oppressive regime. He charged that the United States, in seeking to suppress that revolt, had adopted a policy tantamount to neocolonialism.[17]

As the war escalated in 1965, King met Arthur Goldberg, President Johnson's envoy to the United Nations, and recommended that the bombing of North Vietnam be stopped and peace negotiations initiated. He also told reporters that the United States should end its opposition to the admission of the People's Republic of China to the United Nations. This direct challenge to government policy damaged his relations with the White House and led to divisions among his New York allies. Randolph believed that King had no mandate from the Negro masses to oppose the war, and he was right. A poll commissioned by *Newsweek* showed that only 18 percent of blacks surveyed favored American withdrawal. Rustin was amazed at the negative reaction of Harlemites to King's position. They wanted King to stop talking about Vietnam and concentrate on racial justice.

Delegates to the SCLC convention in August 1965 voiced overwhelming opposition to King's proposal that he write a personal letter to Ho Chi Minh, the North Vietnamese leader. Wachtel and Rustin concluded after the convention that King should drop his Vietnam initiative altogether, and Rustin warned that if he did not, his opponents would come swarming down on him. Levison, too, wanted King to pipe down, to concentrate on being a civil rights leader. King finally retreated, admitting that he had gone too far in thinking that he had the strength to fight against the war and for civil rights at the same time.[18]

On September 28, following another conference call with his New York advisers, King agreed to drop the idea of writing Ho Chi Minh. Levison was annoyed, however, when King suggested that he should once again condemn the war as immoral. "Martin," he said, "we've just gone over this and decided that you're not the person to do this."

Throughout 1966 King saw that his peace thrust was hurting him. Levison and Wachtel recommended he respond to press questions by saying that he had spoken his piece on the war and China and would say no more. For a while he agreed. But his conscience would not let him remain silent. In speeches and public demonstrations he kept sounding his opposition to the war. Harry Belafonte was among the advisers urging this course, and King told Levison that the entertainer believed the issue was of such transcendent importance that only King could save the nation. Belafonte wanted King to resign from SCLC and lead the peace movement. Levison, who was close to Belafonte but thought him naive, felt this was a terrible idea and said so. He wanted King to impress on Belafonte that when he (King) spoke as a man whom 90 percent of Negroes regarded as a leader, his was a big voice; but when he spoke as a man whom some scattered members of peace movements regarded as a leader, it was not so big.[19]

Levison, Wachtel, and other New York advisers urged King to distance himself from the New Left and associate only with the more moderate elements of the peace movement. Levison told King that he would move ten times as many blacks by associating with the Kennedys, the Reuthers, and the Fulbrights than he would by associating with Norman Thomas and Dr. Benjamin Spock, about whom most blacks knew nothing.

King listened but went his own way. He joined Joe Rauh in a new peace group called Negotiation Now and promised Allard Lowenstein that he would not support President Johnson for another term in 1968. Lowenstein wanted King and Spock to head a third-party ticket. Even the pragmatic Levison briefly considered the idea but rejected it, as did King. Levison feared that King might suffer the ignominy of Henry A. Wallace, who, backed by a lot of white middle-class leftists, ran futilely on a third-party ticket for president in 1948. To forestall such an eventuality, Levison prepared a statement in which King, characterizing his role as being "outside the realm of partisan politics," declared he would not run for the presidency.[20]

By this time the infighting among King's aides had intensified. FBI tapes show that when Lowenstein, a fierce and outspoken anti-Communist, was invited to join SCLC's board, Levison was far from happy. He did not welcome a rival for the special relationship he enjoyed with King and probably thought Lowenstein a red-baiter. Young, in turn, thought Levison had become too conservative, particularly on Vietnam. And Levison told Wachtel that he thought Young was pulling King too far to the left. He said that Young thought in terms of fundamental change and had much in common with the radicals, though he was not so crazy. When a *New York Times* story of July 9, 1967, named King as principal speaker at the upcoming New Politics convention that Martin Peretz was bankrolling in Chicago, Levison complained to King that the item effectively pigeonholed King as part of the New Left, in fact as one of its leaders.

Levison reminded King that when he went on the New Politics board, he had agreed to review his position from time to time. Accordingly, the following month King agreed to play down his connection with the conference. Young, too, seemed disillusioned by its extremism. "Those cats don't seem to know the country has taken a swing to the right," he wrote Peretz and his wife.[21]

King's attitude toward black militancy, however, remained ambiguous. On March 25 King, marching alongside Spock, led an antiwar demonstration in Chicago. Levison and many other advisers had urged him to distance himself from the demonstrators. Early in 1967 King's advisers had pulled in opposite directions over his participation in the so-called Spring Mobilization, a peace demonstration scheduled for the United Nations on April 15. One of his aides, James Bevel, had been named national director of the protest. Bevel and Young were among those urging King's participation, while Rustin, Levison, and Wachtel were among those opposed. Rustin feared that King's involvement would end his already shaky access to President Johnson, and Levison saw a danger of King's isolation in both the peace and civil rights movements.

Then, in an effort to distance himself from radical fringe elements in the upcoming mobilization, King agreed to speak earlier at the Riverside Church in New York. Levison was pleased with the plan since he saw King becoming too closely associated with a lot of young people at war with the established society. He told King he could not be identified with that. But once King took the pulpit at Riverside Church, instead of positioning himself far from the leftist elements, he embraced them. Speaking from notes he had prepared with the help of black nationalist Vincent Harding, King expressed his underlying sympathy for the Vietcong insurgents and for revolutionary movements throughout the Third

World. Communism, he said, was primarily a revolt against the failures and injustices of capitalism, which had left a legacy of revolutionary nationalism. It was the duty of the West to support these revolutions now, since the United States had been the greatest purveyor of violence in the world. He compared American action in Vietnam to what the Germans had done during the Holocaust. He said that the nation should withdraw from Vietnam, recognize the Communist-led National Liberation Front, and pay war reparations for the damage done.

Young, who contributed to the speech, thought it a brilliant rationale for King's position on the war, but most mainstream organizations thought otherwise. The *Washington Post* dismissed it as sheer fantasy. The *New York Times*, which opposed the war, chided King for linking the issue with the civil rights effort. Wachtel reported that many contributors to SCLC were threatening to end their support as a result of the speech. An official of the Jewish War Veterans, angry at the Holocaust reference, said the speech could have been written in Hanoi. It was condemned also by the NAACP and the Urban League as well as by Thurgood Marshall and King's fellow Nobel laureate, Ralph Bunche.

Rustin, too, disapproved of the speech and broke with King's inner circle by making his opposition public. Though a lifelong pacifist, Rustin advised blacks to shun the peace movement. The problems of blacks were too vast and crushing for them to waste time and energy on international crises.

Although King was stunned by the reaction his speech had drawn, his inner-circle Jewish advisers were not surprised. Levison complained that King had been too radical, too frank, too moralistic. He told Wachtel that King should realize he was confronting the State Department and the Pentagon and not some local southern sheriff. King, it appears, knew how to play opposition politics, but he did not have as firm a sense of the necessity for widespread public support—coalition support—which Levison and the others saw as paramount. Such support and the need for it remained central issues dividing Jews and more militant blacks.[22]

King's Riverside Church speech strengthened the FBI's conviction that he had fallen into the hands of Communists. And although taped conversations show conclusively that Stanley Levison's was a voice of moderation within King's circle, the bureau continued to focus its attention on him. Without naming Levison, Carl Rowan, a widely read black columnist with close ties to the White House, wrote that King had been listening closely to a man who was clearly more interested in embarrassing the United States than in the plight of either black or Vietnamese people. In a confidential memorandum to President Johnson, J. Edgar Hoover reported that King's recent utterances had shown him to be an instrument of subversive forces seeking to undermine the nation.[23]

Despite the criticism King held his ground. When Levison complained about the speech, King insisted that though politically unwise, it was morally necessary. Likening his role to that of the ancient Hebrew prophets, he suggested that he *ought* to be unpopular. Levison, though certainly no expert on the Old Testament, pointed to a significant difference: the prophets lived in a small country and spoke directly to their people, while King addressed a vastly larger population with the aid of forces that controlled and distorted what he said, namely, the media.[24]

As preparations went forward for the Spring Mobilization, King agreed to address it on condition that Carmichael not be allowed to speak; a promise was given but later broken. Lowenstein started to prepare King's speech, but with personal rivalries welling up again, Wachtel and Levison sought to ease him out. Meanwhile, Young had carved out a key role in defining SCLC's relationship to the basically white antiwar movement. Levison again grumbled that Young was pulling King to the left on this issue.

In a conference call on April 9, Levison and Wachtel pressed King to dissociate himself from Bevel's view that Vietnam was a racist war. King refused to do so; he said he agreed with Bevel and added that it was an unpleasant fact that future wars would be waged against nonwhite people in Latin America or Asia. Levison was appalled. He feared that this pro-Vietcong position would isolate King just as Paul Robeson's pro-Soviet position had isolated him.

Both Levison and Lowenstein continued to work on King's mobilization speech. Liberal columnist James Wechsler also pitched in. Levison pressed King to align himself with such liberals as Jacob Javits and Robert Kennedy, but King declined. He needed to take a leadership role at the demonstration; after that he would move in the direction advocated by Levison.[25]

The Sunday protest attracted 125,000 people to the United Nations Plaza. (It was just a few months before the New Politics convention in Chicago.) King marched at the front of the procession with Bevel, Spock, and Belafonte. According to David Garrow, the speech written by King's haggling aides was not a "memorable oration" although its concluding refrain, "stop the bombing, stop the bombing," generated enthusiasm.[26] Even though the speech was cautious, King's fellow marchers caused further problems for him. Carmichael and Floyd McKissick, the radical head of CORE, were featured speakers, and Carmichael led a group that carried Vietcong flags. For the first time since the 1940s, according to David Dellinger, the march organizer, members of the Communist party marched under their own banner.[27]

Following the demonstration King, Carmichael, and some of their advisers repaired to Belafonte's apartment. King and a surprisingly cooperative Carmichael exchanged views on future plans. They agreed, as Levison later put it, to leadership-level meetings to discuss joint actions they deemed necessary, although Levison felt this to be only an agreement to consult from time to time. After the meeting broke up, Gloria Cantor, Belafonte's secretary, phoned Levison. She feared that her boss was pushing King to embrace SNCC views. Levison agreed but thought it would not work. King would listen to *him*, said Levison, rather than to Belafonte or SNCC. Anyway, Carmichael had no program. "You don't call for insurrection," he said, "in a place where you're outnumbered, outgunned."[28]

It was not Belafonte or Carmichael but Andrew Young who concerned Levison. In the heady days of Montgomery and shortly thereafter, Rustin and Levison had been King's primary advisers and tacticians. After Selma it was Young, who saw and urged the possibility of expanding SCLC across the country and overseas. Young had come to believe that what started as a simple matter of political reform had become a total fight for economic justice and world peace. Levison's views were still sought, and his opinions were valued. But now King seemed more in tune with Young's grandiose visions than with Levison's unexciting pragmatism.

Young's thinking moved King closer to the Third World ideology that Jesse Jackson would develop in the 1980s.[29]

The Six-Day War that broke out in June 1967 posed additional problems for King. American Jews had supported him strongly, and he had consistently defended them. In May 1958 he had addressed the American Jewish Congress in Miami, noting that segregationists made no distinction between blacks and Jews. When black rioters destroyed ghetto businesses in 1964, King had pointed out reproachfully that many of the looted stores were owned by "our Jewish friends." He noted that as a group, Jewish Americans had always stood for freedom, justice, and an end to bigotry. And in response to the pleas of Jewish leaders, in December 1966 he had spoken out in support of Jews barred from leaving the Soviet Union.[30]

King had always admired Israel; he saw it as the source of the Judeo-Christian tradition embraced by most blacks. Indeed, he had urged blacks to learn from and promote a pragmatic version of Zionism. Privately, however, he was less comfortable with the situation in the Middle East. As a pacifist, he felt it necessary to oppose killing, whether it occurred in Vietnam or the Middle East. Moreover, he had to concern himself now with the pro-Arab views of black nationalists and separatists. They already distrusted him, and his endorsement of Israel's preemptive attack on Egypt would make matters worse. King's position came to public attention shortly before the outbreak of the war when an advertisement signed by King and other Christian leaders appeared in the *New York Times*. The ad called for the United States to champion Israel's continued independence and its right to unimpeded passage through the Straits of Tiran, then threatened by Egypt.

In a conversation with Levison and his other New York advisers the following day, King admitted to being confused. He had never actually seen the ad before it appeared, he told them. When he did, he was not happy with it. He felt it was unbalanced and pro-Israel, although he observed that it would probably help him with the Jewish community.[31]

After carefully weighing the situation, his advisers, even the Jewish ones, suggested in effect that King carry water on both shoulders. Since war settles nothing, as Levison put it, King could adopt a peace position without taking sides. While agreeing that the territorial integrity of Israel and its right to a homeland were incontestable, King should urge that all other questions be settled by negotiation. Such a position, said Levison, would serve to keep the Arab friendship and the Israeli friendship. King agreed.[32]

Two days later, in a conference call with Young, Wachtel, and Levison made just prior to a speech on Vietnam, King again asked for their views. SNCC and others in the black community had attacked him for signing the advertisement in the *New York Times*. He was in a real dilemma, he said. Jews liked his earlier statement, but some in the black community had been disappointed, including SNCC. A news article in the *Times* had described the ad as a "total endorsement" of Israel, King said.

His advisers suggested that he simply back the UN call for a cease-fire. King did not have to worry too much about losing the support of the Jewish community, Wachtel told him, so long as he strode very lightly and stressed an end to violence.

The issue arose again one month later when King contemplated leading a pilgrimage of blacks and whites to the Holy Land. He questioned whether such a trip, coming so soon after the Six-Day War, made sense in light of the fact that the Arab world, and probably Africa and Asia too, would interpret the action as endorsing everything Israel had done and he did have doubts. Asked by Wachtel how such a trip would be an endorsement of Israel's position, King replied that most of his stay would be in Jerusalem. The Israelis had annexed the city, "and any way you say it, they don't plan to give it back." Young chipped in that he felt it important that King develop a strong point of view and personal contact with the Middle East situation since the Arab position had never had a hearing in this country. Levison agreed.[33]

Throughout this period Rauh saw no inconsistency in King's backing Israel while opposing the American involvement in Vietnam. For his part Lowenstein hoped the Israelis would not yield Jerusalem. At one point the FBI recordings report Levison as saying that Jews had never been more in danger of extinction, but he was apparently more troubled by the role of "the Zionist Jew" in the Middle East conflict. He wondered what the average ghetto black would think of King's taking a group of middle-class black and white people to the Holy Land.

In the final analysis Levison did not want to dissipate King's energies, whether on Vietnam or Jewish concerns. Levison was the prototypical "non-Jewish Jew" described by Isaac Deutscher; that is, a man with no strong Jewish identity who sought a world free of all forms of group identity that interfered with class solidarity.[34]

Despite King's doubts about Israel's position in the Middle East conflict, its relations with its neighbors, and his own desire to reach out to Third World supporters in the United States, he continued to support Jews and Israel strongly. Several months after the Six-Day War, ten Jewish agencies asked King to disavow the malevolent language of the Chicago New Politics convention. King's response, probably his most comprehensive statement on black-Jewish relations, came in a four-page letter to Morris B. Abram, president of the American Jewish Committee. In it he indicated that he had spoken at the New Politics meeting and then left. Had he stayed he would have reiterated the SCLC stand on the Israel-Arab conflict—namely, that Israel's right to exist as a state was incontestable—and he would have rejected any motion that unequivocally endorsed the position of the Arab powers and rebuked Israel.

He also pledged that SCLC would continue to denounce anti-Semitism frequently and vigorously. Not only was anti-Semitism immoral—though that alone was enough—but it was used to divide blacks and Jews, who had effectively collaborated in the struggle for social justice. He went on to specify that anti-Semitism among blacks was limited in scope and was concentrated almost exclusively in the northern ghettos. Its focus was on "marginal business entrepreneurs" rather than on Jewish ethics or beliefs. King denied that there had ever been an instance of black anti-Semitism that went uncondemned by virtually all black leaders or by the overwhelming majority of black people. He asserted that he had attacked it himself and would continue to do so because of its immoral and destructive nature.[35]

Although King was becoming increasingly amenable to certain more radical views, he never endorsed anti-Semitism or anti-Israel feeling, believing firmly that the black-Jewish alliance was fundamental to civil rights progress. The resolution adopted at the Chicago meeting and the new direction of SNCC therefore reflected a major difference between SCLC and SNCC and represented a dramatic split between the older and more established leadership and the younger elements unwilling to submerge ideological differences in the interest of coalition politics. This split would be played out in increasingly bitter terms in the coming years. Before long even moderate blacks were forced into silence or went along with the new breed. Indeed, King was the last major black leader to promote the legitimacy of Zionism within the black community.

Following his testimony before the Kerner Commission on October 23, 1967, King told reporters that the causes of urban rioting were obvious. Since the government had failed to act, SCLC intended to organize protests in Washington. Poor people by the thousands would travel to the capital to press for action. If necessary, SCLC was prepared to disrupt the city through a campaign of civil disobedience. King envisaged an interracial alliance of the poor that embraced Indians, Puerto Ricans, Mexican Americans, and Appalachian whites.

Levison, Wachtel, and Young supported King, but Rustin opposed any form of massive civil disobedience, as did Rustin's associates Norman Hill and Michael Harrington. They thought such a tactic would attract the most irresponsible and uncontrollable people.[36] The FBI too thought that King's project could easily get out of control. Aware of these concerns, King softened his rhetoric. He told a conference of black ministers in Miami that he would not try to close down the Pentagon. SCLC would instead develop practical proposals that would gain wide public backing, he promised. He asked Harrington, whose socioeconomic study *The Other America* sparked Washington's war on poverty, to draft a manifesto for the campaign. Harrington was amused that King had assigned him, a white man, to prepare the draft, and he mentioned this to King. Laughing, King told Harrington, "We didn't know we were poor until we read your book."[37]

As King readied plans for the Poor People's Campaign, his attention was drawn to a strike of sanitation workers in Memphis. Most of the hourly workers were black, and they lacked job protection. Their strike had gained the support of the Washington-based American Federation of State, County, and Municipal

Workers (AFSCME). Jerry Wurf, the union's Jewish head, told King that the Memphis strike was important to every poor workingman, black or white, in the South. Wurf and local strike leaders invited King to get directly involved, and to the dismay of his staff, who did not want him to be diverted from the Washington effort, he accepted the challenge.

King's initial visit to the city was well received, and the mass meeting he addressed was a triumph. Rustin's warning of dangers in the volatile ghetto neighborhoods appeared baseless. King told Levison that he had never seen such a unified community. Not long after, however, violence disrupted a march King was leading; he had to be rushed from the scene. Shaken and extremely depressed, he phoned his wife, Ralph Abernathy, and then Levison. Fearing even greater disorders in Washington, he spoke of calling off the Poor People's Campaign. Levison calmly assured him that SCLC's experienced Washington staff would prevent such outbreaks.[38] What King needed, his adviser said, was a good night's sleep. Next day, Levison called King in a further attempt to dissuade him from canceling the Washington protest. He drew an analogy to the labor turmoil of the 1930s. Should labor have abandoned its fight because violence occasionally erupted in those days? That would have played into the hands of the employers. In King's view, however, the Poor People's Campaign was doomed.[39]

King left Memphis with no plans to return. On March 30, 1968, his executive staff met to decide whether he should go back or not. Those present included Young, Abernathy, Jackson, Levison, and Joseph Lowery, as well as King himself. King, they believed, should return to Memphis, and he concurred. On his return King, addressing a small audience at the Masonic Temple, invoked the image of Moses and the experience of the ancient Hebrews as, unwittingly, he delivered his own epitaph. He alluded to the time he had been stabbed in New York and noted that only that morning his flight had been delayed by a bomb scare. After referring to the difficult days ahead and to his desire simply to do God's will, King declared that God had allowed him to go up to the mountain. "And I've looked over. And I've seen the Promised Land," he said. "So I'm happy tonight. I'm not worried about anything. I'm not fearing any man. Mine eyes have seen the glory of the coming of the Lord."

The microphone failed to catch his last words: "His truth is marching on."[40]

Martin Luther King's assassination on April 4, 1968, cost the civil rights movement its greatest leader and the black-Jewish alliance its most influential black advocate. As King had wished, Ralph Abernathy succeeded him at the helm of SCLC. His first decision was to press forward with the Poor People's Campaign. Initially it seemed like the right move. A nation stunned by King's murder contributed generously to SCLC. A single advertisement signed by Harry Belafonte and published in the *New York Times* produced $320,000. "The people are responding," Levison exulted. "The poor for the first time almost in this century are really assembling to go to Washington." On May 11 buses started delivering poverty-stricken men, women, and children to the settlement near the Washington Monument that would be called Resurrection City. Tents were pitched; demonstrations were planned. It soon became apparent, however, that the organizers were incapable of running a small city of some three thousand poor people. Conditions quickly deteriorated. Rains swept the area, and before long, gangs roving the muddy streets began robbing and intimidating their neighbors. (In his memoirs Abernathy wrote that the street gangs were simply reliving "the nightmare of the ghettoes.")[41]

By the end of the month, the issues that SCLC wanted to dramatize had been totally obscured. The press was focusing on the mud, the disorganization, and the bickering among the staff. An SCLC board member who visited the camp early in June was appalled, observing that the staff was living at a comfortable hotel while the poor people were living in hip-deep mud.

James Bevel, Resurrection City's first "mayor," was soon succeeded by Jesse Jackson, who was given the more modest title of city manager. His penchant for personal publicity was said to have angered the staff. Adam Fairclough, SCLC's historian, writes that Abernathy first demoted Jackson and then dismissed him. It may have happened, but Abernathy's own book makes no mention of it. So much else went wrong that a change at the top may have gone unnoticed.

At one point Michael Harrington paid a call. He came away totally disillusioned. Far from being a brotherhood and sisterhood of the poor, Resurrection City was a tense and violent place where all the disintegrative forces present in the lower depths of society were tearing the movement apart. After being attacked as if he were "a Dixiecrat senator," Harrington fled the nightmarish wreck of the "beloved community" that he and others in the black-Jewish-labor alliance had tried to create in the mid-1950s.

In desperation Abernathy asked Rustin to help coordinate a mammoth Solidarity Day demonstration on June 19. Rustin agreed but said that it had to be peaceful; he would not tolerate civil disobedience. In drawing up a list of demands for the campaign, Rustin pointedly omitted any reference to Vietnam, an omission that infuriated the more militant members of King's entourage, who viewed him as an Uncle Tom. Levison himself was now deeply suspicious of Rustin and thought he was much too conservative to run the Washington campaign.

Sorely beset and lacking Abernathy's support, Rustin resigned. Abernathy pleaded with Levison to help remedy the situation. Levison refused, saying it was beyond repair. The hapless organizers had come to Washington with a million dollars and a degree of support no other organization had heretofore enjoyed. With bitter irony Levison said that it had required real genius to squander such assets.[42]

Five days after Solidarity Day, Resurrection City came to an unmourned end as police emptied the site and confiscated SCLC's mule train, the symbol of the Poor People's Campaign.* The coalition that had been formed in Montgomery and New York in 1956 and reached its zenith with the 1963 March on Washington—producing the civil rights and voting rights acts of the succeeding two years—had now been fractured beyond hope of repair.

---

*Jack Greenberg and his Legal Defense Fund lawyers handled the campaign's legal matters prior to and after King's death. Its final work included negations of the government claim of $71,795 for use of equipment, damage to trees, and razing the shanties in Resurrection City, which was settled for $2,197.

12

THE LATE SIXTIES

The Conflict Deepens

As the 1960s drew to a close, black power rhetoric grew more radical and New Left politics more extreme. Shortly after the debacle of the New Politics convention, angry student demonstrations disrupted Columbia University in New York and bloody rioting shook the Democratic National Convention in Chicago. Students for a Democratic Society recognized the Black Panther Party as the "vanguard force" of black liberation, and SDS adherents spoke openly of their admiration for North Vietnam.[1]

In this overheated atmosphere a series of highly publicized quarrels between New York's blacks and Jews left a bitter aftertaste that lingers to this day. These quarrels developed in large measure because the interests of the two groups came increasingly to diverge. Unlike earlier confrontations that grew out of landlord-tenant and merchant-customer relations, the new ones occurred within New York's sprawling school bureaucracy and pitted neighborhood blacks against Jewish educators just a step or two above them socioeconomically. The result was a bitter strike in the fall of 1968 that kept one million children out of class for thirty-six school days. Worse still, the strike severed generations-old political understandings among blacks, Jews, and unions that had kept the peace and promoted social progress in New York.

Our big cities are a mix of various socioeconomic, racial, religious, and ethnic groups, all seeking to improve their lot. They all struggle with one another for a bigger piece of the pie and for their at times differing goals and values. In this process collisions inevitably ensue. But as the 1960s drew to a close few conflicts were as poignant as that between the two groups allied for so long—blacks and Jews.

Facing exclusion from mainline banking, law, insurance, and other businesses, great numbers of New York Jews had entered the field of public education in the 1930s and 1940s. By the fifties and sixties, Jewish vice-principals, principals, and higher-level administrators were spread throughout the system. Together with thousands of rank-and-file Jewish teachers, they held, in effect, an ethnic monopoly of leadership and control.[2] Nevertheless, the predominantly Jewish United Federation of Teachers perhaps best exemplified the old liberal-socialist vision that the interests of the poor and of the working and lower-middle classes of whatever color were one and the same. This vision, though shared by many groups, had as its most important defenders blacks and Jews. It was an outlook that saw New York City as a unified, organic whole; it emphasized the shared humanity of all people, sought to establish acceptable boundaries of racial or ethnic particularism within a capitalist system, and advocated a color-blind, equal-opportunity approach to social and economic reform.

Notwithstanding this vision, the city's black population had been historically underrepresented and continued to be so even after black enrollment rose to record numbers. At one point in the 1950s, there was one black principal in a city with more than nine hundred schools. With the growth of the black power movement, popular support had developed for the notion that local communities should control the selection of their own educators. It was this issue that eventually led to ugly clashes between black parents and Jewish teachers.

Albert Shanker, president of the UFT, seemed an unlikely opponent of those pushing for black advancement. As a student at Columbia, he had belonged to the socialist Student League for Industrial Democracy, and later, as a union leader, he raised money for the Freedom Summer, marched with King in Selma, and served on the steering committee of the Conference for Quality Integrated Education. He was perhaps the leading integrationist in the labor movement. Some of King's earliest supporters had joined his staff at the UFT, including Bayard Rustin's young associates Rachelle Horowitz and Tom Kahn, who had both been active in the youth integration marches of 1956 and 1957.[3]

The issue of community control gained the support of militant blacks in the area. Les Campbell, one of the leaders of the Afro-American Teachers' Association and a teacher at J.H.S 271, placed black power and sometimes anti-Semitic materials on the association's bulletin board. The Rev. C. Herbert Oliver, whose son was receiving failing grades, felt no one cared about the schools. Community control now also received backing from an unexpected source: New York's patriciate.

Mayor John V. Lindsay, Governor Nelson Rockefeller, and Ford Foundation president McGeorge Bundy were stirred by the plight of blacks and worried about increasing racial disorder. Lindsay, a former congressman representing a well-to-do Manhattan district, had been elected mayor as a liberal Republican in 1965. Soon after taking office, he turned his attention to the schools. New York's board of education was religiously diverse, with Jews, Roman Catholics, and Protestants all represented, but it had no black or Puerto Rican members, even though these two groups made up by this time about 75 percent of the public school enrollment in Manhattan.

Lindsay saw to it that blacks and Puerto Ricans finally gained seats on an enlarged school board, which nevertheless—and not incidentally—came to be dominated by Jewish board members. The mayor then called on Bundy, a former Harvard dean and Kennedy administration official, to recommend ways of decentralizing the system. The Bundy Report, published in 1967, proposed breaking up New York's school system into neighborhood districts that would be governed by community boards.[4]

Lindsay, following the recommendations of Bundy's staff, designated the heavily black Ocean Hill–Brownsville area of Brooklyn, a center of Jewish radicalism in the thirties, as one of the districts. The UFT was not opposed. In fact, it had earlier advised the Ford Foundation that Ocean Hill–Brownsville would be a good place to start the experiment. Furthermore, the union had previously organized a joint action by parents and teachers (spearheaded by Sandra Feldman, who later succeeded Shanker) that led to the dismissal of a disliked junior high school principal in the district and provision of special services for schools there. Nor were Jewish groups initially opposed to the principle of decentralization. In a 1968 statement, the metropolitan council of the American Jewish Congress described the movement as a way of bringing schools closer to the communities and making them more relevant to the needs of the city's children.[5]

Problems arose with the appointment of a superintendent for Ocean Hill–Brownsville. By arrangement with Ford, the parents chose Rhody McCoy, who had been acting principal of a school for seriously disturbed boys on Manhattan's west side. An angry and determined black man with a deep distrust of whites, McCoy was an outspoken admirer of Malcolm X and frequent visitor to the Harlem mosque where Malcolm vilified whites and urged blacks to take control of their own destiny. He had also visited Malcolm at home and patterned his own thought after Malcolm's. McCoy was sold on the idea that a racist, capitalist America had made the education of black, poor white, and Third World children nearly impossible. Violent revolution was his prescription for making America's public institutions serve all its peoples—a formula, according to Jim Sleeper in *The Closest of Strangers*, that moved beyond community control to separatist nihilism.[6]

McCoy encouraged appearances of "community activists" such as Les Campbell, and Robert "Sonny" Carson, who utilized race-based violence and intimidation against both blacks and whites. (Carson earned further notoriety in 1991 when he exhorted blacks to attack Hasidic Jews in Crown Heights after an accident that resulted in the death of a black child.)[7] McCoy believed his career had been stymied by whites, especially Jews in the school establishment. Soon after taking over the Ocean Hill–Brownsville district, he moved against those supervisors and teachers he considered uncooperative, dismissing nineteen, most of them Jewish.* The

*Jerald E. Podair, a doctoral student studying the Ocean Hill–Brownsville controversy, reported that when one teacher with a Jewish-sounding name turned out to be black, he was quickly reinstated.

community board supported him, but the district was thrown into turmoil. Three hundred fifty teachers walked off their jobs and threatened to stay out until their colleagues were reinstated. Shanker then prepared to shut down the entire city school system.

McCoy responded by hiring 350 substitutes to fill the vacancies. (Half of them were radical activist Jews; McCoy's attorney, Morton Stavis, was a Jewish member of the National Lawyers Guild.) Meanwhile, an unshaken UFT continued to express support of school decentralization in a full-page advertisement in the *New York Times*. But when anti-Semitic leaflets were placed in the school boxes of Ocean Hill-Brownsville teachers—they declared that black children should be taught by Afro-Americans rather than "Middle East murderers of Colored People"—an enraged Shanker printed 500,000 copies of the leaflets and distributed them widely. He acted despite the community board's condemnation of anti-Semitism and an investigation that showed that the scurrilous material had come from outside the district. He said that he wished to show what kind of people wanted to take over the schools.[8]

The New York City chapter of the American Civil Liberties Union accused Shanker of exacerbating an already tense situation. The ACLU noted that the UFT was defending an area of institutional life in New York City in which Jews held real power, two thirds of the UFT membership being Jewish, as was Shanker himself; even in black areas a majority of supervisors and administrators were Jewish, including a majority of the Board of Education.[9]

Shanker denied that he was exaggerating the degree of anti-Semitism that the school conflict had engendered. He charged that over 100,000 pieces of anti-Semitic propaganda had been distributed before the strike, mainly by other extreme black groups, and that this was having a great impact on the young people in the area. The time had come to expose the situation. Sleeper argues that though Shanker may have embroidered his account, not all Jewish fears were disproportionate.[10]

Not surprisingly, media coverage of the two-month strike focused on its anti-Semitic aspects. One radio broadcast in particular stirred passions to fever pitch. Julius Lester, the former SNCC activist, was the host of a half-hour program on listener-supported WBAI-FM in New York. On one show he encouraged Campbell to read an anti-Semitic poem written by one of his fifteen-year-old students. It was dedicated to Shanker and entitled "Anti-Semitism." It expressed nothing but rage and hate.[11]

Lester apparently thought that broadcasting such venom to a wide audience would bring the city to its senses. He badly miscalculated. The poem was seen simply as a vicious example of black bigotry, and Lester himself was labeled an anti-Semite. In a later memoir, he examined his motives:

> I hear an anger within me, an anger that my suffering as a black person is not understood as I feel the suffering of Jews is. I am angry, too, that Jews, the people I thought most able to understand black suffering, do not understand, do not care, even, to try to understand. Once I see my anger staring at me, I cannot deny that part of my motivation in airing the poem had been to hurt Jews as they had hurt me. If such unspoken anger becomes a comfortable habit, there is no way I can prevent myself from sliding into anti-Semitism as if it were a cool lake at the bottom of a grassy slope.[12]

Lester had given perhaps the best explanation of the underlying cause of black anger with Jews.

Shanker, however, was not without support among older elements of the black-Jewish-labor alliance. Randolph backed the union, fearing that if one community school district could violate its contract not to dismiss teachers without cause, others would do the same; union security, seniority, and collective bargaining could be wiped out. On September 19, 1968, the A. Philip Randolph Institute and Bayard Rustin sponsored an advertisement in the *New York Times* signed by twenty AFL-CIO–affiliated black trade union members; it declared that the real issues in the dispute revolved around the integrity of the union movement and had no relationship to race. Later, as the racial dimension of the conflict grew, a number of them backed off.[13]

Ultimately, with the experiment a failure, the Ocean Hill–Brownsville school board was suspended. The district was placed under the supervision of a state-appointed trustee but not before the issue had wrecked the liberal consensus that had prevailed in New York City since the end of World War II. Blacks felt betrayed—Jews had always expressed their support for civil rights in terms of aiding others, not themselves; but now the teachers and many others in the Jewish community were seeking to protect their own interests. This was hardly surprising, but it contravened the "self-abnegating liberal" signals they had previously sent. Blacks had taken them at their word and saw them now as cynically turning their back on the cause of civil rights after having won their own.[14]

The bitterness, distrust, and outright hate engendered by the controversy over community board control of schools spread to other areas of life in New York. The gulf between blacks and Jews grew so wide that any incident could unleash citywide charges and recriminations.[15] The black director of the Martin Luther King Center at New York University stated as a fact that black children were being intellectually castrated by the Jews who controlled the educational bureaucracy of the New York public school system. He was subsequently fired. The catalog for the Metropolitan Museum of Art exhibit "Harlem On My Mind," which opened in January 1969—it was then the largest exhibit ever mounted by the museum—described frictions that had developed between blacks and Jews. The catalog, written by a black woman, declared that "behind every hurdle that the Afro-American has to jump stands the Jew who has already cleared it." She went on to declare that contempt for the Jew made blacks feel more completely American in sharing a national prejudice. When the publication drew criticism, Thomas Hoving, the museum's patrician director, feeling he could not censor it, declared, "Her statements are true. So be it." He later admitted that he had been indiscreet.[16]

As the 1960s drew to a close, the Jewish community felt a mingled sense of panic, confusion, and outrage at these manifestations of hostility. In a book published at that time, *Black Power, Anti-Semitism and the Myth of Integration*, Max Geltman wrote that despite all the support Jews had given to blacks from Harlem to Watts, they had been rewarded only with hatred. Such Jewish groups as the Anti-Defamation League and the American Jewish Committee, which had been active in post–World War II efforts to broaden civil liberties for all minorities, reverted to their original role of combating anti-Semitism. In a widely publicized 1969 report, the ADL concluded that "raw, undisguised anti-Semitism had reached a crisis level in New York City where, unchecked by public authority, it had been building for more than two years." *Time* magazine declared in a cover story that the black-Jewish alliance was ended; others had earlier reached the same conclusion.

Anxieties about encroachments on their neighborhoods and the growth of black anti-Semitism was felt especially by working- and lower-middle-class Jews at this time. Though postwar affluence had permitted great numbers of Jews to move from cities to suburbs throughout the Northeast and Middle West, not all Jews participated in the exodus. Along with other ethnic whites, many remained behind in what one Jewish official called the urban frontier—increasingly black, older neighborhoods plagued with crumbling housing, rising crime rates, and other social pathologies.

Yona Ginsberg, who studied the formerly Jewish enclave of Mattapan in Boston, found that between 1968 and 1972 its population had declined from 10,000 to 2,500. She characterized the Jews she interviewed as living in fear. Yet it would be a misleading oversimplification to explain their feelings as merely an expression of prejudice. For the Mattapan Jews' attitudes were mixed: They regarded blacks as both good and bad and clearly distinguished between those they considered respectable and those they did not.[17]

A 1970 study of Wynnefield, a demoralized and dissolving Jewish section in Philadelphia, reported a widespread conviction that the Jewish community there was declining. To the Jews faced with this situation and to an increasing proportion of blacks, everything seemed more difficult.[18] A similar picture emerges from sociologist Jonathan Rieder's study of the Canarsie section of Brooklyn. Rieder described working-class whites who moved out of decaying neighborhoods just ahead of blacks, each group seeking better housing and safer streets. A Jewish woman in Canarsie, a veteran of local reform politics, lamented the lost innocence of an earlier generation when the family read the *Jewish Daily Forward* and books in Yiddish on socialist Eugene V. Debs and her brothers worked to help the Scottsboro boys. She felt herself to be a compassionate person, but one day there was an ugly scene in the laundry room of a nearby project, and she felt it was time to heed her husband's plea to move out.[19]

Just as blacks and Jews came to distrust one another in this period, so did poorer Jews in many instances come to distrust their more affluent brethren, signaling a series of new rifts within the Jewish community itself. Earlier, working- and lower-middle-class Jews had been willing to accept the leadership of the cosmopolitan Jewish upper class and the professionals running the Jewish social service agencies. In the tumultuous sixties this relationship deteriorated. Less affluent Jews increasingly came to feel that their social betters were indifferent to their problems and really more concerned about poor blacks. It was Jewish liberals in Manhattan, for example, who seemed to provide most of the support for forced busing and community control of the schools. Most of these Jews would be unaffected by such educational changes since their children, if they had any, attended private schools. And as Hillel Levine and Lawrence Harmon noted in their study of older Jewish neighborhoods in the Boston area, *The Death of an American Jewish Community*, mainstream Jewish organizations sometimes seemed to sociologize away lawless conduct and provided little support to the Jews still living in those neighborhoods.*

The Jewish schism now developing was evident in a Harris poll conducted in July 1969. The poll found that by a two-to-one margin, more Jews living in Manhattan considered New York blacks justified in their demands than did Jews living in Brooklyn, the

---

*In this respect, the willingness of intellectuals and social scientists—some of them Jewish and far removed from the fray—to accept and even justify lawless behavior should be noted. In August 1964 rioting destroyed many Jewish stores in north Philadelphia. As director of the American Jewish Committee's Philadelphia office, I commissioned a study of the underlying causes of the disturbances. In his foreword to the analysis, Dean Alex Rosen of NYU's Graduate School of Social Work in effect absolved the rioters. He described violence as "a form of inarticulate language in which one group of people communicates with other significant groups about its feelings, its problems, its life circumstances." Looking back, I am more than a little surprised by his and my own insensitivity.[20]

heartland of the city's Jewish lower middle class. Milton Himmelfarb wrote in *Commentary* in January 1970 that for the first time in forty years, class differences among American Jews were showing signs of emerging as class conflict.

This conflict spilled over into politics in 1969 when Mayor Lindsay, running for reelection, defeated Mario Procaccino. A CBS poll found that most upper-income Jews voted for Lindsay, the Protestant reformer, while lower-middle-class Jews backed his white ethnic opponent. Two years later, about half of Philadelphia's Jewish voters backed Frank L. Rizzo, the city's hard-line police commissioner, in his successful race for mayor. Jews voted for his liberal opponent, however, much more heavily than other whites.[21] Even now, a generation later, this internal conflict continued in New York's 1989 and 1993 elections, where David L. Dinkins received considerable support in Manhattan but was heavily opposed by Jews in the outer boroughs.

Jews on the "urban frontier" feared that as black radicalism increased, upper-class Protestants would join with the Jewish elite in purchasing social peace at their expense. This had happened in Ocean Hill–Brownsville and in Boston, where WASP bankers, fearful of community upheavals, had steered blacks into Jewish neighborhoods to the disadvantage of both groups. One who warned of such a political truce was Earl Raab, who saw the possibility of a "manipulative symbiosis" between the privileged WASP community and the underprivileged black masses. The developing anti-Semitic ideology in the black movement seemed eminently suited to such purposes.[22]

Agreeing with Raab, a number of Jewish intellectuals broke with their more radical past to embrace what came to be known as neoconservatism. Such figures as Norman Podhoretz, Irving Kristol, Joseph Epstein, Midge Decter, Nathan Glazer, and Milton Himmelfarb helped neoconservatism blossom into a full-scale political force. In 1974 Martin Peretz purchased the previously left-liberal *New Republic* and shifted it to advocacy of a "muscular Judaism" and more conservative themes. Podhoretz's *Commentary*—founded by the American Jewish Committee but editorially independent—provided the primary intellectual vehicle (along with the *Public Interest*, edited by Kristol and Glazer) for most of the Jewish neoconservatives, as well as such non-Jewish political scientists as Daniel Patrick Moynihan, James Q. Wilson, and Paul Seabury.

Commentary changed political direction in the early sixties. Until then, its orientation had been left of center, and its orthodoxy had been predictable. Podhoretz, who had grown up in a working-class section of Brooklyn, welcomed the radicalism of the period. As late as 1961 he ran a piece sympathetic to a black militant who had resorted to the use of arms in North Carolina. (The article was so inflammatory that the NAACP censured Podhoretz for publishing it.) Not long after that, troubled by what he viewed as a radical takeover of the black power movement, Podhoretz switched sides.

He worried that community control was, in effect, a turning over of the schools "to a new breed of leader—the kind . . . who lived on the ghetto streets and who led riots rather than the kind [like Martin Luther King and Bayard Rustin] who came in from outside and tried, unsuccessfully, to stop them once they had started." Along with many other Jews of his generation, he feared that black anti-Zionism coupled with New Left radicalism would set off a fresh wave of anti-Semitism in the United States.

In December 1964 Nathan Glazer, writing in *Commentary*, warned that while frictions between lower-class blacks and Jews were nothing new, such feelings were now more widely shared by the new black middle class and white-collar and leadership groups. He foresaw an ominous future for what had been the special black-Jewish relationship. In April 1969, he coupled criticism of black anti-Semitism with an even stronger attack on Jewish radicals, like William Kunstler, who advised and abetted black militants.

Beginning in the June 1971 issue and continuing with extraordinary intensity in the coming years, *Commentary* began to strike out sharply in its defiantly provocative style at these perceived dangers. The first piece, "Quackery in the Classroom," took aim at radical, educational theorists. Subsequent articles targeted the Black Panthers, "literary revolutionism," women's liberation and other "new age" notions.

Blacks, of course, responded bitterly to Jewish neoconservatives. They felt that the former Jewish liberals, having completed their integration into American society, had come to identify with its prevailing racist patterns in exchange for inclusion in the white majority. The suspicion that Jews had backed off from civil rights activities because they were "making it"—the title, not incidentally, of Podhoretz's autobiography—would remain a primary cause of black anger against Jews.[23]

If *Commentary* spoke for Jewish neocon intellectuals, the Jewish Defense League became the voice for militant elements of the Jewish working and lower middle classes. The league came into existence during the Ocean Hill–Brownsville strike, and by 1972 it had fifteen thousand members in New York, Philadelphia, Los Angeles, and elsewhere. In seeking to dispel the passive-victim stereotype of Jews, the JDL somewhat resembled the Black Panthers. Its founder, Rabbi Meir Kahane, had grown up in a Brooklyn household steeped in Zionist tradition (Ze'ev Jabotinsky, patriarch of the Israeli right, had been an occasional visitor). Kahane had joined the youth movement of the Herud party when it was led by future Israeli prime minister Menachem Begin, and he had received paramilitary training in the Catskill Mountains of upstate New York.

In the mid fifties, after his ordination as a rabbi, Kahane headed a congregation in Howard Beach, New York, while simultaneously working as a sports columnist and general writer for *Jewish Week*. According to a recent biographer, Kahane developed close ties with the FBI at this time and infiltrated the extremist John Birch Society on its behalf. But in the tumultuous 1960s he emerged as a defender of embattled Jews in high-crime, rundown urban neighborhoods.[24] Kahane set up a weapons camp and martial arts training center in the Catskills, then and now an area of Jewish resort hotels.

One of those attracted to his movement was a seventeen-year-old Brooklyn yeshiva student named Leon Wieseltier. Wieseltier, subsequently the literary editor of the *New Republic*, later wrote that Brooklyn Jews were as besieged as their ancestors had been and as their brothers and sisters in Israel still were. They too were fighting for their lives. With the start of the Six-Day War, he said, all classes at the yeshiva were suspended, and as some of the teachers wept, radio coverage of the war was broadcast over the school's public-address system.

What also drew Wieseltier to the JDL was the New York City teachers' strike and the concurrent shock of black anti-Semitism. He felt that he and those like him in Flatbush, Borough Park, Bensonhurst, and Crown Heights had found their real enemy, adding in all candor, "I will not pretend that we were betrayed liberals. Still, a young paranoid needs an enemy, and we had agreed to let Kahane train us in paranoia."[25]

A master of media manipulation, Kahane established chapters in Philadelphia, Los Angeles, and other cities. He was sharply criticized by established Jewish organizations for advocating the use of violence; but as Chaim I. Waxman has pointed out, his initial success stemmed from addressing issues of which the large Jewish organizations were seemingly unaware.[26]

Haskell Lazere, director of the American Jewish Committee's New York chapter, made a similar point, laying the responsibility for the rise of Kahane on those Jewish agencies that had lost touch with the rank and file. Lazere wrote that the Jewish establishment was out of step with the neighborhoods and the streets.

Kahane not only preached violence but used it. In 1971 several JDL members drew prison sentences for bombing the offices of Jewish impresario Sol Hurok, who had booked Soviet ballet dancers in New York. A secretary was killed in the bombing. Kahane himself fled to Israel after being indicted on conspiracy charges and founded a radical political party whose platform called for the expulsion of Arabs from Israel. He was later shot to death while delivering a speech in New York in 1990. Though Kahane's violent methods were unacceptable to the great majority of Jews, it seems safe to say that his influence was far greater than many would admit. The JDL's motto, "Never Again," caught the mood of many Jews and expressed their desire never again to respond passively to mortal threats either at home or abroad.

Even as some Jews were drawn variously to neoconservatism and to Meir Kahane's JDL, radical Jewish elements remained firm in their support of the new black extremism. A group led by attorney Victor Rabinowitz with past links to the Communist party kept SNCC financially viable for a while. Others, like New Left intellectual Arthur Waskow, distrusted political liberalism with its emphasis on compromise and coalitions and gave their leftist ideology a fresh Jewish cast. In organizations such as Jews for Urban Justice and the Jewish Liberation Project, "new Jews" found in the Jewish tradition a rationale for their continuing social commitment.[27] They created Havurahs and other vehicles of informal Jewish expression and community. Waskow, an assimilated Jew and civil rights activist, joined with friends to write a "freedom seder." Published first in the left-wing magazine *Ramparts* and then as a book, Waskow's text gave a contemporary resonance to the ancient Jewish fight for freedom, the theme of the original seder, and proved popular with young Jews, especially radicals. In other writings, Waskow identified with black urban rioters, arguing that blacks who emptied stores of food and watches in the Washington, D.C., racial disorders of April 1968 were merely emulating the children of Israel, who looted Egypt of gold and jewels as reparations for four centuries of slavery.[28]

Another "new Jew" who was even more outspoken than Waskow was Michael Lerner. The son of middle-class parents—his father was a state court judge and his mother an aide to a U.S. senator—Lerner had been radicalized at Berkeley, where he became a leader of the Free Speech Movement. Appalled by what he perceived as rampant political corruption, he attacked his fellow Jews for forsaking their religion. In the Fall 1969 issue of *Judaism*, Lerner denounced the entire Jewish community as racist, internally corrupt, and an apologist for the worst aspects of American capitalism and imperalism. He singled out the synagogue and Jewish religious bodies, arguing that as currently constituted, they would have to be smashed. Black anti-Semitism was directly attributable to oppression by Jews of ghetto blacks, Lerner said, and called it "an earned anti-Semitism."[29]

In 1986 Lerner founded the Jewish magazine *Tikkun* as a left-wing response to *Commentary*. (*Tikkun* is a Hebrew word meaning "to mend, repair, and transform the world.") The magazine proclaimed itself the voice of "progressive" Judaism, and in its pages Lerner ardently supported the Palestine Liberation Organization and other radical causes. (In 1989 he retracted his earlier blanket condemnation of the entire Jewish community, describing it as mere adolescent rebellion. Interestingly, Lerner wrote that he had been pressured to disguise his Jewish identity in order to gain credibility as a New Left leader, opining that he had been guilty of internalized anti-Semitism.)[30]

"Black power," Shelby Steele has written, "evoked white guilt and made it a force in American institutions." White guilt, he declared, lay behind the efforts of many civil rights activists to end discrimination against blacks in the fifties and sixties. But later, guilt led some of these same whites to condone social behavior and policies that were unfocused and dysfunctional.[31]

Henry Schwartzchild, a refugee from Nazi Germany, was appalled by what he had seen at the New Politics convention in Chicago in 1967. Nevertheless, he expressed the view that since there was massive, historical victimization in American society not unlike that endured by Jews in Europe, the victims—in his "Jewish judgment"—could draw upon a large account of moral credit. Speaking explicitly for himself (and presumably others), he indicated that even hostile and violent behavior could not exhaust that credit balance.[32]

Jewish Currents, a magazine edited by the long-time leftist Morris Schappes likewise sprang to the defense of the newly radicalized SNCC, declaring in its July-August 1966 issue that it was particularly important for Jews, who were ever alert to the dangers of racism when it affected them, to avoid misjudging an idealistic, heroic movement like SNCC, whose purpose was to abolish racism. Freelance journalist I. F. Stone, who in the late forties had been associated with the left-wing New York newspaper *PM*, saw psychological therapy rather than practical politics in the phrase "black power." And as Julius Lester came under sharp attack for his use of the inflammatory poem on the radio, he received strong backing, publicly and privately, from Carolyn and Robert Goodman (the parents of Andrew Goodman) and from the brother of Michael Schwerner.[33]

In one of the decade's most controversial essays, novelist Norman Mailer published "The White Negro," an extraordinary elegy to ghetto violence, in *Dissent* magazine. Perhaps imitating Jean-Paul Sartre and the French existentialists, Mailer at one point praised the "courage" of two eighteen-year-old hoodlums who beat in the brains of a candy-store owner. He later admitted having second thoughts about the piece, saying that he had been using drugs at the time, was afflicted by self-doubt, and had written the essay more for ego gratification and symbolic catharsis than to influence anyone's opinion. Socialist intellectual Irving Howe, who edited *Dissent*, said that though he later regretted having published the piece, he did so because of its "bounce and brilliance." He also said it helped sell a lot of copies of the magazine.[34]

For Leonard Bernstein, another Jewish member of the cultural avant-garde, it was apparently a sense of personal guilt coupled with a genuine desire to promote racial justice that prompted him to stage his controversial Park Avenue fund-raiser for the Black Panthers. The famous conductor and composer had been a lifelong liberal activist, according to his biographer. His acceptance of the post of music director of the New York Philharmonic in 1958 forced him to muzzle his humanitarian impulses for the next ten years. In 1969 Bernstein—a friend of Sammy Davis, Jr., and James Baldwin and a contributor to the NAACP's Legal Defense Fund—was humiliated by a discrimination suit brought by a black musician against the Philharmonic. New York City's Human Rights Commission subsequently ordered the orchestra to end its racial bias. Bernstein's need to reestablish liberal credentials resulted in a party for the Black Panthers that prompted Tom Wolfe, in a satirical article in *New York* magazine, to coin the term "radical chic."[35]*

While left-wing Jewish artists and intellectuals sought to keep alive their commitment to social progress in this period, most establishment Jewish religious organizations and civic bodies also supported what the Synagogue Council of America called "the prophetic injunction to do justice." In 1967 the Anti-Defamation League had published *Protest and Prejudice*, a five-year study by Gary T. Marx, which found that most blacks were not anti-Semitic, or were at least not more virulently so than most non-Jewish whites. Where such prejudice existed, it resulted from actual con-

---

*One little-explored aspect of the history of black-Jewish relations is Jewish support for the Black Panther party, which, unlike militant separatists, sought alliances with radical whites. They helped the party and its leaders gain national attention. According to David Horowitz, a former *Ramparts* magazine editor, Bert Schneider, the producer of *Easy Rider*, introduced him to Huey Newton in 1973. Horowitz went on to develop and head up the party's Oakland Community Learning Center before breaking with it.[36]

tact with Jews in the sphere of economic relations. Deplorable as this was, Marx wrote, it was certainly more understandable than white anti-Semitism. A year later the National Jewish Community Relations Council declared that it would not disengage from the struggle for liberal measures in race relations just because some Negroes were violent, ungrateful, or anti-Semitic.[37]

Albert Vorspan, a leader of Reform Judaism's social action movement, wondered why Jews who had withstood the fulminations of Gerald L. K. Smith and the violence of the Ku Klux Klan were panicked by indications of anti-Semitism on the part of black militants. He concluded that the hysteria was an excuse to justify Jewish disengagement from social concerns. Backing President Johnson's War on Poverty, Vorspan called for the creation of two million jobs for unemployed blacks. If private enterprise could not or would not provide them, he said, it was the responsibility of government to do so.

Even Max Fisher, president of the United Jewish Appeal and perhaps the nation's leading Jewish Republican, supported such programs. When race relations in New York were shattered by the teachers' strike, Fisher called for continuing assistance to blacks, noting that Jews who truly believed in the advancement of social justice should harbor no lingering doubts about whether helping people in the inner city represented a genuine Jewish commitment.[38]

Despite the harsh rhetoric of black power advocates and the growing reservations at the grass roots level, Jews all across the political spectrum struggled to keep this commitment alive and to maintain their own sense of self as liberals or progressives at the close of the 1960s. They did so even as Jewish and black interests were beginning to diverge and conflicts deepened. In the coming years the gap would widen. But before discussing this, it is necessary to examine another segment of the Jewish community, one cut off, to some degree, from the main body of Jews and how they responded to the civil rights and race revolutions—Jews living in the South.

13

THE NINETEEN MESSIAHS

Southern Jews Caught in the Middle

Throughout the turbulent sixties Jews living in the South were caught squarely in the middle of the civil rights struggle. Their generally muted response to the protest movement reflected their unusual position.

A single incident may serve to illustrate the predicament of southern Jews. In 1958 the Anti-Defamation League's Virginia–North Carolina office sent a parcel of educational materials dealing with racial understanding to a conference sponsored by the NAACP in Charlottesville, Virginia. The materials included portions of the film *Songs of Friendship*, a "Dolls for Democracy" kit, a comic book entitled *About People*, a pamphlet asking *Shall Children Be Free?* and a set of "Bible on Brotherhood" posters.*

The mailing was innocent enough, but the subliminal message provoked outrage. The message was that a Jewish community-relations agency, based in New York but with an office in Richmond, backed the Supreme Court's epochal decision barring school segregation. That was not what the white South wanted to hear just then. Although the court ruling was four years old, little had been done to implement it. Instead, much of the South was openly defy-

*I had personal knowledge of this incident because I headed that office at the time.

ing the court, and any individual or group favoring desegregation was automatically suspect.

In resolutions adopted by their legislatures, eight southern states had brushed aside the decision and sought to interpose their own authority, arguing that they had never yielded their sovereignty at the founding of the Republic. Three other states passed similar proclamations, and the South now threatened to shut down its schools rather than integrate them. Nine public schools in Charlottesville, Norfolk, and other sections of Virginia were, in fact, already preparing to lock their doors. In Washington 101 out of the 108 congressmen from eleven Southern states signed a "southern manifesto" against integration. Virginia's governor J. Lindsay Almond spoke for many when he told the Virginia legislature that he would never willingly be a party to the destruction of education by the mixing of races in the classrooms.[1]

In this climate of fear and suspicion, segregationists had a field day. When James J. Kilpatrick, then editor of the *Richmond News-Leader* (and more recently a syndicated conservative columnist and television personality), got wind of the ADL's involvement in the NAACP's conference, he sprang into action. In consistently opposing the court ruling and urging resistance to it, Kilpatrick had become the intellectual leader of southern resistance. Now he attacked the Anti-Defamation League and specifically the Richmond office. In an editorial on July 7, 1958, he observed that anti-Semitism appeared to be on the rise in a section of the country that was traditionally hospitable to Jews, suggested that southern Jews themselves should search out the reasons for this phenomenon, and pointed to the ADL's Richmond office. By deliberately involving itself in the school desegregation controversy, he wrote, it was identifying all Jews with the unjust cause of compulsory integration.

Kilpatrick conceded the agency's right to interest itself in any form of bigotry but warned that militancy invited retaliation. He then put a question to what he termed the South's many esteemed and influential Jews. What use could they possibly have for a Jewish organization that actively foments hostility to Jews?

The widely read editorial stunned Jewish communities throughout the South. Kilpatrick had struck a nerve. He seemed to be suggesting that, if southern Jews failed to support the campaign of massive resistance to desegregation or even remained neutral, they would arouse further anti-Semitism, possibly even acts of violence. Though Kilpatrick had no anti-Jewish record prior to or after this episode and very likely he sought only to curb opposition, Jews felt threatened.[2]

Kilpatrick's theme was picked up by southern segregationists. When Rabbi Emmet A. Frank criticized massive resistance in a Yom Kippur sermon from his pulpit in Arlington, Virginia, the local citizens council cautioned that his comments would cause irreparable damage to interfaith relations. Shortly thereafter, a bomb threat emptied a Unitarian Church in Arlington just before Rabbi Frank was to speak.

Alarmed, a group of Jewish leaders in Richmond met with Kilpatrick. According to his later account, the Jewish group expressed regret that he had written the editorial but stated their belief that it would do a lot of good, and they promised to use their influence to minimize the ADL's future involvement in the segregation controversy. A local ADL board committee subsequently reviewed materials to be disseminated and recommended that the league cease dealing in racial themes and stick solely to Jewish matters. For a time, that was what the ADL's Richmond office did. But some months later, when Virginia capitulated to a court order calling for termination of segregated education, the office returned to its normal operations.[3]

In the 1950s there were about two hundred thousand Jews living in the eleven states of the old Confederacy—a little over one-half of one percent of the region's population. Though few in number, southern Jews had deep roots in the region and were highly regarded. As Kilpatrick himself accurately noted, the South had a strong tradition of philo-Semitism. According to folk philosopher Harry Golden, rural southerners treated the Jewish population almost as a private possession. "He is 'our Jew' to small-town Southerners," Golden wrote, "and they often take care of him with a zeal and devotion otherwise bestowed only on the Confederate monument in the Square." Beyond this, there were historical and cultural congruities in the experiences of both groups. Both were outsiders in the larger society, Jews because of their religion, southerners because of their defeat in the Civil War and the widely held perception that they were backward and bigoted.[4]

Cities like Richmond, Savannah, and Charleston were home to some of the oldest Jewish communities in the nation. Charleston, in fact, had been the first municipality in the New World to permit Jews to vote. But southern Jewish settlements differed markedly from those in the North and West. Whereas the other areas received vast numbers of eastern European Jews at the turn of the century, many of the southern Jews had emigrated earlier from Germany. They tended to be more homogeneous and also more conservative, both socially and politically, than their counterparts elsewhere.[5]

Jews in the South were often community leaders. In 1954 there were only five or six thousand Jews in the entire state of North Carolina, but both Durham and Gastonia had Jewish mayors, as Greensboro had previously had. Durham's mayor, E. J. Evans, took office in 1950 and was reelected six times. He ran the city out of his department store and didn't hesitate to demonstrate his Jewishness. His wife was a national leader in Hadassah, a Jewish women's organization.[6]

While many Americans tended to view the South as a sinkhole of racial and religious intolerance, southern Jews considered anti-Semitism there less pervasive than in other parts of the country. Passions aroused by the South's stormy race relations may have diverted attention from the small Jewish population that seemed so much like the white majority. As Hodding Carter put it, "It takes perseverance to hate Jews and Negroes and Catholics all at the same time." Yet the affection felt for individual Jews as neighbors did not necessarily extend to the group. William Faulkner made this point in *The Sound and the Fury*, when he had one of his characters declare, "I have nothing against Jews as individuals. It is just the race."[7]

More than anything else, what southern Jews tried to do was fit in. "Fitting in" required conforming to the region's often curious social and cultural mores. Texas-born Diane Ravitch has written that the Jews she grew up with took pains not to antagonize other whites. Their goal, she said, was to become, "just as Texan as other Texans."[8] Stephen J. Whitfield found that the strongest body of anti-Zionist sentiment among American Jews in the first half of the century was found in the South. The rule seemed to be that the older a family's roots in the region, the more anxious they felt about relations with their neighbors.

The black-Jewish alliance did not exist in Dixie for good reasons: the South, during most of this period, functioned as a closed system. "Fitting in" meant, most of all, avoiding any challenge to the racial status quo, and that meant accepting segregation. Silent acquiescence thus became standard behavior for many southern Jews. There were no Joel Spingarns here. For such an isolated group to flout authority on the explosive issue of race was to court social ostracism and, in the Deep South, possibly risk one's life.

Except in the Deep South, however, few Jews living below the Mason-Dixon Line were ardent segregationists. A 1965 survey found that southern Jews were twice as likely as southern white Protestants to feel that desegregation was both inevitable and desirable in the long run. Only about one-third as many Jews as WASPs were inclined to believe that blacks were inherently inferior. As one local black told a rabbi in Birmingham in the strife-filled 1960s, "a Jew can't make a good racist."[9]

Judah Benjamin's biographer wrote that, as a southern Jewish leader in the Civil War, he had to be more loyal to the Confederate cause than anyone else, more outspoken in the cabinet, more courageous, and more willing to meet the demands that total war required. The same might have been said of the comparatively small number of southern Jews who supported massive resistance.[10]

Despite their social and political conservatism, southern Jews cast few votes for Alabama's segregationist governor, George C. Wallace, in his runs for the presidency. It seems safe to say that when the civil rights movement took hold, most southern Jews would have preferred living almost anywhere but there where the fiercest battles were fought. Try as they might to win acceptance, they never fully gained it. And they were keenly aware of the violent strain in the southern temperament. While the targets of the terrorists were usually blacks, acts of anti-Semitism were not uncommon. According to Janice R. Blumberg, wife of an Atlanta rabbi, the murder of Leo Frank by an angry mob in 1915 was a "ghostly idol," reminding Jews that they would be safe only so long as they remained in the back room and kept silent. Southern

Jews grew up with the thought of Frank's lynching never far from their minds.[11]

Political discourse in the South was also unnerving for its Jewish population. Throughout the 1940s two Mississippians, Senator Theodore G. Bilbo and Representative John E. Rankin, filled the halls of Congress with anti-Semitic tirades. In their lexicon "Jew" was synonymous with "Communist," and they often attacked Jews as subversive allies of the Negro. Rankin, who once described the Fair Employment Practices Commission as a product of "alien influences directed by a foreign comintern that is based upon hatred for Christianity," actually introduced legislation to outlaw the ADL but got nowhere with it. Both he and Bilbo, it should be pointed out, distinguished between "good" southern Jews, who backed white supremacy, and New York Jews, who supported the NAACP. Rankin said the "better element" of Jews throughout the South and West was not only ashamed but also alarmed by the activities of Jewish Communists, who were responsible for the rapes and murders of white girls by "vicious Negroes."[12]

Such views were not confined to demagogic politicians, redneck farmers, and the Ku Klux Klan. In 1948 a prominent member of the Daughters of the Confederacy's North Carolina chapter circulated a letter charging that most of the Communists in the United States were Jews and that most agitators stirring up southern Negroes were of Jewish origin. Jews also supplied most of the money for such activities, she said.[13]

In the decades before World War II, hotels and resorts discriminated against Jews in the South, just as they did in the North.[14] Leonard Dinnerstein, who has studied southern Jewry closely, has concluded that, contrary to other Jewish accounts, southern anti-Semitism was far more widespread than previously acknowledged.[15]

Between individual southern Jews and blacks there often were remarkable relationships, such as that depicted in *Driving Miss Daisy*, Alfred Uhry's play (later a prize-winning film). While these relationships were hardly a meeting of equals, within the constraints of the system, Jews often tried to help. The relatively friendly feelings between the two groups were enhanced by warm memories of the support Julius Rosenwald had given to black education in the South. When Rosenwald's daughter married New Orleans businessman Edgar Stern, the Stern Family Fund continued the tradition of support. In the sixties it would provide major organizing grants for the voter-education project of the Southern Regional Council, which played an important role in registering three million new black voters.

Each group, however, knew its place. Even Martin Luther King, Jr., dared not violate the southern code. Janice Blumberg tells of the time she and her rabbi husband, Jacob Rothschild, invited King and his wife to their Atlanta home for dinner. The guests were late. King explained that they had had difficulty reading street numbers and asked nearby residents for directions to the rabbi's house. King assured his hosts that "we were careful not to embarrass you with your neighbors. I let Coretta go to the door so they'd think we were just coming to serve a party."[16]

Black-Jewish relations in the South were generally more harmonious than those in the North. The type of anti-Semitism that flared from time to time in the ghettos of New York, Detroit, and Chicago was not found in Atlanta, Charlotte, or Birmingham. Southern cities were smaller and their slums less daunting. Jewish landlords in the South were rarely accused of rent-gouging, nor were Jewish merchants regularly cited for exploitation. In the North young blacks might attack Jews; in the South, as E. J. Evans wrote, the southern Jewish kid knew that the black kid would not lay a hand on him. Jews and blacks did not compete for jobs in the South, and there were no Bronx "slave markets" there. Noting northern black hostility towards Jews, a southern black observed: "There is no Jew hatred among us . . . there are many things we must hate before we get to so lovable a people as the Jew." Southern black newspapers sometimes criticized the Jew-baiting of some northern blacks. Typical was the *Atlanta World*, which warned (on August 13, 1938) that blacks were playing with dynamite when they condemned all Jews for the alleged transgressions of a few. Thirty years later Gary T. Marx found that blacks in Atlanta and Birmingham scored far lower on his index of anti-Semitism than did those in New York and Chicago.[17]

The reign of terror that followed the Supreme Court's 1954 school decision mainly targeted southern blacks. But it was a nightmare, too, for the small and isolated Jewish communities of the South.[18] The Klan stepped up its activities, and scores of citizens councils were formed to block enforcement of desegregation orders. According to James Silver in *Mississippi, The Closed Society*, the citizens council in Jackson created a card file listing the racial views of nearly every white person in the town. A Jewish resident of Jackson compared the council's activities to those of the Gestapo—neighborhood canvassing, with questions like, Would you send your child to an integrated school?

Historian C. Vann Woodward described the scene this way:

> Books were burned, libraries purged, news suppressed, magazines excluded, TV programs withheld, films banned. Mob violence accompanied the first desegregation of schools in the border states of Texas, Kentucky, Tennessee, and West Virginia in the fall of 1956. Some cities closed their public schools entirely. Lower South states made no gestures of compliance at all, and, in fact, boasted of their defiance. In September 1957, Governor Orval Faubus of Arkansas carried resistance to the point of using the state militia to halt token integration at Little Rock. Under a court order, he withdrew his troops but their place was taken by hysterical, spitting white mobs who forced the removal of nine black children.[19]

From 1954 to 1965, according to records kept by the Anti-Defamation league, there were 227 bombings of black homes, churches, and other places of worship. Forty-three murders were linked to civil rights activities, and more than one thousand instances of racial violence, reprisals, or intimidation were reported. Southern Jews found themselves in the midst of a social revolution, and as always in such periods of turmoil, they were blamed. Temples and other Jewish facilities were bombed in Atlanta, Nashville, Jackson, and Jacksonville, while undetonated dynamite sticks were found on the steps of synagogues in Birmingham and in Charlotte and Gastonia, North Carolina.

Jews living in the Deep South were pressured to join local white citizens councils. The small number who did so rationalized their actions by arguing that as insiders, they would be in a better position to control "excesses." Paul Anthony, former director of the liberal Southern Regional Council, insisted that Jewish merchants had little choice; they had to join their local councils or go out of business. "It was a real blackmail deal," he declared.

A few Jews needed no urging, however, to expound segregationist views. Charles J. Block, a respected lawyer in Macon, Georgia, wrote to congratulate Kilpatrick for his attack on the ADL and urged him to write another editorial attacking the American Jewish Congress and the American Jewish Committee as well. Another Jew eager to sign on with the white supremacists was Rabbi Benjamin Schultz. According to Silver, one of the citizens councils in Mississippi "eagerly clasped to its bosom" a rabbi who moved there from New York—undoubtedly Schultz—and who soon began denouncing both intellectuals and pro-Communists.[20]

The ADL, with its network of staffed offices in the region, was a major watchdog of Jewish defense at this critical time. On May 11, 1958, it convened a meeting of seventy-five Jewish leaders of community relations agencies, both North and South, to consider steps in the wake of synagogue bombings and other terrorist acts. It is perhaps most significant that southern Jews resented the interference of certain Jewish agencies that, from safe havens in New York, kept condemning segregation and demanding that the South quit defying the Supreme Court. Some attributed the increase in overt anti-Semitism and bombings to a Southern white backlash against the positions proclaimed by these Jewish agencies.

To assuage his Southern wing, Benjamin R. Epstein, ADL's national director, sent senior staff members into the South to consult with Jewish leadership there. In one month during 1958, ADL staff representatives visited 143 communities. In each case, local ADL leaders were promised that they would have final determination on implementation of the agency's national program. ADL's relations with its southern branches improved after that.[21]

Sociologically, economically, and politically, the South was no place to develop strong Jewish civil rights efforts in this period. And yet a few leaders did emerge. Georgia's *Gainesville Times*, edited by a Jewish journalist named Sylvan Meyer, was one of the first newspapers in the South to support the *Brown* decision. Jewish store owners continued to back Hodding Carter III's *Delta Democratic Times* in Greenville, Mississippi, when the local citizens council began a house-to-house drive to destroy the newspaper's circulation and frighten away advertisers.[22]

The most outstanding Jewish civil rights leader in the South was Morris B. Abram, an Atlanta lawyer who later served as vice-chairman of the U.S. Commission on Civil Rights. Abram grew up in the small town of Fitzgerald, Georgia, in the aftermath of the Frank lynching, an event that shaped his life, and later served on the American legal staff that tried Nazi war criminals at Nuremberg after World War II. He would never be the same after Nuremberg, Abram wrote in his autobiography, for he now understood "that when the veneer of civilization is cracked, even in the twentieth century, the Jew was the first victim."[23]

Returning home, Abram coauthored a pamphlet with ADL's southern director, Alexander F. Miller. *How to Stop Violence in Your Community* suggested ways of curbing the Ku Klux Klan; five states and fifty-five cities subsequently enacted the legislation it recommended. One such measure prohibited the wearing of masks in public. Another barred the burning of crosses except with the written permission of the owner of the site. Largely because of his civil rights activities, Abram lost a race for Congress.

His greatest victory came later in the battle over Georgia's "county unit" voting method. This system gave disproportionate strength to eight thinly populated Georgia counties that were the largest in land area. Few blacks lived in these rural districts, which often held the key to statewide elections. The 550,000 people in heavily black Fulton County, most of them residents of Atlanta, shared just six votes, for example, while all-white Echols County, with a population of only nineteen hundred, was assigned two votes. On winning Georgia's governorship in 1948, Herman Talmadge boasted that he and the county unit system were the only bulwark protecting Georgia against the federal courts' race-mixing plans in grade schools and colleges.

In launching his attack on the segregationist system, Abram coined a slogan that would gain national and even international currency: one man, one vote. He filed a succession of suits in the Supreme Court, sustaining one loss after another, although with each defeat he gained more public support. In 1958 he brought a suit with William B. Hartsfield, the liberal mayor of Atlanta, which they lost by a narrow 5–4 margin. Vindication came on March 18, 1963, when with only one dissent the Supreme Court ruled that "within a given constituency there can be room for but one constitutional role—one voter, one vote." Abram's persistence and determination had thus advanced a political slogan into a constitutional principle.[24]*

Jewish journalist Harry Golden was an unlikely activist. Short and stout with a cherubic face and a cigar sticking out of his mouth, he could have been taken for a peddler on the lower east side of Manhattan, where he grew up. In his thirties Golden moved to Charlotte, North Carolina, established the *Carolina Israelite*, and built a name for himself as an original talent. There was no other publication quite like his seriocomic journal; it was pure, unadulterated Golden, without photos or advertisements. He would jot down notes on southern history, Jewish life, anti-Semitism and toss them in a bin. When the bin was full of notes, he published them in the *Carolina Israelite*, which was then mailed to a growing list of subscribers all over the country.

One of the subjects that fascinated Golden was the South's curious contradictions on race. He noted, for example, that as long as whites and blacks stood on their feet, there was no danger of a race war. They stood together at supermarket counters and in bank lines. They even ate standing up together at lunch counters. But when black schoolchildren sat down with white schoolchildren in public school classrooms, the entire South erupted. To solve this problem, he proposed the Golden Vertical Integration Plan. Under this plan all the public schools in the South would be equipped with

---

*Abram figured prominently in an episode involving his friend Martin Luther King, Jr. that may have helped John F. Kennedy win the presidency in 1960. After being arrested for picketing Rich's department store in downtown Atlanta that year, King was convicted for an earlier traffic violation and sent to an isolated prison known to be especially vicious in its treatment of blacks. The King family, fearing he would be murdered, sought Abram's help in getting him released. Abram contacted Kennedy's civil rights adviser, Harris Wofford, who talked to the candidate. Kennedy, risking the loss of votes in the South, subsequently telephoned Coretta King, expressing sympathy and support. The widely publicized call apparently led to King's release. Instead of costing Kennedy votes, it won him the backing of liberals who had questioned his sincerity and may have been an element in Kennedy's narrow victory over Richard Nixon.[25]

old-fashioned stand-up desks of the kind used by bookkeepers. Education, he reckoned, could then proceed in peace and quiet.[26]

Golden's White Baby Plan was based on the clever ploy of two black schoolteachers. To avoid being segregated in the balcony of a movie theater, they had "borrowed" the small children of two white friends and, posing as nursemaids, sat in the theater's downstairs whites-only section. Golden suggested that sympathetic whites provide a pool of children to make it possible for blacks to desegregate movie houses.

After his schemes were reported by the national media, Golden gained celebrity as a lecturer and author. He had the nation chuckling, including the South, which was the butt of most of his joshing. He was even admired by James Kilpatrick. Jonathan Daniels, publisher of the *Raleigh News and Observer*, referred to Golden as the "old imp." "The remarkable thing," said Daniels, "is the extent to which the South accepted him." What Golden did, with his northern liberalism and Jewish sense of incongruity, was to make even the most ardent segregationists laugh at themselves. When that happened, segregation's days were clearly numbered.

Jacob Rothschild of Atlanta was one of a small group of Southern rabbis who spoke out against segregation. When another rabbi cautioned him against taking such a strong stand, Rothschild acknowledged that his activism might set off a wave of anti-Semitism in the tense environment of that time. But since Jews expected others to risk their lives for just causes, he said, how could they ask any less of themselves?[27]

His outspokenness on racial issues undoubtedly led to the most spectacular bombing of a Jewish institution in the South. On Sunday, October 12, 1958, shortly before the children were to arrive for school, a loud blast rocked Rothschild's synaogue, leaving a gaping hole sixteen feet wide. Walls were smashed, pillars broken, and glass shattered. Tons of water from a broken main poured through the sanctuary. The reaction provoked by the blast, however, was the opposite of what the bombers had expected. There were no casualties, but the bombing was highly publicized and outraged the nation. President Eisenhower expressed shock and directed the FBI to join the investigation. Led by Mayor Hartsfield and Ralph McGill of the *Atlanta Constitution*, citizens of

Atlanta rallied behind the Jewish community. In her reminiscences Rabbi Rothschild's wife, Janice, entitled the chapter on the incident "The Bomb That Healed" and said that Jewish fears engendered by the Frank case had remained strong until the bombing. "One ended what the other started," she wrote.[28]

Rabbis Perry Nussbaum of Jackson, Mississippi, Emmett Frank of Arlington, Virginia, and Charles Mantinband, who had synagogues in Alabama, Mississippi, and Texas, also criticized segregation publicly. Few others did, however. Most southern rabbis lived and worked in small communities where racism was deeply ingrained. While a few preached in support of desegregation and said the courts had to be obeyed, most were careful not to utter such sentiments publicly.[29]

Southern branches of the Jewish agencies played a quietly constructive role in backing the forces of moderation, but they did not get directly involved in the work of the NAACP, SCLC, or other civil rights groups. At one point Andrew Young asked attorney Henry Schwartzchild, an ADL staff member and a volunteer in the black protest movement, to help out in Birmingham over a weekend. Schwartzchild so advised Benjamin Epstein and Arnold Forster, who were running ADL headquarters in New York. According to Schwartzchild's account, the two officials looked at each other and then told him to go if he felt impelled to do so, but not to bother coming back. Schwartzchild went anyway, ending his relationship with the league.[30]

As a means of monitoring extremist threats against blacks and Jews alike, ADL developed close ties with the FBI in the South. Schwartzschild believes these links to the bureau kept the league from a more forceful role in civil rights matters, but they were a necessary precaution in a situation fraught with danger. In *Terror in the Night: The Klan's Campaign Against the Jews*, Jack Nelson describes an alliance forged by the local police, the FBI, the ADL, and the local Jewish community following a series of bombings of Jewish institutions in Mississippi in which two white Klan adherents were lured into a deadly ambush when they tried to bomb the home of a Jewish businessman in Meridian. It seems clear that where Jews were involved—especially after the deaths of the three civil rights activists—the response of law enforcement authorities was usually swift and strong.

For the most part, the ADL sought to function as an honest broker between the races and to shore up the forces of moderation. While such a stance was hardly heroic, the ADL's presence added to the strength of those who favored change and were aggressively working for it.

With its organizational know-how, the ADL helped such groups as the Southern Regional Council, the Georgia Council for Human Rights, the Urban League, and the Women's Christian Social Action Committee of the Methodist Church to launch their race relations programs. While not directly involved in the desegregation fight, ADL was certainly involved indirectly through its efforts on behalf of the Save Our Schools movement. This movement sought to keep open those schools threatened with closings over desegregation. Though Save Our Schools committee meetings were sometimes held in ADL offices, the league remained wary about its activism. For example, the director of its New Orleans chapter wrote a pamphlet explaining the meaning of the Supreme Court decision and urging citizens to abide by it; but the pamphlet was distributed, not by the ADL office, but by certain board members and other Jews acting anonymously. These precautions were deemed necessary to avoid retribution, since such involvement raised suspicions among extremists who kept close tabs on ADL staff.[31]

Of course, the blacks faced dangers considerably greater than Jews did. Still, threats to the more outspoken Jewish leaders were not uncommon. After A. I. Bortnick, the ADL director in New Orleans, was advised that a notorious white supremacist named Byron de la Beckwith had targeted him for assassination, police stopped Beckwith's car. In it they found a Bible, a city map on which Bortnick's home was marked, and a box with a clock and sticks of dynamite set to go off. Beckwith was later sentenced to five years in prison for transporting explosives into the state without a license. (In 1993, after a third trial, he was finally convicted for the 1963 ambush slaying of civil rights leader Medgar Evers.)

While Charles Mantinband was abroad in 1958, the local citizens council in Mississippi urged his temple to fire the "mischief-making rabbi." The council said that it could not be responsible for the consequences if Mantinband continued speaking out against segregation. His congregation refused to buckle, but on Washington's Birthday in 1963, Rabbi Mantinband, in great distress, wrote that all around him there was a lack of courage and true spirituality and that he was very lonely. A few months later he moved to Texas.[32]

In the summer of 1964, southern terrorists bombed a Jewish temple in Jackson, Mississippi, and another bomb was placed under the bed of a rabbi there. Fortunately he and his wife were away when it went off. At about the same time, a young Klansman was caught placing a bomb in the carport of a Jewish businessman in Meridian, Mississippi. He was promptly tried and sentenced to thirty years in the state penitentiary. (This was unusual. More often the violators went unpunished.)

Ironically, it was not racists but rather the Jewish civil rights protesters from the North and West whom southern Jews feared most. In demonstrating on behalf of blacks, the out-of-staters stirred fierce resentments among southern whites, including indigenous Jews who feared that their livelihoods and even their lives might be jeopardized by the "troublemakers." After the murders of Goodman, Schwerner, and Chaney, a fourth-generation German-Jewish merchant in Mississippi said that though he felt sorry for the boys, nobody had asked them to come down and "meddle with our way of life."

Following the annual convention of the Rabbinical Assembly of America in 1963, a major conflict arose between northern rabbis and southern Jews. During the course of the meeting in the Catskill Mountains, nineteen rabbis volunteered to join King's Birmingham crusade. News services picked up the story, and when Birmingham's Jews heard about it, they panicked. A delegation of these Jews, many of them merchants whose businesses had suffered from King's boycott, met the rabbis' plane and urged them to turn around and go home, according to Evans. The astonished rabbis conferred with the delegation until dawn, but the two groups could not reconcile their differences.

The "nineteen messiahs" (as they were called by local Jews) took rooms at a motel owned by a black businessman named A. G. Gaston, which served as King's headquarters. They spoke at black churches and taught the Hebrew melody "Hava Nagilla." When word leaked out that they planned to march at the head of one of King's demonstrations, angry local Jews demanded another meeting. One woman accused the rabbis of wanting to go home as heroes while leaving the others behind to suffer the consequences. The rabbis sought to make clear that they were there only at the request of the Negro leadership, but the meeting ended inconclusively. Later, when Gaston's motel was bombed, Birmingham's Jews blamed the out-of-town rabbis for stirring up trouble.

Even more vexing to southern Jewish communities were the militant civil rights workers, many of them Jewish students from the North and West, who converged on the South at this time. Evans said that although the young volunteers lacked commitment to the South and any knowledge of the poverty, deprivation, and desperation of rural blacks, they were nonetheless ready to bind themselves over to the concept of equality. The Jewish demonstrators fraternized mainly with other activists rather than with local Jews. Occasionally they would hold a "freedom seder" during Passover, but Jewish residents never joined them.

The protest movement exposed with startling clarity what Stephen J. Whitfield has labeled the aura of make-believe regarding the acceptance of Jews in southern society. The Jewish fear that the civil rights movement might disrupt their presumably excellent relations with Christian neighbors suggested that these relations were less solid than had previously been acknowledged.[33] Nor was their position with blacks made any easier as the movement became more militant, though some blacks were truly sympathetic. One black leader in Atlanta said that the temple bombing was understood as a warning from the other whites to the Jews. Since black churches were frequently so treated, black identification with the Jews increased. Fred Shuttlesworth, who was involved in local protests, said that the response of southern Jews to the civil rights movement compared favorably with that of numerous other white groups. Other blacks criticized the Jews for not doing more, however. Aaron Henry told one Jewish leader that since the Jews themselves had suffered so much over the centuries, they should have been more willing to fight for the rights of black people.

As the black power movement gained strength, black-Jewish relations worsened even in the South. The separatists' fiery rhetoric often appeared to foster anti-Semitism. One day in 1968, Rabbi Rothschild discussed his concerns with members of the Hungry Club, a group of prominent black businessmen and professionals who met regularly for lunch in Atlanta. Having braved considerable local criticism for accepting the cochairmanship of a testimonial dinner to honor King for winning the Nobel Peace Prize, Rothschild believed he had earned the right to speak openly to the black audience. With deep emotion he protested the effort by certain radical blacks to exclude Jews from the battle over civil rights. Jews had participated from the beginning and did not want to be shunted aside now, he said. He argued that it was his fight, too, since as a Jew, he was committed to justice, dignity, and equality and would not forgo this religious commitment even in the face of black separatism.

His audience, instead of applauding his remarks, booed and hissed. Rothschild was crestfallen. He told a white friend who had heard the speech that it might well be too late to convince the black community of Jewish determination and sincerity. When he was honored at a dinner two weeks later, not one of his black friends showed up. The message could not have been clearer.[34]

14

CHARLESTON

One More Battle

The fracas in Ocean Hill–Brownsville and other developing collisions clearly demonstrated the rupture between blacks and Jews. Despite the strains, significant elements of the Jewish community, including most establishment and left-wing organizations, joined black moderates in continuing to seek a way of keeping the alliance intact.

When Bayard Rustin and Stanley Levison—the chief architects of the modern phase of the partnership—joined Martin Luther King in Montgomery in early 1956, their primary aim was to tap a new source of energy and help bring order and direction to the budding civil rights movement. Their loyalty to King and commitment to his cause kept them involved until, and even after, his assassination twelve years later. From the outset, however, their long-term goals transcended the protest effort. Besides challenging America's racial laws and attitudes, Rustin and Levison sought to link the black protest movement to a broader campaign for social and economic justice in a nation with a long history of discrimination against its minority populations.

In the process, whether consciously or not, these veterans of the black-Jewish radical community did much to revive and rebuild the fortunes of the shattered left from which they had emerged. Indeed, they enjoyed far greater success than they had any reason to expect. The series of victories that culminated in the dramatic "freedom summer" of 1964, followed by the enactment of civil rights legislation in Washington, created a veritable sea change in American life. Even the Old Left witnessed some renewal.[1]

Likewise, there can be little doubt that King's close association with Rustin and Levison was a significant factor in bringing him closer to the left and particularly to the trade union movement. In the years after the Montgomery bus boycott, King had become especially close to unions like the United Packing House Workers, District 65; the American Federation of State, County and Municipal Workers (AFSCME), and the Hospital Workers' Union, Local 1199—unions led by Old Left Jewish radicals. Local 1199, especially, offered King the opportunity to reknit ties between Old Left progressives and anti-Communist liberals both within and outside the labor movement. These unions were also leaders in organizing the public employee revolution, the involvement of low-paid (often minority) public-sector service employees—municipal sanitation workers, professionals, teachers, federal employees—in the labor movement.[2]

King appeared at every District 65 convention after the Montgomery bus boycott. He would often interrupt his civil rights activities to assist in organizing drives among black and Puerto Rican workers. His aim was to forge an alliance between unions and the SCLC, and he was on just such a mission on behalf of sanitation workers when he was murdered in Memphis in 1968. His efforts here were a good example of King's ability to cross boundaries between groups and build coalitions. His actions stemmed from a fundamental belief in the need to merge the energies of various groups in common causes, a view that sharply diverged from that of black nationalist separatists like Malcolm X and others.

After Operation Dixie ground to a halt in 1953, efforts at union organization lost steam throughout the South. In 1968 SCLC joined AFSCME's unionization efforts in Atlanta and St. Petersburg. At its 1968 national convention AFSCME voted to launch a nationwide organizing effort, and although the campaign in Memphis was only partially successful, business and political leaders there ultimately agreed to a voluntary dues checkoff. That had been the key goal. AFSCME's president Jerry Wurf felt that if his union could organize in Memphis, it could organize anywhere.[3]

Efforts were simultaneously underway to organize hospital workers in Charleston, South Carolina. After twelve organizers were fired by Charleston hospital authorities, a union delegation sought the help of Local 1199, which was based in New York and affiliated with AFSCME. It was one of the few remaining organizations in which radicals played any part at all. *New York* magazine writer Joe Klein described it as "the last haven for old Communists, fellow travelers, and the romantic left."[4] Somehow it survived the red purges of the fifties and emerged with more than half of the independent drugstores in New York under contract. Under Leon Davis and Moe Foner, one of four radical Jewish brothers prominent in labor and academic circles, 1199 comprised a tough, tight-knit crew, confident of itself but distrustful of others, even within organized labor.[5]

Local 1199 retained a vision of social reform based on radical ideology. It supported rent strikes, helped in the legal defense of the Black Panthers, opposed the war in Vietnam, and criticized Israeli settlements in Arab-occupied areas. It also remained in contact with Third World elements—most of its membership was black or Puerto Rican—that were at the core of 1960s radical politics. At the same time, it was able to gain support from such powerful New Yorkers as Nelson Rockefeller and union moderate Harry Van Arsdale, Jr., president of New York's Central Labor Council. But its habits of mind, its remnants of party discipline, and its network of associations were rooted in the "good old days."

Moe Foner had met and begun to work with Stanley Levison in the 1957 youth marches led by Randolph and Rustin, and it was through Levison that Martin Luther King forged strong ties to the union. Supporting its successful effort to unionize New York City's hospital workers in 1959, King told the strikers that their struggle was, above all, a fight for human rights and human decency. He frequently visited 1199's New York headquarters, spoke or sent messages to its rallies, and referred to it as "my favorite union." When, after King's murder, 1199 formed its National Organizing Committee of Hospital and Nursing Home Employees, it made Coretta King its honorary chairman. Abernathy and other SCLC leaders served on the committee. When black union representatives in Charleston sought its help in 1969, 1199 proved that part of the black-Jewish alliance was still in place.[6]

With King gone, Foner now turned to Levison for help in Charleston. At first, Young doubted that Charleston's black workers could win the unionization battle, but Levison advised him that victory was possible if he was prepared to settle in for a siege.[7]

Working mainly through Young, who was in constant telephone contact with him, Abernathy was persuaded to bring SCLC into the strike.[8] With Levison acting as go-between, SCLC and 1199 coordinated strategy. The union gathered national backing for the strikers and trained the SCLC staff in labor-organizing techniques while SCLC directed a campaign of civil disruption in the community. Between April and July of 1969, more than a thousand people were carted off to jail including Abernathy and Davis. As always, Levison remained in the background, but Foner, Young, and William Rutherford, SCLC's executive director, frequently called on him for advice and assistance.

Telephone conversations monitored by the FBI showed Levison's close involvement. Never one to pull his punches, he was often critical of the work of his associates. In one such conversation with Young on May 1, 1969, Levison made it clear that both he and Coretta King were dissatisfied with arrangements for a meeting she had just addressed in Charleston. There were no loudspeakers in the downstairs section of the hall, and the rally lacked cohesion. He was not surprised, said Levison, that South Carolina's governor had "pulled his curfew business." Young simply was not giving the governor enough trouble. He was not getting the community organized.

In his own defense Young pointed to the lack of manpower. There were only three or four full-time people to do the organizing; the others pitched in when they felt like it. The two-headed leadership made matters worse, he said, because nobody really understood the division of responsibility between the union and SCLC.

Levison was not appeased. He said that another defeat would probably mean that the leadership of SCLC would have to go. "You can't take two defeats, the Poor People's Campaign and then this. . . . Why aren't your best agitators in there?" He urged Young to increase his personnel by half to get across the sense of urgency and to bring back Coretta King, Rosa Parks, and Fanny Lou Hamer.

(Often a word from Levison was enough to kill a proposal. At one point Young suggested a boycott of Detroit's 1970 line of automobiles. When Levison responded negatively, Young backed off, and the idea was dropped. On another occasion Rutherford said SCLC was thinking of raising bail money to free Abernathy and Hosea Williams from their Charleston cells. Levison told him not to do it. The union, he said, would take care of the matter.)[9]

Despite its organizational problems, however, the Charleston strike temporarily united the moribund civil rights movement. Late in April the heads of nine civil rights organizations and five elected officials, all led by Coretta King, issued a joint statement in support of the strike. It marked the first time black leaders had come together on a single issue since the murder of King. Feuding between the AFL-CIO and black leaders over the slowness of union efforts to integrate blacks halted as well. Randolph moved away from his attack on the organization and took the position that alliance and cooperation were imperative.[10]

After months of heavy media coverage, Charleston became a cause célèbre for northern liberals. Late in April 1969 twenty-five congressmen, led by New York's Ed Koch, called upon President Nixon to intervene. The request was brushed aside, but several weeks later seventeen senators, including New York's Jacob Javits and Minnesota's Walter Mondale, appealed for federal mediation.

A Mother's Day rally on May 11 drew a throng of thousands to Charleston, including a biracial group of congressmen. From New York came Koch, Allard Lowenstein (now a congressman), and William F. Ryan; from Michigan, John Conyers and Charles Diggs. According to Fink and Greenberg, the hospital workers' campaign had revived a spirit of interracial cooperation at a time when cooperation between blacks and liberals (especially Jewish liberals) was undergoing severe strains.[11]

Koch, reflecting later on the scene, contrasted the security guard of neatly dressed, well-mannered young black men in Charleston with the black-jacketed Panthers he had seen at home. He said that his hostility toward the inflammatory Panthers made him feel a rapport with men who were clearly capable of defending a march without frightening the marchers. He contrasted the warmth and brotherhood he felt in Charleston with the coldness and racial separateness in New York City.

Earlier that day Koch had lunch with Abernathy and Abernathy's son, Ralph III. Asked what he wanted to be when he grew up, the ten-year-old replied that he wanted to be a minister, an attorney, or a freedom fighter. On his return to New York, Koch wrote that he intended to be a congressman *and* a freedom fighter.[12]

While SCLC was enjoying some success in Charleston, however, its leadership was in turmoil. Abernathy, despite a full measure of courage and dogged determination, was often a disruptive force. Personally vain and seen by his close colleagues as dominated by his wife, he lacked his predecessor's charismatic qualities and could not sustain a movement that was collapsing even before King's assassination. Young, speaking to Levison on July 8, expressed concern for Abernathy's emotional state. He said that Abernathy seemed to get better in jail but relapsed after his release.[13]

Levison's phone calls made clear his annoyance at the failure of Young and others to dump Abernathy. He reprimanded Andy one night, he told Harry Belafonte, and asked Young when he was going to do some fighting. Levison himself, however, perhaps out of recognition that he should not try to manipulate the leadership of a black organization, never confronted Abernathy directly. (He did write a harsh letter to him but received no reply. When Levison asked Young how Abernathy had reacted to the letter, Young replied that he seemed apathetic. "I guess Stan figures I flunked already," he told him.)[14]

In Levison's view, therefore, Abernathy in a Charleston jail was a more effective leader for SCLC than Abernathy free. When Coretta King asked Levison if she should seek to persuade Abernathy to accept bail—she was being pressed by "Daddy" King and Martin's brother, who felt he presented a pitiful figure in jail—he told her not to go anywhere near the jail. The imprisoned Abernathy provided a figure people could rally around, he said. That was the role of a leader. She should send him a telegram of support but not appear to be seizing control of SCLC while its head was incarcerated.[15]

After four months, almost one thousand arrests, and millions of dollars lost in damaged property and boycotted sales, the Charleston strikers returned to work. Though they had failed to win union recognition, they claimed victory anyway, on the grounds that grievance procedures had been established.

As the widow of the most celebrated black man in American history, Coretta Scott King struggled to find a role for herself after her husband's murder. An intelligent, strong-willed woman devoted to nonviolence, she sought to play a role in a collective leadership of SCLC. Unable to get along with Abernathy and out of place in the male-dominated organization, she turned her energies to the development of the Martin Luther King Center for Non-Violent Change in Atlanta.

Increasingly she turned to Levison, her husband's old friend and adviser, for guidance. She often called simply to complain of her day-to-day frustrations. She wanted a Jamaican couple to handle household chores and help care for her children, but she was encountering red tape. Her lack of privacy—people came to her house and treated it as a tourist attraction—troubled her. She was uncomfortable shaking hands with strangers and signing autographs. People kept staring at her. What could she do? Hearing this litany, Levison was invariably calm, sympathetic, and understanding.[16]

On other occasions Coretta King sought help on more substantive matters. Levison frequently counseled her before public appearances and wrote speeches and articles for her. One of the speeches he wrote was for a convention of Protestant and Catholic writers in Atlanta. After completing it, Levison laughingly told Young—in a phone conversation taped by the FBI—that he considered himself one of the foremost religious writers in America. He also helped with her book of reminiscences, *My Life with Martin Luther King, Jr.*[17]

An essay that Levison and Belafonte wrote for the *McGraw-Hill Encyclopedia of Biography* was included verbatim in Coretta's memoir. "Our piece ends the book," Levison told Belafonte in a conversation overheard by the FBI. "It's a darn nice book," he added, "considering that it's written from the point of view of a 'white liberal.' "

As the deadline for the book neared, Levison told another friend that he managed to include some material that the publisher had wanted kept out. One section that apparently made the publisher nervous was the observation that King did not have a one-dimensional, negative attitude toward black militants and black nationalists; rather, he had respect for them as they did for him. There was a crisis over Vietnam that the publisher did not want to deal with, but Levison insisted that these troubling passages also be kept in.[18]

Levison and Coretta were on the phone constantly. She was well prepared for questions on the television program "Meet the Press," for Levison gave her materials to read beforehand and told her what to expect from her interrogators. When she was asked to head the 1970 fund drive of Antioch College, Levison advised against it. Kenneth Clark had just resigned, he said, and this might bring her into collision with him; she should concentrate instead on plans for the Martin Luther King Center. When NAACP head Kivie Kaplan requested her appearance at a Massachusetts social work conference, Levison again advised a rejection. Kaplan had done nothing for SCLC, he said.

Not infrequently, Levison boasted privately of his influence with Coretta King. After James Forman pressed the National Council of Churches for financial reparations for the nation's racist past, Levison confided to Young that he had had Coretta say that this was not enough to ask of the churches, whose eighty million members could forcibly push for significant legislative changes.[19]

Levison and Mrs. King enjoyed reminiscing about her late husband and gossiping about his staffers, particularly the clumsy Abernathy, of whom they shared a poor opinion. Coretta feared that Abernathy was killing the SCLC program and that his aides were not performing well, either. Levison agreed, noting that they lacked direction. He thought that Young had a good mind and fine qualities; but he was indecisive, he avoided problems, he wanted to keep the peace.

"The reluctant conclusion I've come to," Levison told Coretta, "is that the courage of SCLC died with Martin. I don't think Ralph or Andy has courage." Coretta replied that her husband had had the quality of love that gave him the ability to heal all wounds, but Abernathy did not know the meaning of love. She said she felt this keenly at Resurrection City, where poor people badly needed someone to care about them.[20]

For years the FBI's bugging of Martin Luther King's telephones had been an open secret. Finally, in a Houston courtroom in June of 1969, an FBI agent let the cat out of the bag. He said he had supervised the eavesdropping of King's calls and those of Elijah Muhammad, the Black Muslim leader. During his lifetime Robert Kennedy had issued ambiguous and inconclusive denials that as attorney general he had authorized the bugging of King. Following the Houston episode, President Nixon promptly checked to see whether J. Edgar Hoover, in carrying out the wiretaps, had acted "on his own or with proper authority." Nixon subsequently reported that the taps had "always been approved by the Attorney General." Hoover himself indicated that they had been ordered by Robert F. Kennedy over FBI objections—an assertion that was vigorously denied by former Kennedy administration officials and disbelieved by all those familiar with the FBI chief's devious ways.

In the furor over the wiretapping, Stanley Levison's name did not surface as a key adviser to King. Reference was made only to the involvement of a New York lawyer. Not until 1975 was Levison identified as the "mysterious political influence" over the slain civil rights leader. Questioned by the press, he denied ever having engaged in subversive activities or being a member of the Communist party. To his associates Levison professed unconcern about the bugging. He told Young that he did not have anything to hide. He had never made telephone calls to discuss conspiratorial actions; he had talked openly about strategy in the movement and if that was what they wanted to record, he said, let them record it.

After the bugging was made public, Coretta King phoned Levison to report that Ethel Kennedy had called to say that she was sorry about what had been in the paper; she hoped it would not interfere with their relationship. Taken aback by the call and a bit awed, Coretta assured Ethel that though she knew the press could be divisive, she would not let the reports color her attitude toward the Kennedy family in any way. She emphasized that she considered Hoover the man most responsible for the wiretaps. "Oh, I'm so glad!" Ethel Kennedy responded.

Levison told Coretta that she had handled the conversation just right. They both knew that her husband, whether he felt that Robert Kennedy had been involved or not, had always maintained a friendly relationship with Kennedy. "In other words," Levison went on, "if he [King] felt that Bobby Kennedy had done anything, he forgave him for it." That was the position she ought to take. King admired Kennedy's capacity for growth. Coretta agreed. Levison added that her husband had been planning to support him for the presidency in 1968. She agreed with that as well.[21]

After King's death black militancy became even more shrill and extreme, further narrowing the base of black activism. While some militants became reformers, others were content to drop out of the movement or spout empty rhetoric. Ella Baker had dropped out early from the SCLC, feeling that its hit-and-run style did not permit the development of grass roots strength. By 1968, she had joined the Southern Conference Educational Fund. Leroi Jones was now Professor Amiri Baraka. Stokely Carmichael, living mostly abroad, had become Kwame Touré. Eldridge Cleaver continued to rant about "Zionist motherfuckers" and "the Jewish Mafia," becoming finally a born-again religious fanatic.[22]

Levison meanwhile watched helplessly as SCLC disintegrated. Tragedy in Memphis, ineptitude in Washington, chronic financial problems, and divisive internal wrangling left the organization impotent. Local 1199 disparaged the SCLC staffers who were sent to Memphis, Levison told Coretta. The union was keeping only one of fifteen. "Moe Foner said they don't work," Levison reported. "They just sit around and talk."[23]

Within SCLC rival lieutenants battled for the scraps of power. Each functioned like "a little feudal lord that had been given a principality," Levison told Rustin. Jesse Jackson's strength was among blacks in Chicago, where he ran Operation Breadbasket. Young appealed to Northern white liberals, while Abernathy's following was drawn largely from the black poor in the South.

Levison and Rustin, who helped to give SCLC organizational coherence earlier, felt that it needed a complete overhaul. To unify these disparate elements, Levison favored some form of collective leadership and a greater degree of democracy within the organization. But none of those jockeying for position would take direction from anyone else. It quickly became apparent that only King, no one else, could hold together the clashing egos.[24]

Jackson's independence and his unwillingness to perform as a team player had long irked King. Before his death King directed Rutherford to deal with Jackson once and for all, making it clear to him that he had to choose between being a part of SCLC or being out of it.[25]

King got nowhere, however. He had wanted Jackson to quit his base in Chicago and set up Operation Breadbasket nationally. But according to SCLC's historian, Jackson's reluctance to leave Chicago even for regular board meetings amounted to insubordination. Levison had initially been drawn to Jackson because of reports of his "successes" in Chicago. (Levison had been active in support of a self-help program for blacks through the American Jewish Congress.) His view cooled considerably when it became evident that many of the jobs that Jackson claimed to have found for blacks never materialized.[26]

Even so, Jackson's personal dynamism and his quotability won him constant press coverage; colorless Ralph Abernathy could not compete with Jackson in canniness or charisma. By 1969 Levison was warning Rutherford that he had to get rid of Jackson, "or SCLC will just break up and fall into the ocean." Eventually the problem solved itself. In December 1971 financial improprieties were reported within Operation Breadbasket. When Abernathy sought to discipline him, Jackson resigned from SCLC, taking the Chicago branch with him.[27]

One by one the old-timers left SCLC. Rustin departed to become executive director of the A. Philip Randolph Institute in New York. (Randolph decided to provide him with an organizational base rather than let him float around as an itinerant reformer.) Ella Baker and Bob Moses had left earlier, Moses to become active in SNCC. In 1966 his opposition to the Vietnam war and decision to avoid the draft caused him to flee to Canada. Later he moved to Tanzania. James Bevel went through a series of evolutions, finally ending up as a vice presidential candidate on the ticket headed by political zealot Lyndon LaRouche. Wachtel was dropped from the board of SCLC following an internal wrangle. Although Andrew Young never formally broke with Abernathy, his popularity with white liberals and his friendship with Coretta King raised questions about his loyalty. "We're an exhausted organization," Young declared, and in 1970 he left SCLC to enter politics, eventually becoming mayor of Atlanta.[28]

With Young's departure Levison's active role in the organization he had done so much to create came to an end. He continued to raise money for SCLC, however, and spoke proudly of his close association with King. He told his son Andy that at a meeting in New York, Belafonte had introduced him as "Martin Luther King's superior practically." Such praise obviously meant a lot to him.[29]

Levison kept in touch with his old friends, and the FBI conscientiously recorded his pungent comments. He remained hostile to black nationalist movements and the ersatz revolutionaries on college campuses. In his view the students were a problem for everyone. After armed black undergraduates were photographed leaving Cornell University's administration building, Levison told his son that white spines would be trembling for a month. The students represented an image of twenty-two million armed black men, women, and children. They had provoked hysterical terror among the white middle class. He feared that the students, in disrupting the establishment, were laying the groundwork for a right-wing, even fascist, takeover.

Blacks, he believed, were as confused as whites about what was happening in the country. They did not recognize the necessity of class solidarity and an approach to social change based on the older, New Deal—the pragmatic left—model: programs with broad rather than race-based appeal.[30] Levison exaggerated the threat of fascism, but he clearly anticipated one of the elements that would bring the conservative wing of the GOP to power for more than a generation. This confusion, together with the inward turn both Jews and blacks were now taking, the worsening of economic conditions that generated so much black anger and resentment, and persistent Jewish concern over the safety and security of Israel and the several million threatened Soviet Jews, effectively doomed the remnants of the black-Jewish alliance.

Always the supreme tactician, Levison sought to mold all shades of opinion into the causes he served. Though he had earlier helped persuade King to criticize the slogan "Black Power," he expressed admiration when Rabbi Arthur Lelyveld, the newly installed president of the American Jewish Congress, spoke respectfully of the term. Lelyveld, said Levison, "has a pretty advanced type of thinking."[31]

Levison knew that black-Jewish relations were deteriorating. He knew that something had to be done about it. It was clear, however, that his focus was less on newly emerging black-Jewish tensions that on the impact of black extremism on continuing efforts in behalf of social justice.

Levison favored coalitional politics that would bring blacks into alliance with such politicians as Edward Kennedy on the national scene, John Lindsay in New York, and Tom Bradley in Los Angeles. He shared Belafonte's concern about right-wing tendencies in the United States but disagreed with the singer's contention that the country needed "a more rigid social system" to keep things under control.[32]

In some respects (not all) Levison's evolution paralleled that of the Jewish community in the postwar civil rights era. He had been a New Dealer (according to his brother) who found his way into Communist party circles as a result of the threat of anti-Semitism and fascism, the social dislocation of the Great Depression, and the dangers to civil liberties during the McCarthy era. His activities reflected the addiction of many Jews to utopian solutions for their own and the broader society's problems. For a while the Soviet Union seemed to embody these hopes, and he clung to them until the failures of Communism finally became apparent to him around 1956, at which time he linked up with Martin Luther King and the civil rights movement. King quickly came to represent for him a new force for realizing the dream of a more just social and economic system. His loyalty to King would never waver.

Throughout everything, Levison remained a man of the left, and this fact undoubtedly animated the deep concern that J. Edgar Hoover and the FBI felt about him. The FBI continued to bug Levison's phones and follow his activities through informants until at least 1971, despite the fact he had no Communist party associations and there had been no information from any source indicating party influence in his activity on behalf of SCLC. Why the FBI continued to monitor Levison when it conceded he had no Communist ties is a mystery.[33]

With King gone, Levison returned more openly to his older left-wing associations. He was no longer forced to protect his leader from charges of disloyalty and subversion, no longer obliged to remain in the shadows. He was free at last to be his own man. A "progressive," he remained suspicious of liberals. When Young asked if union leader Walter Reuther had at one time been a red-baiter, Levison replied that Reuther was like a weather vane: he was bad when times were bad. He told Coretta King black capitalism was still a "mirage" but argued nevertheless that blacks had to get into the mainstream of industry and trade.[34]

In a discussion with Moe Foner about mounting a political attack on Senator Strom Thurmond of South Carolina under the aegis of the Leadership Conference in Washington, Levison warned that its executive head, Arnold Aronson, "is a conservative liberal [whose] hero is Bayard Rustin." Levison felt, nevertheless, that his help should be sought.[35] And in the Angela Davis case of 1971, which had been taken up by the anti-Communist left, Levison finally did in fact shed his anonymity and take a public stand, as opposed to operating privately behind the scenes.

Davis, a high-ranking Communist functionary—more recently described as a "black activist"—had been charged with murder, kidnapping, and conspiracy to supply the guns used in a bloody shootout in Marin County, California, whose victims included a judge. The U.S. Communist party and its national chairman, Harry Winston, came to her defense, as did a number of mainstream organizations. Americans, stunned by student disruptions at Kent State and Jackson State, convict rioting at Attica (New York) state prison, and the continuing struggle in Vietnam, were transfixed by this black woman whose radicalism seemed to epitomize the violence that was tearing the nation apart. Her trial drew wide attention here and abroad.

Bettina Aptheker, the daughter of Communist scholar Herbert Aptheker and a Communist herself, was a leader in the movement to defend Davis. She helped secure funds from Levison and Moe Foner, who saw providing a black activist with a legal defense as a civil liberties issue. Levison agreed to approach members of SCLC's board of directors. A few days later, he reported to Aptheker that the board had agreed to appeal to its entire national mailing list of more than one hundred thousand people. Levison and Foner raised enough money to pay for the mailing.[36]

The Davis case split the NAACP's Legal Defense Fund. Jack Greenberg, its head, and his longtime black colleague James Nabrit recommended she go elsewhere for legal help. Younger black lawyers, however, wanted the fund itself to defend her. They charged that Greenberg did not understand how important it was to defend a black woman who epitomized resistance to white oppression.[37]

The issue was taken to the fund's board of directors, which, over heated opposition from young black and white attorneys, sided with Greenberg. A black woman thereupon resigned and joined the Davis defense team. The episode reflected the widening black-Jewish schism. Greenberg, one of the true stars of the civil rights movement, was now dismissed by many blacks as overly conservative and out of step with the times.[38]

Levison set up a defense fund for Davis and asked Gloria Steinem, the editor of *Ms* magazine, to serve as its treasurer. A committee met in Levison's home to prepare a fund-raising letter, which was sent to everyone on SCLC's list. Signers included Steinem, Moe Foner, and actor Ossie Davis, who served as fund chairman. Also signing the letter was Levison. It was one of the rare occasions when he permitted his name to be used publicly in connection with a cause that he believed in. The fund-raising effort brought in some fifty-thousand dollars, and a jury ultimately acquitted Angela Davis.

Following a long illness, Stanley Levison died in New York in September 1979. A crucial link in the black-Jewish alliance, Levison, like King, was unique in his ability to synthesize elements of an earlier generation of radicalism with the energy of black demonstrators. Efforts to reconstitute the alliance after his death never coalesced as they had during the King era. The two groups had undergone considerable change; nor did the conditions that had brought blacks and Jews together as partners still exist.

A memorial service was held, appropriately, at the Martin Luther King, Jr., Labor Center in Local 1199's headquarters. Moe Foner and Andrew Young were cochairmen. Young, who had just resigned as ambassador to the United Nations after a controversial meeting there with a PLO official, paid tribute to his longtime ally. "Stan Levison was one of the closest friends Martin King and I ever had," he later told the *New York Times*. "Of all the unknown supporters of the civil rights movement, he was perhaps the most important. He never pushed his own views on us."

From Atlanta, Coretta Scott King sorrowfully paid tribute to her husband's trusted friend. "Because he was such a modest man," she said, "few people know of the magnitude of his contributions to the labor, civil rights, and peace movements. He was truly one of the great unsung heroes in the nonviolent struggle for justice and social decency in twentieth-century America."[39]

15

THE SEVENTIES AND EIGHTIES

Racial Quotas and the Andrew Young Affair

Throughout much of the history of the black-Jewish alliance, the partnership was defined by the issues that united the groups. By the 1970s, however, and in subsequent years, the relationship came increasingly to be defined by issues that drew them apart. Nowhere was this more evident than in the conflict over racial preferences as a primary means of assuring blacks full access to American life.

To Jews, the movement to utilize racial preferences to assure minorities a fair share of jobs, elected offices, and other evidence of inclusion brought back memories of anti-Semitic quotas governing admission to prestigious American universities and law and medical schools. To many Afro-Americans so long denied opportunities, however, such measures offered a catch-up. The opposition mounted by Jews was therefore unexpected and appeared to them to be hypocritical.

Racial preferences by this time had come to be seen by many blacks as the next stage of the civil rights revolution. With the battle over quotas clearly in mind, revisionist historians Mary Berry and John W. Blassingame wrote in *Long Memory: The Black Experience in America* that in the seventies every advance blacks made was challenged by Jewish groups.

The Civil Rights Act of 1964, the high point of the civil rights revolution, had promised equal opportunity for job seekers regardless of race, creed, sex, nationality, or background. Its sponsors and supporters had argued that the doctrine of equal opportunity prohibited discriminatory treatment but did not promise preferential treatment. Yet from the outset critics of the act contended otherwise.

When the bill was debated in the Senate in 1963, Hubert H. Humphrey, one of its chief supporters, felt compelled to assure his colleagues that the plan's proponents had carefully stated that Title VII of the act did not require an employer to achieve racial balance in the work force by giving preferential treatment to any individual or group. Title VII established the Equal Employment Opportunity Commission (EEOC) to monitor compliance.[1]

Even after enactment of the legislation, however, vast numbers of blacks remained outside the nation's economic system. Frustrated by the lack of progress, civil rights bodies like the NAACP sought to move beyond the concept of equality of opportunity to achieve equality of results. President Johnson, in his historic address at Howard University just prior to passage of the Voting Rights Act, pointed out that opening up the gates of opportunity was not enough. It was necessary to move on to the next and more profound stage of the battle for civil rights, affirmative action.

According to historian Hugh Davis Graham, the effort was led, albeit not exclusively, by "a heavily Jewish brain trust" at the EEOC and other bodies. This group included civil rights activists like Herbert Hill, the highest ranking white figure in the NAACP, and Jack Greenberg of the Legal Defense Fund. Many other professionals who had honed their skills in Jewish community-relations organizations or city and state governmental bodies also moved on to leadership roles in the new federal agencies that they had had a hand in creating.

In pushing for group-based rights in the workplace, the activists expected no help from Congress, and so they concentrated on the courts. Individual instances of job discrimination were often hard to prove, however, and prosecution was time-consuming. Herman Edelsberg, Washington director of the Anti-Defamation League and later EEOC's staff director, compared case-by-case litigation to trying to fill a bucket with a medicine dropper.[2] This view was shared by the Jack Greenberg.

The activists thus sought instead to provide justification for preferential treatment of minorities by demonstrating statistical inequality in the distribution of jobs and other benefits. To do that, however, they needed to obtain the personnel records of thousands of employers. Although the Civil Rights Act barred public release of personnel records, it permitted such "notation" on the records as might be necessary to reconcile state and local laws with the new federal statute. This was the loophole, wrote Graham, that a zealous, activist bureaucracy needed.

Alfred W. Blumrosen, a Rutgers University law professor and a committed "people's lawyer," joined the staff of the newly formed EEOC during his 1965/66 sabbatical year. Blumrosen managed to obtain a list of sixty thousand federal government contractors with few or no minority employees through a "creative reading" of the law. He later acknowledged that his interpretation of the 1964 civil rights act was contrary to its plain meaning. But conservatives in Congress who might have been expected to object to such actions were distracted by urban rioting and the war in Vietnam. Blumrosen and his colleagues were thus able to establish a uniform national system of employment reporting, policed by the EEOC, that provided data to support racial preferences.

A critical decision in favor of such preferences was handed down by Federal District Judge Charles R. Weiner in 1970. Weiner, a former majority leader of the Pennsylvania state senate, where he had earlier helped to shepherd through much of the state's civil rights legislation, upheld the so-called Philadelphia Plan, which set quotas for minority hiring on all government contracts. Following attacks on its constitutionality, the plan (originally adopted by the Johnson administration) was modified to establish percentage goals for minority hiring in place of quotas. It was aimed at ending racial discrimination in the building trades, which had traditionally kept their membership all white. In supporting the Philadelphia Plan, Weiner said that the strength of a society was determined by its ability to make economic opportunities available to all who could qualify. Civil rights without economic rights were merely institutional shadows of equality. Weiner viewed the protection of these rights as the whole point of constitutional and statute law.

Later in the year the Nixon Labor Department issued a new set of rules extending the Philadelphia Plan to virtually all activities and facilities of all federal contractors. One Labor Department estimate put this at a third to a half of all the workers in the United States.[3]

During the Nixon years other policies promising preferential treatment for minorities were set in motion and institutionalized. Under the EEOC guidelines racial imbalances that existed in a workplace for whatever reason came to be accepted as sufficient proof of racial discrimination. This line of reasoning in turn provided grounds for group remedies, such as the establishment of racial quotas to address presumed as well as real discrimination. Thus, the outcome that Hubert Humphrey had explicitly sought to avoid while lobbying for the Civil Rights Act became a very real possibility. The fears he had sought to allay resurfaced as well.

Jews and Jewish organizations strongly opposed any movement in which quotas played a central part. They also knew that Jews, a highly educated and successful group representing less than 3 percent of the U.S. population, would be heavily disadvantaged if racial preferences gained widespread acceptance and society's benefits were divided along ethnic lines rather than on the principle of merit. Indeed, some workplaces—such as the New York City school system—were heavily dominated by Jews. They would be the ones to suffer if racial quotas were established.* Jewish opposition was thus partly motivated by self-interest. Accordingly, the American Jewish Committee's letter to President Nixon in 1973 urged him to reject quotas and proportional representation in implementing affirmative action programs.

Jewish groups took the lead in 1973, for example, in a case upholding preferential admission in the state of Washington. The case involved a Phi Beta Kappa, magna cum laude Sephardic Jewish student named Marco De Funis, who had been denied admission to the University of Washington law school. Clarence Mitchell, director of the NAACP's Washington bureau, maintained that the

---

*As early as 1968 Daniel Patrick Moynihan had warned that demands for proportional representation in New York City's school bureaucracy would have a special effect on Jews. The quota process, once started, would never stop, he said, and in American educational institutions, it would be Jews who would be driven out.[4]

inevitable effect of the opposition of Jewish groups and others was that most blacks, who have been handicapped by discrimination in their education, would never be admitted to law school.

It was not just Jews, of course, who feared quotas. Many of America's working-class whites, who formed the base of support for the Nixon administration and later for Ronald Reagan's, were similarly alarmed. Jews, however, seemed to be the most vocal opponents of racial preferences. In the process they positioned themselves against blacks and the black organizations with whom they had been working for so many years.

In 1974 Allan P. Bakke, a Marine Corps veteran who had served in Vietnam, applied for admission to the University of California Medical College at Davis. After being rejected both times, Bakke filed suit, charging that the medical school's special admissions policy unconstitutionally set aside sixteen out of a hundred places for racial minorities. Bakke, a Minnesotan of Norwegian ancestry, claimed that he was better qualified than some of those who were admitted under Davis's special program. The program thereby violated the Constitution's Fourteenth Amendment guarantee of equal protection.

After the California Supreme Court ruled in Bakke's favor in 1976, the university's board of regents appealed to the Supreme Court. When the ADL, the American Jewish Congress, and the American Jewish Committee filed briefs on behalf of Bakke, the stage was set for another major black-Jewish confrontation. (Not all Jewish groups supported Bakke. The Union of American Hebrew Congregations and the National Council of Jewish Women supported the position of the University of California.)

On June 28, 1978, Bakke won his case. The high court's 5–4 decision, leaning on the equal-protection clause of the Fourteenth Amendment, ordered the university to admit Bakke. Yet while outlawing Davis's system, the Court upheld the constitutionality of flexible college-admissions programs that used race as one factor in weighing the qualifications of applicants. That vote was also 5 to 4. The swing vote in each case was cast by Justice Powell.

What the Court seemed to say was that carefully crafted affirmative action programs were acceptable, but explicit quotas were not. Justice Brennan addressed this point when he wrote that government could take race into account only to remedy disadvantages placed on minorities by past racial prejudice.

"I think we won," said the ADA's Joseph Rauh. Moynihan regarded the decision for Bakke as promoting "a good, sensible mainstream idea" of affirmative action. Arnold Forster, the ADL's general counsel, said that his organization was relieved that the Supreme Court had declared racial quotas flatly illegal.

Jack Greenberg thought the decision was too narrow both in vote count and interpretation, leaving the validity of many affirmative action programs uncertain while giving the concept a clear legal basis.[5] The *New York Times* editorialized on June 29 that the ultimate outcome depended on how the nation responded to the decision. Discrimination would find other means of expression if prejudiced whites failed to understand that the Court had given its blessing to affirmative action. On the other hand, if blacks and others felt that "the white guy" had won again, grave problems could ensue.

Some blacks did react as the *Times* feared they might. A day after the decision, the headline in New York's *Amsterdam News* read, "Bakke: We Lose!" The paper concluded that the case placed every affirmative action program in jeopardy, whether in colleges and graduate schools or private business and industry. Jesse Jackson likened the decision's impact on blacks to a Nazi march in Skokie (The Chicago suburb where many Holocaust victims had settled) or Klan marches in Mississippi. Angry protesters rallied in San Francisco, Los Angeles, and New York.

Jewish groups were singled out for attack. Joseph Lowery of the enfeebled SCLC charged that Jews "cribbed, cabined and confined" by their own historical encounters with quotas had led the opposition to affirmative action. Louis Clayton Jones, an *Amsterdam News* columnist, blamed Bayard Rustin and "his friends from B'nai B'rith and the American Jewish Congress" for undoing enforceable affirmative action programs. He warned that overtures would be made encouraging blacks and Jews to get together. Deriding such moves, he suggested that a black-Jewish coalition might be called JEWSAC, an acronym for Jews to Support Affirmative Action Committee.[6]

The American Jewish Committee responded that while it was still opposed to racial quotas, it was not opposed to goals and timetables as affirmative action tools. If these goals were not reached despite serious effort, no one would be held culpable. Some observers thought this a distinction without a difference, since they believed such an approach would inevitably lead to quotas. What black groups remembered, however, was that Jews and Jewish agencies had backed Allan Bakke—and won. The damage had been done; many blacks felt they were like shackled runners suddenly allowed to enter the competition.[7]

The battle over quotas had one additional effect. By creating legal distinctions based on race and by encouraging blacks to seek group compensation rather than equal rights, the Court had institutionalized a general sense of black grievance and entitlement that gave a way out to those who felt most damaged by the society. In doing so, the stage was set for the most aggrieved—the purveyors of the more radical strains of Afrocentrist and revisionist thought and the extremists who have always fed on black frustration—to gain a degree of authority they would not have otherwise enjoyed.[8]

Ironically, the bruising battle over quotas, while deepening conflict between blacks and Jews and solidifying white opposition to minority activism, did little for blacks at the bottom of the social scale. It was not the truly disadvantaged, sociologist William Julius Wilson pointed out, but members of the expanding black middle class who were the principal beneficiaries of affirmative action programs, since it was they and not the underclass who were most able to take advantage of civil rights gains and fresh economic opportunities.[9]

With the hope of social progress fading for many of the black urban poor, there was a renewed thrust toward black political autonomy. Many blacks, embittered by their struggles with the system, withdrew from interracial coalitions. A widely publicized incident at the Harvard Law School underlined the extent to which distrust and suspicion had poisoned relations between blacks and Jews. For years a black professor, Derrick Bell, had taught a popular course on race and law at Harvard. When he left to become dean of the University of Oregon Law School in 1982, the course was discontinued. After several years Harvard, under pressure from a group calling itself the Third World Coalition, decided to offer the course again and asked Julius Chambers, president of the board of the NAACP Legal Defense Fund, to teach it.

Chambers, who was heavily engaged in his own law practice, suggested that Jack Greenberg shoulder half the teaching load.

On its face such a collaboration appeared ideal: Chambers was black and Greenberg Jewish. They were both highly respected and they were friends. Chambers had interned at the fund, and Greenberg was a legendary figure in the civil rights movement. Along with Thurgood Marshall and other NAACP lawyers, he had argued and won a number of school desegregation cases in the fifties. Succeeding Marshall as head of the fund in 1961, he proved to be astonishingly effective as both a litigator and fund-raiser. In 1963 alone, his team of 102 cooperating lawyers had defended 10,487 civil rights demonstrators, initiated 168 cases in fifteen states, and took thirty issues to the Supreme Court.

At the same time, Greenberg boosted the fund's annual income from $560,000 to $3 million in nine years. He found time to launch a poverty law project, which provided government-funded legal representation for the poor, and to battle successfully against the death penalty. He was also a strong supporter of affirmative action programs, some of which he felt were being wrongly opposed by Jewish agencies like the Anti-Defamation League and American Jewish Committee as reverse discrimination.[10]

Notwithstanding these qualifications, the announcement of his appointment to teach the course with Chambers provoked an immediate protest and a call for a boycott. The Third World Coalition demanded that a black professor be named instead. Jonathan Kaufman reported that Greenberg's presence reawakened differences that had simmered beneath the surface of black-Jewish relations for years, including affirmative action, Jewish feelings of betrayal, and black resentment of Jewish paternalism. Chambers and Greenberg ultimately went ahead with the course, but the furor surrounding it clearly exposed the widening gulf between blacks and Jews and suggested that an effort to erase the contributions of Jews to the civil rights movement was now under way.[11]

Other veteran battlers for civil rights were similarly repudiated. When Allard Lowenstein attended the fifteenth anniversary of the "freedom summer" in Jackson, Mississippi, in 1979, he found himself the object of deep hostility. Michael Thelwell, a civil rights activist from Jamaica (now a novelist and professor of African-

American studies at the University of Massachusetts, Amherst), shouted Lowenstein down, accusing him of trying to redefine the movement from a struggle to realize the needs of black people to a series of "touchy-feely" sensitivity sessions. Many whites at the conference were troubled by Thelwell's tirade, and some believed that the ensuing debate on the role of whites in the movement was anti-Semitic.[12]

Even as some younger black intellectuals became more radical and moved away from interracial cooperation, a number of Jewish intellectuals turned increasingly conservative in this period and by their writing strongly influenced an entire generation. Nathan Glazer took aim at racial preferences in a widely discussed book, *Affirmative Discrimination*, as did Norman Podhoretz in a number of articles. Podhoretz, who as much as anyone personified Jewish neoconservatism, argued that the billions spent by the federal government on Great Society programs had produced negligible results; everyone could see that the war on poverty was a failure and that the only disagreements concerned the placement of blame.[13]

Most startling of all was the conversion of a number of onetime Jewish liberal and socialist writers to the virtues of American capitalism. Here Irving Kristol, cofounder with Glazer of the magazine *Public Interest*, led the way. He wrote in the *Wall Street Journal* and elsewhere that all citizens, including minorities, benefited both in material well-being and individual freedom from unrestricted market economics.[14] Podhoretz's *Commentary* would support President Reagan's policies abroad and at home in the 1980s. He, too, viewed the Soviet Union as an evil empire and backed efforts to make America and its allies militarily strong enough to meet the challenge. The *New Republic*'s editor in chief and publisher, Martin Peretz, had also by this time switched allegiances, saying he had realized in 1967 that the American Left contained strands of anti-Semitism, not least among Jewish leftists themselves, and that for the first time he had come face-to-face with black anti-Semitism.[15]

A politician who exemplified the contradictions in black-Jewish relations in this period was New York's outspoken three-term mayor, Edward I. Koch. Koch, who referred to himself as "a liberal with sanity," was one of the first to understand that the liberal idealism of the 1960s had been exhausted. His own political odyssey was linked to his success at coping with the anger and resentments welling up among working-class white ethnics and the new fiscal constraints imposed on a New York that had just about gone broke.

Born in the Bronx in 1924, he lived in Newark and later Brooklyn as a youth. Following World War II service, he took an accelerated course at New York University Law School, practiced law in a small Wall Street firm, and lived with his parents on Ocean Parkway in Brooklyn. He entered politics as a Greenwich Village reform Democrat and supporter of Adlai Stevenson in 1952 and 1956. Reluctantly, he crossed party lines to support John Lindsay and shortly thereafter was elected to the City Council without the mayor's endorsement. Later, running against a patrician WASP who claimed a Virginia background—Koch claimed during the campaign that his own heritage went back to Ellis Island—he unexpectedly won the congressional seat that he held until elected mayor in 1977.

The Ocean Hill–Brownsville flare-up between lower-middle class Jewish teachers and black militants reawakened in Koch an awareness of his own youth in the Bronx and Newark, and he found himself responding sympathetically to the struggling Jews he had left behind (they had moved up a bit on the economic rung themselves).

Koch's differences with blacks dated from his first successful run for mayor, when he accused "poverty pimps" of causing a sharp escalation in New York's welfare costs. As mayor he mounted a drive with Blanche Bernstein, his human resources head, to remove ineligibles from the welfare rolls. During his tenure Koch once openly charged that most black people were anti-Semitic.[16]

Despite his loose and sometimes inflammatory rhetoric, Koch probably appointed more blacks to responsible posts in city government than any of his predecessors. His choices, however, reflected an older Jewish liberalism that was out of step with the ideology of the new black leaders. Few of his black appointees had real bases of power within the black community. For this reason Koch was perceived by many blacks as simply the Jewish mayor.[17] Ultimately, his opposition to Jesse Jackson's 1988 presidential bid played a crucial role in Koch's 1989 Democratic primary defeat by black challenger David N. Dinkins, who went on to win the mayoralty race.

At the close of the 1970s, the American Jewish Committee commissioned two studies by William Schneider (then a political scientist at Harvard and now a resident scholar at the American Enterprise Institute in Washington, D.C.) to survey and summarize research findings on anti-Semitism and Israel. His findings were never made public. However, scholars were able to use his materials, and bit by bit they became known and were reported.[18]

Schneider found that while anti-Semitism among both blacks and whites had declined sharply after World War II, a disturbing trend had recently emerged. By 1964, he reported, young blacks had become significantly more anti-Semitic than their young white counterparts, and the gap between them increased over the next decade. Another social scientist, Ronald Tadao Tsukashima, had reached a similar conclusion based on his 1970 study of blacks in Los Angeles; there he found 73 percent of blacks in their twenties were highly anti-Semitic. The figure declined to 59 percent among blacks in their thirties and forties, and 35 percent among those fifty and older. As young black intellectuals multiplied, Tsukashima concluded, commitment to ghetto control in the name of collective welfare might portend a political basis for anti-Semitism in the 1980s.[19]

Blacks, it is true, to some extent still identified with Jews, and Schneider reported that they were more likely than whites to recognize that Jews had faced discrimination. They continued to support Israel, but not to the same extent as whites. Significantly, their support divided along age lines, with young blacks being the least sympathetic to Israel and most opposed to American military aid to Israel.[20]

These findings were striking. Since the end of World War II, survey research had consistently shown that anti-Semitism was declining among younger, better-educated segments of the overall population. In his earlier study for the Anti-Defamation League, Gary Marx had found black anti-Semitism either nonexistent or occurring only among the less educated and as a result of direct negative experiences with Jewish landlords and merchants in slum areas.[21]

Schneider's second report to the American Jewish Committee (March 6, 1979) was even more disquieting. A 1978 survey by Louis Harris and Associates had given evidence for the first time that black anti-Semitism was increasing on an absolute basis. Schneider found as well that national black leaders held significant negative stereotypes of Jews. Of fifty-three such leaders interviewed, 81 percent agreed that Jews choose money over people, and 60 percent that Jews constitute the largest number of slumlords. Schneider concluded that the relative increase in anti-Semitism among younger blacks was political rather than educational or religious in origin, the result of an increase in ideological militancy and conflicting interests between Jews and blacks.[22]

Jewish attitudes toward blacks were also hardening. Neighborhood confrontations in Brooklyn, Queens, Boston, and elsewhere and the organization and activities of the militant Jewish Defense League gave ample evidence of this phenomenon. The JDL stepped up its picketing in high crime areas. It also actively opposed busing to achieve integration. The JDL's willingness to consider and at times utilize violent means to achieve its ends, however, worried most Jews. While fear of physical threats and loss of status lay behind some of the Jewish response, negative feelings toward blacks, which had always been present, were also clearly reemerging.* The defensive mood of the Jewish community was more broadly evident, too, in the movement that now got under way to obtain the release of Soviet Jews who sought to emigrate.

---

*Such feelings rarely show up in public opinion polls, but they are described in novels by Jewish writers like Wallace Markfield (*Teitelbaum's Window*) and Philip Roth (*Portnoy's Complaint*). Occasionally they surface. Jewish comic Jackie Mason referred to David Dinkins in his first race for mayor as a "fancy schvartze with a mustache" while campaigning for his opponent, Rudolph Giuliani. A memorandum prepared for City Councilman Zev Yaroslavsky, who was preparing a campaign to unseat Los Angeles mayor Tom Bradley, declared, "You've got 50 IQ points on him (and that's no compliment)." Most Jews are highly embarrassed when such forms of gross bigotry occur. Yaroslavsky apologized and dropped out of the race; Mason apologized, too, but routinely continues to deride blacks.

For many Jews, however, the key to the breakdown of black-Jewish relations was the growing black hostility to Israel. A Yankelovich survey of black leaders in 1975 found that approximately two thirds were indifferent to whether Israel existed as a state; if war broke out in the Middle East, 41 percent expected blacks in the United States to support the Arab nations.[23]

To bridge the growing chasm, Bayard Rustin formed a new organization, Black Americans in Support of Israel (BASIC) in June 1975. Arnold Aronson, the most durable of the old-line Jewish civil rights activists, helped with the fund-raising. When the UN General Assembly adopted a resolution equating Zionism with racism in November of that year, Aronson arranged for Clarence Mitchell, the NAACP's Washington representative, to be a speaker at a protest rally in New York. Mitchell, with whom Aronson had worked closely in securing passage of the Civil Rights Act of 1964, was then a member of the U.S. delegation to the United Nations.

"Only in Israel," BASIC's statement of principles declared, "among the nations of the Middle East, are political freedoms and civil liberties secure." While expressing compassion for the Palestinian people and championing their right to self-determination, BASIC criticized the "terrorist" PLO for its uncontrolled violence. Meanwhile, ten black congressional defenders of Israel expressed shock at the move to ostracize the Jewish state. They argued that, just as the southern African liberation movements sought self-determination and nationhood for the oppressed black majority, so Israel sought the same things for the Jewish people. Among the distinguished black educators, clergymen, athletes, labor leaders, and editors who joined BASIC were David Dinkins, later mayor of New York, and Congressman Andrew Young.

Young became the focus of the most significant black-Jewish confrontation of the decade a few years later, when President Carter appointed him ambassador to the United Nations.[24] Young's appointment had initially been greeted with enthusiasm by Jews. He was seen as King's lieutenant, a man whose strength and courage had been demonstrated on the battlefields of civil rights engagements.[25] But in August 1979, stories in the *New York Times* and *Newsweek* reported that Young had met in New York with the PLO's UN ambassador, Zehdi Labib Terzi. At first, this meeting was said to have occurred accidentally. In subsequent reports it became clear that the Young-Terzi meeting was in fact a full-scale exchange. This seemed a violation of the administration's policy not to negotiate with terrorist groups, and Jewish leaders, already disturbed by the adoption of the UN's Zionism-equals-racism resolution, considered the meeting an attempt to legitimate the PLO. They reacted sharply, and Young, after admitting that he had not told the whole truth about it, resigned. "Whatever I did, I did because any number of people I respected a great deal felt that something had to be done to address the Palestinian question, and they couldn't do anything about it," he later told the *Chicago Tribune*.[26]

Recognizing that they would be blamed for Young's departure, Jewish groups acted to head off a confrontation. Theodore Mann, chairman of the Conference of Presidents of Major American Jewish Organizations, wrote to Carter, emphasizing that Young's resignation had neither been sought nor desired, nor should it be an issue between the Jewish and black communities. The organization's objections were aimed at the State Department.[27]

Young's conduct at the United Nations seemed to bear out Stanley Levison's earlier description of him as moving altogether too far to the left. In an interview with a Paris newspaper in July 1979, Young said, in response to a question about prisoners in the Soviet Union, that the United States was holding hundreds, possibly thousands, of political prisoners. In another interview he described Soviet-supplied Cuban forces as a stabilizing influence in Angola. In a third he praised the Ayatollah Khomeini. Young's impulsive statements, which seemed directly to contradict U.S. foreign policy, quickly became an embarrassment to the Carter administration. Morris B. Abram, wrote in his autobiography that he watched with amazement as the president was effectively held hostage by a member of his own administration who acted like a Third World representative in the United States.[28]

Blacks, on the other hand, were understandably proud of Young, the former congressman from Atlanta, who had become the highest-ranking black official in the country; many were furious at his loss of a post once held by such notables as Adlai Stevenson and former Supreme Court Justice Arthur Goldberg. On August 22 an emergency meeting of black leaders was convened at the offices of the NAACP in New York. Some two hundred people showed up, including representatives of virtually every major black organization in the United States. They released a statement declaring that while Jews and Jewish organizations had worked closely with blacks over the years, they had only done so when it served their own interest. The statement also alleged that some Jewish organizations had recently become apologists for the racial status quo and had opposed the interests of the black community in affirmative action cases.[29]

The Young affair thus widened the growing split between blacks and Jews. Jesse Jackson, then leader of PUSH, described Young's resignation as a capitulation to Jews, who had lost interest in sharing the good things of a decent society when blacks started competing with them for real power.[30] Kenneth Clark, the black psychiatrist who had worked closely with the American Jewish Committee and other Jewish groups in leading the social-scientific attack on racist ideology in the fifties, made a personal declaration of black independence from Jewish influence. And novelist James Baldwin, once the recipient of aid and assistance from Jewish editors who helped launch his career, now propounded in the left-wing *Nation* the hardly original theory that American Jews were white men doing the Christian establishment's dirty work. Baldwin also wrote that Israel had been created not as a haven for European Jews but as an instrument of Western imperial interests.[31]

Andrew Young's own attitude toward the reaction occasioned by his resignation was ambiguous. The night of his resignation—according to Robert G. Weisbord and Richard Kazarian, Jr., in *Israel in the Black American Perspective*—he held an hour-long conversation with the black mayors of Los Angeles, Atlanta, Detroit, Newark, New Orleans, and Washington, urging them to prevent any rupture between blacks and Jews. Later, though, he would point to a kind of paternalism in the black-Jewish coalition, a situation in which blacks were totally helpless and dependent on Jews, who made all the important decisions. When blacks began to think for themselves and challenge Jewish liberal views and leadership, he said, "things changed."[32]

Young's ambivalent attitude may be taken to represent a more widespread ambivalence in the black community. On the one hand, blacks wished to maintain the useful ties they had formed with Jews; but they were also understandably upset. A number of blacks, including Vernon Jordan of the Urban League, columnist Tony Brown, Jewish convert Julius Lester, and activist Bayard Rustin, attempted to sound conciliatory notes. Rustin was quickly condemned by Rev. William Jones, president of a Baptist convention, who declared him a creature of the Jews. The NAACP was moved to action by the intensity of feeling Young's resignation engendered. At the end of its annual meeting that year, the group called on the Carter administration to reexamine its pledge to Israel that it would not negotiate with the PLO. Its board also endorsed the intemperate August 22 statement adopted by the national black leaders in New York.

The following March, Young's successor at the United Nations, Donald McHenry, also a black man, supported a Security Council resolution declaring Jerusalem occupied territory and charging Israel with extraordinary human rights violations on the West Bank. President Carter backed away from McHenry's position, saying it resulted from a mix-up in instructions. But Morris Abram, who had earlier served at the United Nations, was convinced that Carter's reelection would have led to a fundamental change in U.S. policy toward Israel. Accordingly, Abram voted that fall for Ronald Reagan. It was the first time in his life that he had voted for a Republican presidential candidate.[33]

Abram's change of heart was symptomatic of a growing conservative mood among a number former Jewish social activists (most Jewish agencies and religious bodies continued to support liberal reform measures, however). Abram had fought the Klan, worked with the Kennedy brothers to free King from a Southern jail, and pressed the litigation that led to the Supreme Court's momentous one-man, one-vote ruling. Later, while he was president of Brandeis University, students pressing for curriculum control of Afro-American studies sought to take over the administration building. Sheets billowed from second-floor windows proclaiming Brandeis to be Malcolm X University.[34]

The siege profoundly affected Abram. Fearing student upheavals and the ensuing violence, he grew distrustful of Democratic leadership, which, he believed, had lost faith in America. In his opinion, liberals had wrongly dismissed the whole of American society as racist, exploitive, and imperialist. Abram felt proud of what had been accomplished to increase opportunities for blacks and women. He fretted over what he saw as the nation's leftward drift, and he deplored those left-wing circles where the Jewish state was considered a satellite of the contemptible West while neighboring Mideast societies, even the most authoritarian, commanded automatic sympathy. President Reagan later appointed Abram to the U.S. Civil Rights Commission, where as vice-chairman he waged a vigorous and highly visible campaign against racial quotas and preferences.[35]

Even in a period of changing loyalties, Abram's dramatic shift from liberal Democrat to Reagan supporter was unusual. Most Jews continued to vote for Democratic candidates, though without their former enthusiasm. But many blacks viewed these developments as ominous. It appeared to them that Jews had become smug and complacent, seeking to preserve their own gains while displaying an increasing insensitivity to the continued suffering of so many blacks.

16

GARVEY'S GHOSTS

The Final Fracturing of the Alliance

While the Young affair, the clash over racial preferences, and other such conflicts that had erupted since the mid-1960s increased tensions between blacks and Jews, blacks nevertheless continued to draw on the Jewish experience for inspiration and uplift. If American Jews could provide such united support to the Jewish state, it was reasoned, why couldn't American blacks be loyal to their blood brothers in the Middle East and Africa? The idea was seized on as part of the Third World ideology adopted by a growing number of black civil rights leaders, including Joseph Lowery, Benjamin Hooks, and Jesse Jackson, according to Jackson biographers Thomas Landess and Richard Quinn.[1]

The internationalization of black political consciousness was reflected in mounting anger against the relationship of Israel to South Africa and the identification of black leaders with the PLO. The Young affair itself may be seen retrospectively as marking the final phase in the fracturing of the black-Jewish alliance.[2]

The extension of black American race consciousness to world affairs was a phenomenon with a mixed payoff. For the first time, African-Americans were asserting their political independence on a national stage, and the awakening of black activism was certainly part of the growth and development process. Yet increasingly, black leaders proved disinterested in—or incapable of—restraining some of the demagogic tendencies that this awakening sometimes yielded, both on the domestic and international levels. The result was a weakening of black political strength with the destruction of traditional alliances. The point is that the fracturing of the black-Jewish alliance did not occur in a vacuum: It was a concomitant of rising black social and political autonomy.

The first move in this new and independent post-Young direction was made by the SCLC's Lowery. He first upstaged the others by meeting with Zehdi Labib Terzi, the PLO ambassador, and then leading a delegation of blacks to the Middle East. Joining him for the trip were Julian Bond and Benjamin Hooks. The group presented a medal, The Decoration of Martin Luther King, to Libya's Muammar Qaddafi. The *New York Times* reported the presentation dismissively in two sentences.

It was Jesse Jackson who captured the headlines. A mercurial figure—distrusted by many blacks as well as whites, yet a man of considerable talent, ambition, and personal magnetism—Jackson had remained an outsider to the King movement, carefully cultivating his base in Chicago. (Barbara Reynolds, another Jackson biographer, said that he often seemed to be chasing his own identity.)

Through local antipoverty programs like Operation Breadbasket and People United to Save Humanity (PUSH), Jackson pressured white businesses in Chicago to hire more blacks. King had wanted him to expand his operations to other cities, but Jackson refused to yield to SCLC discipline. Reynolds described him as a more than occasional source of embarrassment to King, who would somehow have to cope with his escapades and shame him back into line.[3] It was in Memphis at the time of King's murder that the two men had begun to patch up their differences.

Jackson's enterprises encountered financial difficulties and his reliability was questioned (by Reynolds among others), but he rose above these setbacks to claim the leadership of much of black America. His call to blacks not to despair in the face of obstacles created by a racist society had strong appeal to blacks and even to some whites. In the post-King era, an era highlighted by newer empowerment goals and the internationalization of black activism, Jackson was an authentic reflection of the black America that was taking shape.

Like a number of other black leaders, Jackson had an uneven history where the Jewish community was concerned. In 1974 he convened a meeting with Jewish leaders at which he urged both groups to rise above the angry rhetoric of recent years. Along with his family, Jackson had joined in a demonstration to protest a march by neo-Nazis in mostly Jewish Skokie, Illinois. When the chairman of the Joint Chiefs of Staff, General George C. Brown, declared in a speech at Duke University that Jews owned the banks in this country, Jackson wrote to tell him that this was the language of Adolph Hitler. But he was also clumsy, even callous, during the period of his freewheeling public militancy, referring to "Jewish slumlords" and "fight promoters" and denouncing Andrew Young's resignation from the UN as a capitulation to the Jews. The writer Marshall Frady would later write that Jackson's sentiments were recklessly ambivalent.[4]

In the fall of 1979, Jackson paid his first widely publicized visit to the Middle East, stopping first in Israel. Prime Minister Menachem Begin snubbed him, but Jackson, undeterred, toured Yad Vashem, the memorial to the murdered Jews of Europe. According to *Newsweek*, he said that after seeing the memorial, he better understood "the persecution complex of many Jewish people that almost invariably made them overreact to their suffering, because it is so great." Jackson's reference to a "persecution complex" in the shadow of a Holocaust memorial was breathtakingly insensitive, and many Jews were infuriated. Two Jews who accompanied Jackson later quoted him as stating privately on the trip to the Middle East that he was tired of hearing about the Holocaust and of having America put on a guilt trip. It was further claimed that he had said Jews did not have a monopoly on suffering. Jackson would later deny these remarks.[5]

Jackson forged ahead. He urged Palestinians on the West Bank to adopt the American civil rights movement as their model. He cautioned them, however, not to engage in terrorism. On the final day of his trip, Jackson met with Yasser Arafat, and upon emerging he offered his services as an intermediary between the PLO leader and the American government. He listened as the crowd shouted, "Palestine is Arab," and "Our revolution shall triumph." The next day the *New York Times* and papers across the country published a photograph of Jackson and Arafat embracing.[6] The image was to endure in the minds of Jews even as Jackson went on to run for the presidency.

On his return Jackson told the SCLC convention that it was not the Ku Klux Klan that had forced the removal of Ambassador Young. He made it clear that he blamed American Jews. And when the Democrats supported Israel's incursion into Lebanon to root out the PLO in 1982, Jackson described the position as overreaction to the Jewish element in the party. He further charged that the relationship between Jews and Democrats was a kind of glorified bribery that swapped financial support for moral bankruptcy.

In a 1980 speech to an Arab-American organization in Birmingham, Jackson drew a sharp distinction between Judaism and Zionism. The former, he said, was a religion, while the latter was a "poisonous weed" that was choking Judaism. Asked by an interviewer for *New York* magazine during his 1984 race for a comment on the quote, Jackson defended it, noting that to the degree that the prophetic side of Judaism was silenced by the policies of Zionism, it was a threat to the Jewish religion. In effect, he seemed to be endorsing the United Nations's Zionism-is-racism resolution.[7]

Increasingly, Jackson positioned himself as an American spokesman for the Third World. In 1979, seeking funding for PUSH from Arab businessmen, he warned that their failure to contribute could result in the elimination of the letters "P-L-O" from the alphabet. Jackson told the Arab representatives that money and men were needed if they wanted to be part of the human rights struggle.[8] Jack O'Dell, who maintained his far left connections after being ousted from King's entourage, accompanied Jackson on his Middle East forays. He would remain an adviser on foreign policy in Jackson's presidential campaigns.

Jackson's race for the 1984 Democratic nomination was one of the most extraordinary events in recent political history. As the first black candidate to make a serious run for the presidency, he became a messenger of hope for many blacks. His appeal was direct and effective, rejecting self-pity and urging hard work, self-reliance, and responsibility.[9] Despite the opposition of most black politicians and establishment civil rights leaders (like the NAACP's Benjamin Hooks, who feared Jackson's run would weaken their goal of defeating Ronald Reagan), he managed to build a supportive bloc made up mainly of outsiders—his Rainbow Coalition—which called for jobs, peace, a clean environment, and better public services.

But his real message, as author Jim Sleeper has noted, was that real black empowerment would only come with bloc voting. Once unified, blacks could join others, where appropriate, to address issues of mutual concern effectively. Sleeper described Jackson's rallies as exercises in "therapeutic self-assertion." Jackson was more interested in making blacks feel good than in illuminating the political and economic landscape.[10]

Blacks cheered him on; a few New York politicos like David Dinkins and Percy Sutton supported him as well. But Jackson's highly publicized "Hymietown" remark—a private statement characterizing New York City as a center of Jewish influence; it was reported by the *Washington Post*—brought his relations with Jews to a point of no return. A "Jews against Jackson" advertisement appeared in the *New York Times*, showing him embracing Arafat.

Jackson gained national attention during the campaign by undertaking a rescue mission to Syria on behalf of a U.S. Air Force pilot who had been forced down in December 1983. With him was Louis Farrakhan, the Muslim minister, then an obscure figure who was providing security through his Fruit of Islam organization. Barbara Reynolds sees Farrakhan as Jackson's trump card in gaining the release of the pilot, who was black. Apparently, while Farrakhan prayed in Arabic, Jackson regaled Syrian president Assad with the story of Saul's conversion on the road to Damascus. Although the performance was effective—the pilot was released—many chided Jackson for publicity-mongering and viewed his mission as illegal.

In the whole history of black-Jewish relations, there has never been a more divisive force than Louis Farrakhan, the calypso singer turned Black Muslim leader. His message, which has not changed much over the years, is decidedly mixed. On the one hand, he relentlessly sermonizes to blacks on the importance of education and family life and warns about the dangers of drugs. He urges his followers not to count on government handouts but to make their own way. In a racist social and economic system, he argues, minorities must be self-reliant because they can't expect help from any quarter. Such inspirational talk has won over many blacks, who see in Farrakhan—tall, handsome, well-spoken, with his hair cut short and his suits conservatively tailored—a leader worth emulating.

Many whites would cheer him too, were it not for the other side of Farrakhan's message: a harsh attack on white society, and particularly on the role of Jews in that society, for what Farrakhan sees as their cruel and constant exploitation of blacks. In the 1980s he delivered this rebuke in cities and on college campuses from coast to coast, and his withering attack seemed calculated to further the distance between blacks and Jews. In certain respects, his rhetoric was similar to that of Marcus Garvey in the 1920s and Malcolm X in the 1960s. In part because of his close association with Jackson, however, Farrakhan reached deeper into the black psyche, and his message was far more vitriolic, especially in his diatribes against Jews. Even worse in Jewish eyes was the fact that some 65 percent of the Jackson delegates at the 1984 Democratic National Convention indicated they had a favorable view of him.[11]

Born in the Bronx in 1933 as Louis Eugene Walcott, Farrakhan grew up in Boston and attended Winston-Salem University in North Carolina. After two years he dropped out to try his luck as a singer of calypso songs and country music. In 1955, at the age of twenty-two, he was recruited into the Nation of Islam by Malcolm X. He was attached to the Harlem mosque and later headed the sect's Boston unit.

In 1964, following a pilgrimage to Mecca, Malcolm denounced the racist doctrines of the movement's founder, Elijah Muhammad. Shortly after that, Malcolm was assassinated in Harlem. Several days before the murder, Farrakhan called openly for Malcolm's death but later denied responsibility for it. Farrakhan continued to hold high positions with the Nation of Islam. Elijah Muhammad died in 1975, and his son, Wallace D. Muhammad, whose guiding philosophy was integrationist, succeeded him. Having been passed over, Farrakhan started his own movement in Chicago, utilizing Elijah's black nationalist theology.[12]

The distressing resurgence of such black nationalist and anti-Semitic philosophy could be largely attributed to a genuine decline in the standard of living among working class blacks in the 1970s and 1980s. The widening gap between rich and poor, the epidemic of teenage pregnancies and single-parent families, the dismal failures of public education, and the terrifying escalation of crime, violence, and drug use in the inner cities across the country created what author Stanley Crouch has called "a black lower class perhaps more despairing and cynical than we have ever seen."[13] Adding to the anger were the successes of the conservative political coalition and the subsequent cutbacks in federal funding for various urban programs of the Reagan years, cutbacks mirrored on the state and local level as well. Farrakhan's appeal was directly dependent on his ability to exploit black suffering and frustration, and there was certainly no lack of such feeling in the black community in the early 1980s. Nor is there today.*

In 1985 Farrakhan embarked on his first nationwide speaking tour, addressing large and enthusiastic crowds in fourteen cities. In Atlanta, seven thousand persons packed the hall, and many more stood outside. In Chicago, his home base, fifteen thousand heard him. He drew five thousand in Houston, seven thousand in Philadelphia, and ten thousand in Washington, D.C. Before a crowd of fifteen thousand in Los Angeles, Farrakhan, insisting that the Jewish people were not God's chosen people, predicted that once they attained true political power, forty million blacks could wield as much influence as Jews now did. He further accused some black leaders in Los Angeles of bowing to pressure from Jews to repudiate him.

Farrakhan's tour climaxed in New York where, on October 7, an overflow crowd of almost twenty-five thousand jammed Madison Square Garden. A "rainbow coalition" of leaders warmed up the audience before Farrakhan's appearance. Speaking as head of the All-African People's Revolutionary party, Kwame Touré, for-

---

*Farrakhan's influence may also be seen to some degree in the genre of black music that took hold in the late 1980s. Rap music also reflected the anger and frustration of the urban black underclass. Like Farrakhan's lectures, its lyrics sometimes taught racial self-respect and encouraged resistance to crime and drugs. But one of its leading groups, Public Enemy, whose members were Black Muslims, also carried a message of hate toward Jews. One of its members, Professor Griff, blamed Jews for most of the wickedness in the world. One of the group's singles, "Welcome to the Terrordome," suggested that Griff (who had been fired and then rehired by the group) had been "gotten" by the same folks who "got" Jesus.

merly Stokely Carmichael, called for war against Israel and recognition of the "sacredness" of Africa. Said Arafat, a Palestinian, urged the total liberation of Palestine. Russell Means, a founder of the American Indian movement, after attacking white treatment of native Americans, charged that the Jews in Hollywood "did a number on Mr. Farrakhan," adding that that was how Hollywood had treated every nonwhite race and people.[14]

When five hours later, Farrakhan finally took the lectern, he confronted his accusers head on. He told the throng that Edward I. Koch (then running for a third term as mayor of New York), Governor Mario Cuomo, and some local black leaders whom he described as "pitiful" had called him a lot of ugly names. He said that such words only served to make him fight harder.

At one point in the evening, while rhetorically asking who was ranged against him, he directly linked the enemies of Farrakhan with the enemies of Jesus. And who were these? "Jews, Jews, Jews," shouted the crowd.

Farrakhan spoke for three hours, until well after midnight. According to the *New York Times* account, he electrified his audience by coupling his message of economic and spiritual renewal with denunciations of his critics.

Seated in the Garden that night was Julius Lester, the former black militant whose late-sixties radio program had once fueled a controversy between blacks and Jews and now a practicing Jew and Zionist covering the rally for the *New Republic*. Lester was appalled by the scene. Noting that Farrakhan was the only black leader today who could command such an audience, he expressed regret that some black people should have made the journey from Martin Luther King to Louis Farrakhan in fewer than twenty years.[15]

Farrakhan's appeal was not limited to working-class and inner-city blacks. He also aroused great interest and a measure of support on many college campuses. Farrakhan and Kwame Touré gave frequent campus lectures in which they continued to condemn Zionist Jews. Touré inflamed black-Jewish relations, for example, in two 1986 speeches on the campus of the University of Maryland at College Park. In one he told the campus audience, "The only good Zionist is a dead Zionist," and "We must take a lesson from Hitler." Jewish students picketed the affair and lodged a complaint with the National Association for the

Advancement of Colored People, since its campus unit had cosponsored Touré's appearance with the Black Student Union. A riot erupted at the second speech when some twenty Jewish students broke through a police blockade to enter the lecture hall.

After Touré addressed a capacity audience at the State University of New York at Albany, a Jewish student confronted him. Describing himself as a Zionist, the student noted that Touré had often said that the only good Zionist was a dead Zionist. Did that mean that Touré wished him and his Zionist friends dead? Without hesitation, Touré answered yes amid great applause.

In his speeches Touré echoed Afrocentrist themes, themes increasingly discussed and admired in black circles. He assured one audience that Farrakhan could not be anti-Semitic because "the first Jews were from Cush," a reference to Egypt.[16]

So intense had the on-campus black-Jewish collisions surrounding these appearances become that in March 1990 Nat Hentoff, a frequent visitor to campuses, wrote an article that discussed strategies for dealing with them. He urged Jewish students to come armed with accurate quotations from previous speeches. He suggested also that black moderates like Eleanor Holmes Norton, a professor of constitutional law, be brought in to counter them.[17] A number of college administrators scheduled discussions between black and Jewish students in an effort to ease tensions.

In their campus forays Farrakhan and Touré reached beyond the ghetto to young, educated blacks and the black intelligentsia. Heretofore, blacks of economic means had often deliberately distanced themselves from the underclass and adopted white middle-class standards. By the end of the eighties, however, some were identifying more closely, at least emotionally, with the black underclass. It was the Muslim minister who brought the two segments together. Dennis King has noted that Farrakhan's rallies attracted well-to-do black professionals, business people, and college students, as well as the poor and unemployed. He quoted an aide to Jackson as saying that there were many young and middle-aged black professionals who felt kicked around by America. Their feelings inclined them to regard Farrakhan as to some extent their spokesman.[18]

Farrakhan's attractiveness to elements of the black middle class may have reflected what law professor Patricia J. Williams has termed a commitment to stop hating those who were poorer and darker-skinned than themselves.[19] Beyond that, however, better-educated blacks suffered anxieties of their own. Many were in precarious financial straits or feared the loss of jobs from cutbacks in the Great Society programs that had given them their entry into the middle class. Not only has a higher proportion of blacks than whites received direct government support in the form of welfare, food stamps, Medicaid, and other programs aimed at the poor in the last three decades, but as many as half of all blacks holding professional and managerial jobs have been employed in local, state, and federal agencies, compared with just over a quarter of whites. A great deal of the expansion of black employment in the previous twenty-five years has been in firms that come under the jurisdiction of the Equal Employment Opportunities Commission. The cutbacks they could be facing, it was felt, resulted from Reagan's success in forging a coalition with former Democratic voters, a coalition that included some Jews.[20] (A *USA Today* poll taken just before Reagan left office found that 60 percent of American blacks believed they were victims of racial prejudice. Interestingly, well-to-do blacks were more likely to have this perception than poorer blacks. Two thirds of blacks polled who earned more than $50,000 a year considered themselves categorized as potential criminals because of their color, and 79 percent complained of discriminatory treatment while shopping.)[21]

As always when the black condition deteriorates, Garvey's Ghosts were there, blaming outsiders—hardly a unique response.[22] Asian businessmen and merchants, who had replaced Jews in many black neighborhoods, were now subjected to boycotts and other forms of harassment by street-corner agitators. The harangues of radical activists like the Rev. Al Sharpton, Sonny Carson, and C. Vernon Mason in New York were echoes of those heard in Harlem in the thirties. When New York's first black mayor, David Dinkins, defied a group of blacks by making a purchase in a Korean store they were boycotting in Flatbush, Mason denounced him as "a lover of white people" who had "too many yarmulkas on his head."[23] In Philadelphia, a group of protestors picketing a Korean store where a black had been shot and killed were told that behind every Korean stood a Jew.

The civil rights revolution and the ensuing race revolution had seen a sharp rise in black political strength at the local, state, and national level. Starting with the election of a number of black mayors in the late 1960s, blacks were holding important political offices nationwide in the 1980s. Black activism was closely related to this political phenomenon.

The old activists had set concrete goals and built coalitions to attain them. Garvey's Ghosts, however, practiced what Jim Sleeper has called the politics of resentment. They refused to cooperate with authorities seeking to investigate crimes against blacks and they shunned such significant interracial groups as the Hospital Workers' Union, Local 1199, and the United Federation of Teachers, whose leader, Sandra Feldman, had played a major role in Dinkins's victory.[24] Instead, they played to the media. The refusal to build coalitions was a sharp break with the tactics of the earlier civil rights organizations and has been an approach that has always led to failure.

Garvey's Ghosts wanted power, which they viewed often as necessitating absolute separation. The new activists even broke with the Jewish Left, which despite underlying frictions had hung on tenaciously to the otherwise collapsed black-Jewish alliance. The conflict was dramatically evident within Local 1199, the union that King and Levison had worked with so closely and one of the few remaining strongholds of the Jewish Left.

Leon Davis, who built the union and made it a haven for old Communists and fellow travelers, had clung to the idea that race solidarity and class solidarity were one and the same thing. When he retired in 1982, he picked Doris Turner, a black union official, as his successor. He admitted that he chose her because she was female, aggressive, and black. "I underestimated the anger blacks feel about having been left out—how overpowering it is, how controlling."

The decision was a disaster for Davis and his hopes. Turner denounced the old regime, citing "the Jews who use political power against me." There followed a series of antiwhite and anti-Semitic incidents. A split developed between the local and the national organization headed by Moe Foner, Davis's former aide.

Historians of 1199 described Turner as lacking a vision or an understanding of the labor movement. As Foner put it to an interviewer, "How do you teach a world view?"[25]

In this atmosphere vicious attacks on Jews became commonplace. In New York a black activist priest blamed Jewish teachers for the damage done to the city's black youth. In Chicago Steven Cokely, an aide to Mayor Eugene Sawyer and a lecturer at Nation of Islam headquarters from 1985 to 1987, declared that Jewish physicians were infecting black babies with the AIDS virus. While a number of black leaders were openly critical of Cokely, only three of eighteen black aldermen called for his dismissal. After vacillating for almost a week, Sawyer, who is himself black, fired him. Gus Savage, a controversial black congressman from Chicago who frequently railed against Israel and American Jewry, lashed out in particular at Jews who had helped finance his black opponent in a primary race (Savage was narrowly returned to office although two years later he was defeated.) Observing several of these episodes, Professor Eugene Kennedy of Loyola University declared that virulent anti-Semitism was rife in Chicago's black community, while Catholic priest and sociologist Andrew Greeley wrote in the *New York Times* that if he were Jewish he would be terrified.[26]

The civil rights revolution had ended with the assassination of Martin Luther King. Malcolm X was dead. The Black Panthers had been defanged. Other leaders had failed to emerge. Farrakhan, though perceived by many blacks as a disruptive force peddling bigotry and hate, seemed to be combating crime and drug abuse in black ghettos. When the Rev. Leon H. Sullivan, a member of the board of General Motors and a civil rights moderate, invited Farrakhan to speak at his church, one of the largest in Philadelphia, leaders of the American Jewish Committee, who had worked with Sullivan for many years, asked to meet with him. One member of the group that went had, many years earlier, sponsored Sullivan's membership in the Jaycees, which up to that point had been segregated; another had helped out in the fundraising campaign to rebuild his church after it burned down.

Sullivan explained to the group that he had not taken his action alone but had cleared it with his board. In defending it, Sullivan—who had created the Opportunities Industrialization Centers to help train black youth for jobs, spread the movement to other cities and overseas, and initiated "Sullivan principles" as a tool for large corporations to overcome apartheid in South Africa—explained that Farrakhan was the only figure who was effectively fighting the problems that plagued his people. Here he echoed Coretta King, who, in a speech before the National Press Club, had said that while some of Farrakhan's statements had been extremely harmful, his philosophy of self-help was something "everyone can agree on."[27]

In 1988 Farrakhan again toured the nation. Jackson was again running hard for the presidency. In the wake of Jackson's Hymietown remark (for which he had apologized at the 1984 convention), his expression of pro-Arab sentiments, and the tart retorts of Mayor Koch, Farrakhan muted his rhetoric. At Rutgers University he told blacks that they needed to work to better their community and the lives of their people. Jewish students at the University of Pennsylvania protested his appearance, but he drew a capacity crowd, and there were no incidents.

Farrakhan had now become a celebrity. Appearances on the television talk and glamour circuit ensued, as did interviews with the *Washington Post* and *Washington Times*. While more soberly stated and smoothly delivered, his message remained the same: Integration was a failure; blacks had to separate from mainstream American life; the U.S. government had to pay reparations to blacks and provide land for them, either in the United States or Africa.

During the 1988 tour, Farrakhan for the most part kept to the high ground, focusing on widely recognized black urban problems. His reward was a series of tributes from urban politicians. In Washington the city council passed without dissent a resolution praising Farrakhan's economic and spiritual leadership. A Jewish member, who could have killed the resolution with a single negative vote, abstained.[28] Similar resolutions were presented in Philadelphia and elsewhere.

Whether they approved of Farrakhan or not, most blacks and those who, like author Derrick Bell, sought to speak for them refused to distance themselves from him simply in order to pacify white liberals and Jews. The inner history of recent black political life in this country has been a struggle to balance a yearning for greater individual autonomy with the group's larger interests, which often called for meeting conditions set by whites. While Jews had difficulty understanding the hesitation to repudiate Farrakhan, the situation was not unlike what they themselves had experienced. (Witness the uneasiness of many Jews with right-wing governments and policies in Israel over the years coupled with a reluctance to speak out publicly against them.) Moreover, neither group has been eager to wash its dirty linen in public; both have been inclined to emphasize unity within the group against what is seen as the hostility of the outside world.

Jackson's race for the Democratic nomination in 1988 saw the coalescing of a variety of leading voices in the black community. The opposition of many black leaders to his 1984 candidacy had all but disappeared. The attitude of Coretta Scott King symbolized this transition. At the 1984 Democratic National Convention she had opposed a minority plank supported by Jackson delegates. Four years later, when Jackson visited her late husband's church in Atlanta, she embraced him.

Against a weak field of Democratic aspirants, Jackson proved little short of phenomenal on the stump. In thirty-three primaries he received more than six million votes, some 29 percent of the total. Put differently, he received one percentage point more than the combined tally of all the other Democratic candidates except the nominee, Massachusetts governor Michael Dukakis, who received 43 percent. A coalition of organized labor, liberal whites, and black and Hispanic voters had delivered New York City to Jackson. True, some two thirds of his support came from black voters; but his share of white voters had tripled since 1984.[29]

Jackson's campaign galvanized blacks. Barbara Reynolds, whose 1975 biography had been critical of Jackson, wrote in the introduction to a new edition that he had opened the electoral process to millions who never cared about politics before. She was undoubtedly correct. Jackson's two campaigns emboldened other black candidates to run for office at all levels of government.

By traveling in elevated diplomatic circles, Jackson also demonstrated that blacks could establish their own foreign policy goals independent of the federal government. He did not openly advocate such a step, but in a series of high-profile foreign visits beginning with his trip to the Middle East in 1979, he moved closer to the concept of black nationhood that Elijah Muhammad and Louis Farrakhan had developed. Two Jackson biographers, Landess and Quinn, saw great significance in this shift. "Not since the days of Marcus Garvey," they wrote, "have vast numbers of blacks thought of creating a new future except within the confines of a more equitable and tolerant America." In their view the Andrew Young affair had catalyzed this new outgrowth of revolutionary sentiment.[30]

By the close of the 1980s, Farrakhan and Jackson had effectively filled the leadership vacuum that had existed among blacks since the death of King. In doing so, however, they managed to alienate much of the American Jewish community and virtually guaranteed that the fractured black-Jewish alliance would not be reassembled. It is true that Jackson sought to be conciliatory. When Ed Koch remarked that Jews would have to be crazy to vote for Jackson, he responded not with anger but with an olive branch. He said that Jews had no basis for being afraid of sharing power with blacks; he even suggested he would not sit down again with Yasir Arafat.

In spite of such efforts, however, many Jews still distrusted him, citing his continued anti-Israel bias: In an interview in the *New York Times*, he had termed the "Israel–South Africa connection" a prime source of international tension. Furthermore, his links to Arab groups were a matter of public record. Jackson forces had helped gain acceptance of pro-Palestinian statements in the Democratic platforms of seven states and were pushing pro-Palestinian referenda in two cities each in California and Massachusetts. After hotly contested campaigns, three of the four referenda were defeated; but the American Israel Public Affairs Committee alerted its membership that pro-Israel forces had been given a warning that they could ignore only at their peril.[31]

In May 1988 Jackson laid a wreath at a statue honoring Holocaust victims in a park overlooking the Statue of Liberty. "The sons and daughters of the Holocaust and grandsons and granddaughters of slavery," he declared, "must find common ground to end racism and anti-Semitism forever."

But most observers felt it was too late. The differences between the two groups were too great, their mutual distrust too deep. Like it or not, Jackson had become the single most divisive force separating Jews from blacks. In a survey of American Jewish voters in the spring of 1988, 59 percent expressed the view that Jackson was anti-Semitic. More than half said they would vote against the Democratic presidential candidate, no matter who was chosen, if Jackson gained second place on the ticket.

EPILOGUE

Beyond the Black–Jewish Alliance

In retrospect we can see that the civil rights battles of the 1960s marked the high point of the black-Jewish alliance. In that period blacks and Jews labored together in common cause—and often at great risk—to end America's version of apartheid. Racist statutes were struck down throughout the South. It was a remarkable achievement, and those who joined the struggle did, in fact, "overcome" state-ordered racism.

During the second half of the decade, however, the alliance showed signs of coming apart. The assassination of Martin Luther King, Jr., in 1968 accelerated divisions that have only widened with the passage of time. Instead of integration, blacks began turning inward. More radical blacks began calling for separation, and a University of Chicago survey in 1994 found growing support among African Americans for the creation of a separate black political party. According to Michael Dawson, the political scientist who conducted the survey of more than one thousand two hundred blacks, in 1988 26 percent supported a separate party. By 1994 he found the black community evenly divided on the issue. This was especially true among younger and poorer blacks, the survey concluded, and an ever more radical black America appeared to be emerging.[1]

In certain respects this dramatic shift could be seen as a maturing of black political thought; a willingness, indeed a desire, of many blacks to strike out on their own without relying on white intermediaries. But to function properly, the American political system requires participation by all ethnic, racial, religious, and income groups in the established party organizations. That is its genius. It would be ominous, indeed, if a group representing roughly 10 percent of the population were to form a new party based solely on ethnic background.

The landmark Supreme Court *Bakke* ruling was written with such ambiguity that it was not clear who won or lost. But it demonstrated with striking clarity the increasing divergence of interests between Jews and blacks. The black-Jewish alliance held together as long as it did because in uniting to oppose discrimination and bigotry, both groups were operating from the same political and ideological premises, which were based on nondiscrimination and integration. Blacks were the big gainers since the struggle was primarily against racism, but Jews gained, too, for in taking the side of those less fortunate than themselves, they lowered barriers they faced and found fulfillment in upholding the historic tenets of Judaism.

Quotas or racial preferences in graduate school admissions and on-the-job concerns introduced a new and divisive element. Probably more than any other ethnic group, Jews believe that in this country one gets ahead a degree at a time. Education is key. Graduate and professional education opens the door of opportunity. With *Bakke* the Jewish community saw a threat to this opened door. Such old civil rights organizations as the American Jewish Committee and the Anti-Defamation League directly opposed black groups on this key issue, and nothing was the same again. It should be noted, however, that not all blacks support quotas. Some prominent black figures oppose or at least worry about quotas today. In recent years a number of black intellectuals have expressed opposition to these programs as being demeaning and counterproductive.

Historically, most American Jews were poor and lived in the nation's big cities. They shared many of the hopes and aspirations of urban blacks. Both blacks and Jews were largely excluded from the business and social institutions that dominated city life. That is no longer true. In the years after World War II, Jews made remarkable gains. Great numbers moved to the suburbs or to more protected areas of the cities, and in so doing, they left most of the blacks behind. Indeed, a number of Jewish intellectuals became actively involved in a new politics, neoconservatism, that caused many blacks to feel that the traditional Jewish liberal concern for the plight of America's poor, black or otherwise, no longer existed.

It is true that the black middle class has expanded in recent decades, and there are probably more black multimillionaires in the United States today than in all the other countries of the world combined. But the growth of the black middle class has not affected urban pathologies of crime, drug addiction, joblessness, and out-of-wedlock births to teenagers.[2] These societal disorders have raged out of control in American's black slums. And the gap between rich and poor has only worsened. Indeed, it can be safely said that black anti-Semitism, directly related as it is to the anger and frustration of black America, will be relieved less by programs to "understand" each other than by improving the conditions of this group.

Economically and socially, few Jews (and, it should be noted, few other whites of any religion or ethnic group) see much to be gained from an alliance with angry, frustrated blacks whose most widely identified leaders are Louis Farrakhan and others of his stripe. So unrest festers, and the alliance is dead.

Given the current mood of distrust, suspicion, and outright hostility, the emergence of demagogues and pseudointellectuals on the campus scene and elsewhere is not surprising. Such as they thrive in an environment of anger and resentment. The reader will recall the presence of street-corner hustlers in Harlem in the 1930s and 1940s, spouting anti-Semitism to largely uneducated, unemployed poor people. What is new, different, and dangerous now is that the hustlers are practicing their demagogy not on street corners but in college lecture halls and increasingly in high school classrooms. Statements are now being made—in all seriousness—by extreme Afrocentrists that the skin pigment melanin makes blacks more humane than and otherwise superior to white people. There are also tales of the incredible feats of Africans, such as ancient Egyptians flying around in gliders. And the audiences of these Afrocentrists consist not of society's castoffs but of young black students, a group growing in numbers.[3]

Thus, Farrakhan's lieutenant, Khalid Muhammad, picked Kean College in New Jersey as his venue for a vicious attack on Jews, labeling them "bloodsuckers of the black nation." Thus, Dr. Leonard Jeffries used his position at City College to charge that Jews financed the slave trade. Thus, Welleseley College Professor Tony Martin informed his students in a recent book, *The Jewish Onslaught*, that Jews were engaged in a conspiracy to destroy him.

In the spring of 1994, anti-Semitism was particularly striking on the campus of Howard University in Washington, D.C., perhaps the nation's preeminent black university and long viewed as a more conservative institution. A student rally for Mr. Muhammad erupted into raucous chants and assertions that Jews controlled America's financial centers. It is not at all clear how representative these students are. Campus authorities and some other students declare that the Jew-baiting students are a small number on a campus of ten thousand. Such was the turmoil, however, that the university administration felt obliged to postpone a lecture by a visiting professor from Yale who had won a Pulitzer Prize for his study of slavery in Western culture. David Brion Davis, a convert to Judaism, was told to put off his visit not because of the subject of his lecture but because campus authorities felt he would be heckled. Paul Logan, associate dean for the humanities at Howard, said of the Jew-baiting students: "They seem to be out of control."[4]

The cowardice and opportunism that have often greeted these fanatics on the campuses have only made matters worse. University officials have hesitated to denounce, let alone limit or ban, their appearances. Only the interim president of Emory University chose to ban Muhammad's appearance there, overriding the invitation of the school's Black Student Alliance. He said Muhammad's views lacked any "basis in factual truth . . . [or] redeeming moral value."[5] The media, though, have tended to lionize these extremists. Following Muhammad's New Jersey speech, the *Today* show invited Tony Martin to discuss the Nation of Islam, identifying him only as a tenured Wellesley professor whose writings were controversial. When the *Washington Post*'s *Book World* printed a Martin review of a group of books dealing with black anger and white racism on March 20, 1994, the *New Republic*'s Leon Wieseltier asked in a letter to the editor whether the *Post* would similarly invite the Grand Wizard of the Ku Klux Klan.[6]

New York, in particular, has been a hotbed of black-Jewish tensions, producing more than its share of incidents and troublemakers. For many Jewish New Yorkers the fractured alliance's defining moment came in Crown Heights in the summer of 1991 when, following the death of a seven-year-old black youth under the wheels of an automobile in a motorcade for a Hasidic leader, angry blacks murdered a Hasidic scholar and terrorized the Jewish community there for four days and three nights.

In a comprehensive report prepared by the state director of criminal justice, Mayor David Dinkins and his police department were subsequently criticized for responding tardily to the criminality. Other officials were criticized for bungling the investigation so badly that the murder trial of a black suspect ended in an acquittal.[7] Meanwhile, Jewish leadership itself was caught flat-footed, viewing the violence at first as an outgrowth of long-standing bad feelings between the two groups rather than as an anti-Semitic episode of major proportions.

In spite of the extraordinary media attention paid these matters, we know little of black and Jewish mutual perceptions. Nobody has asked Jews what they think about blacks, and survey data concerning black views about Jews is sparse and sometimes contradictory. Summarizing what we do know, Tom W. Smith of the University of Chicago's National Opinion Research Center reports that anti-Semitism has declined among Americans generally in recent years, but the drop has been less marked among blacks. His analysis also indicated that black elites, including better-educated blacks, are more inclined than other Americans to endorse negative comments about Jews.[8] This troubling finding may be one reason why the campus harangues by Farrakhan and others may be having some effect.

A 1992 study by the Anti-Defamation League concluded that 20 percent of the general American population and 37 percent of blacks hold anti-Semitic beliefs.[9] Put another way, the study found that the American people overwhelmingly reject anti-Semitism and that most blacks do, too. In light of the nation's history of blatant anti-Semitism in the workplace, on the political hustings, at country clubs, resort hotels, and the like, these findings, while indeed troubling, suggest that relations between blacks and Jews are more complex than current discussions admit.

There are recent indications that while the demagogues are getting the headlines (and sometimes having an effect, especially among younger people), a subtle shift of African-American opinion may be underway, one that rejects extremism and argues that solutions to the problems facing so many blacks today must come from within the black community itself. Often a weathervane of black political thought, Jesse Jackson now terms the rising incidence of black criminals preying on black people "the premier civil rights issue of our time." Jackson, who had dismissed Zionism as a "poisonous weed" in 1980, describes it now as a liberation movement and is welcomed in Israel. And the man who spoke of New York City as Hymietown in 1984 is currently embarked on a campaign of black-Jewish reconciliation, reminding black audiences they had not come this far on their own but "with Jack Greenberg, Joe Rauh, and others working on their side."[10] Although Jackson's star has dimmed somewhat, according to a 1994 *Time*-CNN poll of black opinion, Jackson remains the nation's preeminent black leader at 34 percent, with Farrakhan, his notoriety notwithstanding, considerably behind at only 9 percent.[11]

Jackson's shift may also be seen as reflecting what Paul Berman has called the exhaustion of "third worldism" in the 1990s, as well as the effect of the peacemaking process going forward in the Middle East and South Africa.[12] This shift may ease some of the tensions against Israel, especially among elements of the black intelligentsia.

Mention was made in the Introduction of Henry Louis Gates's 1992 *New York Times* op-ed piece, which broke new ground with an attack on "pseudointellectuals" who sought to sow discord between blacks and Jews. Gates has been joined in his opposition to racist rhetoric by Harvard Theologian Cornel West, commentator Roger Wilkins, former NAACP official Michael Meyers, and such black newspaper writers as Clarence Page, Cynthia Tucker, Joseph Perkins, and Juan Williams.[13]

What is often lost sight of, indeed, is that there is no monolithic body of black thought. To the contrary, it is increasingly clear that a group of new and independent thinkers (and some older ones with fresh visions) now seek to move beyond both the stale civil rights formulas of the past and the racial chauvinism of Farrakhan and others.

Thus, sociologist William Julius Wilson has argued in two widely discussed books, *The Declining Significance of Race* and *The Truly Disadvantaged*, that racism is no longer the central issue facing American blacks. In his view, the most critical problems are changes in the economy, which send jobs overseas, and automation, which makes those with few or no skills unemployable.

Economist Glenn Loury has urged blacks to move away from traditional civil rights remedies and focus on family dislocation, crime, the breakdown of values—what Loury labels the "struggle within."[14]

Syndicated columnist William Raspberry has questioned whether it is ever justifiable, as a matter of public policy, to choose black job applicants over better-qualified white ones. His answer appears to be no.

Social critic Stanley Crouch has denounced agitators Al Sharpton, Alton Maddox, and their ilk as opportunists who are quick to condemn blacks (like Crouch) who oppose them as traitors to their race. Black college teachers who fail to protest race baiting on their campuses are, in Crouch's view, "demons in the black community."[15]

Television personality Tony Brown has observed that blacks who blame Jews for all the evils of the past are, in effect, embracing anti-Semitism "as an excuse for our status in this country" and are thereby "emulating the very racism that has crippled our people for centuries."[16]

The fact is that blacks, in the mass, are among America's most conservative citizens. Within this minority group there is a silent majority that may approve of Louis Farrakhan's emphasis on self-discipline and self-help (as a *Time*-CNN poll suggests); but it is hardly clear that most blacks endorse his racism and anti-Semitism. When in his autobiography the late tennis star Arthur Ashe lamented the neglect of religion and morality in black life, he spoke for many church-attending and other blacks, as did former chairman of the Joint Chiefs of Staff, General Colin L. Powell, in declaring (in a commencement address delivered at Howard University just a few weeks after Khalid Muhammad's speech there) that blacks could not afford "a detour into the swamp of hatred."[17] And when the National Political Congress of Black Women, joined by members of the Black Leadership Forum and such prominent clergymen as the Rev. Calvin Butts of Harlem's historic Abyssinian Baptist Church, launched a nationwide campaign against vulgar rap entertainment on grounds that it was undermining black self-esteem, their drive resonated among countless black Americans.[18]*

Reflecting such views, a number of black politicians have won office in recent years by eschewing racial separatism and building coalitions with white groups, including Jewish ones. Former Philadelphia Congressman William Gray used this strategy effectively both in his home district and in the House where, as Democratic whip, he ranked third in the hierarchy before resigning to head the United Negro College Fund.

Political scientist Martin Kilson has described such figures as Gray, Georgia congressman John Lewis, Brooklyn congressman Major R. Owens, and former Virginia governor Douglas Wilder as "transethnic politicians" who successfully cross the racial divide.[20] David Dinkins is another. In his first mayoralty race in 1989, he denounced Farrakhan as a rabble-rouser, and shortly after his victory he flew to Israel to express his solidarity with the Jewish state. Despite criticism that he failed to act decisively in Crown Heights, his support among Jews remained virtually intact in his losing bid for reelection in 1993.

It is worth noting, too, that, New York City being a world center for print and electronic journalism, its serious black-Jewish

---

*According to the *Time*-CNN poll, the proportion of blacks who see Jews as having too much power is fairly low (28 percent), considerably lower than whites (80 percent) and big corporations (69%). Moreover, only 16 percent feel relations between blacks and Jews have grown worse.[19]

conflicts receive the widest coverage. But as historian Marshall Stevenson has pointed out, for the most part ethnic explosions there have not been replicated elsewhere. In Philadelphia, Atlanta, and other cities, a measure of cooperation continues to exist between blacks and Jews. Thus, Kansas City's first black mayor, Emanuel Cleaver, credited Jews for important assistance in his 1991 election.[21]

In Congress, too, black and Jewish legislators continue to vote together in support of liberal economic and social measures. Two Jewish congressmen, Howard Wolpe, of Michigan, and Stephen Solarz, who represented New York until redistricting cost him his seat in 1992, were among the leaders of the campaign for economic sanctions against South African apartheid. And the congressional Black Caucus has consistently and overwhelmingly favored foreign aid to Israel—this as recently as 1993.[22] Such backing has come in the face of strong pressure to redirect federal expenditures from overseas to American inner cities, where so many of the caucus's constituents live in poverty and despair.

Nevertheless, it would be a mistake to minimize current black-Jewish tensions or to read into some of these more positive developments the likelihood of a revival of the black-Jewish alliance. Time has not narrowed the breach or ended the estrangement between these groups. Neither side really trusts the other. It was a mutual sense of abandonment that brought them together in the first place, and a similar sense of abandonment now keeps them apart.

The partnership they formed to overcome racial hatred and discrimination existed in an era that itself no longer exists. High-tech America in today's postindustrial age bears little resemblance to the small-town, largely agricultural America of 1909 when Jews helped to form the NAACP and other social justice organizations.

Both groups have undergone tremendous changes since then and respond now to different pressures. What is missing today are the "shared visions"—in Glenn Loury's phrase—that stood at the heart of the old alliance. Jews have joined the American mainstream. This does not mean they have become more racist, but as an in-group they now have more to protect. They should not be stigmatized for defending what they worked so hard to obtain, for in a capitalist society that is what one is expected to do. In protecting what they have gained, however, Jews often find themselves in conflict with blacks and other nonwhites who, while increasing in numbers, are still largely outside the mainstream.

At the turn of the century, millions of European immigrants flocked to these shores. In contrast, current demographics point to a growing nonwhite presence in America. As Arthur Hertzberg has pointed out, seven of the ten largest cities now have black, Hispanic, and Asian majorities; by the year 2000 more than half of the total U. S. population will be nonwhite. Consisting largely of people either new to the nation or newly emerging in their political self-consciousness, this nonwhite majority has no connection, sense of guilt, or obligation to Jews; hence the tendency among some to minimize the significance of the European Holocaust. Indeed, Jews are seen most often as an elite, one that must be challenged.

It bears repeating that in recent years African Americans have enjoyed remarkable political successes. Black mayors have won election in all of the nation's largest cities—New York, Los Angeles, Chicago, Philadelphia, Detroit—and in such smaller ones as Atlanta, Baltimore, and Newark. But the performance of these mayors has been mixed at best, and the socioeconomic problems they have faced so far defy solution. As a result, their triumphs have not translated into substantially improved conditions for their black constituents.

Forty years after the *Brown* decision two out of three black children still attend segregated schools. Housing segregation appears endemic. Job discrimination still exists. Even successful blacks complain that while society has opened up for them, they experience discrimination in their day-to-day lives. Small wonder that, with the old liberal rules of the game having failed to bring so many blacks into the mainstream, the idea of going it alone and an independent black political party should have wide appeal and that black students, who feel increasingly isolated on white campuses, increasingly go to black colleges.[23]

What is currently underway is an intense debate within the black community to rethink the strategies for black inclusion—to sort out its leaders, goals and tactics. As transethnic politicians seek to build coalitions with Jews and other white groups, they often must deal with racial bigots breathing down their backs. In the 1992 New York's senatorial Democratic primary, one such figure, the Rev. Al Sharpton, gained 67 percent of the black vote. Although he lost the election, Sharpton established himself as a political force in the new racial politics.*

Columnist Juan Williams has a term for the ability of demagogues such as Sharpton to disfranchise or silence black leaders. He calls it the Farrakhan Paralysis. Historically, Williams notes, educated black leaders were the social engineers of the black movement. "Today," he notes, "black America is increasingly led by people who can only be described as characters, such as Al Sharpton in New York." At the height of the Kean College episode, he says, the congressional Black Caucus came down with a bad case of Farrakhan Paralysis. On the one hand, it embraced Farrakhan with "covenants," and on the other, it repudiated his "venomous sentiments" in defending Khalid Muhammad.[25] And during a June 1994 weekend, the NAACP's Rev. Benjamin F. Chavis, Jr., convened a summit conference of black leaders for three days in Baltimore, in order to map the next stage of the black liberation struggle. Among those attending were Farrakhan and Sharpton, as well as Jesse Jackson, congressional black caucus head Representative Kweisi Mfume, and the black author Cornel West. Criticized by Jews and others, Chavis declared that he had denounced bigotry but the NAACP would not be dictated to.[26]

The ambivalence reflects the internal struggle currently underway among blacks. Of course, not all black leaders have been par-

---

*Politicians must also deal with the anger and frustration of their core constituents, who are told that racial preferences in government hiring and ethnic redistricting to remedy past discrimination will provide needed relief. In 1992, Congressman Stephen J. Solarz, running in a newly created congressional district fashioned for a Puerto Rican (and opposed by Mayor Dinkins), was defeated despite his strong civil rights record. The following year, at the Human Resources Administration, Mayor Dinkins was forced to agree to give raises and higher rank to some seventy-five supervisors—many of them Jewish—who had contended they had been passed over for advancement because they were white.[24]

alyzed. But the question remains as to what views will prevail in the larger struggle for the mind of the black community.

Just as African Americans are struggling with their own identity, so too are American Jews. How they relate to their ethnicity or religious background is a recurring theme. In an article published in the 1970s, psychologist Judith Weinstein Klein examined the attitudes of Jews in the civil rights movement in terms of humanistic psychology. The Jews appeared to her to be "involved in others' search for mental health, for equal rights, for exploration of ethnic identity, but not in their own relationship to their Jewishness. . . . I often sensed in these Jews a vicarious enjoyment of other ethnic groups' new-found identity and self-consciousness, but an *embarrassment* at explicit attention to Jewishness."[27]

This issue took on fresh urgency with the trailblazing National Jewish Population Study of 1990, which warned of a sharp increase in intermarriage and other assimilating forces. It found Jews marrying outside their religion more than half the time. If that trend continues, it could lead to the virtual disappearance of the Jewish community in the United States.[28]

Intermarriage, religious indifference among younger Jews, and other assimilationist forces are matters of growing concern for Jewish leaders. Curiously, despite their extraordinary gains, Jews, like blacks, continue to see themselves as outsiders in a predominantly white Christian society. They certainly have less reason than blacks to feel threatened, but the fact is they do. Surveys indicate that they continue to view anti-Semitism as a serious and even central problem confronting them in everyday life.[29] Such views are continually reinforced by the activities of groups like the skinheads, the political appeal of such figures as David Duke and Pat Buchanan, and the growth of fascism and anti-Semitism abroad. Even as Jews are becoming assimilated into the larger society, many seem to be turning inward.

Clearly, as the century closes, blacks and Jews have their hands full sorting out their own problems and putting their own communities in order. How should they relate to one another as they do so? Perhaps the best they can manage in these difficult times is to become less preoccupied with one another and simply try to stay out of each other's way. While blacks appear to understand this option, many Jews do not. Frequently, they press for dialogue, assuming that present bad feelings can be cleared up if only Jews and blacks get together and talk things out. Blacks will sometimes indulge Jews in these efforts, but such gestures are at best halfhearted. Black leaders are rightfully more interested in dealing with here-and-now problems in black slums, grappling with their own sense of alienation, and seeking to strengthen their communities than in dialoguing with Jews.[30]

Given the increasingly diverse character of American life, Jews would do well to relate to blacks as they do to other groups—like Roman Catholics, for example. When Jews and Catholics agree on social welfare issues, such as aid to the needy or the handicapped, they work together in lobbying for programs in Washington and elsewhere. When they disagree, as on abortion or government aid to parochial schools, they oppose one another without hesitation.

Similarly, Jews and blacks tend to support the liberal agenda, including health-care and tax reform, and part company on other issues, such as racial preferences, set-asides, and political redistricting along racial lines. But Jewish organizations have sometimes been reluctant to stake out positions that blacks oppose for fear of appearing racist or insensitive. For example, they were slow to confront the violence in Crown Heights as a dangerous manifestation of anti-Semitism. Afterwards, Abe Foxman, executive head of the Anti-Defamation League, acknowledged the mistake. He said it resulted from self-imposed restraint as well as the Jewish search for social justice and a desire not to hurt those who were already suffering so much. He vowed, however, never to repeat the error.[31]

Clearly, Jewish groups are becoming less patient with racial extremism. Following Khalid Muhammad's speech at Kean College, the ADL printed his remarks in a full-page advertisement in the *New York Times*, thus precipitating the public outcry against the Nation of Islam leader. The American Jewish Committee followed with an ad proclaiming, "We Are All Americans," which was sharply critical of Muhammad's remarks. It was signed by numerous black and white leaders. And when the NAACP's president,

Benjamin Chavis, responded ambivalently to Farrakhan and called for a summit meeting with him, the AJC, in an unprecedented move, broke publicly with its old ally in the civil rights movement.

One thing should be made perfectly clear: For each group to go its separate way for a while does not mean that Jews should adopt a policy of "benign neglect" toward the urban crisis. It hardly needs saying that Jews cannot and should not abandon their traditional concern with social justice beyond their own community. Only those with hearts of stone could turn away from parents struggling against almost impossible odds to raise children in crime-ridden neighborhoods and failure-prone schools. They must not be left to fight this war alone. What new urban strategies should be devised to address these problems goes beyond the scope of this volume. One can only hope that they prove more realistic and useful than those of the past.

And as they deal more directly with their own internal problems, the two groups must be frank and open so that each knows exactly where the other stands on every issue and can negotiate the differences that have increasingly divided them.

Some blacks blame Jews for the failings of a society that is oppressing them. Jews who believe they have done their part to achieve racial justice react with a special bitterness. Given this rancor and distrust, it may not be possible to normalize relations between blacks and Jews anytime soon. Yet out of the turmoil and pain of the last thirty years, perhaps a new realism—a sense of what can and cannot be accomplished in this increasingly diverse and economically challenged society—may yet emerge.

In any case, as blacks and Jews continue to chart their unique individual destinies, one can only hope that American history itself is not rewritten. Once upon a time, Jews and blacks together wrote some of the finest pages in that story, shedding their blood to redeem the promise of American life. That is a fact, and it should not be forgotten.

NOTES

Introduction

1. The text of Jeffries's speech can be found in *New York Newsday*, August 18, 1991. On his removal as chairman and the federal court action that required City College to pay damages to him of $360,000 because of violation of his free speech rights, see *New York Times*, May 19, 1993. A federal appeals court later reversed the award. *JTA Community News Reporter*, April 29, 1994.
2. Martin has recently published a private account of his travails at Wellesley, *The Jewish Onslaught: Despatches from the Wellesley Battlefront*. *New York Times*, April 28, 1993; *Jewish Times* (Boston), April 1, December 9, 1993.
3. *New York Times*. September 8, 1993.
4. July 20, 1992. For the negative reaction to his piece, see Henry Louis Gates, Jr., "Memoirs of an Anti-Anti-Semite," *Village Voice*, October 20, 1992.
5. Ross, *J. E. Spingarn and the Rise of the NAACP*, New York: Atheneum, 1972; Claybourne Carson, Jr., "Blacks and Jews in the Civil Rights Movement," in Joseph R. Washington, Jr., *Jews in Black Perspectives: A Dialogue*, Cranbury, NJ: Associated University Presses, 1984. See also Leonard Dinnerstein, "The Origins of Black Anti-Semitism in America," *American Jewish Archives*, November, 1986, pp. 113–122; Stephen J. Whitfield, "A Critique of Leonard Dinnerstein's 'The Origins of Black Anti-Semitism in America,'" *American*

Jewish Archives, November 1987, pp. 193–202. For a bibliography on black-Jewish relations, see Lenwood G. Davis, *Black-Jewish Relations in the United States*, 1752–1984, Westport, CT: Greenwood Press, 1984. A recent journalistic account is Jonathan Kaufman, *Broken Alliance: The Turbulent Times between Blacks and Jews in America*, New York: Scribners, 1988.

6. For a discussion of the new black history, see Darlene Clark Hine, *The State of Afro-American History: Past, Present and Future*, Baton Rouge: 1986, and August Meier and Elliott Rudwick, *Black History and the Historical Profession, 1915–1980*, Urbana: University of Illinois Press, 1986, pp. 101–109. Novick, *That Noble Dream: The Objectivity Question and the American Historical Profession*, Boston: Cambridge University Press, 1988, p. 470.
7. "My Jewish Problem and Theirs," in Nat Hentoff, *Black Anti-Semitism and Jewish Racism*, New York: Richard W. Baron, 1969, pp. 147, 150.
8. Bazel E. Allen and Ernest J. Wilson III, 1984. Christopher Lasch is quoted by the editors as writing at the time that "when all the manifestos and polemics of the Sixties are forgotten, this book will survive as a monument of historical analysis." Stevenson, "Points of Departure, Acts of Resolve: Black-Jewish Relations in Detroit, 1937–1962," doctoral dissertation at the University of Michigan, Ann Arbor, 1988, p. vi. Meier and Rudwick, however, find it difficult to assess Cruse's importance among professionally trained historians but mention several who have consciously used his analysis, p. 205. See also Playhell Benjamin, "African-Americans and Jews: A Tattered Alliance," *Emerge*, October 1990, pp. 73–78, for a contemporary journalist who utilizes Cruse as his starting point in the discussion of black-Jewish relations.
9. "Shortcuts to the Mainstream: Afro-American and Jewish Notables in the 1920s and 1930s," in Joseph R. Washington, Jr., *Jews in Black Perspectives: A Dialogue*, Cranbury, NJ: Associated University Presses, 1984, pp. 83–84. See also Lewis, "Parallels and Divergences: Assimilationist Strategies of Afro-American and Jewish Elites from 1910 to the Early 1930s," *Journal of American History*, December 1984, pp. 543–564.
10. Laurenz, "Racial/Ethnic Conflict in the New York City Garment Industry, 1933–1980," graduate dissertation, SUNY Binghamton, 1980. For a more sympathetic examination of the role of the ILGWU, see Diner, *In the Almost Promised Land*, Westport, CT: Greenwood, 1977, pp. 199–203.
11. Unpublished paper, "Blacks and Jews in the Civil Rights Movement," Conference on Black-Jewish Relations, University of the District of Columbia, November 18, 1985.

12. Williams, "Franz U. Boas and the Conflict between Science and Values, 1894–1915," in *Newsletters on Philosophy Association* 92, 1 (Spring 1993), pp. 7–16.
13. New York: Free Press, 1984.
14. For a fuller discussion of this, see Karen J. Winkler, "Debating the History of Blacks and Jews," *Chronicle of Higher Education*, January 29, 1994, p. 2.
15. William Toll, "Pluralism and Moral Force in Black-Jewish Dialogue," *American Jewish History*, September 1987, pp. 88.
16. Robert G. Weisbord and Arthur Stein, *Bittersweet Encounter: The Afro-American and the American Jew*, Westport, CT: Negro Universities Press, 1970. On how Jews responded to Hitler, see Rafael Medoff, *The Deafening Silence: American Jewish Leaders and the Holocaust*, New York: Shapolsky, 1987, pp. 32–33.
17. "Toward a Research Agenda on Blacks and Jews in United States History," *Journal of American Ethnic History* 12, 3 (Spring 1993), pp. 60–67.
18. "The International Factor in Black-Jewish Tension," unpublished paper delivered at University of the District of Columbia Conference on Black-Jewish Relations, 1985, pp. 30, 34–35.
19. P. 487.
20. *Notes for an African World Revolution: Africans at the Crossroads*, Trenton, N.J.: Africa World Press, 1991. Clarke charges also that the Israeli raid on Entebbe in Uganda, rather than being a heroic act of rescue of people in a hijacked airliner, was "an act of aggression against an African state" (pp. 279–280).
21. Schlesinger, *The Disuniting of America: Reflections on a Multicultural Society*, New York: Norton, 1992; "A Special Issue, Race on Campus," *New Republic*, February 18, 1991. Leon Janoff, "Teaching Reverse Racism," *Time*, April 4, 1994, pp. 74–75.
22. Barry Mehler, "African-American Racism in the Academic Community," *Review of Education* 15, pp. 341–353. Another Afrocentric writer who has come to the defense of Leonard Jeffries is Molefi Kete Asante, chairman of the African-American studies program at Temple University. See Asante, "The Hysteria around Leonard Jeffries," *Philadelphia Tribune*, October 11, 1991.
23. Mehler, pp. 344–345.
24. *Long Memory: The Black Experience in America*: New York: Oxford University Press, 1982, p. 291.
25. The English Jewish press, as well as local newspapers, has been filled with accounts of these visits and the collisions that have resulted between black and Jewish students. For a sample, see "Jew-

ish Groups Protest Security at N.J. College Campus" and "Tempest on New York Campus in Wake of Student's Article," Jewish Telegraphic Agency, December 10 and October 22, 1993; *Jewish Exponent* (Philadelphia), May 15, 1992. Nat Hentoff, a frequent visitor to college campuses, has described as serious the tensions between the two groups there (*Village Voice*, May 1991). The *Jewish Daily Forward* reported on November 26, 1993, that Jewish faculty at Kean College in New Jersey ran programs to sensitize students to anti-Semitism following a speech the previous month of Leonard Jeffries.

26. Murray Friedman, "Jews, Blacks and the Civil Rights Revolution," *New Perspectives*, Fall 1985, p. 2.
27. Claybourne Carson has suggested that there should be a moratorium on the discussion of the history of black-Jewish relations because of the scarcity of historical materials. See Winkler, "Debating the History of Blacks and Jews," p. 11.

Chapter 1: Early Black–Jewish Relations

1. Joann Byrd, "The Timing of News," *Washington Post*, October 31, 1993; Earl Caldwell, *New York Daily News*, October 20, 1993; Voice of the People, *New York Daily News*, November 16, 1993.
2. Letter to writer, November 11, 1993.
3. "Jews in the Slave Trade," *Culturefront*, Fall, 1992, vol. 1, no. 2, pp. 42–45. For Davis's fuller discussion of this, see *Slavery and Human Progress*, New York: Oxford University Press, 1984, pp. 83–101. An earlier and highly polemical revisionist discussion of the role of Jews in slavery is by Oscar R. Williams, Jr., "Historical Impressions of Black-Jewish Relations Prior to World War II," *Negro History Bulletin*, July-August, 1977, pp. 728–731. Morris U. Schappes responds in "Another Comment," pp. 891–892.
4. Seymour Drescher, "The Role of Jews in the Transatlantic Slave Trade," *Immigrants and Minorities*, vol. 12, no. 2, July 1993, p. 117; Davis, "Jews in the Slave Trade," *Culturefront*, p. 44.
5. Ibid., pp. 43–44.
6. Drescher, p. 120.
7. Vol. 2, Detroit: Wayne State University Press, 1970, p. 703.
8. Korn, "Slave Trade," *Encyclopedia Judaica*, Vol. 14, pp. 1661–1663. For his fullest discussion of this subject, see *Jews and Negro Slavery in the Old South, 1789–1865*, Reform Congregation Keneseth Israel, Elkins Park, Pa., 1961. This can be found in Abraham J. Karp, ed., *The Jewish Experience in America*: Selected Studies from the

Publications of the American Jewish Historical Society, 1969, Vol. 3, and Leonard Dinnerstein and Mary Dale Palsson, eds., *Jews in the South*, Baton Rouge: Louisiana State University Press, 1973. The figures on individual cities are from Frederick Bancroft, *Slave Trading in the Old South*, Baltimore, 1931. On Jews as store owners, see Korn, "Jews and Negro Slavery in the Old South," in Dinnerstein and Palsson, p. 93. Korn's view that it was hard to find Jewish overseers stands in sharp contrast with Bracey and Meier's recommendation for further research on the Jewish role here.

9. Korn, "Jews in Negro Slavery," in Dinnerstein and Palsson, p. 61.
10. Leonard Dinnerstein, *The Leo Frank Case*, New York and London: Columbia University Press, 1968, p. 56; Eli N. Evans, *Judah P. Benjamin: the Jewish Confederate*, New York: The Free Press, 1988, p. 48; Korn, *American Jewry and the Civil War*, Philadelphia: Jewish Publication Society of America, 1951, p. iv; Korn, "Jews and Negro Slavery in the Old South," in Dinnerstein and Palsson, p. 134.
11. Jacob Marcus, ed., *Memoirs of American Jews, 1775–1865*, Philadelphia: Jewish Publication Society, 1955, II, p. 291.
12. Arthur M. Schlesinger, ed., *The Cotton Kingdom: A Traveler's Observations on Cotton and Slavery in the American Slave States*, New York: Knopf, 1984, p. 196; Harold David Brackman, "The Ebb and Flow of Conflict: A History of Black-Jewish Relations through 1900," doctoral dissertation at the University of California, Los Angeles, 1977, p. 14; Harry Golden, *Forgotten Pioneer*, Cleveland and New York: World, 1963, p. 14.
13. Peter and Vina Still, *The Kidnapped and the Ransomed*, with an introductory essay on Jews in the antislavery movement by Maxwell Whiteman, Philadelphia: Jewish Publication Society, 1970; Schappes, *Negro History Bulletin*, pp. 890–891. Schappes mentions several others in his account, as does Korn in "Jews and Negro Slavery in the Old South," in Dinnerstein and Palsson, pp. 100–101.
14. Brackman, p. 271; Cyrus Adler, *I Have Considered These Days*, Philadelphia: Jewish Publication Society, 1941, pp. 4–5.
15. Whiteman and Still, p. 25.
16. Jayme A. Sokolow, "Revolution and Reform: The Antebellum Jewish Abolitionists," *Journal of Ethnic Studies*, Spring 1981, pp. 27–41; Brackman, p. 271. Hugh H. Smythe and Martin S. Price, "The American Jew and Negro Slavery," *Midwest Journal*, vol. 7, Winter, 1955–1956, p. 316.
17. Whiteman and Still, pp. 39–41.
18. Sokolow, p. 33.
19. Ibid, p. 33.

20. Morris U. Schappes, *Documentary History of the Jews in the United States, 1654–1875*, New York: The Citadel Press, Rev. ed., 1952, pp. 405–418. Heilprin's reply, pp. 418–428.
21. Sokolow, p. 35; Whiteman and Still, p. 57; Eli N. Evans, *The Provincials*, New York: Macmillan, 1976, p. 302; Arthur Hertzberg, *The Jews in America*, New York: Simon and Schuster, 1989, pp. 124–126.
22. Bertram W. Korn, "Isaac Mayer Wise on the Civil War," in *Eventful Years and Experiences*, Cincinnati: American Jewish Archives, 1954. Lance Sussman, doctoral dissertation, "The Life and Career of Isaac Leeser (1806–1868): A Study of American Judaism in Its Formative Period," HUC-JIR, Cincinnati, 1987, pp. 316, 367, 369; Schappes, *Documentary History*, p. 686.
23. Korn, "Isaac Mayer Wise on the Civil War," p. 124; Evans, *The Provincials*, p. 303. Winthrop Jordan discusses the "curse of Ham" or "Ham myth" in *White Over Black, American Attitudes toward the Negro, 1550–1812*. This holds that as Noah lay in a drunken sleep in his tent after the Flood, his son Ham looked at his nakedness while his other sons covered him (Genesis 9 and 10). When Noah awakened, the story goes (often attributed to Talmudic and Midrashic sources), "Ham was smitten in the skin" and Ham was told "your seed will be ugly and dark skinned." There is clearly no discussion of skin color in the biblical tale, but over the centuries the story has gained extraordinary tenacity. Jordan speculates that the myth developed out of the need of the English to find an explanation for enslaving blacks (p. 20). According to David Goldenberg in an unpublished paper, it is now regularly and sometimes approvingly discussed in the literature on black history. Dr. Goldenberg declares in his paper that "racism towards blacks is a concept as foreign to rabbinic literature as it is to the Old Testament." I am grateful to Dr. Goldenberg for sharing his analysis with me. For a discussion of this subject see also Harold Brackman, letter to the New York *Times*, February 14, 1994.
24. Whiteman and Still, p. 62.
25. Whiteman and Still, p. 89. At least one scholar suggests that Wise went too far in his broadside attacks on the abolitionists. See Louis Ruchames, "The Abolitionists and the Jews," *Publications of the American Jewish Historical Society*, XLII, December 1952, pp. 131–155.
26. Julius Lester, "Lovesong: Becoming a Jew," *Moment*, December 1987, pp. 33–41; Arnold Shankman, ed., *Ambivalent Friends: Afro-Americans View the Immigrant*, Westport: Greenwood, 1982, p. 115.
27. For a fuller discussion of this matter, see Albert J. Raboteau, "Black

Americans," in Moshe Davis, ed., *With Eyes Toward Zion*, II, New York: Praeger, 1986, Chap. 10.

28. *Black Boy*, New York: Harper and Bros., 1945; Perennial ed., 1982, pp. 70–71.
29. As quoted by Leonard Dinnerstein in "Black Antisemitism," in Dinnerstein, *Uneasy at Home: Antisemitism and the American Jewish Experience*, New York: Cornell University Press, 1987, p. 220.
30. Evans, *The Provincials*, p. 304.
31. As quoted in Brackman, "The Ebb and Flow of Conflict," p. 305.
32. *The Negroes and the Jews*, New York: Random House, 1971, p. 17.
33. Korn, as quoted in Brackman, "The Ebb and Flow of Conflict," p. 287. Howard M. Sachar puts the Confederate figure at two to three thousand. *A History of the Jews in America*, New York: Knopf, 1992, p. 74.
34. Sussman, "Isaac Leeser;" Korn, *American Jewry and the Civil War*, Chap. 7.
35. Bertram W. Korn, "American Judeophobia: Confederate Version," in Dinnerstein and Palsson, *Jews in the South*, pp. 153–169; Howard N. Rabinowitz, "Nativism, Bigotry and Anti-Semitism in the South," *American Jewish Archives*, March 1988, pp. 1–2, 44; Mark I. Greenberg, "Ambivalent Relations: Acceptance and Anti-Semitism in Confederate Thomasville," *American Jewish Archives*, vol. xlv, no. 1, Spring/Summer, 1993, pp. 13–29.
36. Eli N. Evans, *Judah P. Benjamin*, p. xx.
37. Leonard Dinnerstein, *The Leo Frank Case*, p. 67; Evans, *Judah P. Benjaman*, pp. 38–39, 149, 156.
38. Evans, *Judah P. Benjaman*, pp. 274–278.
39. Evans, ibid., p. 286.
40. Barry E. Supple, "Business Elite: German-Jewish Financiers in Nineteenth-Century New York," *Business History Review* 31, Summer 1957, pp. 149–151; Naomi W. Cohen, *Encounter with Emancipation: The German Jews in the U.S., 1830–1914*, Philadelphia: Jewish Publication Society, 1984, p. 19; Dinnerstein, *The Leo Frank Case*, p. 67; Thomas D. Clark, "The Post–Civil War Economy in the South," in Dinnerstein and Palsson, *Jews in the South*, p. 163.
41. Brackman, "The Ebb and Flow of Conflict," p. 335.
42. P. 14. For an account of one Jewish peddler and his warm relationship with his black customers, see Louis Schmier, "For Him the 'Schwartzers' Couldn't Do Enough: A Jewish Peddler and His Black Customers Look at Each Other," *American Jewish History*, September 1983, vol. lxxxiii, no. 1, pp. 39–53. Occasionally, the relationship became more intimate. Julius Lester, the black writer,

discovered that his great-grandfather was a Jewish peddler who had emigrated from Germany and married an ex-slave, an act that would have been unthinkable for a white Christian in the South. "Lovesong: Becoming a Jew," p. 35.

43. Cohen, *Encounter with Emancipation*, p. 204; Korn, "Isaac Mayer Wise on the Civil War," pp. 168–169.
44. Evans, *The Provincials*, p. 309; Golden, *Forgotten Pioneer*, p. 14.
45. Shankman, *Ambivalent Friends*, p. 120.
46. John Dollard, *Caste and Class in a Southern Town*, New York: Anchor, 1957, pp. 128–129; Golden, *Forgotten Pioneer*, p. 14.
47. Cohen, *Encounter with Emancipation*, p. 23; Baker, "Following the Color Line," in Shankman, *Ambivalent Friends*, p. 123; Steven Hertzberg, *Strangers Within the Gate City: The Jews of Atlanta, 1845–1915*, Philadelphia: Jewish Publication Society, 1978, p. 184.
48. "A Socialist View of the Jews of the South: The Observations of Baruch Charney Vladeck," translated by Franklin L. Jones, first published in the *Jewish Daily Forward*, March 22, 1911; reprinted in *American Jewish Archives*.
49. Isabel Boiko Price, "Black Responses to Anti-Semitism: Negroes and Jews in New York, 1880 to World War II," doctoral dissertation, University of New Mexico, 1973, pp. 29, 56, 60; Seth M. Scheiner, *Negro Mecca: A History of the Negro in New York City, 1865–1920*, New York: New York University Press, 1965, p. 131; Stephen J. Whitfield, "A Critique of Leonard Dinnerstein's 'The Origins of Black Anti-Semitism in America,'" *American Jewish Archives*, November 1987, pp. 193–202.
50. Philip S. Foner, "Black-Jewish Relations in the Opening Years of the Twentieth Century," *Phylon*, Winter 1975, pp. 359–360; Price, "Black Responses to Anti-Semitism," p. 36.
51. Foner, "Black-Jewish Relations," p. 361. For additional comment of this kind, see August Meier, *Negro Thought in America, 1880–1915*, Ann Arbor: University of Michigan Press, 1963, pp. 56–57, 248; Scheiner, *Negro Mecca*, p. 132.
52. Diner, *In the Almost Promised Land*, p. 17.
53. Louis R. Harlan, "Booker T. Washington's Discovery of Jews," in J. Morgan Kousser and James M. McPherson, eds., *Region, Race and Reconstruction: Essays in Honor of C. Vann Woodward*, New York: Oxford University Press, 1982, p. 275; Shankman, *Ambivalent Friends*, pp. 114–115.
54. Louis R. Harlan, ed., *Booker T. Washington Papers*, III, pp. 408–409; September 26, 1914, in Shankman, *Ambivalent Friends*, p. 118. Meier, *Negro Thought in America*, pp. 56–57, 105.
55. Harlan, "Booker T. Washington's Discovery of Jews," pp. 275–276;

Harlan, *Booker T. Washington: The Wizard of Tuskegee, 1901–15*, New York: Oxford University Press, 1983, p. 260.

56. David J. Hellwig, "Black Images of Jews: From Reconstruction to Depression," *Societas—A Review of Social History* VIII, Summer 1978, pp. 209–218; Berson, *The Negroes and the Jews*, p. 21 ff.
57. Berson, pp. 19, 25–26.
58. Dinnerstein, *The Leo Frank Case*, p. 65; W. J. Cash, *The Mind of the South*, New York: Doubleday Anchor, 1956, p. 334. "Double-Lynching of a Jew and a Negro, News-story, The Franklin, Tenn., Double Murder," *The Israelite*, Cincinnati, August 28, 1868, in Schappes, *Documentary History of the Jews in the United States*, pp. 515–517; Shankman, *Ambivalent Friends*, p. 141.
59. Berson, p. 28; Dinnerstein, *The Leo Frank Case*, p. 68.
60. Foner, "Black-Jewish Relations," p. 360.
61. As quoted in Scheiner, *Negro Mecca*, pp. 130–131. "Surely the United States government cannot be more sensitive over the wrongs inflicted on the Semitic people in Romania than over the ignominious disgraces heaped upon the Afro-Americans, its citizens, by white citizens," the *Voice of the People* declared on November 1, 1902. The paper, published by Henry Tanner, bishop of the A.M.E. church in Atlanta, pointed out that just as the government could "issue a note" on behalf of persecuted Romanians, "it could issue an order to the various states for a better treatment of its colored citizens" (Foner, "Black-Jewish Relations," p. 362); Hertzberg, *Strangers within the Gate City*, p. 195.
62. Price, "*Black Responses to Anti-Semitism*", pp. 33–34.
63. Harlan, *The Booker T. Washington Papers*, VII, pp. 168–169.
64. Harlan, "Booker T. Washington's Rediscovery of Jews," p. 70; Foner, "Black-Jewish Relations," p. 363.
65. Stephen J. Whitfield, "The Jewish Vote," *Virginia Quarterly Review*, Winter, 1986, p. 8.
66. Foner, "Black-Jewish Relations," pp. 363–364.
67. Ibid., pp. 363–365; Brackman, "The Ebb and Flow of Conflict," p. 337; Hertzberg, p. 200.
68. Joan Dash, *Summoned to Jerusalem: The Life of Henrietta Szold*, New York: Harper Row, 1979, p. 9; Brackman, "The Ebb and Flow of Conflict," p. 337.
69. Charles Reznikoff, ed., *Louis Marshall, Champion of Liberty: Selected Papers and Addresses*, vol. 1, 1957, pp. 425–426.
70. "Black Images of Jews," p. 210.
71. Pp. 35, 48.
72. Brackman, "The Ebb and Flow of Conflict," pp. 441–446.

73. Ibid., p. 337; Lloyd P. Gartner, "Candidates, Messiahs and Aristocrats," *Midstream*, XIV, October, 1968, p. 27.
74. Brackman, "The Ebb and Flow of Conflict," p. 458; Cyrus Adler, ed., *Jacob Schiff: His Life and Letters*, I, Garden City: Doubleday, 1928, p. 314; Irving Howe, *World of Our Fathers*, New York: Harcourt Brace, 1976, pp. 90–93.
75. Brackman, "The Ebb and Flow of Conflict," p. 461; Scheiner, *Negro Mecca*, pp. 150–151.
76. Gilbert Osofsky, *Harlem: The Making of a Ghetto*, New York, Harper & Row, 1968, p. 36; Scheiner, *Negro Mecca*, pp. 176–177.
77. Harlan, "Booker T. Washington's Discovery of Jews," p. 271.
78. Ibid., p. 273; James D. Anderson, *The Education of Blacks in the South, 1860–1935*, Chapel Hill: University of North Carolina Press, 1988, p. 158.
79. "Rethinking the American Jewish Experience: A Peculiar Alliance: Julius Rosenwald, the YMCA, and African-Americans, 1910–1933," *American Jewish Archives*, vol. xliv, no. 2, Fall/Winter, 1992, pp. 585–605.
80. Harlan, *The Booker T. Washington Papers*, VIII, p. 97.
81. At one point, Du Bois approached Schiff for help but got nothing because he thought most of Schiff's friends were advocates of Tuskegee. Brackman, p. 465; August Meier, *Negro Thought in America*, p. 133; Hellwig, p. 214; Harlan, "Booker T. Washington's Discovery of Jews," p. 268. On greater respect for Washington more recently see Howard Brotz, *Black Jews of Harlem*, New York, Free Press of Glencoe, 1964.

Chapter 2: Origins of the Black–Jewish Alliance

1. Charles F. Kellogg, *NAACP*, Baltimore: John Hopkins Press, 1967; John Hope Franklin, *From Slavery to Freedom: A History of Negro Americans*, 4th ed., New York: Knopf, 1974 p. 328.
2. Kellogg, p. 10; Franklin, p. 328; Mary White Ovington, *The Walls Came Tumbling Down*, New York: Harcourt Brace, 1947, pp. 101–102; James M. McPherson, *The Abolitionist Legacy: From Reconstruction to the NAACP*, Princeton: Princeton University Press, 1975, p. 385.
3. Hellwig, "Black Images of Jews," p. 210.
4. Francis L. Broderick, *W. E. B. Du Bois: Negro Leader in a Time of Crisis*, Stanford, CA: Stanford University Press, 1959 (reprinted 1966), pp. 26–27.
5. Hellwig, p. 217.

6. Chicago (A.C. McClung edition), pp. 170, 204.
7. Herbert Aptheker, "The Souls of Black Folk: A Comparison of the 1903 and 1952 editions," *Negro History Bulletin* 34, p. 16; Dinnerstein, *Uneasy at Home*, p. 226. On Du Bois's apology, see also Du Bois, *The Souls of Black Folk*, KTO, 1973, p. 41.
8. I am grateful to Professor Dinnerstein for sharing his research with me on this matter. See also Henry Louis Gates's discussion of this in Nat Hentoff's column in the *Village Voice*, August 20, 1991.
9. On Du Bois's role, see Broderick, p. 92; Diner, p. 122.
10. Broderick, p. 92.
11. Franklin, p. 330; Kellogg, p. 129; Scheiner, p. 59; Guichard Parris and Lester Brooks, *Blacks in the City: A History of the National Urban League*, New York: Little, Brown, 1971, p. 34.
12. Richard Hofstadter, *Anti-Intellectualism in American Life*, New York: Vintage Books, 1962, p. 123.
13. Naomi Cohen, *Not Free to Desist: A History of the American Jewish Committee, 1906–1966*, Philadelphia: Jewish Publication Society, 1972 p. 144; John Higham, *Send These to Me*, New York: Atheneum, 1975 p. 167.
14. W. E. B. Du Bois, *The Autobiography of W.E.B. Du Bois*, New York: International Publishers, 1968, p. 254. Du Bois noted that Villard's wife was from Georgia, the implication being that she grew up with southern-style antiblack biases and passed them on to her husband. Du Bois said that neither he nor any of his black associates ever set foot in Villard's home, and he doubted that any Jews had either. Du Bois may not have been wrong. Exasperated at one point, Villard referred to blacks as a "child race."
15. B. Joyce Ross, *J.E. Spingarn and the Rise of the NAACP 1911–1939*, New York: Atheneum, 1972, pp. 68, 110.
16. Broderick, *W. E. B. Du Bois*, p. 99.
17. Kellogg, p. 101.
18. Diner, p. 120.
19. Ross, pp. 10, 14, 20; Kellogg, pp. 61, 93.
20. Ross, pp. 26–27.
21. Ibid., p. 29.
22. Ibid., p. 29.
23. Ibid., pp. 26–27; Kellogg, pp. 93, 128.
24. Ross, p. 46; Kellogg, pp. 86–87.
25. Kellogg, p. 208; Franklin, p. 337; David Levening Lewis, *W.E.B. Du Bois: Biography of a Race*, New York: Henry Holt, 1993, Chapter 18.
26. Cited by D. L. Lewis in "Shortcuts to the Mainstream: Afro-American and Jewish Notables in the 1920s and 1930s," in Joseph R.

Washington, Jr., *Jews in Black Perspectives: A Dialogue*, Cranbury: Associated University Presses, 1984, p. 85.

27. Ross, p. 26.
28. "Parallels and Divergences: Assimilationist Strategies of Afro-American and Jewish Elites from 1910 to the Early 1930s," *Journal of American History* 71, 3 (December 1984), pp. 554–555.
29. "Shortcuts to the Mainstream," pp. 84–85. Despite his doubts about the usefulness of Jews in the black struggle, Lewis does cite the positive role on racial issues of the *Forward*'s Abraham Cahan and notes it was "necessary and natural" for blacks and Jews "to believe fervently in the mystique of a special racial bond, an altruistic conspiracy of the dispossessed."
30. As quoted by Larry Cohler, "Finally, the Politicians Listen," *The Jewish Exponent Centennial Edition, 1887–1987*, p. 76.
31. Diner, pp. 28–41.

Chapter 3: The Twenties

1. Dinnerstein, *The Leo Frank Case*, p. 6.
2. Eugene Levy, "Is the Jew a White Man?: Press Reaction to the Leo Frank Case, 1913–1915," *Phylon*, June 1974, p. 214.
3. Stephen J. Whitfield, *Voices of Jacob, Hands of Esau: Jews in American Life and Thought*, Garden City, NY: Anchor, 1984, p. 235; Levy, p. 214.
4. Steven Bloom, "Interactions between Blacks and Jews in New York City 1900 As Reflected in the Black Press," doctoral dissertation, New York University, 1973, p. 59; Levy, p. 216.
5. Dinnerstein, *The Leo Frank Case*, p. 150; "Not the Work of a Day," Anti-Defamation League of B'nai B'rith *Oral Memoirs* V, New York: ADL, 1987, p. 85.
6. Levy, p. 221; Charles Reznikoff, *Louis Marshall: Champion of Liberty* I, Philadelphia: Jewish Publication Society of America, 1957, p. 426.
7. Levy, p. 218.
8. Diner, p. 134; Ross, p. 38.
9. Diner, pp. 129, 157; Franklin, p. 329.
10. Lewis, "Shortcuts to the Mainstream," pp. 93, 129; Juanita Mitchell, "The Black-Jewish Alliance: Reunion and Renewal," Colloquium, November 28–29, 1988, sponsored by Religious Action Center of Reform Judaism, Atlanta.
11. Morton Rosenstock, *Louis Marshall, Defender of Jewish Rights*, Detroit: Wayne State University Press, 1965, pp. 69–70.

12. Reznikoff, *Marshall* I, p. xxviii.
13. Diner, p. 130; Reznikoff, *Marshall* I, p. 465.
14. Walter White, *A Man Named White*, New York: Viking, 1948, pp. 8, 89.
15. Cruse, p. 152.
16. Ibid., p. 153.
17. Ibid., p. 158.
18. Ibid., p. 152. For more on his animus against Jews, see "My Jewish Problem and Theirs," in Nat Hentoff, *Black Anti-Semitism and Jewish Racism*, New York: Baron, 1969, pp. 143–188.
19. Ibid., p. 160.
20. Reznikoff, *Marshall* II, p. 464.
21. Howard Brotz, *The Black Jews of Harlem*, New York: Schocken, 1970, p. 71.
22. Philip S. Foner, *Business and Slavery: The New York Merchants and the Irrepressible Conflict*, Chapel Hill: University of North Carolina Press, 1941, pp. 204–205; Brackman, "The Ebb and Flow of Conflict," p. 251.
23. Foner, *Business and Slavery*, pp. 198–199.
24. Osofsky, *Harlem*, pp. 87–89; Jeffrey S. Gurock, *When Harlem Was Jewish, 1870–1930*, New York: Columbia University Press, 1979, p. 167.
25. For a discussion of this, see Deborah Dash Moore, *At Home in America*, New York: Columbia University Press, 1981.
26. Gurock, p. 149.
27. Gurock, pp. 146, 167; Scheiner, p. 30.
28. *American School Board Journal*, February 1991; reprinted in Albert Shanker column, *New York Times*, March 10, 1991; *Philadelphia Tribune*, February 15, 1991; *Washington Jewish Week*, March 21, 1991.
29. Brotz, p. 9; Diner, p. 69.
30. Pp. 11–12.
31. Franklin, p. 365; Price, "Black Responses," p. 119; Roi Ottley, *New World A'Coming: Inside Black America*, Boston: Houghton Mifflin, 1943, p. 73.
32. Franklin, p. 365; Brotz, pp. 99–101.
33. Brotz, p. 101.
34. As quoted in Robert G. Weisbord and Richard Kazarian, Jr., *Israel in the Black American Perspective*, Westport, CT: Greenwood Press, 1985, p. 16.
35. Price, "Black Responses," p. 135.
36. Judith Stein, *The World of Marcus Garvey: Race and Class in Mod-*

ern Society, Baton Rouge: Louisiana State University Press, 1986, pp. 202–203; Price, "Black Responses," p. 131.

37. Price, "Black Responses," pp. 136–137; Weisbord and Kazarian, p. 17.
38. As quoted in Weisbord and Kazarian, p. 17.
39. Ibid., p. 17.
40. Feingold, "Finding a Conceptual Framework for the Study of American Antisemitism," *Jewish Social Studies*, Summer-Fall, 1985, p. 317; Feingold, speech, Philadelphia, December 16, 1987; Weisbord and Kazarian, p. 18. On black ambivalence, David J. Hellwig writes, "Little will be gained by seeking to determine whether blacks have been pro- or anti-Jewish. Their view of Jews reflected [their] insecurity" since "Jews symbolized both hope and oppression." "Black Images of Jews from Reconstruction to Depression," *Societas*, 1978, pp. 205–223.
41. Price, "Black Responses," pp. 138, 347; Anderson, p. 149.
42. As quoted in Shankman, *Ambivalent Friends*, p. 131.
43. Anderson, p. 179.
44. Ibid., chapters 5 and 6; for educator Bond reference, p. 177.
45. Levy, p. 217.
46. Shankman, p. 129.
47. Price, "Black Responses," p. 92.
48. Diner, pp. 72–73.
49. Price, "Black Responses," pp. 172–173.
50. Jervis Anderson, *A. Philip Randolph: A Biographical Portrait*, New York: Harcourt Brace Jovanovich, 1972, pp. 62–63.
51. Diner, pp. 205, 229; Anderson, p. 94.
52. Diner, p. 203.

Chapter 4: The Thirties

1. Kate Simon, *A Wider World: Portraits in an Adolescence*, New York: Harper & Row, 1986, pp. 3, 123–124.
2. Simon, p. 125. For an examination of victimization of blacks, see Ella Baker and Marvel Baker, "The Bronx Slave Market," *Crisis*, November 1935, pp. 330–331; Ottley, *New World A'Coming*, p. 127. For the origin of the term "schvartze," see Leo Rosten, *The Joys of Yiddish*, New York: McGraw-Hill, 1968, p. 377.
3. Cruse, "My Jewish Problem," p. 48.
4. Howard University Studies in the Social Sciences, The Graduate School, Washington, DC, 1942, p. 12. For a discussion of Jews who for reasons of poverty could not move from Harlem and were "a vilified minority within a minority," see Irving Louis Horowitz,

Daydreams and Nightmares, Jackson: University Press of Mississippi, 1990.

5. Price, p. 190.
6. *New York Times*, March 22, 1930. Some very good medicine was being practiced in Harlem at this time. Famous doctors and surgeons from Berlin and Vienna were fleeing Europe and finding places there. Horowitz, p. 10.
7. Gilbert Osofsky, *Harlem: The Making of a Ghetto*, New York: Harper & Row, Second Edition, 1971, p. 121. There is a considerable literature on the cultural systems of groups and the support they have provided for business achievement; see Ivan Light, *Ethnic Enterprise in America: Business and Welfare among Chinese and Blacks*, Los Angeles: University of California Press, 1972.
8. Wedlock, p. 8.
9. Price, pp. 22, 226.
10. *Uneasy at Home: Anti-Semitism and the American Jewish Experience*, New York: Columbia University Press, 1987, p. 228; Price, p. 197. See also Ottley, p. 125.
11. Price, p. 236; Ottley, pp. 117, 119; Judd L. Teller, *Strangers and Natives*, New York: Delacorte, 1968, pp. 185–186.
12. Harold Brackman, "Splash! Farrakhan's Big Belly Flop," *Jewish Exponent*, January 8, 1986, p. 7; Ottley, p. 119; Price, pp. 235–236; Winston C. McDowell, "Conflict and Cooperation: African-Americans, Jews and Harlem Job Boycotts, 1932–1935," a paper prepared for the conference, "Blacks and Jews: An American Historical Perspective," Washington University, St. Louis, December 2–5, 1993, p. 7.
13. Wedlock, pp. 126–127.
14. Price, p. 247.
15. Ottley, p. 118; Price, p. 247. For a fuller discussion of Harlem boycotts and the role played by various organizations, see Cheryl Lynn Greenberg, *Or Does It Explode: Black Harlem in the Great Depression*, New York: Oxford University Press, 1991, pp. 126–128.
16. Thomas Kessner, *Fiorello H. LaGuardia*, New York: McGraw-Hill, 1989, pp. 328–329; Franklin, pp. 408–409; Price, pp. 254–258.
17. Franklin, pp. 408–409; Wedlock, p. 167; Diner, p. 238. It is an indication of how little black-Jewish tensions engaged the attention of historians that John Hope Franklin, in discussing the 1935 riot in his one-volume history of blacks in America (4th ed., 1974), makes no mention of them.
18. *Amsterdam News*, April 16, 1938.
19. Wedlock, p. 145.

20. Wedlock, p. 80. For discussions of the response of famed black track star Jesse Owens, see William J. Baker, *Jesse Owens*, New York: Free Press, 1986, pp. 91–104; Price, p. 276. The headline on an article in a *Philadelphia Tribune* story of October 29, 1936, declared, according to Wedlock, "Hitler Praised above Roosevelt by Jesse Owens at G.O.P. Rally." Referring to FDR's failure to support the antilynching bill, it quoted him as saying, "I think Hitler's a noble man" (p. 47). For Olympic leaders' treatment of Jewish track stars and Owens's sympathetic response to the Jewish runners, see also Glickman in Howard Simons, *Jewish Times: Voices of the American Jewish Experience*, Boston: Houghton Mifflin, 1988, pp. 339, 388; Duff Hart Davis, *Hitler's Games: The 1936 Olympics*, New York: Harper & Row, 1986.
21. "My Jewish Problem," p. 48. On Communism among blacks during this time, see Mark Naison, *Communists in Harlem during the Great Depression*, New York: Grove Press, 1983, pp. 11–13.
22. Lawrence D. Reddick, "Anti-Semitism among Negroes," *Negro Quarterly*, Summer 1942, pp. 112–122; Ottley, p. 128.
23. Arnold Rampersad, *The Life of Langston Hughes, I, 1902–1941*, New York: Oxford University Press, 1986, p. 273.
24. "As the Crow Flies," September 1933, p. 197. I am grateful to Leonard Dinnerstein for calling my attention to this article. Price, p. 311; *Amsterdam News*, November 29, 1941.
25. Dominic J. Capeci, Jr., "Black-Jewish Relations in Wartime Detroit: The Marsh, Loving, Wolf Surveys and the Race Riot of 1943," *Jewish Social Studies* 47, 3–4 (Summer-Fall 1985), p. 224.
26. Price, p. 286.
27. Price, pp. 287–288.
28. *New York Age*, September 19, 1936.
29. Price, pp. 235–236; see also B. Z. Sobel and May L. Sobel, "Negroes and Jews: American Minority Groups in Conflict," in Peter Rose, ed., *The Ghetto and Beyond: Essays on Jewish Life in America*, New York: Random House, 1969, p. 389.
30. Price, pp. 295, 302.
31. Wedlock, p. 83.
32. See a discussion of this in Patrick S. Washburn, *A Question of Sedition: The Federal Government's Investigation of the Black Press during World War II*, New York: Oxford University Press, 1986, pp. 32–33. Price, pp. 238, 284; Sobel and Sobel in Rose, p. 388; Weisbord and Kazarian, pp. 17–18.
33. Diner, p. 127.
34. Price, p. 348; Whitfield, "Braided Identity," p. 379; Dan Carter,

Scottsboro: A Tragedy of the American South, Baton Rouge: Louisiana State University Press, 1969, pp. 156–158, 161–163, 235–241, 322–324. For conflict between Liebowitz and the Communist-dominated International Labor Defense (ILD) attorney Joseph Brodsky, see Quentin Reynolds, *Courtroom: The Story of Samuel S. Liebowitz*, New York: Farrar, Straus, 1950, p. 286; James Goodman, *Stories of Scottsboro*, New York: Pantheon, 1994.

35. Price, p. 265; *New York Times*, July 22, 1942.
36. Reddick, pp. 112–122; Ottley, pp. 128–129.
37. September 15, 1942, in Price, p. 322.
38. Price, pp. 318, 328.
39. Ibid., p. 454.
40. Franklin, p. 455.
41. White, *A Man Called White*, p. 235.
42. Price, pp. 330–339. See also the description in Dominic J. Capeci, Jr., *The Harlem Riot of 1943*, Philadelphia: Temple University Press, 1977.
43. Capeci, p. 225. For the later recollection of the riot, see Noam M. M. Neusner, "The Sleepwalker," *Detroit Jewish News*, January 20, 1992.
44. Price, p. 339.
45. Sobel and Sobel, p. 389. For black-Jewish tensions in Chicago, see St. Clair Drake and Horace R. Cayton, *Black Metropolis: A Study of Negro Life in a Northern City*, vol. 2, New York: Harcourt, Brace, 1945, pp. 435–456.
46. Capeci, "Black-Jewish Relations in Wartime Detroit," pp. 229–230.
47. *Amsterdam News*, February 14 and 21, 1942.
48. *Philadelphia Inquirer*, November 11, 1992; *Philadelphia Jewish Times*, December 31, 1992.
49. Richard Kluger, *Simple Justice, Vol. I, Brown v. Board of Education and Black America's Struggle for Equality*, New York: Knopf, p. 163 (1975 edition).
50. Roy Wilkins, *Standing Fast*, p. 148; Auerbach, *Unequal Justice: Lawyers and Social Change in Modern America*, New York: Oxford University Press, 1976, p. 213; Jack Greenberg, *Race Relations and American Law*, New York: Columbia University Press, 1959, pp. 35–37; Mark V. Tushnet, *The NAACP's Legal Strategy against Segregated Education, 1925–1950*, Chapel Hill: University of North Carolina Press, 1987, pp. 26–27. In practice, the Margold report is described by Kluger as a "conservative instrument," since the NAACP moved forward to equalize facilities in the higher education cases rather than launch an immediate assault on public school education. I, p. 169; White, p. 142.

Chapter 5: Blacks and Jews as Allies in the Arts and Social Sciences

1. *Jewish Exponent* (Philadelphia), August 10, 1990; Michael Elkin, "Spike Shots," *Jewish Exponent*, June 14, 1991.
2. *Philadelphia Inquirer*, July 13, 1990.
3. Cruse, pp. 516–517; *New York Times*, September 2, 1990.
4. On Hollywood's early attack on prejudice, see Richard Weiss, "Ethnicity and Reform: Minorities and the Ambience of the Depression Years," *Journal of American History*, December 1979, p. 569. See also Thomas Cripps, *Slow Fade to Black: The Negro in American Film, 1900–1942*, New York: Oxford University Press, 1977.
5. Rampersad, *Langston Hughes, I*, p. 105.
6. Rampersad, I, pp. 67, 189, 291.
7. *Philadelphia Inquirer*, December 3, 1987.
8. Rampersad, I, pp. 281–285.
9. "The Fire This Time," *New Republic*, December 30, 1985, p. 41; W. J. Weatherby, *James Baldwin: Artist on Fire*, New York: Donald L. Fine, 1989, p. 51.
10. Weatherby, p. 55.
11. February 1948; I am indebted to Nathan Glazer's reading of this piece in "The Fire This Time," p. 42.
12. For Podhoretz's discussion of how the piece came to be written and his anger at its being sold to the *New Yorker*, see Podhoretz, *Breaking Ranks: A Political Memoir*, New York, Harper & Row, 1979, p. 121; Weisbrot, *Freedom Bound*, p. 225.
13. Rampersad, I, p. 381.
14. *Gershwin: His Life and Music*, Indianapolis: Bobbs-Merrill, 1973, p. 72.
15. Schwartz, p. 245.
16. Edward Rothstein, "George Gershwin's Heav'nly Lan'," *New Republic*, March 18, 1985, p. 28. On the Toronto controversy, see "Letter from Toronto," *Forward*, May 7, 1993; *New York Times*, May 1, 1993.
17. *Crisis of the Negro Intellectual*, p. 52; *Plural but Equal*, p. 136.
18. "Parallels and Divergences," pp. 560, 564.
19. *New York Times*, September 30, 1988. For a recent discussion of Josephson, see Lewis Erenberg, "Greenwich Village Nightlife, 1910–1950," in Rick Beard and Leslie Cohen Berlowitz, *Greenwich Village: Culture and Counterculture*, New Brunswick, NJ: Rutgers University Press, 1993.
20. Allida M. Black, "Championing a Champion: Eleanor Roosevelt and the Marian Anderson Freedom Concert," *Presidential Studies Quar-*

terly, Fall 1990, pp. 719–732; *New York Times*, May 18, 1993. In a letter to the *Times* on June 7, 1993, Scott A. Sandage argued that the idea for the use of the Lincoln Memorial originated with a group of black activists.

21. *New York Review of Books*, April 27, 1989.
22. Yaacov Luria, "Kaddish for Paul Robeson," *Friday* (a forum of literature and opinion published by the *Jewish Exponent*), undated.
23. Ibid., p. 67.
24. Taylor Branch, *Parting the Waters: America in the King Years, 1954–63*, New York: Simon & Schuster, 1988, p. 170; Mark Naison, *Communists in Harlem during the Depression*, New York: Grove Press, 1983, p. xv. On local 1199, see Leon Fink and Brian Greenberg, *Upheaval in the Quiet Zone: A History of Hospital Workers' Union, Local 1199*, Urbana: University of Illinois Press, 1989.
25. Richard Wright in Richard Crossman, ed., *The God That Failed*, New York: Bantam Books, 1965, p. 105.
26. Naison, p. 323.
27. As quoted in Lee Congdon, "Anti-Anti-Communism," *Academic Questions*, Summer 1988, p. 46. Alice Citron and Morris Schappes, who also were active in the party's Harlem section, remembered that the two "org-secs" (organization secretaries) and most of the Communist teachers and relief workers from 1933 to 1939 were Jewish. They were young, poor, and "willing to take substantial risks on behalf of black neighborhood residents or black victims of injustice." A number faced "social ostracism" after dating and marrying blacks. Teachers, like Alice Citron, sent into Harlem from impoverished Jewish backgrounds, closely identified with their black students. They joined black teachers in calling for Negro History Week observances in the public schools. Naison, pp. 321–323. See also Ruth Jacknow Markowitz, *My Daughter the Teacher; Jewish Teachers in the New York City Schools*, New Brunswick: Rutgers University Press, 1993, p. 163.
28. Meier and Rudwick, *Black History and the Historical Profession*, p. 108.
29. Meier and Rudwick, p. 109.
30. E. Digby Baltzell, *The Protestant Establishment*, New York: Random House, 1964, pp. 170–171.
31. Baltzell, Introduction to W. E. B. Du Bois, *The Philadelphia Negro: A Social Study*, New York: Schocken Books, 1987, p. xix.
32. Charles U. Smith and Lewis Killian, "Black Sociologists and Social Protest," in James E. Blackwell and Morris Janowitz, *Black Sociolo-*

gists: Historical and Contemporary Perspectives, Chicago: University of Chicago Press, 1974, pp. 29, 197.

33. Ibid., p. 29.
34. Peter Rose, *The Subject Is Race*, New York: Oxford University Press, 1968, p. 39; *New York Times*, November 16, 1978; Diner, pp. 146–148; Jane Howard, *Margaret Mead, A Life*, New York: Simon & Schuster, 1984, p. 53.
35. Diner, p. 149.
36. Kluger, 1976 edition, p. 309; Diner, p. 148.
37. Boas to Horace Kallen, November 2, 1933, in Richard Weiss, "Ethnicity and Reform," p. 571.
38. John Higham, *Send These to Me*, New York: Atheneum, 1975, p. 213; Weiss, p. 572.
39. Weiss, p. 571; Rose, pp. 40, 77–78; Higham, p. 213.
40. David W. Southern, *Gunnar Myrdal and Black-White Relations: The Use and Abuse of an American Dilemma, 1944–1969*, Baton Rouge: Louisiana State University Press, 1987, p. 48.
41. Weiss, p. 573.
42. As quoted in Peter Novick, *That Noble Dream: The "Objectivity Question" and the American Historical Profession*, Cambridge: Cambridge University Press, 1988, p. 471.
43. Higham, p. 217.

Chapter 6: The Origins of the Civil Rights Revolution

1. Charles Herbert Stember et al., *Jews in the Mind of America*, New York: Basic Books, 1966, p. 121. Edward S. Shapiro, *A Time for Healing: American Jewry since World War II*, Baltimore: Johns Hopkins University Press, 1992, pp. 5–6.
2. David G. Singer, "An Uneasy Alliance: Jews and Blacks in the U.S. 1945–1953," *Contemporary Jewry*, 1978.
3. *Jews and American Politics*, New York: Doubleday, 1974, p. 30. For a discussion of how Jewish newspapers expressed this strong sense of idealism, see Singer, "An Uneasy Alliance."
4. Interview with Arnold Aronson, February 25, 1990.
5. Interview; for a discussion of earlier hesitation on the part of some Jewish groups to join blacks and neglect Jewish interests, see also Will Maslow, "The Postwar Years," *Congress Bi-Weekly*, May 6, 1968, p. 13.
6. Rosenstock, p. 23.
7. Interview, February 17, 1976. Murray Friedman, "John Slawson

(1896–1989)," *American Jewish Yearbook*, Philadelphia: Jewish Publication Society, 1991, pp. 555–558.

8. Berson, *The Negroes and the Jews*, p. 99; author's notes, "The Black-Jewish Alliance: Reunion and Renewal," Colloquium, November 28 and 29, 1988, Religious Center of Reform Judaism, Atlanta.
9. Stephen Wise, *Challenging Years: The Autobiography of Stephen Wise*, New York: Putnam, 1949, p. 212.
10. Berson, p. 110.
11. John Slawson and Marc Vosk, *Unequal Americans: Practices and Politics of Intergroup Relations*, Westport, CT: Greenwood Press, 1979, p. 114. The first workers were John Cosgrove at the AFL and Edward Brock, CIO. Undated letter from Harry Fleischman to Murray Friedman.
12. Robert Coles, "Understanding White Racists," *New York Review*, December 30, 1971, p. 12; H. Stuart Hughes, *The Sea Change: The Migration of Social Thought, 1930–1965*, New York: Harper & Row, 1975.
13. Cohen, *Not Free to Desist*, p. 176.
14. *The Role of Science in Intergroup Relations*, New York: Institute of Human Relations Press, April 1962, p. 5.
15. Conference on Research in the Field of Anti-Semitism, Summary of Proceedings and Suggestions for a Program, Biltmore Hotel, American Jewish Committee files, Series 1–5, March 1945; interview with John Slawson, February 17, 1976.
16. Nathan Glazer, Letter to the editor, *Commentary*, December 1985, p. 17; Slawson, *The Role of Science*, p. 13.
17. Feingold, *Zion in America*, p. 272. For examples of sociological studies that grew out of this research, see Melvin M. Tumin, *An Inventory and Appraisal of Research in American Anti-Semitism*, New York: Anti-Defamation League, 1961.
18. "Public Education and American Pluralism," in *Parents, Teachers & Children*, San Francisco: Institute for Contemporary Studies, 1977, p. 92.
19. "Multiculturalism," *American Scholar*, Summer 1990, p. 341. Ravitch has characterized this form of multiculturalism as "a bad idea whose time has come." See also Arthur Schlesinger, Jr., *The Disuniting of America*, New York: Norton, 1992.
20. Susan Dworkin, *Miss America, 1945: Bess Myerson's Own Story*, New York: Newmarket Press, 1988.
21. White, p. 201.

22. As quoted in Dinnerstein, *Uneasy at Home*, p. 188.
23. Nathan C. Belth, *A Promise to Keep: A Narrative of the American Encounter with Anti-Semitism*, New York: Times Books, 1979, p. 177.
24. Herbert Garfinkel, *When Negroes March*, New York: Atheneum, 1969, pp. 150, 153. For a discussion of Rauh's role as a civil rights activist, see his obituary in the *New York Times*, September 6, 1992.
25. White, p. 193; interview with Arnold Aronson, January 11, 1989, and February 25, 1990.
26. Garfinkel, p. 163.
27. Interview with Aronson, February 25, 1990; Garfinkel, p. 163.
28. Garfinkel, p. 163; interview with Aronson, February 25, 1990.
29. Interview with Aronson, February 25, 1990; Wilkins, *Standing Fast*, New York: Viking, 1982, p. 190, 208; profile of Aronson, *Washington Times*, January 17, 1986.
30. See Greenberg, p. 2, for a discussion of this issue.
31. Berson, pp. 109–110.
32. Maslow, "The Postwar Years," p. 14.
33. Nathan Glazer and Daniel Patrick Moynihan, *Beyond the Melting Pot: The Negroes, Puerto Ricans, Jews, Italians, and Irish of New York City*, Cambridge: MIT Press, 1963, pp. 74–75; James Q. Wilson, *Negro Politics*, Glencoe, IL: Free Press, 1960, pp. 152–153; Maslow, "The Postwar Years," p. 14. For a discussion of the role of Jewish builders and social activists like Richard Ravitch, Morris Milgram, and Roger Starr in open-housing efforts at this time, see James Sleeper, *The Closest of Strangers: Liberalism and the Politics of Race in New York*, New York: W.W. Norton, 1990, pp. 80–85; and Morris Milgram, *Good Neighborhood: The Challenge of Open Housing*, New York: Norton, 1977.
34. For a discussion of this in Philadelphia, see Murray Friedman and Carolyn Beck, "An Ambivalent Alliance," in Friedman, *Philadelphia Jewish Life, 1940–1985*, Philadelphia: Seth Press, 1986, pp. 143–165.
35. Reed, *The Jesse Jackson Phenomenon*, New Haven: Yale University Press, 1986, pp. 98–99; Cruse, *Plural but Equal*, p. 122; Lewis, "Shortcuts to the Mainstream," pp. 83–97; Carson, "Blacks and Jews in the Civil Rights Movement," pp. 1–16.
36. *Jewish Exponent*, July 6, 1945.
37. "Civil Rights: A Program for the President's Committee," May-June, 1947, author's file; Will Maslow to Friedman, March 13, 1989; interview with Maslow, October 3, 1985.
38. Eli Ginzberg, *My Brother's Keeper*, New Brunswick, NJ: Transaction, 1989, p. 127.

39. Kluger, *Simple Justice* I, pp. 488–491, 504–505; of the half-dozen white lawyers who signed the brief in *Brown* v. *Board of Education*, Charles Black was the only non-Jew. Jack Greenberg, " The Making of an Activist," *Forward*, May 13, 1994. This is an excerpt from the forthcoming book by Greenberg, *Crusaders In the Courts: How a Dedicated Band of Lawyers Fought for the Civil Rights Revolution* (New York: Basic Books).
40. Leonard Baker, *Brandeis and Frankfurter: A Dual Biography*, New York: Harper & Row, 1984, p. 473.
41. Baker, pp. 404–405.
42. Joseph P. Lash, *From the Diaries of Felix Frankfurter*, New York: Norton, 1975, p. 73.
43. Alfred H. Kelly, "The School Desegregation Case," in John A. Garraty, ed., *Quarrels That Have Shaped the Constitution*, New York: Harper & Row, 1964, p. 259; Hadley Arkes, "The Problem of Kenneth Clark," *Commentary*, November 1974, pp. 37–46; Kenneth B. Clark, *Prejudice and Your Child*, 2nd ed., Boston: Beacon Press, 1955, p. 210; Kluger, I, pp. 397, 637.
44. Kluger, II, p. 891.
45. Clark's defense against this criticism is contained in appendix IV in *Prejudice and Your Child*.
46. Arkes, p. 40.
47. Kluger, II, p. 778.
48. Kluger, II, pp. 937–939. The phrase was actually inserted by Philip Elman, a former clerk of Frankfurter's and continuing confidant. Frankfurter had used the phrase in two opinions in the 1940s.
49. Kluger, II, p. 943.
50. Wilson, p. 157; Dinnerstein, *Uneasy at Home*, p. 232.
51. Paula F. Pfeffer, *A. Philip Randolph, Pioneer of the Civil Rights Movement*, Baton Rouge: Louisiana State University Press, 1990, p. 230.
52. For a view that subsequent black-Jewish difficulties had their origins in these collisions in the labor movement, see Nancy L. Green, "Juifs et noirs aux Etats-Unis, la rupture d'une 'alliance naturelle,'" *Annales ESC* 2 (March-April 1987), pp. 445–464; Tom Brooks, "Negro Militants, Jewish Liberals and the Unions," *Commentary*, September 1961, pp. 209–216; and chapter 22 in Foner, *Organized Labor and the Black Worker*. The revisionist attack on the ILG from a Marxist perspective is contained in Robert Laurentz, "Racial/Ethnic Conflict in the New York City Garment Industry, 1933–1980," a dissertation in the Graduate School of the State University of New York at Binghamton, 1980. On the progressive role played by the

ILGWU in racial reform, see Diner, *In the Promised Land*, pp. 223–224.

Chapter 7: The Civil Rights Revolution and the Crisis of the Left

1. Aldon D. Morris, *Origins of the Civil Rights Movement*, New York: The Free Press, 1984, pp. xi, 25, 132.
2. Coretta Scott King, *My Life with Martin Luther King, Jr.*, New York: Holt, Rinehart and Winston, 1969, pp. 41–42.

   King himself was little known at the time, even in the South. Both he and his wife, however, had broader backgrounds than many of their colleagues there. Following undergraduate work at Morehouse College in Atlanta, he studied at Crozer Theological Seminary, outside of Philadelphia, and later earned his doctorate at Boston University. Among those who greatly influenced him were the pacifist A. J. Muste, who introduced him to the concept of civil disobedience, and Reinhold Niebuhr, from whom he learned an awareness of Christian pragmatism. Coretta in the 1940s studied music at Antioch College in Ohio, where a sizable portion of the student body was Jewish. For a year she went steady with a Jewish student. Kluger, I, p. 9; Martin Luther King, Jr., *Stride toward Freedom: The Montgomery Story*, New York: Ballantine, 1958; David L. Lewis, *King: A Critical Biography*, Baltimore: Penguin, 1970, p. 37. See also David J. Garrow, *Bearing the Cross: Martin Luther King, Jr., and the Southern Christian Leadership Conference*, New York: William Morrow, 1986; and Taylor Branch, *Parting the Waters: America in the King Years, 1954–63*, New York: Simon & Schuster, 1988.
3. Claybourne Carson, Jr., "Blacks and Jews in the Civil Rights Movement," in Washington, *Jews in Black Perspectives*, p. 117.
4. Carl Bernstein, "My Parents Belonged to the Communist Party," *Moment*, August 1989, p. 407. See also Bernstein, *Loyalties: A Son's Memoir*, New York: Touchstone, 1989.
5. Maurice Isserman, *If I Had a Hammer: The Death of the Old Left and the Birth of the New Left*, New York: Basic Books, 1987, p. 4.
6. "Still Taking the Fifth," *Commentary*, July 1989, p. 53.
7. Branch, *Parting the Waters, 1954–63*, p. 211; Isserman, p. 9.
8. Howe, "New Styles in Leftism," *Dissent* 12 (Summer 1965), pp. 300–301.
9. Isserman, p. 33.
10. *Fragments of the Century*, New York: Saturday Review Press/Dutton, 1973, p. 95. In varying ways Michael Harrington's memoirs, William Barrett's *The Truants: Adventures among the Intellectuals*,

and Paul Hollander's *Political Pilgrims*, all dealing with this period, have commented upon the need of intellectuals for some form of meaning in a society that has lost its sense of religion.

11. "Blacks and Jews in the Civil Rights Movement," p. 117.
12. Harrington, p. 99.
13. Jervis Anderson, "Randolph, Martin, and the March on Washington Movement," *American Educator*, Winter 1988, p. 16; interview with Arnold Aronson, January 11, 1989, Oral History Library, American Jewish Committee.
14. Branch, p. 170; Harrington, p. 99.
15. James Farmer, *Lay Bare the Heart: An Autobiography of the Civil Rights Movement*, New York: Arbor House, 1985, p. 162; Morris, p. 159; Harrington, p. 99.
16. Branch, p. 168; Harrington, p. 101.
17. Howell Raines, *My Soul Is Rested*, New York: Putnam, 1977, pp. 53, 56; Garrow, *Bearing the Cross*, p. 73; Morris, p. 157.
18. Branch, pp. 56, 208; Garrow, *Bearing the Cross*, p. 72.
19. *Of Kennedys and King*, New York: Farrar Straus Giroux, 1980, p. 115.
20. David J. Garrow, *The FBI and Martin Luther King, Jr.: From Solo to Memphis*, New York: Norton, 1981, p. 15; *New York Times*, September 14, 1979; Branch, p. 208.
21. Interview with Roy Bennett, October 26, 1989, and telephone interview, October 28, 1989. Levison's first wife, however, describes him at this time as a Stalinist who followed every twist and turn in Soviet policy. When she criticized the Hitler-Stalin pact of 1939, she claims, he reacted sharply. "It was like criticizing the Pope," she says. Telephone interview with Janet Kennedy, January 27, 1991.
22. Levison, Filner says, never let him take him out to expensive restaurants. "Travel economy and give the first-class difference to social and political charities," he said; interview, January 27, 1991.
23. Levison Headquarters FBI file, sec. 2, June 9 and 19, 1953; also, undated, probably 1953, p. 20.
24. Levison Headquarters FBI file, sec. 7, p. 17. See also Paul Lyons, "Philadelphia Jews and Radicalism: The American Jewish Congress Cleans House," in Murray Friedman, ed., *Philadelphia Jewish Life, 1940–1985*, Philadelphia: Seth Press, 1986, pp. 107–123; telephone interview with Will Maslow, May 20, 1988. Levison would retain his links with the congress even as his ties to King deepened and began to absorb most of his energies.
25. Garrow, *The FBI and Martin Luther King*, p. 32.
26. Garrow, *The FBI and Martin Luther King*, pp. 34–40.

27. Garrow, *The FBI and Martin Luther King*, pp. 34, 43. See also his endnote, p. 239. Levison had close business ties with Joseph Filner, a left-wing businessman. Sometime in the mid fifties, Filner made contact with Victor Lessiovski, a Russian national widely believed to be connected with the KGB, the Soviet intelligence service. Lessiovski was then an assistant to United Nations Secretary General U Thant. Filner prepared a memorandum for Lessiovski on the failures of the Soviet Union to market effectively its rich resources of nickel and other precious metals around the world. Lessiovski passed the memo to Moscow, according to Filner. It was the start of Filner's major and continuing international business relationship with the Soviet Union, which continued into the 1990s. Garrow claims that Lessiovski offered his services to the FBI as an informant in 1962. Roy Bennett was then a UN correspondent for the British Labour weekly, the *London Tribune*. He introduced his brother to Lessiovski in 1965, and the two met occasionally for lunch thereafter. Levison, who must have known about the other man's dubious background, told relatives that he viewed Lessiovksi as a comic figure, interesting to talk to but hard to take seriously. Bennett, shortly before his death, said that the two men met only once and there was no ongoing relationship between them. Still, one wonders why Levison, in light of his own ties with King and his knowledge of the FBI's relentless surveillance of both of them, would have any contact with this shadowy figure. Interview with Filner, January 22, and by telephone, January 27, 1991.
28. When the question of Levison's party associations arose in subsequent years, Rustin dismissed them. He made the point that Levison took positions that the party could not be happy about. Rustin told the writer in an interview on October 3, 1985, that Levison was not a Communist during the time Rustin worked closely with him. Rustin's close associate Norman Hill makes the same point. Interview, May 16, 1990, American Jewish Committee Oral History Library, p. 5. See also Branch, p. 209. Joshua Muravchik, in a book review of *Parting the Waters*, challenges Branch's benign treatment of Levison. He argues that Levison was hardly an independent thinker and the *Brown* decision resulted in "a quick change in the party line" on school desegregation. *Commentary*, April 1989, p. 63.
29. Lillian Gates—an upper echelon leader of the New York State Communist Party in the 1950s, whose husband, John, was editor of the *Daily Worker*, the party organ—claims Levison attended one or more meetings of the party convened late in 1956 or early in 1957, when

it was split into three warring factions and faced extinction. The meetings, she reports, were convened to hear the views of Levison and one other person, neither of whom was a formal party member. Lillian Gates believes Levison was a "submarine" in the King movement, that is, a secret party agent whose mission was to infiltrate the civil rights organization to promote party purposes. Janet Kennedy, Levison's first wife, believes this, too. But neither woman can produce hard evidence, and Levison's subsequent behavior suggests this is hardly likely. Telephone interview with Janet Kennedy, June 8, 1990. Telephone interviews with Lillian and John Gates, February 22, and with Lillian, June 7, 1990. Branch has an account of an interparty meeting, pp. 211–214, 945. It was Lillian, not John Gates, who was present. The latter claims not to have been involved at this "truce" meeting or meetings. According to Branch and my own interviews with Lillian, there is no indication that Levison expressed any view on the party's future. Branch reports that at one point Levison took a call from King, causing those present to become worried. They feared, he claims, the FBI was listening in and might use such a conversation to destroy King as they did Paul Robeson. Garrow doubts that Levison attended the truce meetings or that King would call him in such a setting. Interview, October 19, 1991. Interview with Bennett, October 26 and by phone October 28, 1989; interview with Navasky, Novermber 14, 1989. Navasky was the first, or among the first, to break the story of the FBI wiretaps on the telephones of King and Levison. "The Government and Martin Luther King," *Atlantic Monthly*, November 1970, pp. 43–52.

30. Levison FBI Headquarters File, sec. 7, pp. 82, 84. Adam Fairclough, *To Redeem the Soul of America: The Southern Christian Leadership Conference and Martin Luther King, Jr.*, Athens: University of Georgia Press, 1987, p. 31. Interview with Taylor Branch, June 23, 1989. In an interview in 1970, Levison said In Friendship was formed early in 1955. This would be when he was still actively involved in party activities. February 14, 1970, Civil Rights Documentation Project, Moorland-Spingarn Research Project, Howard University, Washington, D.C., pp. 1–2.
31. John Britton interview with Ella Baker, June 19, 1968, Civil Rights Documentation Project, Moorland-Spingarn Research Project, Howard University, Washington, D.C. *New York Times*, December 18, 1986.
32. Arthur Kinoy, *Rights on Trial: The Odyssey of a People's Lawyer*, Cambridge: Harvard University Press, 1983, pp. 2, 41–51, 82, 116.
33. Ibid., pp. 151–153.

34. Morris, p. 120; Garrow, *Bearing the Cross*, p. 490; Mosby interview with Levison, p. 20.
35. Harrington, *Fragments of the Century*, p. 104; interview with Rachelle Horowitz, January 11, 1988, Oral History Library, American Jewish Committee, p. 13; Branch, p. 216.
36. Kinoy, pp. 155–157. Coretta Scott King, *My Life with Martin Luther King*, p. 159; Branch, p. 217.
37. Branch, pp. 216–217; Garrow, *Bearing the Cross*, p. 93; Harrington, p. 104. The ideas in a Levison letter to King and Rustin's working paper, "The Next Step for Mass Action in the Struggle for Equality" served as the basis for King's speech.
38. Isserman, p. 186.
39. Harrington, pp. 106–107.
40. Pfeffer, *A. Philip Randolph*, p. 169.
41. Branch, p. 245.
42. Garrow, *Bearing the Cross*, p. 235.
43. Interview, January 11, 1989.
44. Branch, pp. 227, 860.
45. Garrow, *The FBI and Martin Luther King*, p. 28.
46. Garrow, *Bearing the Cross*, pp. 111–112.
47. Garrow, *Bearing the Cross*, p. 649.
48. Britton interview with Baker, pp. 34–37.
49. Fairclough, p. 29. Ralph David Abernathy, *And the Walls Came Tumbling Down*, New York: Harper & Row, 1989, p. 311.
50. Britton interview with Baker, p. 8.
51. Mosby interview with Levison, February 14, 1970, in Civil Rights Documentation Project, Moorland-Spingarn Research Project, p. 16; Morris, pp. 83, 302.
52. Fairclough, pp. 33, 38, 44.
53. Eugene P. Walker, "A History of the Southern Christian Leadership Conference, 1955–1965: The Evolution of a Southern Strategy of Social Change," doctoral dissertation, Duke University, p. 45. According to Walker, SCLC recording secretary Fred Shuttlesworth and first vice-president C. K. Steele did not know at all about Levison's counsel to King "nor his suggestions for the organization."
54. Fairclough, pp. 38–39.
55. Mosby interview with Levison, p. 18.
56. Interview, January 11, 1988.
57. Branch, p. 575.
58. Branch, pp. 285, 575; Garrow, *Bearing the Cross*, p. 168. Garrow does not agree with Branch as to O'Dell's importance to King.
59. Interview with Harry Wachtel, October 24, 1985.

60. Branch, p. 300.
61. McAdam, *Freedom Summer*, p. 237.

Chapter 8: The Jews Who Went South

1. Carson, "Blacks and Jews in the Civil Rights Movement," p. 117; Branch, pp. 272–273.
2. Robert Weisbrot, *Freedom Bound: A History of America's Civil Rights Movement*, New York: Norton, 1990, p. 56; Isserman, p. 189; McAdam, p. 21.
3. Farmer, p. 162; Morris, p. 120.
4. Jonathan Kaufman, *Broken Alliance*, New York: Scribners, 1988, pp. 66, 86; Seth Cagin and Philip Bray, *We Are Not Afraid*, New York: Macmillan, p. 106.
5. Branch, p. 490.
6. Claybourne Carson, *In Struggle: SNCC and the Black Awakening of the 1960s*, Cambridge: Harvard University Press, 1981, pp. 23–24; Weisbrot, p. 34.
7. Weisbrot, pp. 37; Branch, p. 290; Mary Rothschild, *A Case of Black and White: Northern Volunteers and the Southern Freedom Summers, 1964–1965*, Westport, CT: Greenwood Press, 1982, p. 6.
8. On Goodman's motivation, see Jules Chametzky and Sidney Kaplan, *Black and White in American Culture*, University of Massachusetts Press, 1969, p. 71.
9. As quoted in Murray Friedman, *The Utopian Dilemma: American Judaism and Public Policy*, Washington: Ethics and Public Policy Center, 1985, p. 24. Chaim Waxman, *America's Jews in Transition*, Philadelphia: Temple University Press, 1983, pp. 105–106; Arthur Liebman, *Jews and the Left*, New York: Wiley, 1979, p. 68.
10. As quoted in Friedman, p. 24
11. Evans, *The Provincials*, p. 324.
12. Isserman, p. 110.
13. Jervis Anderson in *The American Educator*, p 18.
14. Kaufman, p. 89.
15. Kinoy, pp. 191, 233.
16. Interview with Charney Bromberg, December 21, 1987; telephone interview with Jerome Shestack, May 24, 1988.
17. Kenneth O'Reilly, *Racial Matters: The FBI's Secret File on Black America, 1960–1972*, New York: The Free Press, 1989, pp. 181–182.
18. Evans, *The Provincials*, p. 324.
19. Edward I. Koch with William Rauch, *Politics*, New York: Simon & Schuster, 1985, pp. 84–85.

20. Richard Cummings, *The Pied Piper: Allard E. Lowenstein and the Liberal Dream*, New York: Grove Press, 1985, p. 245.
21. Ibid, p. 285; Kaufman, pp. 15, 110. See also Seth Cagin and Philip Dray, *We Are Not Afraid*, New York: Macmillan, 1988, p. 51.
22. Hendrik Hertzberg, "The Second Assassination of Al Lowenstein," *New York Review*, October 10, 1985, p. 34; Gregory Stone and Douglas Lowenstein, eds. *Lowenstein: Acts of Courage and Belief*, San Diego: Harcourt Brace, 1983, p. 23.
23. Cagin and Dray; William Bradford Huie, *Three Lives for Mississippi*, New York: WCC Books, 1965, pp. 44–45.
24. Branch, p. 329.
25. Cummings, p. 285.
26. Branch, pp. 328–329; David Harris, *Dreams Die Hard*, New York: St. Martin's Press, 1982, pp. 24, 32–33.
27. Hertzberg, p. 34.
28. Cagin, *Jewish Exponent*, June 3, 1988; Henry, Notes, Colloquium, p. 5; Cummings, pp. 240–242.
29. Cummings, p. 239.
30. Ibid., p. 243; Hertzberg, p. 34.
31. Charles Silberman, "A Jewish View of the Racial Crisis," *Conservative Judaism*, Summer 1965, p. 6; Judith Weinstein Klein, "Ethnotherapy with Jews," *International Journal of Mental Health*, Summer 1976, p. 26; Cagin and Dray, pp. 410–411; Kaufman, p. 18. On Lowenstein's discomfort as a Jew, see William H. Chafe, *Allard Lowenstein and the Struggle to Save American Liberalism*; New York: Basic Books, 1993.
32. This symposium provides an excellent discussion by highly assimilated Jewish leftists of their attitudes toward their Jewishness. "Jewish Young Freedom Fighters and the Role of the Jewish Community: An Evaluation, A Public Dialogue," *Jewish Currents*, July-August 1965, pp. 4–33.
33. Huie, pp. 44, 49.
34. Kaufman, p. 18.
35. "Blacks and Jews in the Civil Rights Movement," pp. 4–5.
36. Interview with Schwartzchild, October 7, 1989.
37. Sara Bershtel and Allen Graubard, "Mystique of the Progressive Jew," undated reprint p. 21. For a fuller expression of their views, see *Saving Remnants: Feeling Jewish in America*, New York: Free Press, 1992.
38. As quoted in Friedman, *The Utopian Dilemma*, pp. 25–26.
39. Jack Reimer, "Abraham Joshua Heschel," *Present Tense*, Summer 1983, pp. 39–42; Friedman, p. 27.

40. Taylor Branch, "The Uncivil War," *Esquire*, May 1989, pp. 89–116.
41. Vorspan, "Martin and the Jews: A Look Then and Now," *Philadelphia Tribune*, April 8, 1986; Vorspan, *Jewish Values and Social Crisis*, pp. 118–119.
42. Wilkins, *Standing Fast*, pp. 270–271.

Chapter 9: The Alliance Peaks and Splits

1. Fairclough, p. 65.
2. Ibid., p. 66; Branch, p. 688.
3. Branch, p. 835.
4. Edwin O. Guthman and Jeffrey Shulman, *Robert Kennedy in His Own Words: The Unpublished Recollections of the Kennedy Years*, New York: Bantam, 1988, p. 141; Branch, pp. 833–838.
5. Wofford, pp. 216–217; Branch, pp. 845, 851. It is not surprising perhaps that the FBI would want to keep a close watch on some of King's associates, given their leftist backgrounds and the threat of nuclear war between the world's two superpowers. Burke Marshall, no friend of J. Edgar Hoover, told Victor Navasky that if he had been attorney general, he, too, would have authorized the taps. What is unconscionable is that when it was clear that there was no conspiracy to use the King movement on behalf of a foreign power, the taps continued and the attempt to undermine King was stepped up. At what point Levison began to shift his loyalties away from the Communist movement is not clear. He always denied he was a member of the party, which was true but disingenuous, given his earlier associations with its underground apparatus. In an interview with the *Washington Post* on December 15, 1975, he acknowledged past associations with the party but shrugged them off, saying that in the 1930s and 1940s one could hardly be an intellectual in New York without knowing some Communists. See Victor S. Navasky, "The Government and Martin Luther King," *Atlantic*, November 1970, pp. 43–52.
6. Interview, October 26, 1989.
7. Schlesinger, *Robert Kennedy and His Times*, pp. 360–361; Garrow, pp. 300–304.
8. Isserman, p. xviii.
9. Fairclough, p. 152.
10. Interviews with Arnold Aronson, May 17, 1988, and May 20, 1990.
11. Jervis Anderson, "Randolph, Rustin, and the March on Washington Movement," *American Educator*, Winter 1988, pp. 14–19.
12. Joseph Rauh, Jr., "Martin Luther King's Idealism, Faith Taught

Blacks to Hope, Whites to Care," *Jewish Exponent*, January 13, 1989, p. 3.

13. Interviews with Arnold Aronson, May 17, 1988, and May 26, 1990. Denton L. Watson, *Lion in the Lobby*, New York: William Morrow, 1940; Charles and Barbara Whalen, *The Longest Debate: A Legislative History of the Civil Rights Act*, Cabin John, MD: Seven Locks Press, 1985, p. 95.
14. Benjamin Zelenko, general counsel of the House Judiciary Committee, in author's notes, "The Black-Jewish Alliance," Colloquium, Atlanta, p. 5.
15. Interviews with Arnold Aronson, May 17, 1988, and May 26, 1990. Whalens, p. 46.
16. Whalens, p. 223.
17. Carson, "Blacks and Jews in the Civil Rights Movement," p. 115.
18. Ibid. p. 118.
19. Hertzberg, pp. 34–40; James Forman, *The Making Of Black Revolutionaries*, New York: Macmillan, 1972, p. 356.
20. Liebman, *Jews and the Left*, p. 565; Cummings, p. 237.
21. Cagin and Dray, p. 252; Paul Cowan, *The Making of an Un-American*, New York: Viking, 1967, p. 37.
22. James Forman, *The Making of Black Revolutionaries*, p. 383.
23. P. 154.
24. Cagin and Dray, pp. 391, 415.
25. Cummings, p. 266; Garrow, p. 346.
26. The King comment is from Forman, *Black Revolutionaries*, p. 392; Garrow, *Bearing the Cross*, p. 349. Garrow generally agrees. Cummings reports King remained strangely neutral; p. 269.
27. Gitlin, *The Sixties*, p. 161.
28. *The River of No Return: The Autobiography of a Black Militant and the Life and Death of SNCC*, New York: William Morrow, 1973, p. 111.
29. Kinoy, pp. 259, 263, 267.

Chapter 10: The Race Revolution

1. Alex Miller, "Not the Work of a Day," ADL Oral History Memoirs (unpublished), V, p. 226; Jack Nusan Porter, "Mr Goldberg and John Henry: The Relationship Between Afro-Americans and American Jews" in Porter, *The Sociology of American Jews: A Critical Anthology*, Washington: University Press of America, 1980, p. 234; Friedman, in Rose, *Through Different Eyes*, p. 155.

2. Donald F. Dixon and Daniel J. McLaughlin, Jr., "Do the Inner City Poor Pay More for Food?" *Economic and Business Bulletin*, Temple University, Spring 1968, pp. 6–12. See also U.S. Department of Labor, Bureau of Labor Statistics, "A Study of Prices Charged in Food Stores Located in Low and Higher Income Areas of Six Large Cities," February 1966, Washington, D.C.: "Many Landlords Abandon Solid Inner City Building," *Philadelphia Inquirer*, November 2, 1970.
3. Murray Kempton, *New York Review*, June 29, 1972, p. 4.
4. *Down the Line: The Collected Writings of Bayard Rustin*, Chicago: Quadrangle, 1971, p. 231.
5. *An Autobiography*, New York: Dutton, 1964, p. 49.
6. *Philadelphia Inquirer*, August 28, 1989.
7. *Philadelphia Inquirer*, July 29, 1990.
8. *Breaking Ranks*, pp. 124–127.
9. The *New Yorker* article appeared November 17, 1962. *The Fire Next Time*, New York: Dell, 1962. See also Henry Gates, Jr., "The Fire Last Time," *New Republic*, June 1, 1992, p. 41.
10. "Racial Perversity in Chicago," *Commentary*, December 1988, pp. 32–33. Gates makes the same point in "The Fire Last Time."
11. Morris Dickstein, "Call It an Awakening," *New York Times Book Review*, November 29, 1987, p. 1.
12. "American Judaism Thirty Years After," *American Jewish History*, December 1987, p. 284.
13. Weisbrot, p. 170.
14. For a good discussion of the evolution of his role, see *Philadelphia Inquirer*, March 3, 1990. A sometimes less flattering account of Malcolm's life, including the falsification of some of his autobiographical claims, can be found in Bruce Perry, *Malcolm: The Life of a Man Who Changed Black America*, New York: Station Hill Press, 1991.
15. Weatherby, p. 362; Kaufman, p. 75. On Malcolm meeting with the Klan, see Marshall Frady, *New Yorker*, October 12, 1992, p. 70.
16. Claybourne Carson, Jr., *Malcolm X: The FBI File*, New York: Carroll and Graf, 1991, p. 176; Kaufman, p. 135; Raab, "Poisoned Goods," *Moment*, January-February 1986, p. 15; Lenni Brenner, *Jews in America Today*, Secaucus, NJ: Lyle Stuart, 1986, p. 235; Weisbord and Kazarian, p. 45; Earl Raab, "American Blacks and Israel," in Robert S. Wistrich, ed., *Anti-Zionism and Anti-Semitism in the Contemporary World*, New York: NYU Press, 1990, p. 159.
17. Stanley Crouch, "Huey Newton, R.I.P.," *New Republic*, September 18 and 25, 1989, pp. 10–11. On the gangster tendencies of the

group, including intimidation, sexual harassment, beatings, and routine violence, see Hugh Pearson, *The Shadow of the Panther: Huey Newton and the Price of Black Power in America*, New York: Addison-Wesley, 1994.

18. Langston Hughes, *Selected Poems*, New York: 1974, p. 190.
19. P. 229.
20. Murray Friedman, "Black Anti-Semitism on the Rise," *Commentary*, October 1979, p. 33; Baraka as quoted in Brenner, p. 240.
21. *Philadelphia Inquirer*, August 22, 1988.
22. Peter Novick, *That Noble Dream: The "Objectivity Question" and the American Historical Profession*, New York: Cambridge University Press, 1988, p. 477.
23. See Darlene Clark Hine, *The State of Afro-American History*. For a critical analysis of the new black history, see Novick, chap. 14.
24. Adam Begley, "Black Studies' New Star," *New York Times Magazine*, April 1, 1990, p. 50.
25. For a discussion of the personal experience of one individual, see statement of Martin Goldman at Hearings before the Special Subcommittee on Education of the Committee on Education and Labor, Part 2 A, Washington, D.C., August 8–15, September 17–25, 1974. pp. 591–612. Meier and Rudwick discuss this subject but come to no conclusion. They quote a Jewish historian as saying, "The signs are up: 'No Jews Need Apply' "; p. 295
26. *New York Times*, September 7, 1991.
27. Meier and Rudwick, *Black History and the Historical Profession*, p. 292; Novick, p. 475.
28. On Gutman being shouted down, Meier and Rudwick, pp. 292–293; Novick, p. 479.
29. P. 147.
30. Meier and Rudwick, pp. 291–292. At heart also was a struggle over turf. To the victors went prestige and pay. A black professor at a white institution, speaking candidly to Meier and Rudwick, questioned the motivation of some of his colleagues. He said it was difficult to determine how much of their anger was genuine and "how much was tactical, articulated to obtain the jobs opened up by the black studies programs through intimidation and by playing upon feelings of guilt of white academicians."
31. *Down the Line*, p. xi.
32. Southern, *Gunnar Myrdal and Black-White Relations*, pp. 267–268.
33. Kaufman, p. 76; Weisbrot, p. 242; Carson, *In Struggle*, p. 186.
34. Interview with Will Maslow, October 28, 1988; Robert G. Weisbord and Arthur Stein, *Bitter Sweet Encounter*, Westport, CT: Greenwood

Press, 1970, pp. 139, 144; Friedman and Beck, "An Ambivalent Alliance," in Friedman, *Philadelphia Jewish Life, 1940–1985*, p. 156.

35. *The River of No Return*, pp. 146–147.
36. Cagin and Dray, p. 422; Julius Lester, "Notes of a Journey," in John J. Bunzel, ed., *Political Passages*, New York: The Free Press, 1988, p. 69.
37. Carson, "Blacks and Jews in the Civil Rights Movement," p. 118.
38. Interview with Arnold Aronson, May 17, 1988; *New York Times*, April 6, 1967.
39. Lester in Bunzel, p. 72.
40. Carson, "Blacks and Jews in the Civil Rights Movement," p. 122.
41. Ibid., p. 124; Kaufman, p. 80; Sellers, pp. 201–202.
42. Carson, "Blacks and Jews," p. 126; Carson, *In Struggle*, pp. 266–267.
43. Stuart E. Knee, "Ethnic Anti-Zionism in The U.S.A., 1917–1941," *Patterns of Prejudice* 11, September/October, 1977, pp. 32–33; Weisbord and Kazarian, pp. 23–24.
44. "Black-Jewish Alliance Alive," a response to Lenni Brenner, in *Freedomways*, February 1985, pp. 8–9.
45. Sellers, p. 202; Belth, p. 223; Carson, "Blacks and Jews," pp. 120, 127.
46. McAdam, p. 115.
47. Interview with Arthur Waskow, March 12 and 23, 1990; Gitlin, p. 226.
48. Kaufman, pp. 206–208.
49. Carson, "Blacks and Jews," p. 126; Carson, *In Struggle*, p. 269.

Chapter 11: Martin Luther King

1. Levison to King, the Martin Luther King Center, Atlanta, April 7, 1965.
2. Fairclough, p. 257.
3. Ibid., p. 3.
4. *New York Times*, September 14, 1979.
5. *Perspectives*, Spring 1980, U.S. Commission on Civil Rights, pp. 2–3.
6. Levison New York FBI file, June 2, 1965; Fairclough, pp. 339–340.
7. Garrow, *Bearing the Cross*, p. 497; Fairclough, p. 259.
8. Levison New York FBI file, July 19, 25, 27, 29, 1967; Garrow, *Bearing the Cross*, pp. 569–570.
9. Fairclough, p. 274. James A. Colaiaco, *Martin Luther King, Jr.: Apostle of Nonviolence*, New York: St. Martin's Press, 1988, p. 152.
10. Fairclough, pp. 275–277; Halberstam, p. 43.
11. Levison New York FBI file, June 24, 1967.
12. Lewis, *King*, p. 125.

13. Garrow, *Bearing the Cross*, p. 426; C. Vann Woodward, "The Dream of Martin Luther King," *New York Review*, January 15, 1967, p. 8.
14. Levison New York FBI file, April 22, 1967; Woodward, "Dream", p. 9; Garrow, *Bearing the Cross*, p. 572.
15. Halberstam, p. 48; Colaiaco, p. 178.
16. On the idea for the Poor People's Campaign coming from Levison, see *New York Times*, September 14, 1979. Garrow, *Bearing the Cross*, p. 578; Fairclough, pp. 357–358.
17. Garrow, *Bearing the Cross*, p. 429; Fairclough, p. 271.
18. Fairclough, pp. 272–273.
19. Levison New York FBI file, March 25, 1967.
20. Ibid., July 10, August 27, 1967; Garrow, *Bearing the Cross*, p. 559.
21. Levison New York FBI file, July 10, August 22, 27, 1967; Fairclough, pp. 344–345.
22. Levison and Wachtel were furious that Rustin went public with criticism. They viewed him as a tired radical, too eager for respectability and too close to the AFL-CIO and President Johnson. Levison told King he ought to rethink Rustin's role among his inner-circle advisers. Levison New York FBI file, April 6, 1967; Fairclough, p. 339.
23. Garrow, *Bearing the Cross*, p. 555.
24. Levison's wife declined to be interviewed. When I mentioned to her that I thought her husband was influenced in some measure by the Jewish tradition, she responded, "Stanley would have laughed at that."
25. Levison New York FBI file, April 8, 9, 12, 1967; Fairclough, p. 341.
26. It was probably Levison who introduced this phrase into the speech. The FBI tapes show that before delivering the speech, King, listening to sections written by Levison that emphasized the need to end the bombing, told his friend, "It really gets everything I need to say." Levison New York FBI file, April 13, 14, 1967.
27. Garrow, *Bearing the Cross*, pp. 556–557; Nancy Zaroules and Gerald Sullivan, *Who Spoke Up? American Protest Against the War in Viet Nam, 1963–1975*, Garden City, NY: Doubleday, p. 111.
28. Levison New York FBI file, April 17, 1967.
29. Ibid., April 15, 1967; Garrow, *Bearing the Cross*, p. 541; Levison was concerned also that Young was too lackadaisical in his role as King's second in command. On King laying the foundations for Jackson and his Rainbow Coalition, see also Colaiaco, p. 202.
30. *Jewish Week* (Washington), January 14, 1993.
31. Levison New York FBI file, June 6, 1967; Weisbord and Kazarian, p. 38.
32. Levison New York FBI file, June 6, 1967.

33. Levison New York FBI file, July 24, 1967.
34. Ibid., March 24, June 15, 1967. Deutscher used this phrase in his book *The Non-Jewish Jew and Other Essays*, New York: Oxford University Press, 1968.
35. The letter, dated September 28, 1967, can be found in Morris B. Abram's files. See also Weisbord and Kazarian, p. 38.
36. Fairclough, p. 364; Garrow, *Bearing the Cross*, p. 591.
37. Harrington, *Fragments of the Century*, p. 127.
38. Garrow, *Bearing the Cross*, p. 612.
39. Fairclough, p. 376.
40. Fairclough, pp. 380–381; Harrington, p. 127.
41. *And the Walls Came Tumbling Down*, New York: Harper & Row, 1989, p. 529.
42. Fairclough, p. 388.

Chapter 12: The Late Sixties

1. Morris Dickstein, "Columbia Recovered," *New York Times Magazine*, May 15, 1988, pp. 32–35, 64–68; Lester, "Notes of a Journey," p. 78.
2. Martin Mayer, *The Teachers Strike*, New York: Harper & Row, 1969. Diane Ravitch, *The Great School Wars*, New York: Basic Books, 1974, pp. 316–361. Sleeper, pp. 98–104. Jerald E. Podair, "The Failure to See: Jews, Blacks and the Ocean Hill–Brownsville Controversy," Center for American Jewish History, Temple University, July 1992.
3. Mayer, p. 71; Isserman, p. 189.
4. Jack Newfield and Paul Du Brul, *The Abuse of Power*, New York: Viking Press, 1977, p. 152.
5. Sleeper, *Closest of Strangers*, p. 100; Rachel Levy, "N.Y. Teachers Strike—For What?" *Jewish Currents*, December 1968, pp. 4–15, 55.
6. P. 100.
7. Kaufman, p. 129; Sleeper, p. 100; Tamar Jacoby, "The Carson Show," *Forward*, August 30, 1991.
8. Kaufman, p. 153; Henry Hampton and Steve Fayer, *Voices of Freedom: An Oral History of the Civil Rights Movement from the 1950s through the 1980s*, New York: Bantam Books, 1991, p. 505.
9. Lester, *Lovesong*, p. 50; and "Blacks, Jews and the Media: The 1968 New York City Teachers' Strike," unpublished paper delivered at University of District of Columbia conference; Fred Ferretti, "New York's Black Anti-Semitic Scare," *Columbia Journalism Review*, Fall 1969, pp. 18–29.

10. Albert Shanker interview in Melvin I. Urofsky, *Why Teachers Strike: Teachers' Rights and Community Control*, Garden City, NY: Doubleday/Anchor Books, 1970, pp. 156–159; Sleeper, p. 101.
11. Lester, *Lovesong*, p. 51. Campbell, later Jitsu Weusi, was another representative of the older black-Jewish radical culture that was now coming apart. In the 1950s he had attended Camp Kinderland, a leftist Jewish summer camp, "picking up friendships, pinochle and an impressive repertoire of Yiddish idioms from veterans of the Abraham Lincoln Brigade." Sleeper, p. 69.
12. Lester, *Lovesong*, pp. 58, 62. Lester himself later converted to Judaism.
13. Pfeffer, pp. 293–294. Randolph's position among the radicals, already damaged, was weakened further when his Randolph Institute moved into a building owned by the UFT after the strike. Jerald E. Podair, "Crucible at Ocean Hill: The United Federation of Teachers and the Crisis of Social Unionism," Fall 1989; typescript paper. I am grateful to Podair, who is writing his doctoral dissertation on the strike, for sharing some of his materials with me.
14. Podair, "The Failure to See," p. 7.
15. On an incident involving the dismissal of a Jewish chief of pediatrics at Lincoln Hospital in the Bronx much like the Harlem Hospital episode in the 1930s, see *New York Times*, December 21, 1970. Incidents involving black-Jewish tension were not limited to New York. In Detroit the president of Wayne State University declared that the student newspaper edited by a black militant was publishing material "disturbingly reminiscent of Hitler Germany." Geltman, p. 4.
16. Thomas Hoving, *Making the Mummies Dance*, New York: Simon & Schuster, 1993, p. 179; Murray Kempton, "What a Problem!" *New York Review*, June 29, 1972, pp. 3–8; Berson, p. 421; Friedman in Rose, p. 154.
17. *Jews in a Changing Neighborhood*, New York: Free Press, 1975, p. vii. See also Jonathan Rieder, *Canarsie: The Jews and Italians of Brooklyn against Liberalism*, Cambridge: Harvard University Press, 1985, p. 294; and Hillel Levine and Lawrence Harmon, *The Death of an American Jewish Community: A Tragedy of Good Intentions*, New York: Free Press, 1992.
18. Endnote 24 in Friedman, "The Jew," in Rose, *Through Different Eyes*, p. 439.
19. Rieder, *Canarsie*, pp. 23, 26.
20. Lenora E. Berson, *Case Study of a Riot: The Philadelphia Story*, New York: Institute of Human Relations Press, 1966, p. 6.

21. Henry Cohen and Gary Sandrow, *Philadelphia Chooses a Mayor*, Philadelphia: American Jewish Committee, 1971; Kaufman, p. 165.
22. *Commentary*, January 1969, p. 30.
23. *Breaking Ranks*, pp. 92, 247, 304.
24. Robert I. Friedman, *The False Prophet: Rabbi Meir Kahane, from FBI Informant to Knesset Member*, Brooklyn: Lawrence Hill Books, 1990 pp. 61–62, 82; Sherry Ostroff, "Jewish Defense League," in Jack Fischel and Sanford Pinsker, *Jewish American History and Culture*, New York: Garland Publishing, 1992, p. 303; Shlomo M. Russ, "The 'Zionist Hooligans': The Jewish Defense League," Ph.D. dissertation, City University of New York Graduate Center, 1981; Kahane, *Never Again*, Los Angeles: Nash, 1971.
25. "The Demons of the Jews," the *New Republic*, November 11, 1985, p. 24.
26. "An American Tragedy—Meir Kahane and Kahanism: A Review Essay," *American Jewish History*, March 1989, pp. 429–435.
27. Isserman, p. 214.
28. Waskow, *The Bush Is Burning! Radical Judaism Faces the Pharaohs of the Modern Superstate*, New York: Macmillan, 1971, pp. 7–20; Waskow, *The Freedom Seder*, pp. v, 42–45.
29. "Jewish New Leftism at Berkeley," pp. 473–478.
30. Hershel Shanks, "Michael," *Moment*, June 1990, p. 57; *Jewish Voice*, November 14, 1989.
31. *American Scholar*, Autumn 1990, pp. 497–506.
32. Interview, November 7, 1989; Schwartzchild to author, November 9, 1989.
33. Carson, "Blacks and Jews," pp. 121, 129; Lester, *Lovesong*, p. 57. See also David Horowitz's fascination with the Black Panthers. The murder of a young woman whom he recommended to them to keep their accounts finally ended his career in the New Left. Sharon Churcher, "Radical Transformations," *New York Times Magazine*, July 16, 1980, p. 48.
34. Mailer, *Advertisements for Myself*, New York: Putnam, 1959, p. 339; Isserman, p. 234.
35. Joan Peyser, *Bernstein: A Biography*, New York: Ballantine, 1988, p. 408.
36. Peter Collier and David Horowitz, *Destructive Generation: Second Thoughts about the 60s*, New York: Summit, 1989, pp. 17, 269–271, 330; David Horowitz, "Black Murder Inc.," *Heterodoxy*, March 1993, pp. 1, 11–16; telephone interview, June 17, 1993. See also David Hilliard and Lewis Cole, *The Autobiography of David*

Hilliard and the Story of the Black Panther Party, Boston: Little, Brown, 1993; and Elaine Brown, *A Black Woman's Story*, New York: Pantheon Books, 1993.

37. Friedman, *Utopian Dilemma*, p. 40. For a sharp criticism of Marx, see Lucy D. Dawidowicz, "Can Anti-Semitism Be Measured?" *Commentary*, July 1970, pp. 36–43.
38. Hertzberg, *The Jews in America*, p. 379.

Chapter 13: The Nineteen Messiahs

1. Murray Friedman, "One Episode in Southern Jewry's Response to Desegregation: An Historical Memoir," *American Jewish Archives* XXX, 2 (November, 1981), p. 172; Numan V. Bartley, *The Rise of Massive Resistance: Race and Politics in the South during the 1950's*, Baton Rouge: Louisiana State University Press, 1969, pp. 222–224.
2. The editorial was called "Anti-Semitism in the South"; Friedman, "One Episode," p. 174.
3. Murray Friedman, "Virginia Jewry in the School Crisis: Anti-Semitism and Desegregation," *Commentary*, January 1959, pp. 17–22.
4. Golden, *Forgotten Pioneer*, pp. 66–67; Golden, "Jew and Gentile in the South: Segregation at Sundown," *Commentary*, November 1955, pp. 403–404; Allen Krause, "Rabbis and Negro Rights in the South, 1954–1967," in Dinnerstein and Palsson, *Jews in the South*, p. 361.
5. Howard N. Rabinowitz, "Nativism, Bigotry and Anti-Semitism in the South," *American Jewish Archives*, March 1988, pp. 437–451; Evans, *Judah P. Benjamin*, p. 6; Stephen J. Whitfield, "The Braided Identity of Southern Jewish History," *American Jewish History*, March 1988, pp. 363–386; Nathan M. Kaganoff and Melvin I. Urofsky, *Turn to the South: Essays on Southern Jewry*, Charlottesville: University Press of Virginia, 1979.
6. Joseph Cohen, "An Interview with Eli N. Evans," *American Jewish History*, December 1988, p. 237. Evans's father was the mayor of Durham. When I visited him in the 1950s, I noticed that prominently displayed in his office was the Karen Kayemet collection box for coins to reclaim land in Israel.
7. The Carter quote is from Rabinowitz, p. 447; the Faulkner quote is from Stephen J. Whitfield, *Voices of Jacob, Hands of Esau: Jews in American Thought*, Hamden, CT; Archon Books, 1984, p. 217.
8. As quoted in Whitfield, "The Braided Identity of Southern Jewish History," p. 365. Lo and behold, in the summer of 1991, Leonard Jeffries in his tirade against Jews referred to her as a "Texas Jew."

9. Evans, *The Provincials*, p. 320. See also Mark H. Elovit, *A Century of Jewish Life in Dixie: The Birmingham Experience*, Birmingham: University of Alabama Press, 1974, pp. 175ff.
10. Evans, *Judah P. Benjamin*, p. 121. For Jews who supported segregation, see Steven Hertzberg, "The Jews of Atlanta, 1865–1915," doctoral dissertation, University of Chicago, 1973, p. 287; Howard Simons, *Jewish Times: Voices of the American Jewish Experience*, Boston: Houghton Mifflin, 1988, pp. 229–236.
11. *One Voice: Rabbi Jacob M. Rothschild and the Troubled South*, Macon, GA: Mercer University Press, 1985; Dale M. Schwarz and Cecil Alexander, "Still in the Shadow of Leo Frank," *Moment*, March 1989, pp. 12–19.
12. Edward S. Shapiro, "Anti-Semitism Mississippi Style," in David A. Gerber, *Anti-Semitism in American History*, Urbana: University of Illinois Press, 1986, pp. 139–141.
13. Harry Golden, "A Son of the South and Some Daughters: Carolina Epistle with a Happy Ending," *Commentary*, November 12, 1951, pp. 379–380.
14. When Alexander F. Miller opened the ADL's first southern office in 1943 in Florida, he found some 1,800 hotels and tourist resorts still turning away Jews. Most of the resorts made no secret of their "Christian only" policies. One hotel advertised: "Every room with a view. Without a Jew." *ADL Oral History Memoirs*, pp. 22, 52.
15. *Uneasy at Home*, p. 9.
16. *One Voice*, p. 145.
17. Evans, *The Provincials*, pp. 292, 312; Shankman, p. 126; Marx, p. 134.
18. Evans, *The Provincials*, p. 319.
19. "Between Little Rock and a Hard Place," *New Republic*, February 3, 1986, pp. 29–33.
20. On Block, author's file; Silver, *Mississippi: The Closed Society*, p. 131; Krause, "Rabbis and Negro Rights," p. 365.
21. *ADL Oral History Memoirs* V, p. 104. That summer my Richmond office, continuing its regular programming, sent educational materials to the NAACP workshop that brought the Kilpatrick warning.
22. Evans, *The Provincials*, p. 312. See also his reference to Joe Weinberg of Greenville in "Strangers in a Strange Land: The Jewish Communities of Savannah, Mississippi and Atlanta," *The Lonely Days Were Sundays*, Jackson: University Press of Mississippi, 1993, p. 59.
23. *The Day Is Short*, New York: Harcourt Brace Jovanovich, 1982 , pp. 21, 76.

24. Abram, p. 109.
25. Abram, pp. 129, 132; Coretta King, p. 195; Garrow, *Bearing the Cross*, pp. 144–145; Wofford, pp. 16–20.
26. Golden may have gotten this idea from Durham's mayor, E. J. Evans. When told that he could not serve an integrated clientele at his department store's lunch counter, Evans asked his attorney to research the law. The lawyer found that he could serve blacks and whites together as they stood at the counter. Evans then removed the stools. Cohen, "An Interview with Eli N. Evans," pp. 237–238. See also "Golden Rule," *Time*, April 1, 1957, p. 62; Robert A. Hohner, "The Other Harry Golden: Harry Goldhurst and the Cannon Scandals," *North Carolina Historical Review*, vol. 65, April, 1988, pp. 154–172.
27. *One Voice*, p. 76.
28. *One Voice*, p. 79; Evans, *The Provincials*, p. 261.
29. Weisbrot, p. 41; Krause, p. 364.
30. Interview, November 7, 1989.
31. In 1956, for example, I spoke to the Virginia Education Association on classroom teaching materials useful in intergroup relations, hardly an incendiary subject. Yet the *Virginian*, a virulently anti-Semitic, segregationist publication spawned by the state's massive resistance movement, saw in it signs of subversion. Its lead article on my talk was entitled "ADL Attempts Sneaky Invasion of Virginia's Public Schools."
32. *ADL Oral History Memoirs*, pp. 133–135; Silver, pp. 57–58; *Philadelphia Inquirer*, December 19, 1990; *New Orleans Times-Picayune*, December 24, 1992.
33. *Voice of Jacob*, p. 227.
34. *One Voice*, p. 206.

Chapter 14: Charleston

1. Victor Rabinowitz, president of the National Lawyers Guild, conceded in 1970 that prior to the civil rights revolution, his generation was moribund. "Then things began to pick up." Members began to come in in 1963 and 1964. "We started to get out of the status we were in [and in the next few years] grew radically." Interview by Robert Wright, February 26, 1970, Civil Rights Documentation Project, Howard University, p. 5.
2. Leon Fink and Brian Greenberg, *Upheaval in the Quiet Zone: A History of Hospital Workers' Union, Local 1199*, Urbana: University of Illinois Press, 1989, pp. x–xi.

3. Philip S. Foner, *Organized Labor and the Black Worker, 1919–1981*, New York: International Publishers, 1981, p. 385.
4. "Labor Pains, Turmoil Grips an Old Left Union," *New York*, March 25, 1985, p. 41.
5. Fink and Greenberg, p. 130.
6. Fink and Greenberg, p. 103.
7. Fairclough, p. 395.
8. Abernathy, chap. 16; Levison New York FBI file, August 11, 1969.
9. Rutherford telephone call to Levison, Levison New York FBI file, June 22, 1969.
10. Foner, *Organized Labor*, pp. 367, 390.
11. Fink and Greenberg, p. 146.
12. Fink and Greenberg, p. 147.
13. Young telephone call to Levison, Levison New York FBI file, July 8, 1969.
14. Belafonte telephone call to Levison, Levison New York FBI file, April 16, 1969. Levison file, June 19, 1969. Abernathy was conscious of Levison's role in the strike and in SCLC, but in his memoirs he makes virtually no mention of him.
15. Levison New York FBI file, June 23, 1969; Foner had pressed Levison to intercede and keep her away; Fink and Greenberg, pp. 155–157.
16. Levison New York FBI file, August 11, 1969.
17. Levison New York FBI file, May 24, 1969; Wachtel arranged for a substantial advance from her publisher and handled her estate. Interview with Wachtel, October 24, 1985.
18. Levison New York FBI file, July 7, June 18, and April 16, 1969.
19. Levison New York FBI file, June 25, 1969.
20. Levison New York FBI file, March 6, 1969.
21. *Newsweek*, June 16, 1969, pp. 29–30; David Wise, *The American Police State: The Government against the People*, New York: Random House, 1976, p. 301; Navasky, "The Government and Martin Luther King," pp. 43–44; *Washington Post*, December 15, 1975; Levison telephone conversation with Wachtel, Levison New York FBI file, June 21, 1969; Levison New York FBI file, June 20, 1969; *Philadelphia Tribune*, September 29, 1992.
22. Lenni Brenner, *Jews in America Today*, Secaucus, NJ: Lyle Stuart, 1986, p. 141; interview with Baker by John Britton, June 19, 1968, in Civil Rights Documentation Project, Howard University.
23. Levison New York FBI file, March 6, 1969.
24. Fairclough, pp. 390–391.
25. Garrow, *Bearing the Cross*, p. 584.

26. Interview with Harry Wachtel, October 24, 1985; Fairclough, p. 394; Clarence Jones telephone conversation with Levison, Levison New York FBI file July 13, 1967.
27. Levison New York FBI file, June 22, 1969; Fairclough, p. 394.
28. Fairclough, p. 392; *Philadelphia Tribune*, September 29, 1992; Alex Jetter, "Mississippi Learning," *New York Times Magazine*, February 21, 1993, p. 35.
29. Levison New York FBI file, October 21, 1969, and August 25, 1971.
30. Levison New York FBI file, April 27, 1969.
31. Telephone conversation with Tippy Crowder, Levison New York FBI file, May 9, 1967.
32. Levison New York FBI file, June 18, 1969.
33. Levison New York FBI file, August 25, 1971.
34. For a discussion of anti-anti-Communism, see Guenther Lewy, *The Cause That Failed*, New York: Oxford University Press, 1990, chapter 7; Levison New York FBI file, April 21 and June 19, 1969.
35. Levison New York FBI file, June 14, 1969.
36. Bettina Aptheker, *The Morning Breaks: The Trial of Angela Davis*, New York: International Publishers, 1975, pp. 27, 62; interview with Moe Foner, October 7, 1989.
37. Kaufman, *Broken Alliance*, pp. 115–116.
38. Ibid., pp. 115–17. Other "establishment" organizations that joined in the defense of Davis were the Urban League, the ACLU, and the YWCA.
39. *New York Times*, September 14, 1979; interview with Moe Foner, October 7, 1989. It is beyond the purposes of this book, but the need exists to learn more about Levison's role in the development of the "third left" in the years following King's death. Bayard Rustin at one point bumped into Donald McHenry, Young's successor at the UN, and McHenry said he could not stop because he was rushing to visit Levison in the hospital. Asked if he was still seeing Levison, McHenry replied that both he and Young frequently consulted with Levison.

Chapter 15: The Seventies and Eighties

1. Hugh Davis Graham, *The Civil Rights Era: Origins and Development of National Policy, 1960–72*, New York: Oxford University Press, 1990, p. 193; Shelby Steele, "A Negative Vote on Affirmative Action," *New York Times Magazine*, May 13, 1990, pp. 46–49, 73–75.
2. Graham, p. 197.
3. *The Contractors Association of Eastern Pennsylvania, Plaintiff and*

James D. Morrissey, Inc. and others v. The Secretary of Labor, Federal Supplement, March 13, 1970, pp. 1002–1013; *Philadelphia Inquirer*, March 14, 1970; Graham, p. 341.

4. As quoted in Graham, p. 458.
5. *New York Times*, June 29, 1978.
6. Weisbord and Kazarian, *Israel in the Black American Perspective*, p. 140; Murray Friedman, "Intergroup Relations," *American Jewish Yearbook*, 1980, p. 51.
7. Mary Berry and John Blassingame, *Long Memory: The Black Experience in America*, p. 291.
8. Joe Klein, "Deadly Metaphors," *New York*, September 9, 1991, pp. 26–29.
9. *The Truly Disadvantaged*, pp. 110–118, 132.
10. Herbert H. Haines, *Black Radicals and the Civil Rights Mainstream, 1954–1970*, Knoxville: University of Tennessee Press, 1988, p. 84; Kaufman, *Broken Alliance*, pp. 96, 118–123.
11. Kaufman, p. 123. When 1960s activist Julius Lester—now converted to Judaism and teaching courses for seventeen years as a tenured professor in the Afro-American studies program at the University of Massachusetts, Amherst campus—was critical of James Baldwin's statements about Jews a few years after the Greenberg incident, the department voted unanimously to remove him. This followed more than ten years of harassment by department members and others following publication of his first criticism of Baldwin and his autobiography, *Lovesong*, in which he described his growing disaffection from black radicalism. Martin Goldman, *Boston Ledger*, week of June 11–17, 1988, and February 25, 1988.
12. Stanley Crouch, *Notes of a Hanging Judge: Essays and Reviews, 1979–1989*, New York: Oxford University Press, 1990, p. 25.
13. Peter Steinfels, *The Neo Conservatives: The Men Who Are Changing America's Politics*, New York: Simon & Schuster, 1979, p. 173.
14. *Reflections of a Neoconservative: Looking Back, Looking Ahead*, New York: Basic Books, 1983.
15. "Renaissance Man," *Present Tense*, pp. 18–23. Interview with Norman Podhoretz, June 14, 1990.
16. On Koch's background, see Edward I. Koch, *Mayor: An Autobiography*: New York: Vantage Books, 1984, pp. 4–35; Crouch, *Notes of a Hanging Judge*, pp. 13, 34.
17. Friedman, "Intergroup Relations," *American Jewish Yearbook*, 1980, p. 77.
18. I used this material in my article "Black Anti-Semitism on the Rise," *Commentary*, October 1979.

19. The Tsukashima figures are quoted by Schneider in "Rising Black Consciousness May Mean More Hostility to Jews and to Israel," *National Journal*, May 6, 1984; for a full discussion of Tsukashima's findings, see "Chronological, Cognitive, and Political Effects in the Study of Interminority Group Prejudice," *Phylon*, September 1983, pp. 217–231. In his book *Anti-Semitism: The Longest Hatred*, Robert S. Wistrich argues also that anti-Semitism among better-educated blacks has increased; but in a review of the book in the *Forward*, September 4, 1992, Jerome A. Chanes disputes this, arguing that the data suggests anti-Semitism has declined among both better educated groups but that blacks are relatively more anti-Semitic than whites at the same educational level.
20. "Anti-Semitism and Israel: A Report on American Public Opinion for the American Jewish Committee," December 1978, pp. 6–7, 102.
21. For the evolution of attitudes towards Jews, see Charles Herbert Stember, *Jews in the Mind of America*, New York: Basic Books, 1966. For a more recent discussion of the attitudes of younger blacks, confirming the trends noted by Schneider and Tsukashima, see Ernest Spaights, Harold Dixon, and Susan Nickolai, "Attitudes of Black Collegians toward Jews and Economic Matters," *College Student Journal* 19/2 (Summer 1985), pp. 118–122.
22. William Schneider to Milton Himmelfarb on update of data on anti-Semitism and Jewish attitudes, AJC files, p. 6. There has been virtually no systematic research on black-Jewish relations since the early 1980s. The last major study was done by the Yankelovich organization in January 1981, and the findings generally confirmed Schneider's summary of earlier studies. See also Gregory Martire and Ruth Clark, *Anti-Semitism in the United States: A Study of Prejudice in the 1980s*, New York: Praeger, 1982, p. 44.
23. Glenn C. Loury, "Disparate Public Visions: Black-Jewish Relations in the 1980s and Beyond," Luncheon Address to Conference on Black-Jewish Relations, University of the District of Columbia, November 19, 1985.
24. Weisbord and Kazarian, pp. 32, 51; interview with Arnold Aronson, November 18, 1990.
25. Weisbord and Kazarian, pp. 122, 129; Earl Raab, "American Blacks and Israel," in Robert S. Wistrich, *Anti-Zionism and Antisemitism in the Contemporary World*, New York: New York University Press, 1990.
26. Thomas Landess and Richard Quinn, *Jesse Jackson and the Politics of Race*, Ottawa, IL: Jameson, 1985, p. 129; Friedman, "Intergroup Relations," *American Jewish Yearbook*, 1981, p. 123.

27. Weisbord and Kazarian, p. 128; Friedman, "Intergroup Relations," *American Jewish Yearbook*, 1981, p. 124. Young's comment, *Philadelphia Inquirer*, September 14, 1993.
28. Weisbord and Kazarian, pp. 122–123; Abram, p. 254.
29. Friedman, "Intergroup Relations," *American Jewish Yearbook*, 1981, p. 125.
30. As quoted in Weisbord and Kazarian, p. 125. See chap. 6 for a fuller discussion of the Young Affair. Also, Landess and Quinn, pp. 130–131.
31. As quoted by Friedman, "Intergroup Relations," *American Jewish Yearbook*, 1981, p. 126. On Baldwin, see Henry Gates, Jr., "The Fire Last Time," *New Republic*, June 1, 1992, pp. 41–42.
32. Pressed over the years to declare that Israel and Jews did not force his resignation, Young has remained silent. As mayor of Atlanta, he sought successfully to bring Arab business to the city, which fact may have foreclosed his further discussion of this episode. Weisbord and Kazarian, pp. 124, 133; Landess and Quinn, p. 131.
33. Abram, pp. 258, 263.
34. Ibid., pp. 174–185.
35. Pp. 249, 258, 262; see also "Profile," *Baltimore Jewish Times*, June 28, 1985.

Chapter 16: Garvey's Ghosts

1. The Pulitzer Prize-winning black writer James Alan McPherson has written, however, that American blacks are a self-created people who had not been African since the eighteenth century. Their ideals, he declared, have come from the documents of American life, their sacred values from the marketplace of ideas, and their root mythologies from identification with Jews from the Old Testament. "To Blacks and Jews: Hab Rachmones," in Justin Kaplan, *The Best American Essays*, New York: Ticknor & Fields, 1990, pp. 206–213.
2. Landess and Quinn, p. 143.
3. Ibid., p. 23; Barbara Reynolds, *Jesse Jackson: The Man, the Movement, the Myth*, Chicago: Nelson-Hall, 1975; Garrow, *Bearing the Cross*, p. 585.
4. Marshall Frady, "Outsider without Portfolio," *New Yorker*, February 17, 1992, p. 48.
5. Weisbord and Kazarian, p. 148; Arch Puddington, "Jesse Jackson, the Blacks & American Foreign Policy," *Commentary*, April 1984, p. 20.
6. Landess and Quinn, p. 146.

7. Puddington, p. 21.
8. Weisbord and Kazarian, p. 152. In describing this solicitation to a *Chicago Sun-Times* reporter, Jackson said he told the Arab representative that "if they wanted to be part of the human rights struggle . . . they must join it with dollars and bodies." Libya's cash contributions to PUSH were investigated by the Justice Department, which found no evidence of wrongful behavior on Jackson's part. Puddington, p. 26; Friedman, "Intergroup Relations," *American Jewish Yearbook*, 1985, p. 107.
9. Lucius J. Barker and Ronald W. Walters, *Jesse Jackson's 1984 Presidential Campaign: Challenge and Change in American Politics*, Urbana: University of Illinois Press, 1989, pp. vii, 16–17; Crouch, *Notes of a Hanging Judge*, p. 9.
10. *The Closest of Strangers*, p. 274.
11. Barker and Walters, p. 170.
12. *Louis Farrakhan: Continuing the Message of Hate: An Update*, ADL Background Report, June 1988; ADL Research Report, *Louis Farrakhan: The Campaign to Manipulate Public Opnion, A Study in the Packaging of Bigotry*, 1990, pp. 21–22; Kenneth S. Stern, *Farrakhan and Jews in the 1990s*, American Jewish Committee, vol. 2, no. 4, 1992; Dennis King, "The Farrakhan Phenomenon: Ideology, Support, Potential," *Patterns of Prejudice*, vol. 20, no. 1, 1986, p. 13; Playhell Benjamin, "The Attitude Is the Message: Louis Farrakhan Pursues the Middle Class," *Village Voice*, August 15, 1989; "Farrakhan's Mission," *Newsweek*, March 19, 1990, p. 25.
13. "Nationalism of Fools," *Notes of a Hanging Judge*, p. 169.
14. Crouch, p. 170. On anti-Semitic themes in rap and their relationship to Farrakhan, see Nat Hentoff, "Blacks and Jews: Do the Right Thing," *Jewish Week*, August 31, 1989; Henry Louis Gates, Jr., "2 Live Crew Decoded," *New York Times*, June 19, 1990; Terry Teachout, "Rap and Racism," *Commentary*, March 1990, pp. 60–62. For a good discussion of the meaning of rap, see Arthur Kempton, "Native Sons," *New York Review*, April 11, 1991, pp. 55–61.
15. October 28, 1985, pp. 11–12. See also Lester, *Lovesong*, pp. 230–236.
16. *Philadelphia Tribune*, March 30, 1990. See also "Speaker Stirs Concern at Princeton," *Philadelphia Inquirer*, February 7, 1990.
17. Mitchell G. Bard and Rachel Weinberg, "Combating Bigotry on Campus," *Jewish Exponent*, December 7, 1990; Jon Greene, "Touré Speech Sparks Black-Jewish Tensions at the University of Maryland," and Nat Hentoff, "Talking Hate on Campus" *Jewish Week*, February 8 and March 22, 1990.

18. "The Farrakhan Phenomenon," 12.
19. See her review of Shelby Steele, *The Content of Our Character, New York Times Book Review*, September 16, 1990, pp. 12–13.
20. Thomas Byrne Edsall and Mary D. Edsall, *Chain Reaction: The Impact of Race, Rights and Taxes on American Politics*, New York: Norton, 1991, p. 18.
21. Ben Wattenberg, "Does Less Equal More Bias?" *Washington Times*, September 21, 1989; *New York Times*, November 26, 1990.
22. The phrase is from Tamar Jacoby's article, "Garvey's Ghosts," *New Republic*, July 2, 1990, pp. 18–19.
23. "Garvey's Ghosts," p. 18.
24. Sleeper, p. 184.
25. Joe Klein, "Labor Pains," *New York*, March 25, 1985, pp. 18–19; Sleeper, p. 245.
26. *New York Times*, May 7, July 29, July 31, 1988.
27. I attended this meeting, and the account is from my notes. King, "The Farrakhan Phenomenon," p. 12.
28. *Washington Post*, October 27, 1989.
29. Barker and Walters, p. 28.
30. P. 153.
31. Earl Raab, "Intergroup Relations," *American Jewish Yearbook*, 1990, p. 209; Eugene C. Levy, Jr., President, and Thomas A. Dine, Executive Director, August 3, 1988.

Epilogue: Beyond the Black–Jewish Alliance

1. Thomas B. Edsall, "Survey: Backing Growing for Separate Black Party," *Philadelphia Inquirer*, April 16, 1994; *The Sun* (Philadelphia) April 24, 1994. For the growth of nationalism among younger blacks, see *Wall Street Journal*, April 22, 1994.
2. On the frustratons of the black middle class, see Ellis Cose, *The Rage of a Privileged Class*, New York: HarperCollins, 1994.
3. Leon Janoff, "Teaching Reverse Racism," *Time*, April 4, 1994, pp. 74–75.
4. *New York Times*, April 21, 1994.
5. *Forward*, April 29, 1994.
6. "Brother Act," *New Republic*, February 14, 1994.
7. Richard A. Girgenti, *A Report to the Governor on the Disturbances in Crown Heights: An Assessment of the City's Preparedness and Response to Civil Disorder*, 2 vols., New York State Division of Criminal Justice Services, 1993.
8. *Working Papers on Contemporary Anti-Semitism*, New York: Ameri-

can Jewish Committee, May 1994. See also Leonard Dinnerstein, "The Origins of Black Anti-Semitism in America," *American Jewish Archives*, November 1986, pp. 113–122; Stephen J. Whitfield, "A Critique of Dinnerstein's 'The Origins of Black Anti-Semitism in America,'" *American Jewish Archives*, November, 1987, and Dinnerstein's response, pp. 193–202.

9. Caren Benjamin, "Black Anti-Semitism Can Be Hard to Quantify," *Washington Jewish Week*, February 17, 1994.
10. *The Sun* (Philadelphia), March 27, 1994.
11. *Philadelphia Tribune*, April 22, 1994.
12. "The Other and the Almost the Same," *New Yorker*, February 28, 1994, p. 71.
13. Jeffrey Goldberg, "Black Newspapermen Seize Lead," *Forward*, March 11, 1994.
14. "Beyond the Black-Jewish Split," *Commentary*, January 1986, pp. 23–27. See also Loury, "The Alliance Is Over," *Moment*, June 1994, pp. 32–35, 68–71.
15. *Notes of a Hanging Judge: Essays and Reviews, 1979–1989*, New York: Oxford University Press, 1990, pp. x, 8, 257.
16. "Jews as Enemy?" *Philadelphia Tribune*, July 4, 1990.
17. Ashe and Arnold Rampersad, *Days of Grace: A Memoir*, New York: Knopf, 1993; *New York Times*, May 15, 1994. According to a *New York Times* poll taken in February and early March 1994 (reported March 15, 1994), black Americans reject the notion that Louis Farrakhan and the Nation of Islam represent the views of most blacks, and most feel racist statements by blacks and whites should be equally condemned.
18. "Hard-Core Rap Lyrics Stir Black Backlash," *New York Times*, August 15, 1993.
19. William Henry III, "Pride and Prejudice," February 28, 1994, pp. 20–21.
20. On Owens see *Washington Jewish Week*, June 23, 1994; *Forward*, July 9, 1993; Fred Barnes, "Mild Wilder," *New Republic*, August 13, 1990, p. 29; "Problems of Black Politics," *Dissent*, Fall 1989, pp. 528–529.
21. I am grateful to Dr. Marshall F. Stevenson, Jr., for sharing with me his unpublished paper, "Cincinnati Is Not New York: Regional Differences in Black Jewish Relations After World War II." On Mayor Cleaver, see *Jewish Telegraphic Agency News Reporter*, April 5, 1991.
22. Memo to Key Contacts, AIPAC, June 24, 1993; AIPAC Fact Sheet, July 3, 1993. On May 25 1994, every black congressman save two (who did not vote) supported the Foreign Aid Appropriation bill,

which included three billion dollars in economic and military assistance and eighty million dollars for refugee resettlement in Israel. AIPAC Key Contacts and Activists, June 3, 1994.

23. *Wall Street Journal*, April 22, 1994.
24. On Solarz and his successor Representative Nydia M. Velazquez, see *New York Times*, March 20, 1994 and November 2, 1992. On Mayor Dinkins and racial preferences, see *New York Times*, June 8, 1993.
25. *Washington Post*, February 13, 1994.
26. *New York Times*, June 13 and 15, 1994. For a favorable view of a summit convened earlier by the Detroit chapter of the NAACP that included Leonard Jeffries, see Dr. Conrad W. Worrill, "Congratulations to the NAACP for Reaching Out," *Philadelphia Tribune*, May 6, 1994. The Baltimore summit, however, was attacked by Hazel N. Dukes, president of the New York State Conference of NAACP Branches, in a letter to the editor of the *New York Times*, July 4, 1994.
27. "Ethnotherapy with Jews," *International Journal of Mental Health*, Summer 1976, p. 26.
28. Barry Kosmin et al., *Highlights of the CJF 1990 National Jewish Population Survey*, publication of the Council of Jewish Federations, New York: 1991.
29. Steven Cohen who has surveyed opinions of American Jews found seventy-five percent in disagreement with the view that anti-Semitism is currently not a serious problem. *Dimensions of American Jewish Liberalism*, American Jewish Committee, 1989.
30. For a further discussion of this, see Murray Friedman, "Going Our Own Ways," and Glenn C. Loury, "The Alliance Is Over," *Moment*, June 1994, pp. 32–39, 68–72. Jonathan Kaufman expresses a different view in "What's a Jewish Liberal to Do?," pp. 40–42, 73–74.
31. *New York Times*, August 31, 1991; "The Jewish No Defense League," *Village Voice*, August 10, 1993; *Forward*, August 6, 1993.

INDEX